Freud and the Far East

Freud and the Far East

Psychoanalytic Perspectives on the People and Culture of China, Japan, and Korea

Edited by
Salman Akhtar

JASON ARONSON
Lanham • Boulder • New York • Toronto • Plymouth, UK

Chapter 1 was originally published in *Japanese Contributions to Psychoanalysis* 1 (2006), and is being published with the permission of Mrs. Eiko Okonogi, the deceased author's wife, Dr. Kunihiro Matsuki, the journal's editor, and of the Japan Psychoanalytic Society and the Kodera Foundation for Psychoanalytic Study, Tokyo, Japan. Chapter 4 was originally published in *Gonryo* in 1931 and subsequently republished in the *Japanese Journal of Psychoanalysis* 1: 1–8 (1954), as well as *Japanese Contributions to Psychoanalysis* 2: 3–11 (2007); it is being published here with the permission of Mr. Yorio Kosawa, the author's son, and the Japan Psychoanalytic Society and the Kodera Foundation for Psychoanalytic Study, Tokyo, Japan. Chapter 9 is being reprinted from *The Psychoanalytic Quarterly* 75: 163–96 (2006), with the permission of its author. Chapter 15 is reprinted from *The Journal of the American Academy of Psychoanalysis* 17: 427–50 (1996), with the permission of its author. Chapter 16 first appeared in *Japanese Contributions to Psychoanalysis* 2: 158–78 (2007), and is being published here with the permission of its author and of the Japan Psychoanalytic Society and the Kodera Foundation for Psychoanalytic Study, Tokyo, Japan.

Published in the United States of America
by Jason Aronson
An imprint of Rowman & Littlefield Publishers, Inc.

A wholly owned subsidiary of
The Rowman & Littlefield Publishing Group, Inc.
4501 Forbes Boulevard, Suite 200, Lanham, Maryland 20706
www.rowmanlittlefield.com

Estover Road
Plymouth PL6 7PY
United Kingdom

British Library Cataloguing in Publication Information Available

Library of Congress Cataloging-in-Publication Data

Freud and the far east : psychoanalytic perspectives on the people and culture of China, Japan, and Korea / edited by Salman Akhtar.
p. cm.
Includes bibliographical references and index.
ISBN 978-0-7657-0693-5 (cloth : alk. paper) — ISBN 978-0-7657-0695-9 (electronic)
1. Psychoanalysis and culture. 2. Psychoanalysis—Cross-cultural studies. I. Akhtar, Salman, 1946 July 31–

BF175.4.C84O75 2009
150.19'5095—dc22 2009011249

Printed in the United States of America

∞™ The paper used in this publication meets the minimum requirements of American National Standard for Information Sciences—Permanence of Paper for Printed Library Materials, ANSI/NISO Z39.48-1992.

To

Professors Keigo Okinogi (late) and Osamu Kitayama

in gratitude for their hospitality during my visit to Japan

Drs. June Cai and Mikyum Kim

in celebration of our long-term friendship

and

Drs. Lois Choi-Kain and Frederick Huang

in anticipation of their bright futures in psychoanalysis.

Contents

Acknowledgments

I wish to thank the distinguished colleagues whose contributions appear in this volume. I am grateful to Michael Vergare, M.D., the senior vice president for academic affairs and the chairman of the Department of Psychiatry and Human Behavior at Jefferson Medical College, for his unwavering support of my work. I also wish to express my gratitude to the Margaret Mahler Psychiatric Research Foundation and to the Kodera Foundation for their cosponsored invitation for me to speak during the Third International Margaret Mahler Symposium held April 1–2, 2000, in Tokyo, Japan. My wife and fellow psychoanalyst, Dr. Monisha Nayar, coauthored a chapter with me for this book and offered support, editorial comments, love, and friendship that were invaluable in my pursuing this venture.

My dialogue with Drs. Daniel Freeman, Mikyum Kim, Mark Moore, Stuart Twemlow, Adeline van Waning, and Teresa Yuan strengthened my interest in matters pertaining to China, Japan, and Korea. A number of psychoanalytic candidates and psychiatric residents with roots going back to these countries have regularly or sporadically sought my guidance and enlightened me about their respective cultures in the process. Prominent among this group of individuals are Drs. Lois Choi-Kain, Martha Hashimoto, Fred Huang, Jieun Kim, and Jingduan Yang. Ms. Jan Wright prepared the manuscript of this book with diligence, grace, and not-infrequently-required patience and humor.

Finally, I wish to thank the warmhearted camaraderie of the Far Eastern immigrant physicians who entered the United States at the same time as myself and with whom I spent the first year of my psychiatric training at the University of Medicine and Dentistry of New Jersey at Newark, New Jersey. They include Drs. Danielo Campos, Mikyum Kim, Young Ho Kim,

H. K. Lee, S. H. Lee, and D. Shen. And I would be remiss if I did not acknowledge the "holding" function of the near-weekly banter between myself and the owner of the Bala Cynwyd Cleaners, Ms. Hsin-tz ("Rose") Chien, over the last three decades. It is this sort of thing that Kahlil Gibran most likely had in mind when he declared that the morning of the heart arrives amid the dewdrops of mundane happenings.

Introduction

With his characteristic blend of humility and candor, John Klauber, the in-optimally celebrated British psychoanalyst of the mid-twentieth century, recognized "the problems involved in understanding a patient from a remote culture—for example, a Japanese—and of estimating the significance and advisability of possible interventions" (1968, p. 130). However, such clinical reserve is hardly the explanation of the fact that few Japanese individuals, or for that matter, Chinese or Koreans, figured in the history of psychoanalysis on either side of the couch. Other factors perhaps played a greater role in this. The Eurocentric base of the profession's theory and personnel held a lukewarm, if not prejudicial, attitude toward the "Orientals," regarding them as unsuitable for analytic treatment and/or training. The close tie between psychiatry and psychoanalysis in the United States also made it difficult for immigrant physicians from the Far East to enter psychoanalysis. They could only gain entrance to inferior, state-hospital-based psychiatric residency programs and thus had less exposure to psychoanalytic ideas and to psychoanalysts. Their college and medical education as well as their religious tenets were hardly "psychoanalysis-friendly" to begin with. Acting in unison, all these factors led to the numbers of analysts and analysands from Japan, China, or Korea remaining miniscule.

To be sure, there were exceptions going back to the very early days of psychoanalysis. Heisaku Kosawa, a prominent Japanese psychiatrist, for instance, went to Vienna to study analysis and was in training analysis with Richard Sterba from 1932 to 1933. Closer to home, the Topeka Psychoanalytic Society, located on the campus of the renowned Menninger Clinic, did accept many foreign medical graduates (or FMGs, as they were then called) into its didactic fold. Takeo Doi, who later brought the important Japanese concept of *amae* to psychoanalysis, was trained there. The Washington Psychoanalytic Institute holds the credit for training the Chinese psychoanalyst Ping Nie Pao, who went on to make important contributions to psychoanalytic understanding of schizophrenia besides writing highly influential papers on hatred, pathological jealousy, and hypomania. Among other noticeable psychoanalytic trainees from Far Eastern nations who achieved professional prominence are Normund Wong, Yasuhiko Taketomo, and Tetsuro Takahashi.

Such outstanding individuals notwithstanding, the representation of Chinese, Japanese, and Korean individuals in the membership of the IPA (International Psychoanalytic Association) and the "American" (American Psychoanalytic Association) remained insignificant. Worse than this was the profession's bland indifference to this demographic peculiarity. The question, however, is that if the people of these nations constitute a third of the world's population, can psychoanalysis go on ignoring them without appearing to be a narrow, ethnocentric enterprise?

Fortunately, a change is now evident. The rise of these nations as major world economies has brought the West's attention to them with a renewed vigor. Rapid demographic changes due to immigration in the Western countries, especially in the United States, have resulted in a larger "sample size" of potential analytic patients and candidates from such backgrounds; this is especially true of the first and second generations of the Far Eastern immigrants. Cynical though it may sound, the endangerment of psychoanalysis in the West has perhaps also propelled the burst of interest in remote outposts of the psychoanalytic regime; the "conquistador" spirit of Sigmund Freud, the profession's founder, lives on, it seems.

As a result, a reinvigoration of the Japan Psychoanalytic Society (originally established by Yaekichi Yabe in 1930) is in evidence, and, beginning in the mid-1980s, the IPA Congresses have made simultaneous translation from English to Japanese available. The year 1980 saw the birth of the Seoul Psychoanalytic Study Group in South Korea. More recently, interest in exporting psychoanalysis to mainland China has emerged; the inception of the IPA China Committee (Chair: Professor Peter Loewenberg; members: Drs. Alf Gerlach and Sverre Varvin, and Mrs. Maria Teresa Hooke) and founding of the China American Psychoanalytic Alliance (CAPA) in 2001 are but a few outward manifestations of such enthusiasm. A parallel development to these "movements" within (and toward) China, Japan, and Korea is the dramatic increase in Western psychoanalysts traveling to these destinations in order to teach, supervise, and organize clinical seminars. These actions are undoubtedly laudable. However, an important question remains as to whether this export of knowledge is matched by the import of novel ideas that would make us rethink our cherished psychoanalytic notions. In the absence of such heuristic bilateralism and cross-fertilization, the psychoanalytic profession might imperiously advance but psychoanalytic knowledge will remain smugly stagnant.

Talking of knowledge brings up the painful issue of Western, especially North American, geographical ignorance and cultural provincialism. The ordinary masses in the United States can be truly appalling in their lack of knowledge or concern about the "Orient" while driving around the country in their Hondas, Toyotas, Subarus, Hyundais, and Suzukis. The educated classes enjoy the movies of Akira Kurasowa, admire the architectural genius of Ieoh Ming Pei, read the fiction of Kazuo Ishiguro and Amy Tan, savor book reviews by Michiko Kakutani, respect the secular pragmatism of Ban Ki Moon, and swoon over the music of Yo-Yo Ma. They have incorporated acupuncture, bonsai, dim sum, feng shui, haiku, karaoke, origami, and sushi in the alphabet of their cosmopolitan lives, though without adequately mentalized gratitude to the Far Eastern origins of these artifacts and practices. Both groups lead lives that merrily ignore the destruction of Hiroshima and Nagasaki, the Japanese internment camps in the United States during and soon after World War II, the bloodshed during the Korean War, the relentless American bombing of Laos and Cambodia, and its merciless pillage of Vietnam. Disregard of history is coupled with disinterest in the contemporary affairs of the East. Ignorance abounds.

Frankly, we psychoanalysts are hardly more informed than the ordinary folks in this regard. As a thought experiment, let us imagine a group of mental health professionals faced with a "pop quiz" about China, Japan, and Korea. What percentage of them would know the following facts?

- The nation of Japan is comprised of three thousand islands.
- The average life expectancy for the Japanese is over eighty-one years.
- Japan is the world's second-largest economy calculated by the gross domestic product.
- Chinese is the longest continuously written language in existence.
- Paper, compass, gunpowder, and printing were all invented in China.
- Judaism arrived in China in the seventh century BC.
- The literacy rate in South Korea is over 97 percent.
- South Korea has forty-one medical schools.
- The average life expectancy for Korean women is above eighty-two years.

The fact is that few among us well-educated and, to our minds, well-intentioned folk know such facts. This is sad, to say the least. More distressing is our ignorance of the cultural nuances of this vast segment of the world's population. Myths, fables, literature, and traditions evolved over centuries in this region remain outside our awareness and curiosity. The resulting gap in knowledge is detrimental to our fully grasping the complexities of human development, the essential nature of psychopathology, and the unthought diversity of ameliorating interventions that awaits discovery. Consider the following Eastern notions for a moment and you will see what I mean.

- The concept of *amae*, a tender sort of affection that goes a long way toward emotionally refueling the ever-so-vulnerable human psyche.
- The "filial piety complex," which often puts the conventionally known Oedipal situation on its head.
- The pre-Oedipal origins of guilt in the crucible of the mother-child relationship.
- The food-sex equation and, even more important, the depth-psychological significance of good table manners.
- The notion of transience, and its twin, a view of the self as process rather than structure.
- The concept of *wa*, or keeping relationships smooth and rounded by all means.
- The disciplined self-investigation propelled by the meditative methods of Naikan.
- The intricate psychosomatic bond between Zen, martial arts, and psychoanalysis.

One could go on, but the point is made: we can not jettison the knowledge about feelings, thoughts, and human relationships that the East offers us unless we are content with a psychoanalytic theory that ignores some of the richest cultural traditions evolved by humanity. The reverberations of these traditions and the achievements derived from them are truly majestic in their scope and depth. These range from the unifying existentialism of the Buddhist doctrine to the shy exhibitionism of Kabuki theater, from the contemplative mysticism of Zen to the disciplined symbolism of haiku, from the imposing moralism of Confucian thought to the playful corporealism of tae kwan do, from the meditative realism of Li Bai to the firm-fisted socialism of Mao Zedong, and from the sublime spiritualism of Lao Tzu to the sardonic surrealism of Japanese airbrush painting. That the fruits of such rich intellectual trends have not been brought to bear upon the psychoanalytic thinking of the West seems unfortunate. Think about it. Just the way the feminist challenge led to the diminution of phallocentrism of psychoanalytic theory, an open-minded encounter with the Eastern Other can reduce psychoanalysis's confining Eurocentrism.

Broad-minded psychoanalysts have always known this privately and many among them have been pursuing this path in an open, academic manner for years. Following illustrations readily come to mind in this context:

- Daniel Freeman's long-term commitment to psychoanalytic exploration of Japanese and Korean cultures.
- Alan Roland's clinically founded hypotheses about the Eastern self and its object relations.
- Calvin Settlage's studies of Japanese American separation-individuation process.
- Nina Coltart's, Mark Epstein's, David Nichol's, Randall Paulsen's, and Jeffrey Rubin's attempts to integrate psychoanalysis and Buddhism.
- Maria Teresa Hooke's, Peter Loewenberg's, Elise Snyder's, and Teresa Yuan's untiring work to bring psychoanalysis to China.
- Sander Abend's, Allen Compton's, Abigail Golomb's, Richard Lightbody's, Robert Tyson's, and David Sachs's efforts on behalf of the Korean Psychoanalytic Society.

The fact that the IPA China Committee, along with the Psychoanalytic Institute of Eastern Europe and the IPA Centenary Committee, is planning the first IPA Asian Psychoanalytic Conference in Beijing in 2010 is a shining testimony to the international psychoanalytic community's interest in bringing psychoanalysis to the Eastern parts of the world. On a day-to-day academic level, however, more seems needed. Psychoanalytic interest in the Far East, rather than being a "subspecialty" of a select few, should be viewed as an integral part of the curriculum on applied and cross-cultural psychoanalysis in psychoanalytic institutes. Moreover, the traffic of knowledge needs to move in both directions. Western psychoanalysts' help to their Far Eastern colleagues must be matched by an open-minded epistemic drive to acquire, assimilate, and utilize Eastern wisdom to enhance analytic theory and praxis.

It is with this aim in mind that I offer *The Orient and the Unconscious* to the reader. Within its pages, distinguished colleagues from East and West attempt to weave a fine and colorful tapestry of the ubiquitous and idiosyncratic, the plebian and profound, and the neurotically inclined and culturally nuanced. They provide meticulous historical accounts of the development of psychoanalysis in Japan, Korea, and China and, in the process, familiarize the reader with interesting personages, quaint phrases, cultural nuances, foundation of journals, and emergence of groups (and group rivalries!) interested in psychoanalysis. The contributors to the book also discuss the depth-psychological concepts of *amae*, *wa*, Ajase complex, and the filial piety complex, thus underscoring the complex interplay of drive and ego-driven development of personality with the powerful forces of ancestral legacies and their attendant myths and fantasies. The reverberation of these aesthetic and relational paradigms in epic love stories, martial arts, and cinema are also elucidated. In addition, the book offers insights into the psychosocial trials and tribulations of the Western immigrant populations from these countries and their offspring. Finally, the implications of all this to the conduct of psychotherapy and psychoanalysis are addressed.

The book is thus a lexical ambassador with the dual responsibility of bridging the West and East and enhancing psychoanalytic conceptualization in the course of such encounters. By juxtaposing the familiar with the unfamiliar, it seeks to enrich our understanding of both. That it, occasionally, underscores the differences of mentality between the East and the West paradoxically reminds us that only by acknowledging cultural differences do we become ever more deeply knowledgeable about human similarities. Shedding light on the periphery eventually illuminates the center. That is where the book leads us: the core of the human heart with all its innocent idiosyncrasies and its inescapable universality.

I

TALES AND TERRAINS

1

Psychoanalysis in Japan

Keigo Okinogi

Pleasure is the seedbed of pain; pain is the seedbed of pleasure.

Japanese proverb

The history of psychoanalysis in Japan may be roughly divided into two periods: (1) the period before World War II and (2) the period from the end of World War II to the present.

THE PERIOD BEFORE WORLD WAR II

The Introduction of Freud to Japan (1910s)

The first Japanese document on psychoanalysis, an article by Kaison Ohtsuki titled "The Psychology of Forgetfulness," appeared in a journal of psychological research in 1912. The same year, Kyuichi Kimura published "How to Detect the Secrets of the Mind and to Discover Repression," which introduced psychoanalysis as a scientific method of exploring people's thoughts.

Psychologists and educators introduced Freudian psychoanalysis in a variety of forms over the next ten years. The most notable effort was *A Lecture on Psychology,* written in 1914 by psychologist Yoichi Ueno. While in the United States, Ueno had become acquainted with Freudian psychoanalysis through a lecture by Professor Stanley Hall of Clark University. On returning to Japan, he wrote *A Lecture on Psychology,* which included Japan's first systematic outline of psychoanalysis. It contained such chapters as: "The Origin of Psychoanalysis," "Psychoanalytic Therapy," "The Interpretation of

Dreams," "Infantile Sexuality," "The Psychoanalysis of Mythology and Art," "Forgetfulness and Verbal Slips," "Wit," "Psychoanalysis and Education," and so on.

The Publication of Freud's Collected Works in Japanese (1929–1933)

From 1929 to 1933, two collections of Freud's works appeared in Japanese translation. Both were the work of a group headed by literary figures Kenji Ohtsuki and Yaekichi Yabe.

On a visit to London in 1930, Yabe, a psychologist, met the president of the IPA (International Psychoanalytic Association), Ernest Jones. Yabe subsequently established the Tokyo Branch of the IPA. Ohtsuki, a writer, later succeeded Yabe as president. The association, however, promoted psychoanalytic theory to the general public only, as a system of thought, without inviting the participation of psychiatrists. It thus never developed as an association of clinical psychoanalytic psychotherapists and was finally disbanded after World War II.

Kioyuasu Marui and Tohoku School (1920s–1930s)

In the domain of Japanese psychiatry and medicine, Freudian psychoanalysis was originally dismissed as a misguided theory of pansexualism. Kiyoyasu Marui became the first Japanese psychiatrist to study psychoanalysis as a theoretical system of psychopathology.

Marui went to the United States in 1919 to study with Adolf Meyer at Johns Hopkins University. Witnessing the influence of psychoanalysis on American psychiatry, he hoped to introduce psychoanalysis to the Japanese psychiatric community. After returning to Japan, he began teaching at the University of Tohoku in Sendai (in northeastern Japan). Psychoanalysis became the focus of his medical school lectures on psychiatry. Beginning in 1925, he also taught psychoanalytic theory to practicing psychiatrists. Marui furthermore published psychiatric textbooks with a special emphasis on psychoanalysis. Psychiatrists who studied under Marui became Japan's first generation of psychoanalytically oriented psychiatrists, known collectively as the Tohoku School.

The Tohoku School flourished from the late 1920s to 1940. However, this school of psychiatrists led by Marui did not fully comprehend the techniques of psychoanalytic therapy. Rather, they understood psychoanalysis simply as a theory of psychopathology. On the basis of this understanding, members of the Tohoku School presented papers focusing on a psychoanalytical understanding of neurosis in Japan at meetings of the Japanese Association of Neurology and Psychiatry. They also published the *Journal of Psychoanalytic Psychopathology*. However, the mainstream psychiatric circle in Japan at the time was characterized by a German Kraepelinian trend.

Marui's small isolated group was continuously subject to harsh criticism. In 1933, nonetheless, Marui visited Freud in Vienna and received approval for establishing a Sendai Branch of the IPA.

Heisaku Kosawa, "The Father of Japanese Psychoanalysis" (1930s)

Heisaku Kosawa, a student of the Tohoku School, began to question Marui, who taught only theory without understanding Freudian psychoanalytic therapy (which Kosawa himself had been studying directly from the works of Freud). In order to learn psychoanalytic methods firsthand, Kosawa left Japan to study at the Vienna Psychoanalytic Institute from 1932 to 1933. He received training analysis from Richard Sterba and individual supervision on psychotherapy from Paul Federn.

While in Vienna, furthermore, Kosawa visited Freud at his home at Bergasse 19 and interviewed him directly. He presented Freud with a paper explaining his theory of the Ajase complex, which he contrasted with the Western Oedipus complex. (Kosawa's theory will be discussed more thoroughly in part II.) Unfortunately, however, Freud does not appear to have evinced great interest in Kosawa's thesis.

After returning to Japan in 1933, Heisaku Kosawa, now at odds with Kiyoyasu Marui, opened a private clinic in Tokyo. Here he began practicing psychoanalytic therapy as it was known in Europe and the United States.

With the outbreak of World War II in 1939, Japan became an ally of Nazi Germany—which regarded psychoanalysis as a dangerous, Jewish system of thought. Heisaku Kosawa came under constant surveillance from the special police. Nevertheless, he continued to conduct a private practice throughout the war.

THE PERIOD AFTER WORLD WAR II

The Second-Generation Psychiatrists and the Kosawa School (1950s–1960s)

The end of World War II brought an influx of learning and culture from the United States, which greatly influenced all aspects of Japanese society, including the field of psychiatry. It created a generation of young psychiatrists who sought to study the model of American dynamic psychiatry. They chose to receive training analysis and individual supervision from Heisaku Kosawa.

This group of psychiatrists who studied under Heisaku Kosawa became the second generation of Japanese psychoanalysts, known as the Kosawa School. Some leading members included: Takeo Doi from the University of

Tokyo; Makoto Takeda and myself from Keio University; and Shigeharu Maeda and Masahisa Nishizono from Kyushu University. These young psychiatrists from the Kosawa School became members of the Japan Branch of the IPA.

After the death of Kiyoyasu Marui in 1953, Heisaku Kosawa had succeeded Marui as director of the IPA Sendai Branch. Through exchanges with Anna Freud and Heintz Hartmann, Kosawa later changed the name of the Sendai Branch to the Japan Branch. He then established its headquarters in Tokyo, a move approved by the IPA.

The Japan Branch of the IPA is known internationally as the Japan Psychoanalytic Society. Members of the Society have completed studies in training analysis based on rigorous international standards, as well as psychoanalysis through individual supervision. Psychiatrists who received training analysis from Heisaku Kosawa between 1950 and 1960 represent its core members.

At approximately the same time, from the end of the 1940s to the early 1950s, a study group for psychoanalysis was established by Heisaku Kosawa and professors of psychiatry from various universities. With this group as its center, the Japan Psychoanalytical Association was established in 1955.

As far as its focus is concerned, the Japan Psychoanalytical Association should more correctly be called the Association for Dynamic Psychiatry. It was established by psychiatrists and psychologists with a psychoanalytical orientation. Although it includes "psychoanalysis" in its name, the association has no specific eligibility requirements or standards for membership.

Membership for the Japan Psychoanalytical Association has grown steadily over the years. It is currently a major scientific organization with 1,500 members, roughly 70 to 80 percent of whom are dynamic psychiatrists. A number of clinical psychologists also participate.

The founding members of the Japan Psychoanalytical Association, like those of the Japan Psychoanalytic Society, received psychoanalytic training from Heisaku Kosawa. Psychiatrists who have studied psychoanalytic psychotherapy and dynamic psychiatry in the United States and Europe have also become members. The association does not limit itself to any specific school of psychoanalysis; some members adhere to Freudian ego psychology, while others advocate British object relations theory of the Kleinian school. In this sense, various schools cooperate to run the association. Members who have joined after studying psychoanalytic psychotherapy abroad include: Akihisa Kondo, who worked with Karen Horney; Kenji Sakamoto, who studied under Clara Thompson; and Ikuo Miyoshi, who received training from Metard Boss of Switzerland.

The Third-Generation Psychiatrists (1960s–1970s)

In 1969, following the death of Heisaku Kosawa, Michio Yamamura succeeded to the presidency of the Japan Psychoanalytic Society and the Japan

Psychoanalytical Association. The period 1960–1970 also witnessed the return of several Japanese psychiatrists from clinical training abroad. Kiyoshi Ogura, for example, returned to Japan after undergoing complete clinical training at the Menninger Hospital. Third-generation psychiatrists, who had completed training with second-generation psychiatrists such as Nishizono and myself, returned from shorter sojourns in England and the United States. Among these returning third-generation psychiatrists was Tetsuya Iwasaki, who, after studying at the Menninger Psychiatric School, presented Otto Kernberg's theory on borderline personality and its treatment. He also translated the works of Hanna Segal and introduced the Kleinian school of thought to Japan. During the same period, Joji Kandabashi, Sadanobu Ushijima, and others received training from John Padel in London. They introduced the object relations theory of Winnicott to the Japanese clinical scene.

Boosted by the participation of these third-generation psychiatrists, psychoanalysis gradually gained importance in Japan and became a major influence in the field of clinical psychiatry. However, as mentioned before, Japanese psychiatry has traditionally possessed a German—more specifically, a Kraepelinian and biological—orientation. This long-established tradition within Japanese psychiatry resulted in a variety of conflicts with emerging psychoanalytic dynamic psychiatry. It was under these circumstances that clinicians with a psychoanalytic orientation in psychiatry, clinical psychology, and psychosomatic medicine gradually began demonstrating their leadership through the vehicle of the Japan Psychoanalytical Association.

During the period 1960–1970, many important psychoanalytic works were translated into Japanese, in a movement toward internationalization organized by the Japan Psychoanalytic Society under the leadership of myself. The third Japanese translation of Freud's collected works appeared. In addition, most of the leading works on ego psychology by Wilhelm Reich, Heinz Hartmann, Ernst Kris, Anna Freud, and Erik Erikson were translated into Japanese.

The most original research in Japanese psychoanalysis at this time was that of Takeo Doi. As will be discussed later, his theory of *amae* eventually received recognition not only in Japan but also in the international psychoanalytic community.

In terms of clinical practice, it was during the period 1960–1970 that the diagnosis and psychotherapy of borderline cases, as well as classic psychoanalytic therapy, began to attract keen attention. Reflecting contemporary trends in Europe and the United States, psychoanalytic psychotherapists in Japan began actively performing psychotherapy for schizophrenic patients. Soon, psychiatric family study, particularly that of the schizophrenic family, became a theme of major importance. From approximately 1970, however,

Japanese psychiatry came under the influence of the worldwide antipsychiatry movement; as a result, numerous disputes occurred among various psychiatric societies and universities.

The Fourth-Generation Psychiatrists and Increasing International Exchange (Late 1970s–1980)

As disputes among universities and academic societies abated, a new wave of psychiatrists—who might be called the fourth generation—joined the established psychiatric community. This fourth generation, like the third, returned to Japan after studying psychoanalytic psychotherapy and dynamic psychiatry in Britain and the United States. Kuninao Minagawa, for example, received five years of training in psychotherapy at Michigan University from the Nagera group, focusing on the treatment of children and adolescents. Rikihachiro Kano returned to Japan after receiving training in psychoanalytic psychotherapy and dynamic psychiatry for three years at the Menninger Hospital in Topeka, Kansas. Osamu Kitayama received training in psychotherapy with a psychoanalytic orientation at the Department of Psychotherapy of London's Mousley Hospital.

During the 1980s, Japanese translations appeared for most of the essential works of object relations and Kleinian theorists: Melanie Klein, Michael Balint, Douglas Fairbain, D. W. Winnicott, and Hanna Segal. The translation of Bion's work is still under way, although Leon Grinberg and Elizabeth Bianchedi's study, "An Introduction to the Work of Bion," has appeared in Japanese.

From 1980 onward, a growing number of psychoanalysts from overseas, particularly from the United States, began to visit Japan. Leading American psychoanalysts such as Cornell University's Otto Kernberg and Arnold Cooper conducted the first international seminar in Tokyo, on borderline cases and narcissism. Numerous psychoanalysts from other countries followed, resulting in a dramatic increase in the number of seminars and lectures held in Japan. Leading IPA analysts—including former IPA presidents Robert Wallerstein, Serge Lebovici, and Joseph Sandler, among others—came to Japan on various occasions to give lectures and organize seminars. Ramon Ganzarain visited Japan for the congress meeting of the International Association of Group Psychotherapy, Serge Lebovici, Robert Emde and Joy Osofsky for the IACAPAP, and Efrain Bleiberg for the Menninger Workshop Tokyo.

Following the IPA Congress in Hamburg in 1983, the Japan Psychoanalytic Society has implemented English-Japanese simultaneous interpretation at subsequent IPA Congresses in Madrid (1985), Montreal (1987), and so on. The number of Japanese members taking part in the IPA Congress increases each year, and full-scale international exchanges with the IPA have been organized.

During the late 1980s, I became interested in reviving Kosawa's theory of the Ajase complex, seeking to integrate it with my own clinical experience and subsequent psychoanalytic research. Presented at a variety of international conferences, this new interpretation of Kosawa's theory has received widespread attention. Doi's concept of *amae,* presented at the IPA Congress in Montreal as well as the Amsterdam Congress (1993), has also attracted attention for its universal applicability. Osamu Kitayama has made original presentations at several IPA congresses, including the Psychoanalytic Congress in Rome (1989), the IPA Congress in Buenos Aires (1991), and the Amsterdam Congress. His studies are beginning to draw worldwide interest as well.

IMPORTANT CONTRIBUTIONS OF JAPANESE PSYCHOANALYSTS

As studies by leading Japanese psychoanalysts frequently cited in overseas literature, I would like to introduce (1) Takeo Doi's theory of *amae,* (2) the Ajase complex theory, developed by Kosawa and later expanded by myself, and (3) Osamu Kitayama's "The Prohibition of 'Don't Look'" and "Studies on Mourning." In terms of chronology, I should rightly begin with Kosawa's Ajase complex. However, in order to include my own, subsequent research on the Ajase theory, I will follow the order in which the studies drew international notice, and begin by discussing Doi's concept of *amae.*

The Theory of *Amae*: Takeo Doi

The first paper by Doi introducing the concept of *amae* appeared in an American speech journal (the 1956 spring issue of *Western Speech*), under the title, "Japanese Language as an Expression of Japanese Psychology." The relevant passage from this paper appears below.

> *Amaeru* [*amae* is its noun form] can be translated as "to depend and presume upon another's love." This word has the same root as *amai,* an adjective which corresponds to "sweet." Thus, *amaeru* has a distinct feeling of sweetness, and is generally used to express a child's attitude toward an adult, especially his parents. I can think of no English word equivalent to *amaeru* except for "spoil," which, however, is a transitive verb and definitely has a bad connotation; whereas the Japanese *amaeru* does not necessarily have a bad connotation, although we say we should not let a youngster *amaeru* too much. I think most Japanese adults have a dear memory of the taste of sweet dependency as a child and, consciously or unconsciously, carry a lifelong nostalgia for it. (92)

Thus, although *amaeru* has its primary locus in childhood, it may also apply to an interpersonal relationship between adults, if that relationship contains the same desire for dependency and belonging experienced by a child. Doi argued that the visibility or conscious recognition of *amae* might itself be a distinguishing factor of Japanese culture.

Doi furthermore discovered that an unfulfilled desire for *amae* lies behind *toraware* (a state of obsession in which a patient adheres to one idea to the exclusion of all others), often seen among patients of Morita *shinkeishitsu* or "nervousness"—the type of neurosis most prevalent among the Japanese. Doi later concluded that the psychodynamics of *amae* plays a central role in a variety of other psychiatric disorders as well.

Eventually, Doi came to assert that *amae* was not a psychology unique to the Japanese, but rather a universal psychology, appearing in other cultures as well. The psychology of keeping pets, for example, may be understood in terms of *amae*. Doi thus maintains that although the word *amae* originates in the Japanese language, the concept of *amae* possesses universal applicability and represents an important tool for psychoanalytic investigation.

In order to position his theory within the broader context of international psychoanalysis, Doi has compared *amae* with several existing psychoanalytic concepts. He writes:

> It has been my belief at the same time that this concept has a universal applicability inasmuch as the patient's transference can be interpreted in terms of *amae*. In other words, the concept of *amae* can lend itself to psychoanalytic formulation and may even complement the existing theories of psychoanalysts.

I would like to continue with another quotation from Doi:

> *Amae* agrees with object-relations theory and makes it more amenable to introspection precisely because *amae* and its vocabulary refer to inner experience. For instance, passive object love or primary love as defined by Michael Balint can be equated with *amae* in its pure form and as such, his concept becomes something quite tangible. In fact, Balint deplores the inadequacy of the word "love" to catch its essence in nascency, and states as follows: "All European languages are so poor that they cannot distinguish between the two kinds of object-love, active and passive." (1965, 56)

It is then remarkable that the Japanese language has this word *amae*, enabling the infantile origin of love to be accessible to consciousness. Incidentally, I began to correspond with Balint in 1962 and he confirmed that, after reading some of my papers, his ideas and mine were developing in the same direction. I also had the good fortune to discuss the matter with him personally when I went to London in 1964. I was furthermore delighted that he honored me later by citing my work in his last book, *The Basic Fault*.

In this connection, I would like to say a few words about the concept of attachment, which was introduced by John Bowlby into psychoanalysis from ethology, since it obviously covers the same area as *amae*. As is known, Bowlby sharply distinguishes attachment from dependence, saying that a child does not become attached to his mother because he has to depend on her. So he prefers attachment to dependence as a term, as the former can be more precise than the latter in describing behavior. He also mentions the negative value implications of the word dependence as another reason for avoiding it. Even so, it seems to me that he overlooks the fact that attachment involves a dependence of its own, as one necessarily becomes dependent on the object as far as one is attached to it. In this regard, *amae* definitely has an advantage over attachment precisely because it implies a psychological dependence in the sense mentioned above and unlike attachment refers to the feeling experienced rather than to behavior. All in all, one can say, paradoxical as it may sound, that the concept of *amae* makes it possible to discuss what is not verbalized in ordinary communication, hence is something that remains totally unnoticed if you are speaking European languages.

Next, I would like to explain how the concept of *amae* can be related to narcissism, identification, and ambivalence. *Amae* is object-relational from the beginning, therefore it does not quite agree with the concept of primary narcissism. However, it fits in very well with secondary narcissism; in fact, it is particularly well-suited to describe whatever state of mind may be called narcissistic. Namely, of the two kinds of *amae*—primitive and convoluted—that I mentioned before, the convoluted *amae*, which is childish, willful, and demanding, is surely narcissistic. As a matter of fact, if you suspect someone of being narcissistic, you may be sure that this person has a problem with *amae*. In the same vein, a new concept of self-object defined by Kohut as "those archaic objects cathected with narcissistic libido" (1971, 3) will be much easier to comprehend in the light of *amae* psychology, since "the narcissistic libido" is none other than convoluted *amae*. Also, Balint's observation that "in the final phase of the treatment, patients begin to give expression to long forgotten, infantile, instinctual wishes, and to demand their gratification from their environment" (1965, 81) makes perfect sense, because the primitive *amae* will manifest itself only after narcissistic defenses are worked through by analysis.

Doi's *amae* theory has prompted numerous debates and discussions. I myself, for instance, have discussed adult perceptions of *amae* behavior in children. The concept of *amae* as represented by Doi is an intrapsychic emotional state experienced by adults, and it is also a mode of interpersonal relationship. It should be noted, however, that Japanese rarely used the word *amae* subjectively, for example, in the sense "I want to *amaeru*." Rather, the word refers to someone else: "He or she is *amaeru*-ing," "is overly *amaeru*-ing," or "is resorting to *amae*." It is essentially a word used by an adult to refer to a child, or by an older or senior person to refer to a junior, describing the latter's emotions, or mode of interpersonal relationship.

Some adults experience negative feelings toward *amae*. They may want to prohibit or punish it in others, or they may feel ashamed and guilty of their own desire to *amaeru*. In certain cases, the mind may work to ignore or negate feelings of *amae*. In psychoanalytic terms, the conflict with the superego toward *amae*, or the defense of the ego against *amae*, generates a variety of emotions. Part or all of this mental process is then projected onto another person.

Finally, within the context of the parent-child relationship in Japan, the word *amae* frequently carries a sense of reproach: "Stop *amaeru*-ing," "See, you're *amaeru*-ing again," "I've had enough of your *amaeru*-ing," or "You're an *amaeru*-ing child."

The Ajase Complex: Kosawa and Okonogi

The Story of Ajase and His Mother: Heisaku Kosawa's Version

The Ajase complex is an original theory developed by Heisaku Kosawa and subsequently expanded by myself. Whereas Freud based his Oedipus complex on a Greek tragedy, Kosawa developed his theory of the Ajase complex from stories found in Buddhist scripture. The story of Ajase centers on the Buddhist concept of reincarnation.

Well known to the Buddhist world, Ajase's story appears with many variations in the scriptures of ancient India. These scriptures entered Japan by way of China and Korea from approximately 700–1000 AD. Kosawa modeled his theory on the version of Ajase's story appearing in the *Kanmuryojukyo*, a Buddhist scripture centering on the salvation of the mother. In this instance, the woman saved by the Buddha is Ajase's mother, Idaike.

Wife of King Bimbasara, the ruler of an ancient Indian kingdom, Idaike feared that as her beauty faded she was losing her husband's love. She consulted a soothsayer, who told her a sage living in the forest would die in three years' time, to be reborn as her son. However, Idaike was too anxious to wait three years, and, desperate to have a child, she killed the sage. As he was dying, the sage cursed Idaike, telling her that, reincarnated as her son, he would one day kill the king. Idaike became pregnant at this moment. The unborn Ajase had thus already been murdered by his mother's egotism. Moreover, fearing the wrath of the sage reincarnated in her womb, Idaike attempted to kill her son by giving birth to him from the summit of a high tower. Ajase survived; however, having broken his little finger as a result of his fall, he was nicknamed "the prince with the broken finger."

Ajase passed a happy childhood. However, on reaching adolescence, he learned from Daibadatta, the enemy of Buddha, that his mother had attempted to kill him by giving birth from the top of a high tower; he had only to look at his broken little finger for proof. The Sanskrit word *Ajatasatru* means both "broken finger" and "prenatal rancor" (a term to be discussed below). Disillusioned with the mother he had idealized, Ajase attempted to kill her. He was subsequently overcome by guilt, however, and developed a severe skin disease, characterized by festering sores so offensive that no one dared approach him, except for his mother, Idaike. Despite his mother's devoted care, Ajase did not readily recover; he even attempted several times to kill her. Seeking relief, Idaike went to the Buddha and told him of her sufferings. The Buddha's teachings healed her inner conflict, and she returned to continue to care for Ajase. Eventually, the prince was cured to become a widely respected ruler. This is the version of the Ajase story Kosawa wrote in the 1950s, based on the *Kanmuryojukuo*.

Themes of the Ajase Complex

My own research has identified two fundamental aspects of the Ajase story as presented by Kosawa. I will also present, as a third point, Kosawa's own examination of guilt in the Ajase complex.

The Mother's Conflict Between the Wish for a Child and Infanticidal Wishes. Queen Idaike wished to have a child in order to protect her status as queen and maintain her husband's love—she took the extreme action of killing the sage to achieve her desires. However, believing that the birth of the reincarnated sage would bring disastrous results, Idaike began to fear the child in her womb. She then attempted to kill her child by giving birth to him from the top of a high tower.

The story of Ajase illustrates two conflicting emotions on the part of the mother. On the one hand, she wishes to have a child in order to protect herself and to achieve her own desires. On the other hand, projecting persecutory imagery and hatred onto her baby, she becomes fearful of the child's birth and attempts to kill him.

According to Serge Lebovici, such conflict depicts the mother's ambivalence concerning her *bébé imaginaire*. The egocentric conflict of the mother—her wishes both to have a child and to eliminate her baby—arouses persecutory anxiety through projection onto the child she carries. This unconscious maternal conflict appears clearly in the Ajase story.

The Child's Prenatal Rancor and Matricidal Wishes. Ajase experienced rage toward his origins from the moment of conception. As a reincarnation of the murdered sage, that is, he desired to kill his mother even before his birth. In Buddhism, this anger experienced toward birth itself is termed *mishooon*, or prenatal rancor.

Kosawa compared the Oedipus complex and the Ajase complex as follows:

> Freud's Oedipus complex originates in a conflict involving the libido, with the son's love for his mother and hatred for his father. The Ajase complex, on the other hand, concerns the more fundamental question of birth or origins.

Kosawa further contended that whereas incestuous desire and patricide formed the core of the Oedipus complex, the Ajase complex centered on the themes of matricide and prenatal resentment.

Two Types of Guilt and the Mother's Forgiveness. The paper Kosawa originally submitted to Freud concerning the Ajase complex bore the title "Two Types of Guilt." ("The Ajase Complex" was a subtitle.) In this paper, Kosawa asserted the following: When a child makes a mistake or does something wrong, he or she first experiences guilt as a fear of punishment. However, human beings have another sense of guilt, which is of a higher dimension than mere fear of punishment. This second type of guilt is experienced when the child who fears punishment is forgiven his or her wrongdoing.

In terms of the Buddhist legend, Ajase suffered feelings of guilt when confronted by a minister with his desire to kill his mother. Shocked at his own contemplated matricide, he began to shake and became deathly ill. Idaike, however, forgave her son and nursed him devotedly. Under his mother's care, Ajase experienced a more profound sense of guilt, one of heartfelt remorse.

Kosawa termed this guilt resulting from forgiveness *zangeshin* or "repentance." He emphasized the need to differentiate between repentance and the guilt related to punishment. This "repentance"-type guilt compares with Klein's depressive/reparative guilt. The Ajase story may thus be viewed as depicting the transition from a punitive to a reparative type of guilt. (Kosawa may in fact have read Klein's *The Psycho-Analysis of Children* before writing his thesis.)

Ramon Ganzarain, an American psychoanalyst who studied the Ajase complex, has delineated several defense mechanisms in its treatment of guilt: denial, confusion, and so on.

Subsequent Discussions of the Ajase Complex

The most important discussions will be introduced below.

The Mother's Distress Over Losing Paternal Support

I once received the following remarks from Professor Theodore Lidz concerning the Ajase story. In his view, children should be raised by both parents; the conflict of the Ajase story originates in the father's declining an active role and leaving the child's fate in the hands of the mother. Ajase's difficulties, in other words, began with the mother's tragedy of losing her husband's—or, in a broader sense, a man's—support.

I believe this is a very important interpretation. One of the important themes of the Ajase complex is that, although children grow up in a triadic world of father, mother, and the child, a mother such as Idaike carries the burden of raising her child by herself. The world of the Ajase complex is therefore a dyadic world.

Lidz's interpretation is also relevant in light of the sociohistorical background of the Ajase legend in Japan. Early Japanese Buddhism was highly influenced by Chinese philosophy. (As mentioned above, Buddhism arrived from India via China and Korea.) An essentially Japanese, popular Buddhism began to develop during the Kamakura era (1183–1333)—through the efforts of such priests and Shinran and Nichiren. One of the issues in popular Japanese Buddhism was the possibility of women's entry into the Buddhist paradise. Behind this issue lay the problem of guilt over infanticide, particularly abortion, since Japanese women have traditionally been assigned responsibility for disposing of unwanted children. The depiction of Idaike's salvation in the *Kanmuryojukyo* played an important role in assuaging mothers' guilt over infanticide.

On the Origins of the Text of the Ajase Complex

The Ajase story also appears in the *Nehangyo* quoted in the teachings of Shinran, the *Kyogyoshinsho,* with an emphasis on the father-son relationship and patricide as in the Oedipus complex. Kosawa, however, influenced by the *Kanmuryojukyo,* wrote his story as a uniquely mother-child story.

It is interesting to compare this textual history with recent Western studies of Freud's Oedipus complex. For example, attention has recently been focused on Freud's omission of certain aspects of the Oedipus story, particularly the conflict occurring between Laius and Jocasta before Oedipus's birth. Freud omitted this portion of the Oedipus myth and focused only on the conflict between the adolescent Oedipus and his parents, naming this the Oedipus complex. If Freud had included the incidents surrounding Oedipus's birth, his story might have possessed a greater thematic similarity with the Ajase complex. From a cross-cultural perspective, one might suggest that Freud was influenced by the Judeo-Christian tradition, whereas Kosawa was heavily influenced by the oft-cited "maternal" aspect of the Japanese culture.

The Ajase Complex of Sigmund Freud

Balmary (1979) have proposed that one reason behind Freud's radical switch from the psychic trauma theory to the endogenic drive theory lay in defense mechanisms organized against the acknowledgment of his father's failure. They argue that, while married to his second wife, Rebecca, Freud's father had a relationship with a twenty-year-old woman who became pregnant. This child was Sigmund Freud. After Rebecca's flight and subsequent suicide, Jacob married Amalia, Freud's mother. If this hypothesis is correct, Freud would have experienced extreme conflict concerning his existence as his parents' "imaginary baby."

Does the avoidance of origins and of the *bébé imaginaire* in Freud's Oedipus story represent a repression of the Ajase complex? Joan Raphael-Leff, a psychoanalyst based in London, has compared Ajase's mother Idaike in the Ajase story with Oedipus's mother Jocasta in the Oedipus myth. In her paper, Raphael-Leff contends that, like Idaike, Jocasta also displays maternal ambivalence, expressing both the desire to have a child and infanticidal wishes. Further study of the Oedipus myth in light of the Ajase complex might prove to be highly significant.

In sum, the origins of both Oedipus and Freud, as well as Freud's Ajase complex, have recently become the subject of study in the West. The theory of the Ajase complex is thus not applicable to only Japanese mothers and children; it is a universal theme.

The Study of *On*—the Japanese Concept of Debt or Indebtedness—and of the "Don't Look" Prohibition: Osamu Kitayama

As Osamu Kitayama states in "Metaphorization—Making Terms," the analyst's receptiveness to ambiguity is generally thought to be an essential part of his or her psychoanalytical practice. The interpretation of multiple meanings can effectively crate a "bridging function" between personal metaphorical meaning and shared literal meaning. It appears that this ambiguous metaphor fails to function in the treatment of schizophrenics, who experience metaphor in literal terms. Some, however, can utilize metaphors, indicating positive signs (i.e., a nonpsychotic part, an anal retentive tendency, creativity, ambiguity tolerance, etc.).

Kitayama's paper concerns the transitional process from literal experience to metaphorical understanding in schizophrenic patients. In this process, the therapist's role of translating the patient's expressions, which are experienced literally, into metaphorical "here and now" events is essential. Among relevant technical issues, the appearance and usage of the "in-metaphor" and compound metaphor may play an important role in interweaving the words and meanings of the two persons in therapy.

Kitayama (1993) next analyzed several ambiguous metaphorical expressions in the Japanese language: for instance, the Japanese word *on*, which expresses obligation, debt, guilt, and love or kindness. Whereas the English concept of guilt is associated with punishment, *on* implies repayment or "requital." It is interesting to note that concepts such as *oime*, *giri*, and *kari*, which also seem important to Japanese ways of thinking, share with *on* the core meaning of debt or indebtedness.

Intrigued by the importance of debt to Japanese motivational concepts, Kitayama (1985) investigated Japanese myths and folktales, particularly tales of marriage between humans and nonhumans, in order to relate them to his clinical experience. In one tale, the snake-wife, responding to the hero's demand, forfeits her milk-producing eyeballs. The most typical and popular legend is "A Crane's Repayment of her Debt (*On*)." Below is an outline of the tale.

1) The hero rescues an injured crane, which, in the guise of a beautiful woman, then visits his home and offers herself in marriage.
2) The young woman is a talented weaver as well as a devoted wife. However, she prohibits the hero from watching her at work, since, in her original form as a crane, she is weaving cloth from her own feathers.
3) Unable to resist the temptation, the hero ignores the prohibition of "don't look"—only to see the young woman in her original form.
4) He becomes frightened; the crane-woman feels hurt and ashamed. The two separate in the end.

The prohibition of "don't look" is a taboo which, in a two-body relationship, should be broken over time, in contrast to the oedipal incest taboo, the taboo to be kept. Kitayama concluded that the tragic development of the above tale shows a sudden transition, in Kleinian terms, from the paranoid-schizoid position to the depressive position.

Kitayama (1991) further argued that from the viewpoint of "environmental failure," "false charge," or "forced guilt" may occur when the infant is suddenly confronted with its causal relation to the fragile environment, and that maternal prohibition should be withdrawn gradually as the infant develops the capacity to tolerate causality. As an infant's feeling of indebtedness stems from the relative tension between his or her own destructiveness and the mother's survival, it is thus possible to speak of "forced" or "false guilt," generated in infants with masochistic caretakers.

Finally, Kitayama (1993) proposed the value of "indebtedness" as a psychological concept to bridge external charge and internal debt. When analyzing transference and repeated acting-out in the form of masochistic or suicidal behavior, we may discover a conscious or unconscious pathological accumulation of debt.

THE PRESENT STATE OF THE JAPAN PSYCHOANALYTIC SOCIETY

To restate briefly, on succeeding to the presidency of the IPA Sendai Branch in 1955, Kosawa changed its name to the IPA Japan Branch and relocated its headquarters to Tokyo. This IPA Japan Branch later came to be called the Japan Psychoanalytic Society. The society is currently directed by psychiatrists who received training analysis from Heisaku Kosawa, Japan's first generation of psychoanalysts.

Michio Yamamura succeeded Kosawa as president of the society, to be followed by Takeo Doi, and current president Masahisa Nishizono. I myself have served as secretary for many years. Sadanobu Ushijima is the current treasurer, and Tetsuya Iwasaki the current chairman of the Education and Training Committee.

During the transition period between Kosawa's death and the start of training conducted by the first-generation psychoanalysts, training analysis was not actively performed in Japan. The present membership for the Japan Psychoanalytic Society therefore remains quite small, with eighteen active members and thirteen associate members.

Eighty percent of the society members live in the Tokyo area, with the remaining 20 percent in distant Fukuoka (in southern Japan) and vicinity. Although the Japan Psychoanalytic Society has not yet established a psychoanalytic institute integrating these two areas, it hopes to do so by 1994. Members, however, have not yet agreed whether to establish one psychoanalytic institute covering all of Japan, or two psychoanalytic institutes—one in Tokyo and the other in Fukuoka.

The society intends to establish, by 1994, new regulations in line with the education and training criteria set forth by the IPA. It also plans to increase the number of training analysts and to implement training analyses in accordance with international standards.

CONCLUDING REMARKS

The psychoanalytic theory transmitted from the Vienna Psychoanalytic Institute via Kosawa forms the mainstream of psychoanalysis in Japan. From the 1950s to the 1970s, this dominant trend received its greatest influence from the dynamic psychiatry of the United States.

Presently, there is a mounting interest in Japan for Kohutian self-psychology as well as object relations theory, particularly the work of Melanie Klein, D. W. Winnicott, and W. Bion. Establishing the clinical applications of these theories has become a major challenge for numerous Japanese clinicians. The application of psychoanalysis to the fields of adolescent and infant psychiatry is also a focus of interest, and has been the topic of international meetings conducted in Japan. There is finally a growing trend to conduct psychoanalysis independent of either dynamic psychiatry or psychoanalytic theory.

The number of patients receiving psychoanalytic psychotherapy has increased dramatically in the Japanese cities of Tokyo, Osaka, Fukuoka, Kobe, and Hiroshima. There has also been a sharp rise in the number of private psychotherapeutic clinics operating in Tokyo, including five or six psychoanalytic psychotherapy clinics. These trends indicate potential for the future growth of psychoanalysis and psychoanalytic psychotherapy in Japan.

Japanese psychiatrists' and psychologists' study of psychoanalytic thought generated an encounter between Western and Japanese culture. Indigenous Japanese patterns of thought merged with the imported theory of psychoanalysis, paving the way for such theories as those of *amae*, the Ajase complex, and the "don't look" prohibition. These theories aid in understanding the mentality not only of Japanese, but also of people from other cultures; they furthermore promise to contribute greatly to psychoanalytic understanding itself. I sincerely hope that Japanese psychoanalysis will continue to make significant theoretical contributions to the international community.

2

Psychoanalysis in Korea

Do-Un Jeong and David Sachs

> Ten feet-depth of water we can look into; one foot-depth of human mind we cannot.
>
> Korean proverb

We always dream and dreams come true sometimes. Psychoanalysis has been always a dream to Koreans to come true for decades.[1] Where do we begin talking about psychoanalysis in Korea (essentially South Korea; officially Republic of Korea)? Talking about psychoanalysis and Korea is not an easy task, since Korea is a sophisticated country, with its history dating back to 2,333 BC.

SOME FACTS ABOUT KOREA

Korea is a peninsula. It is located between China on the west and north and Japan on the east. South Korea is blocked on the north by North Korea, with the DMZ (demilitarized zone, the product of the Korean War) in between. The total area of South Korea is 98,480 square kilometers with 238 kilometers of land boundary with North Korea and coastline of 2,413 kilometers (World Factbook, 2008). On the north and east it is mostly hilly and mountainous and on west and south it has wide plains. Its biggest island is Jeju Island. There are nine provinces and seven major cities. The major cities include Seoul (capital), Incheon, Busan, Kwangju, Daegu, Daejeon, and Ulsan. South Korea has four distinct seasons: spring, summer, autumn, and winter. Jeju Island, a popular vacation place, has a temperate oceanic climate. South Korea's population is about forty-eight million. Literacy rate is 97.9 percent. GDP per capita is US$25,000 (2007). Korean industries cover electronics, telecommunications, automobile production, chemicals, shipbuilding, and steel. Korea exports US$379 billion f.o.b. and imports US$349.6 billion f.o.b. (2007). Korea has 35.59 million Internet users (2007).

Koreans (South and North Koreans) use Korean as their official language. In South Korea, English is widely taught in schools in addition to elective education in other foreign languages such as German, French, Japanese, Chinese, Spanish, and so on. Hangeul, the official Korean alphabet, was first invented in 1443 and promulgated in 1446 by Great King Sejong of the Joseon Dynasty. (The "King Sejong Literacy Prize" is awarded by UNESCO every year in memory of him.) The modern Hangeul syllabic unit is composed of a selective combination of seven vowels and fourteen consonants.

South Korea is now a modern democratic nation, in contrast to North Korea, the Communist country under one-man dictatorship. In South Korea, people elect the president by vote for a single five-year term. With the consent of the National Assembly, the president appoints the prime minister. The National Assembly, Supreme Court, and Constitutional Court have independent functions. More than four political parties are active in Korea. There are also political pressure groups, such the Federation of Korean Industries, Korean Confederation of Trade Unions, Korean Veterans' Association, and National Council of Labor Unions. Nowadays, NGOs (nongovernmental organizations) are very active and important in Korean politics. South Korea maintains official membership in almost seventy international organizations, including the UN, OECD, APEC, IBRD, IAEA, WHO, and WTO. Examples of internationally notable South Koreans are Ban Ki-moon, the present secretary-general of the United Nations, who is a former minister of foreign affairs and trade of South Korea, and Dr. Lee Jong-wook, now deceased, who is the immediate past director-general of the WHO.

Tae-geuk-gi is the South Korean flag. The center circle in the white background has equally divided red (top) ("the yang") and blue ("the yin") sections. The yang and yin symbolize infinite movement, balance and harmony. Four trigrams (representing universal elements of heaven, earth, fire, and water) surround the circle. The national anthem of South Korea is called *Ae-guk-ga* ("Loving the Country") and the music was composed in 1935 by Eak-Tay Ahn (1905–1965). *Mu-gung-hwa* (*mu-gung*, meaning immortality), Rose of Sharon, represents the endurance and perseverance of the Korean people and culture and is the national flower of South Korea.

South Korea is rapidly entering into a geriatric society, with 10.5 percent of its population occupied by those sixty-five years and over. Population growth rate is 0.269 percent, with a birthrate of 9.09 per 1,000 population and death rate of 5.73 deaths per 1,000 population. Total infant mortality rate is 4.29 deaths per 1,000 live births. Life expectancy at birth is 78.64 years (total), 75.34 years (male), and 82.17 years (female). Ethnic groups are relatively very homogeneous but in recent years there have been an increasing number of immigrants from foreign countries, particularly China, Vietnam, and Japan, mostly by marriage (e-Indices, Korean Government, 2008). Confucianism, adopted in 1394 by the Joseon Dynasty as the country's national religion/ discipline, has exerted profound influence on Koreans in general in terms of morality, ways of life, and legal system, and has produced many Korean Confucian scholars. Confucianism, however, is no longer regarded as a religion. Other religions include Buddhism (23.2 percent, since 372 AD), Protestantism (19.7 percent, circa 1882), and Roman Catholicism (6.6 percent, circa 1784). Interestingly, Koreans became academically interested in Catholic and Protestant beliefs even before the arrival of missionaries to Korea. Traditional shamanism is also a part of modern Korean life and culture (e.g., *gut*, a rite by a shaman at fortune-telling cafes or festivals).

South Korea has 8,344 preschools, 5,813 elementary schools, 3,077 middle schools, 1,493 high schools, 697 occupational high schools, 147 junior colleges, 174 universities/colleges, 10 teachers' colleges, and 13 colleges for industries. There are 433 departments of medical sciences and pharmacy (Center for Education Statistics, 2008). South Korea has 41 medical schools/colleges (The Korean Council of Deans of Medical College, 2008).

Under a long tradition of Confucianism, South Koreans used to have "boy-preference" and expected the eldest son to be in charge of the family matters. Now with revision of the family-related laws, equality for sons and daughters in inheritance and other matters is ensured legally. Industrialization and urbanization have caused the disruption of the extended family system into couple-centered nuclear family system. In spite of this change, Koreans reaffirm their relationship with the ancestors by having *Je-sa* on the anniversary days as well as on special occasions such as *Seol-nal* (Lunar New Year's Day) and *Chu-seok* (Korean Thanksgiving Day).

In Korea, marriage is the most important task of an individual and his or her family. Children take the father's family name but Korean women do not take the husband's family name. The husband's income is expected to be kept and managed by his wife. A divorce is regarded as a disgrace not only for the couple but also for the families on both sides. However, for the past decade the divorce rate has increased rapidly and it has emerged as a major social problem.

Han-ok is a traditional Korean house. Its design is eco-friendly in not only its structure but also its building materials. Traditional Korean rooms serve multiple functions and they are heated with an underfloor heating system, called *On-dol*. *Han-bok* had been the Korean traditional clothing for thousands of years before the import of Western clothing one hundred years ago. The beauty and grace of Korean culture can be still found when Koreans wear the traditional clothing on special occasions.

South Korea is not a small country considering the diversity and differences of food and dishes found throughout Korea. Rice has been and is still the basis of food originating from the agricultural tradition. Notable side dishes are *gimchi* (fermented spicy dish made of vegetables with varied seasonings), *doenjang* (fermented thick paste of soybeans), *namul* (seasoned vegetable/herb/green dish different from *gimchi*), and *jeotgal* (fermented salted seafood). Korean cuisine also includes a wide variety of meat and fish dishes. In Korean table setting, all dishes are served at the same time and a spoon is used more often, compared to neighboring China and Japan.

KOREAN MEDICINE AND PSYCHIATRY

When we talk about psychoanalysis in the world, we talk about North America, Europe, South America, and Australia. Despite the fact that there is an IPA (International Psychoanalytical Association)–accredited Psychoanalytic Institute in Japan, Japan and Korea are separated by the sea and there is a historical animosity transferred from the Japanese occupation of Korea in the early part of the twentieth century (1910–1945).

Asia, in general, has no international access to psychoanalytic training and education except in domestic Japan and India. So psychoanalytic development in Asian countries should be quite different from what has been occurring for the past years in Eastern European countries. Koreans have had no possibility of condensed analysis, shuttle analysis, and other choices. Unlike European languages, Korean, Japanese, and Chinese share very little linguistically.

Korean medicine during the ending part of Joseon Dynasty (1392–1910), that is, the very late part of the nineteenth century and the very early part of the twentieth century, had some initial input from American missionary medicine. But it soon became the domain of Japanese "Western" medicine with the occupation of Korea by Japan (1910–1945). And at that time Japanese medicine was being heavily influenced by German medicine.

Psychiatry was no exception. Kraepelinian descriptive psychiatry from Germany was the mainstream. Freudian psychoanalysis was introduced but in a very scattered, episodic manner in the early part of the twentieth century. Survey of the Korean history database on the Internet (National Institute of Korean History, 2008) produced evidence of the introduction of psychoanalysis to Korea in magazines and newspapers during the 1930s. For example, *Dong—A Daily News* reported in its issue published on August 15, 1939, that Dr. Sigmund Freud was seriously ill in bed in London.

What if Korea had not been occupied by Japan for thirty-six years and if American missionary medicine had continued to influence Korean "Western" medicine? Historically, Korea has been very much able to import ideas from outward, make them part of its culture, and export them to other countries—for instance, Buddhism and Confucianism. So, there is no reason that psychoanalysis should be the exception, if introduced in a consistent manner. In the thirtieth issue of a magazine published on July 1, 1930, a Korean scholar belonging to the Medical Psychology Study Group wrote on "the effects of psychotherapy applied to psychotic patients." He presented a case treated with a psychoanalytic method and discussed anticipatory fear (Lee, 1930).

Koreans' curiosity about and access to psychoanalysis was blocked by Japanese colonial occupation, while the Japanese themselves enjoyed much more freedom to access Freudian psychoanalysis in Vienna (Okonogi, 1995). Historical evidence about Korean interests in psychoanalysis during the early part of the twentieth century is still being discovered from various historical archives and needs to be explored further and described in the near future.

With its liberation from Japanese occupation in 1945 after Japan's defeat in World War II and following the outbreak of the Korean War in 1950, the whole landscape of Korean scholarship changed. The Korean War was a major, tragic deterrent to the development of modern Korea; however, in terms of the importing psychoanalytic ideas, the introduction of American medical officers during the war assisted the Korean scholars to be more and more aware of psychoanalytic ideas and practice. It was a turning point of Korean psychiatry from descriptive psychiatry of German origin introduced by Japanese scholars to American psychodynamic psychiatry. Seok-Jin Yoo, a graduate of the Seoul National University College of Medicine and later one of the early major figures in Korean psychiatry, was one of the converted and was very actively committed to reading psychoanalytic literature and teaching what he had learned to his juniors. Psychoanalysis rapidly caught the attention of Korean psychiatrists. Seok-Jin Yoo, with junior psychiatrists, tried to translate Freud's works in Korean.

The Korean War and the consequent combat-related mental disorders required urgent action and demanded Korean psychiatrists to be trained in psychotherapeutic measures for treating soldiers. Despite this significant historical input, Korea's quest after psychoanalysis could not continue in a consistent way due to lack of resources during the following decades.

SIGMUND FREUD SYMPOSIUM IN SEOUL AND KOREAN ENTHUSIASM ABOUT PSYCHOANALYSIS

In retrospect, the year 1957 might be considered as the first historical year of Korean psychoanalysis. The symposium on psychoanalysis in commemoration of Sigmund Freud's one-hundred-and-first birthday was held by the Korean Neuropsychiatric Association, the oldest specialty organization under the Korean Academy of Medical Sciences (Korean Neuropsychiatric Association, 1957). It is reported that about 2,500 enthusiastic people gathered at the Grand Auditorium of the Seoul National University College of Medicine for the one full-day symposium, and most of them didn't leave until the symposium ended. Well-known scholars, many of them psychiatrists, presented thirteen papers. The proceeding included "Freud's photograph," "brief biography," and "an introduction" by the dean of Seoul National University College of Medicine (Joo-Wan Myung, professor of psychiatry) as well as papers. The papers were on "major conceptions of Freudian psychoanalysis," "the development of psychoanalysis," "Freud's theory of hysteria," "libido and sexual instincts theory," "Freud's theory of dream analysis," "Freud and wit," "psychoanalysis and art," "psychoanalysis and group psychology," "psychoanalysis and religion," "philosophical background of psychoanalysis," "critique of sexual instincts theory," "neo-Freudian Karen Horney," and "Freud in contemporary American psychiatry." In 1959, *The Interpretation of Dreams* by Freud was translated by Yong-Ho Lee and published in Korean.

The first textbook of psychiatry in Korean was published by Dongse Hahn (1969), then an assistant professor of psychiatry at the Seoul National University College of Medicine. Trained in psychiatry in New York City and certified by the American Board of Psychiatry and Neurology, he had far advanced general knowledge, experience, and skills in contemporary American psychiatry. His book was intended to be a general textbook for medical students, doctors, and other scholars dealing with mental issues and contained many psychoanalytic and psychotherapeutic ideas and case examples. For example, rapport, ventilation, suggestion, persuasion, the unconscious, infantile sexuality, repression, free association, transference, countertransference, participant observer, supportive psychotherapy, and intensive psychotherapy were presented, explained, and discussed. He boldly mentioned—whether validly or not—that Koreans had strong oral and weak anal tendencies. He also described how the side effects of Western-style psychotherapies applied to Koreans.

With easily available and stimulating textbooks in the Korean language, university trainees in psychiatry became more interested in dynamic psychiatry. In the 1960s, hospitals opened psychotherapy programs for patients and individual supervisions for trainees were provided. In the 1970s and 1980s, with rapid economic growth, more attention was paid to psychotherapy by the general public as well as mental illness specialists. Psychotherapy training became a mandatory part of board certification in psychiatry. Examinees were required to present their own cases at the examination.

As South Korea arose from being a war-stricken, impoverished nation to a highly successful economy in East Asia, Koreans began to be subjected to the side effects of industrialization and urbanization. With the dissolution of the extended family system into a nuclear one, the traditional value system based on hierarchy collided with westernized ways of thinking, causing the dilution and loss of filial piety and mobilizing other conflicts. Koreans consequently became more interested in and oriented to the psychological origin of illnesses. The need for psychotherapy increased and it subsequently reflected the wishes of Korean psychiatrists and the general public for the "premier version" of all psychotherapies—that is, psychoanalysis.

However, Koreans were still on the unhappy side of the "psychoanalytic divide." They were geographically and linguistically isolated from psychoanalytic training and education. In spite of a scattered introduction of psychoanalytic ideas into Korea in the disciplines of philosophy, literature, education, and medicine, individual efforts did not bring a significant change. Koreans were hungry for psychoanalytic training, but they did not have good teachers. The availability of psychoanalytic books and journals imported from abroad only made them more curious and then frustrated, because the literature contained many psychoanalytic and psychotherapeutic ideas and practical applications that could not be understood without proper education and training. Unanswered curiosity was simply depressing. Teachers had a difficult time saving face when confronted by tricky questions from students.

THE SEOUL PSYCHOANALYTIC STUDY GROUP

In 1980 the second historical era of Korean psychoanalysis began. After many years of thought and consultations with foreign analysts including Jacob Arlow, Marianne Kris, Arnold Cooper, Edward Joseph, and Anna Freud, Doo-Young Cho, a Cornell University Medical Center graduate from the psychiatry residency program and then an assistant professor at the Seoul National University College of Medicine, initiated a movement for organizing a psychoanalytic study group in Seoul (Cho, 1995). He himself had the experience of being in personal analysis during his stay in New York City. He recruited five other psychiatrists (Seung-Hwan Oh, Eyong Kim, Hyun-Woo Kim, Dong-Soo Han, and Jin-Wook Sohn), organized a group, and named it the Seoul Psychoanalytic Study Group (later renamed in 1989 as the Korean Psychoanalytic Society with growing membership). The group was founded on May 6, 1980, in commemoration of Sigmund Freud's birthday. The six members apparently identified themselves with Sigmund Freud's Committee. They held biweekly book-reading seminars on Wednesday evenings. With the steady increase of membership in the following years, Cho was elected as the first president in 1983.

The ambience in Seoul regarding the organization of a psychoanalytic study group was not a favorable one. A Jungian group was already active. A psychotherapy group was also present. They all were watchful and challenged the young, vulnerable students of Freudian psychoanalysis. However, the group grew despite these competing and interrupting influences from outside as well as inward ambivalence and fragility. Biological psychiatry was also a strong emerging opponent.

New members of the group were carefully selected, based on recommendations of active members and discussions among members. The membership has grown rapidly nationwide and now numbers about 150. Also, the society now has many enthusiastic nonmember participants at its biannual congresses and other workshops that are usually fully occupied.

As a small group of several members, there were not much to be done except read the literature in psychoanalysis. It usually ended up in postseminar social gatherings where the group's cohesiveness and identity were strengthened. Later, this family-like ambience inevitably slowed the formation of formal organizational identity. Studying psychoanalysis based mainly on reading could not provide an optimum level of intellectual and emotional satiety. The group realized the necessity of inviting good teachers from abroad. However, it was not easy to invite a foreign analyst to teach the group, because Korea was too new and had never been thought of internationally as fertile soil for psychoanalytic growth. Also, financially, there was no money for that. Even now, there is no sponsored funding for the invited teachers.

Eventually in 1984, the group invited Alan Fraser (United States), Masahisa Nishizono (Japan), and Myunghee Kim (United States). In 1985, Normund Wong (United States) came to visit the group. It is told that at the first encounter with Korean members, Wong was quite upset, since nobody volunteered to talk during the session. Koreans, having been accustomed to didactic education, expected him to talk and teach, while he, with an American educational background, wanted Koreans to ask him questions and make comments. Two cultures collided, but soon mutual understanding occurred. Generally, seminars are intensive for four consecutive days including two weekend days. Besides academic activities, invited analysts are provided ample opportunity to become familiar with Korean history, culture, and customs.

In order to attend the seminars, members travel across the nation. So far, invited analysts from abroad between 1985 and 2008 have been as follows (in alphabetical order): Sander Abend, Harold Blum, Donald Cohen,

Theodore Cohen, Calvin Colarusso, Arnold Cooper, Jim Dimon, Alan Fraser, Raymond Gehl, Sanford Gifford, Nancy Goodman, Edward Joseph, Otto Kernberg, Myunghee Kim, Nadine Levinson, Robert Michels, Robert Nemiroff, Owen Renik, Arthur Rosenbaum, David Sachs, Albert Solnit, Nam-Soo Song, Barbara Stimmel, James Strain, Robert Tyson, Robert Wallerstein, and Normund Wong (United States); Matthew Suh (Canada); Ronald Baker, Dinora Pines, Anne-Marie Sandler, and Joseph Sandler (United Kingdom); Georg Bruns and Peter Kutter (Germany); Collette Chiland (France); Adeline van Waning (Netherlands); Kim Skoglund (Sweden); Elizabeth T. de Bianchedi, Marcello de Bianchedi, and Teresa Yuan (Argentina); Takeo Doi, Masahisa Nishizono, Keigo Okonogi, and Osamu Kitayama (Japan). Some of the above-mentioned analysts came to visit Korea more than once. Koreans have been inviting foreign analysts, mostly world-eminent training analysts, two to six times per year.

The experience of inviting world-famous psychoanalysts and learning from them on the theory and practice of psychoanalysis was very insightful and stimulating. Out of this novel, repeated exposure to highly experienced analysts, Koreans learned that psychoanalysis was real and effective. This clinical approach was far more convincing about the value of psychoanalysis than reading books on psychoanalysis. The Koreans became familiar with the three pillars of psychoanalytic training—that is, training analysis, didactic courses, and supervised control cases. Then, they began to develop their own training program. However, they knew their progress would be slow because at that time, Korea did not have even one certified analyst.

For many years, efforts to invite at least one or two training analysts to be in residence in Seoul were made (*International Psychoanalysis,* October 1998) and necessary funding was collected from those members who wished to be analyzed. Unfortunately it did not work because no qualified analysts were willing to move to Korea and frustration increased among the members of the group. During the 1980s, several junior members initiated their formal and informal psychoanalytic or psychotherapy training abroad in the United States and United Kingdom. In 1988, Do-Un Jeong, on his faculty development project very humbly funded by the Seoul National University College of Medicine, went to San Diego with the recommendation of Edward Joseph. A few days after the arrival with his family, he arranged to meet with Robert Tyson, then chair of the Education Committee of the San Diego Psychoanalytic Society and Institute (SDPSI). The deadline for new candidacy application for the year 1988 at the SDPSI was already over. Not being quite sure about the future and benefit of an analysis that would be incomplete due to the applicant's full-time faculty position in his university in Seoul, Tyson consulted with Robert Wallerstein in San Francisco. With Wallerstein's support, and after a formal process of three interviewers evaluating him, Jeong finally was accepted as a special student. He became the first Korean student of SDPSI.

After years of positive experience with Korean students, SDPSI years ago organized the Korea Committee and developed guidelines for Korean students. So far, those who have had psychoanalytic experience at the SDPSI are Tak-Yoo Hong, Mee-Kyung Kim, Min-Geol Kim, Nam-Hyeon Cho, Eun-Kyung Kim, Weon-Jeong Lim, Sun-Ju Chung, and Jong-Heun Kim. In 2008, Jeong-In Ko, Byeong-Yong Lee, and In-Soo Lee joined the program. Jin-Wook Sohn, Moo-Suk Lee, and Eui-Joong Kim had the experience of personal analysis by SDPSI's analysts. Bum-Hee Yu had psychotherapy training at the SDPSI.

San Diego is not the only place where psychoanalytic training of Korean students occurs. Cleveland has produced one Korean graduate, Jaehak Yu. Young-Sik Yoo had training in New York City. Jee-Hyun Ha and Yu-Jin Lee were in Toronto for psychoanalytic training. The Seattle Psychoanalytic Society and Institute also began training Wang-Gu Roh in 2008. Koreans expect the expansion of training possibilities abroad to continue in order to absorb the diversified viewpoints of contemporary psychoanalysis; however, their long-term goal is to develop training within Korea through the institute development program of the International New Groups Committee of the IPA.

Despite the serious efforts within the confines of Korea, Korean psychoanalysis had no official IPA designation and didn't have international visibility. They were psychoanalytic orphans without surrogate parents to take care of them. In 1985, Koreans attended the Congress of the IPA for the first time. It made them sure that internationally psychoanalysis was alive and well despite persistent attacks on Freud and psychoanalysis within Korea by its competitors. However, it took many years for Koreans' affection for psychoanalysis to be responded to by the IPA. In 1991, at the Buenos Aires congress, the IPA officially recognized the Korean Group as its first Guest Study Group (Sandler, 1991). Compared with the notion of the Allied Center, the successor of the Guest Study Group concept, a guest was a guest—being invited but still basically extramural and not being taken care of and monitored. This status began to change during the 1995 IPA Congress in San Francisco. Do-Un Jeong made a strong plea for more managerial attention for the Korean Group during a session of the Asia Committee meeting of the International New Groups Committee. This appeal received strong support from the International New Groups Committee (David Sachs, chair), which maintained its interest and encouragement for the remainder of the process that ultimately resulted in Koreans reaching Study Group status in 2008. After the San Francisco Congress of the IPA, the Korean Group's immediate next step to be taken was to produce direct members of the IPA from its members, so that there would be a sufficient number to qualify Koreans as a study group. It took thirteen years.

FURTHER DEVELOPMENTS

In 1990, the Korean Group began to publish the only journal of Freudian psychoanalysis in Korea, *Psychoanalysis*. It is now published biannually with about one thousand copies distributed nationally, with many copies sent abroad. It contains original papers, review articles, cases, book reviews, and other topics on psychoanalysis and psychotherapies. Among the contributions that have appeared in this journal are "the 34th Hamburg IPA congress in 1985" by Seung-Hwan Oh (2000), "psychoanalysis: Korea and Asia" by Do-Un Jeong (2000), "a psychoanalytic approach on Chang-Sup Sohn's three short stories" by Doo-Young Cho (2001), "self-image of Tim Burton visualized in the movie, *Scissorhands*" by Hae-Nam Kim (2001), "cultural difference in analytic practice? Experience in interracial analysis" by Jaehak Yu (2002), "a psychoanalytic exploration of Korean folk tales" by Jee-Hyun Ha (2002), "hidden resistance relating to the previous therapist" by Mee-Kyung Kim (2005), "psychotherapy and medication" by Sung-Hee Han (2005), "therapist-patient relationship in self psychology and intersubjectivity theory" by Jin-Wook Sohn (2005), "development of Freudian theory" by Tak-Yoo Hong (2007), "use of contertransference" by Moo-Suk Lee (2007), "on holding environment" by Geon Ho Bahn (2008), "an essay on Freud's view of instincts and its interpretation through Yin-Yang Doctrine of Confucianism" by Ik-Keun Hwang and Jong-Chul Yang (2008), and "a psychoanalytic comment on Woo Jang-Choon and the Seedless Watermelon" by Byung-Wook Lee (2008). In 1997, the *Standard Edition* of Freud's writing was translated and published in Korean.

In 2000, the Korean Group opened a two-year program in advanced psychoanalytic psychotherapy training, the first such program in Korea, with the proposal of Bum-Hee Yu and with the full support of Do-Un Jeong as president of the Korean Group. About fifteen students are admitted each year. As of now, it is mandatory for anyone to become a regular member of the Korean Group to graduate from this program.

During the 2001 IPA Congress in Nice, Do-Un Jeong and Tak Yoo Hong were evaluated by three senior members for direct membership in the IPA. Due to an administrative problem subsequent to political turmoil related to "telephone analysis" the appointments were deferred. This type of analysis had been initiated and was being done to some members of the Korean Group by its former active member, who was an interim training analyst appointed in July 2000. The Korean Group was opposed to this practice and their interim training analyst status was suspended by the IPA Council in

January 2001. To resolve the problem, an Exploratory Committee to Korea was appointed in January 2002, consisting of Allan Compton (chair), Georg Bruns, and Carmen Medici de Steiner. Allan Compton and Georg Bruns visited Seoul from May 22 to May 27, 2002. The committee reported back to the council in July 2002 (Exploratory Committee to Korea, 2002). IPA declared that "telephone analysis" would not be recognized. A further delay in the direct member appointments occurred when the IPA Toronto Congress in 2003 was cancelled due to the SARS (severe acute respiratory syndrome) epidemic. Eventually, Do-Un Jeong, joined by Tak Yoo Hong, became the first direct member of the IPA from Korea at the New Orleans Congress in March 2004.

In 2002, Professor Doo-Young Cho, the founding president of the Korean Group, had the honor of receiving the Mary S. Sigourney Award for the first time in Asia, in recognition of his contribution to the development of psychoanalysis in Korea. He graciously donated his award to the Korean Group for further development of psychoanalysis in Korea.

In 2005, Jaehak Yu became the third direct member and in 2007, Mee-Kyung Kim and Moo-Suk Lee were also recognized as direct members in Berlin. Mee-Kyung Kim became the first woman direct member from Korea. It meant that Korea has five direct members, more than fulfilling the requirement for establishing an IPA study group.

Production of five direct members, historically speaking, owes very much to the efforts and contribution of the Korea Advisory Committee of the IPA (IPA, 2003) as well as individual efforts of many years—in fact, sixteen years. The committee was officially organized in October 2003, following the IPA Executive Council's acceptance of the report of the Exploratory Committee to Korea in July 2002. It was to operate as a subcommittee of the International New Groups Committee in order to foster the development of psychoanalysis in Korea. As stated in the mandate, the intention was "to provide assistance, guidance and advice so as to lead to the appointment of a number of Direct Members of the IPA." Sander Abend was appointed as chair, with Barbara Stimmel and Georg Bruns participating as members. Robert Tyson joined the committee in July 2004.

The Korea Advisory Committee has played an instrumental role in further organizing and advising the development of psychoanalysis in Korea. One major contribution by the committee was the Korea Seminar Weekend, held twice (2004 and 2005) in San Francisco and supported pro bono by many psychoanalysts in the San Francisco, San Diego, and Los Angeles areas. About thirty Koreans participated each time and enjoyed the intensity and depth of a series of group discussions. It was a master class of psychoanalysis.

In terms of IPA activity by the Koreans, Do-Un Jeong was first appointed to the Allied Centers Committee in July 2004. He visited Taiwan in March 2005 to explore the Taiwan group's potential to be an Allied Center. He was reappointed in September 2005. In the same year, Do-Un Jeong presented the first poster from Korea at the IPA Congress in Rio de Janeiro. It was a neuroimaging study of the victims of posttraumatic stress disorder; the subjects were traumatized by a massive subway fire.

RECOGNITION OF THE KOREAN STUDY GROUP OF THE IPA AND APPOINTMENT OF KOREA SPONSORING COMMITTEE

With five direct members, Korea was ready to be considered for IPA study group status. During the American Psychoanalytic Association meeting in New York City, in January 2008, the International New Groups Committee and the Allied Centers Committee convened and came to conclude that the Korean Study Group for five direct members and the Korean Allied Center for the rest of the Korean Guest Study Group could be recognized. The members of the study group elected to remain in the Allied Center according to IPA procedures. The IPA finally approved the decision in April 2008. The Korea Sponsoring Committee then was organized. It comprises Richard Lightbody (chair, United States), Abigail Golomb (Sponsoring Committee function, Israel), and Barbara Stimmel (Allied Center function, United States). The year 2008 marks the third historical era of the Korean psychoanalysis.

In July 2008, the Korean Study Group and the Korean Allied Center had the Korea Sponsoring Committee in Seoul for the first time. Richard Lightbody (Chair) and Abigail Golomb spent four full days with the Korean members. It led to mutual understanding of Korea's developmental process of psychoanalysis and the functions of the Sponsoring Committee. The Korea Sponsoring Committee is expected to visit Korea twice per year. It is predicted that psychoanalytic training within Korea will begin in 2009, with the Korea Sponsoring Committee and the Korean Study Group working together. Korea will leap into another stage of sustainable psychoanalytic development.

Issues raised during Korea's quest to define itself in psychoanalysis have been as follows: very limited accessibility of psychoanalytic training, diluted density of provided information, less availability of unbiased knowledge and experience, surviving competition and biological orientation, slow speed of transition, and sometimes biased understanding of national situation by international psychoanalytic community. It was no less a problem that Koreans have had no world-class curriculum for psychoanalytic education.

Our century is the century of speed. Speedy action and speedy solution are the national and international virtues. Psychoanalysis has competitors, nationally and worldwide. We are not alone in the race. Our competitors, other schools and biologists, are aggressive, speedy enough, and on many occasions well-funded. Korean psychoanalysis has survived and succeeded, but in the process has painfully lost a substantial number of potentially excellent analysts of the future, not only outside the group but also within the group. Frustration is infectious. Early active adoption of (interim) training analysts within new countries will play a key role in expanding psychoanalysis and recruiting future psychoanalysts, generation after generation.

Depending on the Korean experience, the value and power of university-hospital based psychoanalysis cannot be too much emphasized. A major portion of membership of the Korean Group is occupied by professors of psychiatry. Careful and thoughtful development of psychoanalysis in a university hospital setting should be a major objective in new countries of psychoanalysis. University programs are a powerful, lasting source for recruiting young generations of interested people year after year. However, in the age of biological dominance, it is very difficult or sometimes impossible to initiate and maintain a proper and robust psychodynamic program for trainees. University-based psychoanalysts might position themselves in a better way by focusing on dual responsibilities—for example, being committed to consultation psychiatry or student mental health service in addition to being a psychoanalyst.

In the case of Korea, rapid growth of national economy, increased availability of opportunities traveling abroad, and subsequent increasing global awareness all have been very conducive to importing psychoanalytic ideas and obtaining training. Reduced communication cost and innovative technology like Internet phone service have helped supervisions across countries. There are always regrets even when we are pleased with achievement. The Korean quest for psychoanalysis is an excellent case of psychoanalytic development in a linguistically and geographically isolated area and of bridging the psychoanalytic divide. Issues raised during the quest could be wisely looked into and dealt with, we hope, with the initiative of the IPA, so that new countries on the way to the long journey would go through an improved model of psychoanalytic development. Among the issues, for the future of psychoanalysis worldwide, we suggest that speed of commitment by the new country, speed of commitment by the IPA, and speed of interactive cooperation by the two parties should be seriously considered and improved in a systematic and consistent manner.

CONCLUDING REMARKS

No longer on the unhappy side of the psychoanalytic divide, Korea is now an emerging young power of the psychoanalytic movement in Asia. It has been a very slow process since the foundation of the Seoul Psychoanalytic

Study Group in 1980, filled with expectations, frustrations, internal turmoil, sense of achievement, and pride. We think the Korean experience can be referred to and shared for new countries now and in the future for the timely and sustainable development of psychoanalysis and the release from the divide worldwide. The Korean Group very much appreciates the efforts and contributions that have been made by many friends of Korean psychoanalysis, especially Korea Advisory Committee of the IPA and its members, Robert Tyson, Sander Abend, Barbara Stimmel, and Georg Bruns.

NOTE

1. "I [Do-Un Jeong] was in a big room. Three exits. On one side of the room, I found a black couch and in front of that, there were a sofa and other things. The room was almost full with the couch, the sofa, chairs, and bookshelves. There were also two sets of recliners, which I use for psychoanalytic patients. In the room, I found Dr. Edward Joseph and I was supposed to obtain the last analysis of mine from him. Strangely, he and I were distantly apart. He was sitting on the sofa in front of the black couch. I was on the other side of the room, myself rather belonging to bookshelves and sitting on the recliner just like the one I use. Dr. Joseph told me that he had a present for me and that I should find it out from the series of bookshelves. With some efforts, I located the package. I brought it to him and he suggested that I unpack it. In there, there was a set of CDs on which Sigmund Freud's picture was printed. I thought I had already bought a similar one but I did not verbalize it." (Do-Un Jeong had this dream while he was writing this paper. In the spring of 1988, Dr. Edward Joseph, now deceased, wrote him a recommendation letter when he was trying to obtain psychoanalytic training in the United States.)

3

Psychoanalysis in China

Douglas Kirsner and Elise Snyder

> Truth is not only the realization of our own being:
> It is that by which things outside of us have an existence.
>
> Confucius (circa 500 BC)

Since the establishment of the People's Republic of China in 1949, China has undergone massive changes at all levels. The Great Leap Forward, the Cultural Revolution, and the subsequent rapid modernizations have all impacted on the infrastructure and superstructure in far-reaching ways. Construction is ubiquitous in urban areas of a country that now forms the world's fourth-largest economy. The levels of stress and change that accompany capitalist cutthroat competition, rapid technological development, and opening to the world with the need to adapt to new ways, have had major psychological impacts upon a population whose prior assumptions have been constantly under challenge. There has been increasing focus on the individual and self-fulfillment instead of the traditional Chinese approach of serving the family and the group.

The May 2008 earthquake in Sichuan Province that killed at least 87,500 people highlighted the dearth of psychological resources. However, compared with the 1990s, psychiatry and psychology are now respected professions in China. For the past twenty years there has been a burgeoning interest in psychoanalysis and psychotherapy. The number of mental health professionals is expanding and there is a hunger for training. Nonetheless China has only thirty thousand mental health professionals serving its 1.3 billion people. There are only seventeen thousand psychiatrists in China: 1.3 psychiatrists per 100,000 Chinese compared with 13.7 per 100,000 Americans, one-tenth the number (Lawrence, 2008). According to a 2002 report, there were sixteen million people with mental illness in China with thirty million children and adolescents suffering mood or behavioral disorders. China's National Centre for Disease Control has a still higher estimate. They claim that one hundred million Chinese suffer from some kind of mental illness, most of whom are diagnosed and treated by general practitioners too ready to prescribe antidepressants. A 2007 study by the Shanghai Women's Federation found most Shanghai families dealing with serious stress. But only 2 percent of respondents sought psychotherapy, with only 19 percent saying they would ever consider it (*The Economist* [United States], 2007). But as the culture modernizes and changes, so will the felt need. The suicide rate in China is alarmingly high—a Chinese person kills himself or herself every two minutes. The reforms have brought spectacular economic benefits but at the cost of society becoming more complicated. The culture of competition to become rich places major pressure especially on children who, with the one-child policy, often have no siblings and whose parents place them under immense pressure to be successful (AFP, 2008).

This chapter will provide an overview of the history and development of psychoanalysis in China. Chinese philosophical traditions provide a receptive soil for psychoanalysis. Chinese concepts of mind go back as far as the fourth century BC with the "Medicine of Parallels," deriving from the *Handbook of the Yellow Emperor for Internal Medicine* and the *Book of Ailments*. A combination of Oracle and Demon medicine, Confucianism, Daoism, and Buddhism subsequently shaped this system of parallels. It proffered a harmonious and well-ordered life based on the ancient concept of yin and yang. The world of human beings is reflected in the laws of the macrocosm and microcosm, where visible and invisible, external and internal forces are mutually dependent on each other. Advances in knowledge on mental disorders in China have always been integrated within this Chinese perspective (Gerlach, 1995). Notably, in 2006 the Chinese Communist Party Central Committee adopted a strategic plan to construct a "socialist harmonious world" in economic, political, and social domains. The history of psychoanalysis in China is closely intertwined with those of the cognate disciplines of psychology, psychiatry, psychotherapy, and medicine as well as literature and the humanities. It might not be out of place, therefore, to refresh our memories with some basic facts about China and Chinese society before delving into the intricacies of how psychiatry and psychoanalysis have developed there.

SOME FACTS ABOUT CHINA

China is the fourth largest country in the world (after Russia, Canada, and the United States). Its vast and rambling borders abut Afghanistan, Bhutan,

India, Kazakhstan, Kyrgyzstan, Laos, Mongolia, Nepal, North Korea, Pakistan, Russia, Tajikistan, and Vietnam. Its terrain ranges from mostly mountains and plateaus in the west to plains and deltas in the east. The word "China" is derived from the Sanskrit *Cina*, which might, in turn, have been derived from Qin, the westernmost of the Chinese kingdoms during the early Zhou Dynasty. The pronunciation of *Qin* is similar to the phonetic *ch'in* and may have led to the emergence of the word China. While this name has stayed, the fact is that country has been referred to by many different names by Western historians before the modern period.

China's population, as of 2008, stands at 1.3 billion people, with a population growth of 0.6 percent per year. The average life expectancy for men is seventy-one years, and for women is seventy-five years. The main ethnic group in China is Han (nearly 92 percent of the population); other ethnic groups include Buyi, Dong, Huy, Manchu, Miao, Tujia, Uyghur, and Yao. Besides these there are people of Mongul, Tibetan, and Korean descent living in China. Officially, the country is atheistic, but there are people of Buddhist, Christian, Muslim, and Taoist faiths living within its borders. There are many languages and dialects in China; the most prominent are *Putonghua* (Mandarin) and *Yue* (Cantonese). China is a highly educated country with a literacy rate of over 90 percent.

China is an ancient civilization. Archaeological evidence suggests that the earliest humans in China date from over two million years and the so-called Peking Man (circa 500,000 BC) is one of the first-known specimens of the genus *Homo erectus*. Chinese culture extends back to more than six million years and is the source of the world's oldest continuously used written language system. China is the font of many great inventions including paper, the compass, gunpowder, and the printing press. Some historians believe that the game of football (soccer) also originated in China.

After centuries of dynastic rule (with the succession of Xia, Zhou, Qin, Han, Tang, Song, Yuan, Ming, and Qing dynasties), the Republic of China emerged in 1912 under the dominance of the Kuomintang (the KMT, or the Nationalist Party) though it remained a coherent and unified state only for a few years. Warlords in various regions soon regained actual control over their respective territories. In the late 1920s, the Kuomintang, under Chiang Kai-Shek (1887–1975), was able to reunify the country, moving the nation's capital from Peking (now Beijing) to Nanking (now Nanjing). The Sino-Japanese War (1937–1945) forced an uneasy alliance between the Nationalists and the emergent Communist factions. With the surrender of Japan during World War II in 1945, China emerged victorious but monetarily weakened. The ongoing mistrust between the Nationalists and the Communists led to the Chinese Civil War. In 1947, constitutional rule was established, but because of the continued conflict between various factions, many provisions of it were never implemented on the mainland. Then, in a major development, the Communist Party of China (the CCP), under Mao Zedong (1893–1976), gained control of most of mainland China and on October 1, 1949, established the People's Republic of China as a socialist state. The Kuomintang retreated to Taiwan that very year and established their own rule under Chiang Kai-Shek. Visionary "reforms" of the Great Leap Forward (late 1950s) and the Cultural Revolution (the mid-1960s) then followed. Though a certain social stability and homogenization did occur as a result, these movements left the Chinese education system and economy in shambles. With the death of the first-generation Communist Party leaders such as Mao Zedong and Zhou En-Lai, the country began implementing a series of political and economic reforms. The leadership of Deng Xiaoping especially spurred China's rapid economic growth, starting in the 1990s.

Today, mainland China is governed by the Chinese Communist Party and goes by the name of the People's Republic of China. With the expulsion of the Republic of China (Taiwan) from the United Nations in 1971, the People's Republic of China is recognized as the sole legitimate ruler of all "China." A rising economic giant and a mighty military force, China is a permanent member of the United Nations Security Committee. The increasing relaxation of trade and economic barriers it had erected against the West has led not only to greater interchange of consumer and producer goods but also to enhanced tourism, exchange of ideas, and collaborative diplomacy. Consequently, a change is discernable in the Chinese culture at large. While Confucianism was the bedrock of China's traditional values and, to a great extent, remains so today, Western individualism and self-realization have permeated the modal psyche, especially as far as the contemporary youth is concerned. This is simultaneously a source of intrapsychic and interpersonal conflict and rejuvenated striving for personal authenticity and social freedom.

With this thumbnail sketch of Chinese history and culture as a backdrop, we are now prepared to resume the discourse on how psychiatry and psychoanalysis have evolved in this great nation.

EARLY DEVELOPMENTS

From the beginning of the twentieth century until the present, a "pure" form of psychoanalysis was never introduced or received in China. There were always cultural interpretations and adaptations that added Chinese characteristics to the mix. Massive changes in the political, social, and historical contexts greatly impacted the development of psychotherapy and psychoanalysis in China. Consider these: the founding of the republic, colonial involvements, the Japanese invasion, World War II, the civil war and Nationalist Governments, the founding of the People's Republic of China under Mao Zedong, the Great Leap Forward, the Cultural Revolution, the Opening Up and Reforms, and their consequences.

Western medicine was introduced in China during the nineteenth century, and psychotherapy began as part of Western medicine. It spread mainly through Christian missionary societies, which aimed for success with the combination of medical and missionary activities. An American missionary, Dr. John Kerr, opened a home for the mentally ill in Canton in 1898 (Pearson, 1991). During the 1910s and 1920s, psychoanalytic books and papers about the interpretation of dreams and free association were translated into Chinese. In 1917, the first psychology institute was founded in Beijing by Dr. Cai Yuanpai, who was a student of Wilhelm Wundt in Germany (1908–1912) before he returned to China to become the Republic's first Minister of Education. He was appointed as chancellor of Peking University (1916–1926). In 1919 the May Fourth Movement, in which Cai played a part, was sparked by Peking University students. This was an attempt to reform and modernize China and reevaluate Chinese institutions, including curriculum change and new forms of knowledge based on science. It changed the political and cultural climate in China, which allowed for greater influence of outside ideas.

Despite the fact that the Chinese translation of Freud's *The Interpretation of Dreams* reinterpreted the sexual references or removed them completely (Blowers, 1994), this renaissance allowed Freud's theories about sexual tensions in families to be used for modernizing China. Some translations systematically bowdlerized the sexual import of Freud's work because of its challenge to Confucian family values. However, Freud's modern thinking was a fertile ground for Chinese intellectuals intent on breaking with old feudal practices and "superstitions." His influence was nonetheless complex (Blowers and Yuan, 2005). As Jingyuan Zhang (1992) suggests:

> Freudian theory was not transmitted in a single coherent form, but rather in bits and pieces over time and in changing social contexts. It was altered in the course of being translated and explained in China, and it took on a different significance as a result of being grafted onto the country's own rich tradition of psychological explanation in literature. (3)

In 1921 the Chinese Psychological Society (only the seventh to be established in the world) was founded in Nanjing, with Zhang Yao-xiang as its first president. The society published a journal—*Psychology*—but it and the society itself were short-lived during this period (Li and Guan, 1987). As in other parts of the world during the 1920s and 1930s, Freudian ideas percolated into the culture of the Chinese Republic through the interests of literary critics and theorists and also some clinicians, who saw Freud's ideas of the primitive unconscious as challenging the dominant social Confucian mores of "family values." Psychoanalysis was taken up by members of the "Creation Society" in the struggle against Confucian ethics. Although psychology was often deployed, the leading figures of this society, according to Gerlach (2006),

> were interested in the fact that psychoanalysis seeks to understand the misfortune, the "discomfort" of the human being in his culture. In the psychoanalytic theory the conflicts between human nature and forms of socialization are not suppressed, and the theory never justifies a culture which breaks individuals.

Furthermore, the influence of psychoanalysis came via nerve doctors on the margins of medicine that used Freud's theories for various remedies. Freud's image even adorned bottles of popular nostrums. Five of Freud's works were translated before 1949—*The Interpretation of Dreams, Group Psychology and the Analysis of the Ego, Introductory Lectures on Psychoanalysis, New Introductory Lectures on Psychoanalysis,* and *An Autobiographical Study.* There were also a number of translated expositions and critiques of Freudian theory (Zhang, 1992). Zhang maintains that the way Freud was translated into Chinese greatly influenced the reception of psychoanalysis in China. The fact that there is considerable discussion today about the undue influence upon non-German readers of Freud of James Strachey's choices for his "standard" translations of Freud into English underlines this point as to the exact nature of what was received about Freud in China, especially as a number of terms came secondhand via Japanese translations. Zhang (1992, 37–56) provides detailed examples of such translation-related problems. The term "unconscious" stands out in this regard. It finds no easy equivalent in Chinese and conveys different metaphorical meanings that are not infrequently context bound. Moreover, for some odd reason, it seems to have been translated "directly" from German and not from the Japanese renditions of it. Actually there are three broad categories of Chinese terms for the "unconscious" which are often used interchangeably. These include *yin shi, yin ji,* and *qian jia* (referring to unconscious), *xia yishi* (referring to subconscious), and *wu yishi* and *bu qui yi shi de* (referring to nonconscious). However, it seems that *qian yishi,* the metaphorical expression for "submerge," is the term mainly used for the Freudian unconscious today.

The translator of *An Autobiographical Study* was the important dissident intellectual Zhang Shizao. He wrote to Freud while traveling in Germany asking about intercultural cooperation, and suggested writing an article for *Imago.* The original letter is lost but in the only recorded contact with anybody from China, Freud responded:

> Most esteemed Professor,
> In whatever way you wish to carry out your intention, whether it is by paving the way for the development of psychoanalysis in your homeland—China—or

> by contributions to our journal *Imago* in which you would judge against your own language our conjectures about the nature of archaic modes of expression, I will be extremely pleased.
> Very respectfully,
> Yours, Freud (Cited in Blowers, 1993, 264)

Freud mentioned China in his writings importantly in relation to language in terms of parallels between interpreting Chinese characters in context and psychoanalysts interpreting dreams in context, and to the issue of the significance of foot-binding of Chinese women as a case of fetishism (Blowers, 1993; Zhang, 1992).

An American, Dr. Richard S. Lyman, a graduate of Johns Hopkins University, was professor of psychiatry and neurology at Peking Union Medical College Hospital in 1932. He included a course in psychoanalysis in the curriculum. Lyman invited the first psychoanalyst in China, Dr. Bingham Dai (1899–1996), to a teaching post at Peking University Medical College and suggested that he teach psychology and psychotherapy to Chinese doctors. Dai graduated in 1923 from St. John's University College in Shanghai and went on to undertake a PhD in sociology at the University of Chicago. Following the completion of his thesis in 1932, Dai met Harry Stack Sullivan at a yearlong Rockefeller Foundation seminar on "Culture and Personality" at Yale University. Sullivan began to train Dai, as did Leon Saul and Karen Horney at the Chicago Institute for Psychoanalysis. John Dollard, sociologist and psychoanalyst, and Edward Sapir, a prominent anthropologist, were also his teachers (Blowers, 2004). Dai taught psychotherapy at the Peking Union Medical University Hospital from 1935 to 1939. Influenced by Confucianism and later by the neo-Freudian Culturalist School of psychoanalysis, Dai attempted to sensitize his students to different types of therapy and emphasized sociocultural factors rather than the more orthodox sexual ones. He began a small psychoanalytic training group and treated patients. In 1939 following the Japanese invasion, Dai left for the United States, where he worked at Fisk University and then at Duke University. There he rejoined Lyman and became professor of mental hygiene and psychotherapy at Johns Hopkins University from 1943 until the late 1950s (Blowers, 2004; Dai, 1984).

On the last day of 1938, just a few months before Dai left China, Adolf Storfer, a member of the Vienna Psychoanalytical Society and a refugee from Vienna fleeing Hitler, arrived in Shanghai. Shanghai was a free port. Many stateless people, including many European Jews, fled to Shanghai during this period. Storfer participated in the lively intellectual and journalistic life of Shanghai, editing the German language *Gelbe Post*, which covered relationships between Asian culture, psychoanalysis, and linguistics. Storfer was able to escape to Australia just after Pearl Harbor (Blowers,

2004, 100–101). In 1933, an Austrian physician, Dr. Fanny Halpern, followed Richard Lyman at the National Medical College of Shanghai. She was not at all sympathetic toward psychoanalysis (Blowers, 2004, 94). She devoted herself to the care of the mentally ill and opened a clinic for mental hygiene in Shanghai in 1940 (Gerlach, 2006).

In 1936 Wilhelm Reich's controversial book *Dialectical Materialism and Psychoanalysis* together with W. Jurinetz's *Psychoanalysis and Marxism* were published in translation in China. Reuben Osborn's book *Freud and Marx: A Dialectical Study* was translated into Chinese in 1940. Western critics were generally sympathetic to an amalgam of psychoanalysis and Marxism whereas Soviet critics were not (Zhang, 1992). Although discussions of these books reflected differences among Chinese intellectuals as they did in the rest of the world, they should also be seen in the context of the growing influence and power of the Communists in China.

Psychoanalysis had a respectable though not stunning influence in China before 1949 (Dai, 1984). It was part of intellectual currency, as it was in other parts of the world at the time. "By the mid-1930s," as Jingyuan Zhang observes, "Freudian theories were familiar to many Chinese intellectuals and, in reductive forms, to a surprisingly broad sector of the Chinese population. . . . Freudian theory was known fairly well to the Chinese public" (1992, 34). The Japanese occupation, the ensuing war, the civil war between the Communists and the Nationalists (Kuomintang) and the enormous changes in the government put an end to organized interest in psychoanalysis for the next forty years.

AFTER WORLD WAR II

In the United States after World War II interest in psychiatry and psychoanalysis greatly expanded. At the most prestigious medical schools (e.g., Harvard and Columbia University) most of the top 10 percent of the graduating class became psychiatrists. Many of the best and brightest young psychiatrists applied for psychoanalytic training. Yet China's situation was in stark contrast: China had only fifty psychiatrists by 1949 for its five hundred million people (Chen, 2003).

As the Communists' 1949 victory led to rebuilding the university system, the medical accreditation system, and the cultural field in general, psychoanalysis more or less dropped out of common knowledge (Saussy, 2008). But psychotherapy was disparaged after the revolution in 1949 (Lawrence 2008). With the founding of the People's Republic of China, all ties were severed with non-Communist countries. The free intellectual interchange between China and the rest of the world that flowed from 1919 onward was over. Soviet neuropsychiatric models influenced Chinese psychiatry, with the maintenance of public order a political priority (Chang, Tong, Shi, Zeng, 2005). Between 1949 and 1965 only a few professionals conducted psychotherapy. In addition, some other Chinese psychologists tried to use psychotherapeutic ideas to work with their patients during this period. As the World Congress of Psychotherapy website summarized:

> The Rapid Comprehensive Therapy for neurasthenia was the most influential method at this time. The model was a short-term one, developed by some of Chinese psychologists and psychiatrists at the end of 1950s and the beginning of 1960s. Initially it was employed to treat neurasthenia, but later it was also used for treating other kinds of disorders. It combined medical treatment, physical exercises, thematic lectures and group discussion. Patients were treated by interpretation, encouragement, homework assignment and supportive methods. This therapy was reportedly very effective . . . and aroused interest in psychotherapy among mental health professionals. (WCP, 2008)

During the 1950s there were also detailed social-psychological studies employing a psychoanalytical basis on the understanding of Chinese culture. They suggested that Chinese children had a longer, more intensive oral phase and that the solution to the oedipal conflict should be seen as lying "more in submission to the father than in aggressive rivalry with him" (Gerlach, 2006). There was a slow resurgence of interest in psychoanalysis in the 1950s but the Cultural Revolution and the subsequent change in the status of intellectuals ended that. Early in its first decade all psychological work was based on Soviet psychology, and the Chinese paid close attention to Pavlov's work. Then, as Blowers and Yuan (2005) observed,

> When this model proved less than satisfactory for explaining all psychological phenomena, there then followed two very difficult periods in which psychology was criticised and eventually shut down along with many other disciplines in the second of these periods that became known as the "Proletariat or Cultural Revolution." (38)

THE CULTURAL REVOLUTION: 1966–1976

This was a very dark period for almost everybody in China, including intellectuals and mental health professionals. Mental health problems were seen as the result of "wrong politics" and bourgeois influences to be solved by socialist reeducation. Psychiatric treatment was replaced by political education using Mao's *Little Red Book*. Psychology and kindred approaches were attacked as pseudoscience, and Freud for pan-sexualism. The mental health disciplines were all but wiped out. No articles or books related to psychotherapy were published. Many Chinese were traumatized by their experiences during the

Cultural Revolution. There remains a large population of such individuals that puts an even greater strain on the decimated mental health profession.

The death of Mao Zedong in 1976, the ascension of Deng Xiaoping, and the trials and conviction of the "Gang of Four" for their crimes during the Cultural Revolution marked a major turn for the better in ending the Chinese ice age. Deng Xiaoping's Four Modernizations, his opening up to the West, and the freeing of the Chinese economy from the constraints of state control augured well for the future. There can be no doubt as to the increasing space between the market society and the political structure for professional autonomy and openness as well as increasing individual freedom of speech, provided that central authority is not challenged directly head-on.

Psychology emerged with a new agenda and was largely free from political constraints by the government (Blowers and Yuan, 2005). Since the opening, China's Communist system of state-controlled work has become a capitalist free-for-all, with cutthroat competition for education and work, with an increasing gap between rich and poor. Psychotherapy has become increasingly needed to help cope with the stresses and changes (Lawrence, 2008).

During the first years of the opening-up period few publications related to psychotherapy appeared, while books written by famous Western psychotherapists, such as Freud, Carl Jung, and Erich Fromm, were translated and published. A number of workshops, training programs, and academic conferences related to psychotherapy were held. Some scholars explored the profession of counseling and psychotherapy while some psychology clinics opened in the early 1980s (WCP, 2008).

Between 1979 and 1992 the majority of psychotherapy-related publications in China focused on behavior therapy, cognitive therapy, and insight-oriented approaches. Fewer were published on other techniques (Chang, Tong, Shi, Zeng, 2005). As these authors suggest, "with the opening-and-reform policies initiated in the 1980s, China has officially reentered the global fray, experimenting with Western ideas, markets, and institutions, including Western-style counseling and psychotherapy" (110).

Visiting psychoanalysts had the impression that the most commonly employed psychotherapeutic methods were orientated toward behavioral therapy or supportive techniques. This they thought was because of the influence of traditional patterns in Chinese culture such as the notion of shame (Blowers and Yuan, 2005). During this period, interest in psychoanalysis among literary scholars was again rising. For example, Wang Ning, a prominent literary theorist, wrote his doctoral dissertation on "Psychoanalysis and Chinese Literature" at that time. As in most parts of the world, literary critics and theorists found Lacan more congenial and their readings of Freud were limited in scope and sophistication.

In addition to interest in psychotherapy, from the mid 1980s, psychoanalytic and psychotherapy theory has been taken more seriously in China. More psychoanalytic works have been published, including many by current psychoanalytic authors, and are keenly read by sociologists, literary scholars, and other intellectuals (Adolf Gerlach, personal communication, November 19, 2008).

1980S ONWARD

The German-Chinese Psychotherapy Training Program led by Adolf Gerlach was established in 1982. It is located at the Shanghai Mental Center, the largest mental hospital in China, and attracts mental health professionals from all over China. There is a cumulative program (2008–2010). The training takes place in intensive one-week courses during which lectures, seminars, clinical supervisions, and "self-experience" sessions are held. Some Chinese leaders in mental health have gone to Germany for analysis and training. There are courses in Wuhan, Harbin, Xian, and conferences in Kunming. They have been funded by government and private donors in Germany and China and cofounded by the Medical University of Kunming, the University of Beijing, Shanghai Mental Health Center, the Tongji University of Wuhan, and the West China University of Chengdu (Chang, Tong, Shi, Zeng, 2005; Peter Loewenberg, personal communication, 2008). A variety of psychoanalytic groups are actively involved in training in China, for instance, Jungians in Shanghai.

From 1987 on, there has been what has been called a blossoming of the mental health field in China. This growth has been fueled by the government's recent acknowledgment of the social burden caused by mental health problems and a variety of state-sponsored initiatives to improve access to psychological services in the country's hospitals, schools, and prisons (Chang, Tong, Shi, Zeng, 2005). Among young mental health professionals and their teachers, interest in psychoanalysis is very high. They read everything about analysis they can find, but their clinical knowledge lags, limited by access to Western clinicians who speak Mandarin and by the loss of a generation of clinical teachers as a result of the Cultural Revolution. However, there are differences in the training of various mental health professionals, the distribution of mental health care, and the role of the government in these endeavors in China.

Psychiatrists

Students enter medical school directly from high school. The profession is prestigious and admission is difficult. They receive a Bachelor of

Medicine (because they do not have a doctorate in medicine, they cannot find work in the United States, which makes further training in the United States almost impossible) followed by a four-year psychiatric residency. Some then obtain a doctorate, sometimes in medicine, but more often in psychology with varying specialties including psychotherapy. Psychiatrists work in public and private outpatient clinics, psychiatric hospitals, and private practice. A few of the private psychiatric hospitals are more like spas than hospitals with indoor and outdoor swimming pools. Some (for example, the Wuhan Hospital for Psychotherapy) are state-of-the-art institutions with comfortable rooms and innovative psychoanalytically oriented treatment. Patients receive psychotherapy, milieu therapy, and psychopharmacology. They remain in the hospital until they have achieved, at the very least, the level of functioning they had *before* they fell ill (one to three months), and are then followed as outpatients. The hospital fees range from US$1000 to US$2500 per month (that's in the hospital with two pools). Not inexpensive, but affordable for the affluent middle class with insurance.

Psychologists

The training is similar to that in the United States. The Chinese government has been sending psychologists abroad to learn "best practices." The most recent generation of psychologists and psychiatrists are seeking graduate degrees and postdoctoral training overseas with World Health Organization (WHO) financing or in Western universities (Chen, 2003). In 2008, following the Sichuan earthquake, the government authorized the construction of ten new masters'-level departments of psychology in the disaster region. The students must be residents of the area and pledge to return to their hometowns for five years after graduation

Counselors

Most psychotherapy in China is performed by counselors. Counselors may have an undergraduate degree in any field (for many, becoming a counselor represents a career change). After a six-month course at a counseling school, often freestanding, graduates then find work in private, but also public clinics, private practice, middle schools, and university student health services. The range in the quality of their training, both at the counseling schools and also in their on-the-job training, is enormous. The government reportedly has mandated that middle schools have one counselor for each three hundred children. The number in the United States is about one to thirty thousand. The government, aware of the variation in training quality, has recently instituted certification for counselors. There are three levels. Most of the counseling schools are essentially "cram" courses to help people pass the exam. Nonetheless two-thirds of applicants fail the lowest level of certification. The examination for the highest level of certification requires a doctorate.

Social Workers

This is a masters'-level degree. Most, but not all, social workers are involved with social problems rather than psychotherapy. At the most recent Party Congress (October 2007) funding for social work schools was increased so that more social workers would be available to work on such issues as spousal abuse among minority peoples.

Psychoanalysts

This is not a licensed profession in China. As has been the case throughout psychoanalytic history around the world, a number of people call themselves psychoanalysts in China. There is one IPA analyst in Beijing and an IPA training center was opened there in October 2008.

THE CURRENT SCENE

In 2000, Elise Snyder was invited to give two papers on psychoanalysis in Beijing: one at a conference at Beida University and the other to the Academy of the Social Sciences. She learned of a group interested in psychoanalysis in Chengdu, a city of more than ten million people in Sichuan province. There she gave several lectures to audiences of more than one hundred people. The national government had given permission to Sichuan University to offer a nonclinical masters' degree in Psychoanalytic Studies. A person in Chengdu who had had a partial analysis in Paris with a Lacanian analyst, was, under the auspices of the local Philosophical Association, "training" people to become psychoanalysts.

In 2001, Dr. Snyder went again to Chengdu, where she lectured and conducted brief supervisions and consultations. She also established relations with a group in Xi'an and a group in Beijing. Many members of the group in Chengdu who had been involved with the "psychoanalyst" there asked for American analyses. Between 2001 and 2003 Dr. Ubaldo Leli, an analyst affiliated with the Columbia University Psychoanalytic Institute in New York, visited China. He began to analyze someone in Chengdu, via Skype, and this was the beginning of the China American Psychoanalytic Alliance (CAPA). Dr. Leli has since returned to China several times, as have other members of CAPA. The China American Psychoanalytic Alliance Inc., a nonprofit organization, was established to promote psychoanalysis, psychoanalytic psychotherapy, and psychotherapy training in China.

There are now almost two hundred American members (several Canadians and several Australians are also members) of CAPA, most of whom are also members of the American Psychoanalytic Association and the International Psychoanalytical Association. They are treating patients (mainly mental health professionals) and doing supervisions. Initially CAPA members worked in Chengdu, and Xi'an. In 2003 CAPA expanded its work to Beijing and Shanghai and in 2008 to Wuhan. Since 2005, CAPA has been providing low-cost analyses and psychotherapies. Following the initiative of Dr. Leli, these treatments are conducted via Skype. More than thirty Chinese people are in analysis and twelve in psychotherapy. There are long waiting lists in both categories. The analyses are conducted three to five sessions/week and the psychotherapies one to two sessions/week. The fees are whatever is usual in the patient's part of China, generally between $5 and $10 per session. Since 2005 CAPA has been providing once-a-week supervision to almost thirty Chinese mental health professionals. These supervisees include psychiatrists, psychologists, counselors, and student health personnel. Many CAPA members have visited China, lectured, supervised, provided consultations, and assisted in earthquake relief. Two CAPA members (Elise Snyder and Ubaldo Leli) visit for extended periods each year.

In 2007, Dr. Snyder met with perhaps fifty chairs of departments of psychology and psychiatry, directors of psychiatric hospitals, and so on to discuss organizing two-year training programs in psychoanalytic psychotherapy. What had been sorely lacking in China is organized intensive treatment or training that takes place on a weekly or more frequent basis. This is the gap that CAPA is attempting to fill. There are now almost one hundred Chinese affiliate members of CAPA. The Books for China project is another CAPA endeavor. Twenty-five CAPA members donated more than 5,400 books. At the time of the earthquake, CAPA was actively involved in providing disaster training for more than two thousand Chinese mental health professionals, translating and arranging for publication of Gil Kliman's *Children's Workbook*. CAPA continues to organize disaster training and relief.

In September 2008, six two-year psychoanalytic psychotherapy training programs began. One of the six is organized and staffed by the Washington Psychoanalytic Center. There are two programs in Beijing, two in Shanghai, and one each in Chengdu and Wuhano. There are fifty-seven Chinese mental health professionals in training. Each program meets weekly and includes two and a half hours of theory and technique seminars, one and a quarter hours of continuous case seminar and (almost unheard of in China) one session of individual supervision per week. The students meet in a classroom and all the sessions are conducted on Skype. The National Psychologists' Association, in the interest of assuring quality training, has prepared a registration procedure for psychotherapy training programs. The six CAPA programs may be the first foreign programs to be certified.

The World Congress of Psychotherapy, held in Beijing in October 2008, attracted a large number of Chinese mental health professionals in addition to many foreigners. There were many psychoanalytic presentations, including papers by the authors. Presentations included IPA members involved with CAPA (Elise Snyder and Ubaldo Leli from the United States), and IPA members of its China Committee—Peter Loewenberg (chair from the United States), Adolf Gerlach (Germany), Maria Teresa Hooke (Australia), and Sverre Varvin (Norway). Otto Kernberg, a former president of the IPA, and Nancy McWilliams, president of the Division of Psychoanalysis of the American Psychological Association, also presented at the congress, as did other foreign non-IPA analysts and psychoanalytic therapists. A large number of psychoanalytic presentations were made by Chinese mental health professionals. Most of the attendees were Chinese mental health professionals.

During the World Congress of Psychotherapy, the IPA opened its first formal training institution in China (October 9–15), the China Allied Centre. Present from the IPA were IPA President Cláudio Laks Eizirik and the IPA China Committee. The President of the China Mental Health Association had told the group: "We know our therapists are not well enough trained. Please bring us psychoanalytic training." Seminars were held for the nine accepted candidates who are significant academics and clinicians, members of the center and those in analysis there. The candidates have come from the German and Norwegian training programs; some having studied for many years and now administering the programs. On behalf of the Deutsche Gesellschaft für Psychoanalyse, Psychotherapie, Psychosomatik, und Tiefenpsychologie, Alf Gerlach presented each new candidate a grant of €800 toward their training. The IPA training analyst in Beijing is Irmgard Dettbarn (Peter Loewenberg, personal communication, 2008).

CONCLUDING REMARKS

What accounts for the enormous interest in psychoanalysis in China? When people no longer concern themselves primarily with hunger, where there is a growing middle class, where there is rapid change, where there is an increased awareness of anxiety and depression, it does not seem at all surprising that people should be interested in psychoanalysis. If the Chinese fascination with much that comes from the West is factored in, there is another reason. The Chinese government and major figures in Chinese psychology and psychiatry have been very welcoming to the idea of psychotherapy. There is institutional support for psychoanalysis and psychotherapy. There is also a background of Chinese culture in seeing dualities such as yin and yang, the complex frameworks of surface and depth, and an ongoing philosophical, cultural, and literary interest in the nature of human nature. Last but not least, psychoanalysis is in itself a fascinating endeavor. Psychoanalysts from Germany, Norway (Sverre Varvin), Argentina (Teresa Yuan) and the United States (Peter Loewenberg, Elise Snyder) have offered training and workshops in psychoanalytic-oriented psychotherapy (A. Gerlach, personal communication, November 19, 2008).

If the interest of Chinese mental health professionals in psychoanalysis were the only criterion, psychoanalysis will have a very bright future in China. The problem will be to train enough people as psychoanalysts. There are almost no Mandarin-speaking psychoanalysts in the entire world. Luckily, most young Chinese have good English. Competence in English is required for admission to college and greater competence for graduation. Currently many Chinese children begin to learn English in nursery school. This almost bilingual new generation should be able to obtain good psychoanalytic training and perform some much-needed work that will benefit many people in China in the future.

II

TRADITIONS AND TRANSFORMATIONS

4

Two Kinds of Guilt Feelings: The Ajase Complex

Heisaku Kosawa

> The goodness of a father is higher than a mountain, The goodness of a mother deeper than the sea.
>
> Japanese proverb

In discussing religion, Freud first wrote about a scene in which he envisaged the "totem meal," a ritual similar to the bear festival of the Ainus in Japan.[1]

> The clan is celebrating the ceremonial occasion by the cruel slaughter of its totem animal and is devouring it raw—blood, flesh and bones. The clansmen are there, dressed in the likeness of the totem and imitating it in sound and movement as though they are seeking to stress their identity with it. Each man is conscious that he is performing an act forbidden to the individual and justifiable only through the participation of the whole clan; nor may anyone absent himself from the killing and the meal. When the deed is done, the slaughtered animal is lamented and bewailed. (1913, 140)

Freud added the following:

> Psycho-analysis has revealed that the totem animal is in reality a substitute for the father (*Vaterersaty*); and this tallies with the contradictory fact that, though the killing of the animal is as a rule forbidden, yet its killing is a festive occasion—with the fact that it is killed and yet mourned. (141)

He then returned to his thoughts on cannibalism by comparing (1) Darwin's hypothesis on the "Primal Horde" (*Urhorde*) that "there is a violent and jealous father who keeps all the females for himself and drives away his sons as they grow up," and (b) a union of males (*Männerverbande*) that is the most primitive kind of organization that we actually come across (an organization that consists of bands of males; these bands are composed of members with equal rights and are subject to restrictions of the totemic system, including inheritance through the mother).

> One day the brothers who had been driven out came together, killed and devoured their father and so made an end of the patriarchal horde. United, they had the courage to do and succeeded in doing what would have been impossible for them individually. (Some cultural advance, perhaps, command over some new weapon, had given them a sense of superior strength.) Cannibal savages as they were, it goes without saying that they devoured their victim as well as killing him. The violent primal father had doubtless been the feared and envied model of each one of the company of brothers: and in the act of devouring him they accomplished their identification with him, and each one of them acquired a portion of his strength. The totem meal, which is perhaps mankind's earliest festival, would thus be a repetition and a commemoration of this memorable and criminal deed, which was the beginning of so many things—of social organization, of moral restrictions and of religion. (141–42)

Freud wrote further as follows:

> They hated their father, who presented such a formidable obstacle to their craving for power and their sexual desires; but they loved and admired him too. After they had got rid of him, had satisfied their hatred and had put into effect their wish to identify themselves with him, the affection which had all this time been pushed under was bound to make itself felt. It did so in the form of remorse. A sense of guilt made its appearance, which in this instance coincided with the remorse felt by the whole group. The dead father became stronger than the living one had been—for events took the course we so often see them follow in human affairs to this day. What had up to then been prevented by his actual existence was thenceforward prohibited by the sons themselves, in accordance with the psychological procedure so familiar to us in psycho-analysis under the name "deferred obedience." They revoked their deed by forbidding the killing of the totem, the substitute for their father; and they renounced its fruits by resigning their claim to the women who had now been set free. (143)

Thus, created the fundamental taboos of totemism out of the sense of guilt of the son (1—Never kill a totem; 2—Never use for sexual purposes females who belong to the totem), and for this very reason they had to correspond with the two repressed wishes of the Oedipus complex.

Thus, totem religion emerged from a child's sense of guilt, as an attempt to allay this emotion and to reconcile with the deceased father, in compliance with "deferred obedience." All subsequent religions, although they differ depending on the conditions of the culture of the period when such religion had been contrived and the means that were used, were attempts to solve the same problem.

Furthermore, Freud touched on the subject of the origination of the concept of God and on Christian theories, and stated:

> There was one factor in the state of affairs produced by the elimination of the father which was bound in the course of time to cause an enormous increase in the longing felt for him. Each single one of the brothers who had banded together for the purpose of killing their father was inspired by a wish to become like him and had given expression to it by incorporating parts surrogate in the totem meal. But, in the consequence of the pressure exercised upon each participant by the fraternal clan as a whole, that wish could not be fulfilled. For the future no one could or might ever again attain the father's supreme power, even though that was what all of them had striven for. Thus after a long lapse of time their bitterness against their father, which had driven them to their deed, grew less, and their longing for him increased; and it became possible for an ideal to emerge which embodied the unlimited power of the primal father against whom they had once fought as well as their readiness to submit to him. As a result of decisive cultural changes, the original democratic quality that had prevailed among all the individual clansmen became untenable; and there developed at the same time an inclination, based on veneration felt for particular human individuals, to revive the ancient paternal ideal by created gods. (148)

> There can be no doubt that in the Christian myth the original sin was one against God the Father. If, however, Christ redeemed mankind from the burden of original sin by the sacrifice of his own life, we are driven to conclude that the sin was a murder. The law of talion, which is so deeply rooted in human feelings, lays it down that a murder can only be expiated by the sacrifice of another life: self-sacrifice points back to blood-guilt. And if this sacrifice of a life brought about atonement with God the Father, the crime to be expiated can only have been the murder of the father. (154)

> In the Christine doctrine, therefore, men were acknowledging in the most undisguised manner the guilty primaeval deed, since they found the fullest atonement for it in the sacrifice of this one son. Atonement with the father was all the more complete since the sacrifice was accompanied by a total renunciation of the women on whose account the rebellion against the father was started. But at that point the inexorable psychological law of ambivalence stepped in. The very deed in which the son offered the greatest possible atonement to the father brought him at the same time to the attainment of his wishes against the father. He himself became God, beside, or more correctly, in place of, the father. A son-religion displaced the father-religion. (154)

If I were to summarize Freud's discussion, I would have to conclude that religion is an attempt to allay the emotion of wanting to kill one's father, and to reconcile with the father with "deferred obedience," and therefore is a mental state that is manifested from a child's sense of guilt.

But is only this situation representative of all the religions that exist in this world? Is religion that has emerged out a child's sense of guilt the only and universal religion? I am compelled to say that there are other types of religion. What had emerged out of a child's sense of guilt is "religious desire or demand without spiritual enlightenment" and not a perfect, well-established religious state of mind. If so, what is a religious state of mind? I would like to say that it represents a situation whereby a child develops a sense of guilt for the first time after his murderous tendencies are "melted down and dissolved" by the parent's self-sacrifice.

I would like, furthermore, to illustrate this once again, using an ordinary parable. There was a certain child. He was a very obedient child. Suppose that one day, he accidentally (in the truest sense of the word) dropped a plate and broke it. In doing so, a feeling of remorse, of having done a bad thing, welled up in his heart. When he was brought in front of his parents, he must have been trembling with fear. He apologized again and again, from the bottom of his heart, that he had done a bad deed and was sorry. But the stubborn old man continued to reproach the child. The obedient child could no longer stand it, and shouted, "I've apologized this much but still you do not forgive me. Why? I'm a human being, and human beings make mistakes. All right, do as you please, I do not care any more." The child's attitude must have been, as viewed by his parents, that of the most hideous rebel. However, the other parent (mother) said to him, "It is clear that what you did was bad. It is true that people make mistakes, but the bad you did was truly bad. Still, people are people, and a plate is something to be broken. You cannot help that, no matter how hard you try. So, always remember this admonishment and continue working." Hearing this, the obedient child burst out in tears. "Oh Mother, how generous you are for saying such things to me, who have done such a bad thing. I apologize from the bottom of my heart that I have done wrong. Please forgive me; I will never repeat the same mistake, ever again."

Readers—I am sure you have learned that, in this simple parable, a child developed a sense of guilt, but that this sense of guilt was made to change by the parent, to give rise to a different sense of guilt in the child's mind. Earlier, I stated that there are two religions; what I meant by that is a religion that came about by the differences in two mental states such as these. So the religion shown earlier, if seen from one angle, is a "religious desire or demand," and may not be something that should be referred to as religious state of mind. I intend to call the child's first awareness of guilt "a sense of guilt," and the latter awareness of guilt "repentance."

Then, where is such a religion? I believe it is the origin of the Shinshu sect of Buddhism, began by Saint Shinran in Japan, which is the place of Mahayana Buddhism; it is the *Samannaphalasutta* ("unconditional and absolute faith that welled inside a person, like a plant that sprouted despite having no roots") of Prince Ajase who lived in India during the days of the Buddha.

Prince Ajase, young and ambitions, won a serious of victories with neighboring countries. At the instigation of Daibadatta (a cousin of the Buddha), he confined his father King Bimbasara in prison, feeling an ever-mounting wish to exact vengeance. Ajase first reached the prison gate and asked the gatekeeper whether or not his father was still alive. The gatekeeper told him the exact circumstances—that his mother, Queen Idaike, was secretly supplying food to Bimbasara. Immediately upon hearing this, Ajase was enraged. "My mother is a villain. This is because she is the companion of my father, who is a villain." He also shouted, "The priests are villains; they use a variety of black magic in an attempt to prolong the evil king's life." Cursing and shouting, Ajase all at once stretched his left arm to grab his mother's hair, picked up a sword with his right hand, placed it on her chest, and was about to run it through her heart. His mother, astonished, clasped her hands in prayer, bent her body, lowered her head, flung herself on her child's arm, drenched in perspiration, and fainted in agony. A minister by the name of Gakko ("moonlight") and a physician, Jivaka, rushed to stop Ajase and admonished him by saying, "The ministers know that, since long ago, there have been many evil kings. Many princes have killed their fathers to seize the throne. However, they have never, ever heard of a person committing the atrocious act of injuring his own mother. If you, the prince, commit this act, it is a shameful act unworthy of *Kshatriyas* or the nobility. It is a heinous act that we the ministers and your followers cannot bear to hear. This is an act of the *Shundras* who belong to the lowest caste." Hearing these words, Ajase held back and decided not to strike his mother down with his sword. However, he immediately told the attendant to confine her to an inner chamber in the palace and refused to let her go out, even by a step. Later, Prince Ajase became the king, and, purely out of a wish to fulfill all his desires and pleasures unimpeded, killed his father and assumed the throne. As the years passed, these feelings of guilt led him to break out in a severe skill illness (virulent sores) that covered his body with foul-smelling pustules so offensive that no one dared approach him. King Ajase himself admitted that this was clearly a retribution for his bad deed, and that he would fall into the pits of hell at any moment. Indeed, he was at the height of distress, disrepair, and suffering. His mind and body were in such disarray that all the pain and suffering of the present and future loomed over him, all at once, as if a huge mountain had collapsed on him. It was at such a period that six followers—scholars who studied the Indian philosophy of the six schools—came to meet Ajase. Each stated his views in an attempt to console the king, but failed to provide him with peace of mind.

One day, the Minister Jivaka came to meet Ajase and tried to comfort him. At that instant, a voice was heard, coming out of thin air, telling King Ajase, "The Buddha will sooner or later enter nirvana. So go to the Buddha immediately and ask for his redemption. Nobody but the Buddha can save you. I am advising you this because I feel pity for you." On hearing this, Ajase was terrified, his body trembled, and, visibly shaking like a Japanese banana tree, asked the sky, "Who are you who says those things from above the clouds? I cannot see you; I can only hear your voice." The voice replied, "I am your father, King Bimbasara. You are to follow the words of Minister Jivaja; you should not do what your six ministers tell you to do." Hearing his father's kind words, King Ajase became so distressed that he lost consciousness and fainted.

Ajase finally reached the place of the Buddha. The Buddha did not preach anything. However, having killed his innocent father, Ajase was convinced in his mind that he would definitely go to hell, so he doubted that even the Buddha could save him. The Buddha focused on breaking down Ajase's resistance and tried to arouse religious beliefs in him.

> As long as the Buddha, who oversees the past, present and the future, provided—despite knowing that King Ajase would kill his father for the sake of the throne—the father-king with the causality that he must ascend to the throne in response to the offerings that the father-king had given to the Buddha in the past, then, even if the King had killed his father-king, the King's killing of his father cannot be blamed only on the King himself. If the King falls into the pits of hell, other gods must also fall with him. If the gods are not reprimanded for their sins, there is no way that Ajase would be so reprimanded for his sins. Thus, the Buddha must save Ajase from going to hell. How can the Buddha, who receives the wishes of other people for the repose of the souls of the deceased, ever see Ajase go to hell without doing anything about it?

It was as if King Ajase's tightly closed chest of darkness was suddenly thrown open; he felt as if he had been walking along a narrow, winding road and suddenly saw himself out in a wide, open beach.

> Dear Buddha, when I look around me, I see that, from the seeds of that horrible tree called iran, the same iran always grows. However, the beautiful and fragrant chinaberry tree never grows from the seed of an iran. But isn't it strange? Right now, I see that a chinaberry has grown out of an iran seed. The iran is me. The chinaberry is the devotion I just obtained now. If so, then this devotion may be referred to as *Samannaphalasutta* or unconditional and absolute faith.

So, the education of virtue that the compassionate Buddha had given to Ajase has left the confines of logic and reason, filling him with sympathy and thankfulness. And thus, dried-up trees began to blossom, and beans began to sprout. The teachings of redemption provided to such extreme feelings of guilt helped induce this tremendous feeling of repentance in Ajase.

At this point, I wish to briefly describe the differences between the desires of Oedipus and the desires of Ajase.

At the core of Oedipus's desire was the love for his mother, and Oedipus killed his father to make her his. In other words, the murder of his father enabled him to marry his mother. In Ajase's case, however, the killing of his father, a king, did not originate in the former's lust for his mother. Queen Idaike was about to see her youthful years go by, and since she had no child with her husband, the king, she worried that the love of her husband would vanish along with her beauty. Ajase's murder was based on this lamentable agony of his mother.

Idaike consulted a soothsayer, who told her to kill a hermit living in the forest, who was destined to die in three years' time. The hermit was reincarnated in her womb and she became pregnant. She gradually began seeing things the soothsayer had said, such as wanting to suck the blood from her husband's right leg. This brought her tremendous agony, both physically and mentally. It was inevitable that Ajase, who was born this way, would harbor a feeling of hatred toward his parents. Ajase was a hot-blooded youth of unparalleled valor, and other people regarded him as the happiest prince on Earth. However, no matter how hard he tried, he was unable to dispel the mysterious dark clouds that hovered over him day and night. Then, the time came. The ambition of Daibadatta, regarded as the revolutionary of the Buddhist community, finally revealed the true nature of his dark shadow. And so, instigated by Daibadatta, Ajase ended up murdering his father.

According to recent teachings of psychoanalysis, the most primitive form of sadism is oral sadism. Crunching, or crushing with the teeth, is the most primitive form of tyranny; it is an appalling crime. Why? It is because it is about crunching the mother, who is the ultimate source of life.

Ajase's tyranny was the most horrifying, primitive tyranny imaginable—attempting to harm his own mother.

In fact, according to psychoanalysis, in addition to those who wish to kill their father because they love their mother, some psychopaths wish to kill their mothers because they love them. The former is known as the Oedipus complex; I am inclined to name the latter the Ajase complex. Oedipus killed his father; Ajase even tried to kill his mother as well. Even if a father is killed, the ultimate source of life remains. Then, what if a mother is killed? Is the fundamental question on life an answer made toward the ultimate source of life?

Furthermore, I would like to end this manuscript by briefly discussing whether or not neurotics and psychopaths are actually able to acquire a religious state of mind.

A certain analysand began saying the following, moments before ending treatment: "I have always regarded religion in an uncritical fashion. I used the famous proposition made by Marx which I found in a book I had read three or four years ago—that religion is that opium of the masses—to argue uncritically that religion is a reflection of the dissatisfaction of the members of the subordinate class, that was either created in the form of an image, or was a hypothetical things such as heaven. But lately, I don't know exactly why, but I have become very aware of the need to reeducate myself in a critical manner concerning religion."

Since early on, this analysand was raised by his grandparents as their foster child. He experienced all imaginable forms of sexual trauma. On reaching school age, he returned to his hometown to live with his parents. Up to that point, he had lived in a completely different world. His father was a person of high standing in a provincial town. He was also an educator. As a result, the analyst's life created an extremely strange personality in him, whether he liked it or not.

His neurosis originated in his upbringing. His personality was thoroughly murderous and sexual. He was both Oedipus and Ajase. However, his world of the unconscious became his reexperience, and, as he began to recognize this, his disease melted away, like snow under the sun. At the same time, his personality became nonmurderous and changed to a religious character of its own accord.

Although this may appear tedious, I would like to show how his murderous tendencies are manifested.

> On the day of my younger brother's funeral, I was worried if other people would suspect my feelings or attitudes to be those of some happy occasion. Of course, I was influenced by the mood around me, and objectively showed, at least on the surface, that I was overcome with grief. At the funeral, I was sitting at a dining table at the very far end, being served post-funeral dishes. But I got excited, quickly taking a peek at every single dish that was served at the table by removing the plate cover; I remember people sitting near me laugh at me.

You may say that this is the silly, thoughtless behavior of a fifteen-year-old. That is, of course, true. However, if the mourning during those sad events, and rejoicing in joyful events, are manifestations of natural, humane sensitivities, not much influenced by education or any other acquired formalisms that had been added on later in life, then the fact cannot be denied that the analysand was showing abnormal reactions toward the death of his brother.

> The place where we used to live was totally devastated by the so-called Great Kanto Earthquake that struck in 1923. We worked with our father and younger brothers to build a small house. We made everything ourselves, from the foun-

dation stones to walls—we wove one sheet of bamboo after another. We made tremendous efforts to erect a tiny house with a six-mat room. Even though I was a child, I was already a fourth grader in middle school, and physically, I was almost a grown man. Ordinarily, in a case like this, it is perfectly natural to think that, since we made such heroic efforts to build a house, the parents should live in it. But then, after we learned that the children could not live in that house . . . I remember sulking considerably at my mother. I even hoped that another earthquake would strike and smash the house we just built.

His sexual life was also something that matched these tendencies.

One evening, when I was in the third or fourth grade of middle school, my father was late coming home because of some business. My mother put the younger children to sleep and went to the parents' bedroom. In those days, I was living alone in an annex. I got tired of studying, so I left the annex to drink some tea, and, since nobody was around (I guess I should explain to other people that I just wanted to check in on my mother and younger brother, who was sleeping soundly), I went close to my mother and spied on her, overcome with a desire that can never be forgiven.

With descriptions that made his book a world masterpiece, Émile Zola described how "Nana," the heroine, peeks through a keyhole and watches her parents engage in sexual intercourse, and becomes an extremely lewd woman as a result. As for me, in a house that my family had rented when I was in sixth grade of elementary school, I used to sleep in the living room. At one time, unfortunately, we had houseguests, so I spread a mattress in my parents' bedroom and slept there. There, I had the same experience that Nana had. And it was not through a tiny keyhole.

This account provides a glimpse of what is at the fundamental root of his personality. When studies on what are referred to in psychoanalysis as oral or anal stages came to be analyzed in more depth, and many more things became known from various angles, this analysand used to say to me, "Even during this summer vacation, my mother told me how happy she was, seeing me take much better care of my father than before, but I don't know if she was simply praising me, or making ironic remarks about how I used to behave. In any event, she told me something of the sort two or three times."

During the early and middle stages of my interview with him, he used to bite his nails while talking. However, he stopped doing it, and it appeared as if everything was resolved from the heart. His personality changed completely. His perceptions of life also changed dramatically. The way he viewed life changed completely, as if silver had changed to gold. This psychology is the most harmonious state that human beings have managed to attain, to this date, even when seen from contemporary cutting-edge scientific and psychoanalytical perspectives. Lastly, therefore,

I wish to pose the question to thinking people, "What does religion mean for ordinary people?"

NOTE

1. This paper is an old version of the manuscript Kosawa wrote in 1931. It was the first paper that he gave to Freud, after getting it translated into German. Seemingly, they had further communications later on.

5

Amae: East and West

Daniel Freeman

> Children are treasures more precious than a thousand granaries.
>
> Japanese proverb

Amae is a periodic interaction in which from time to time customary rules of social formality are suspended, allowing people to receive affectionate support and indulgence and to symbolically gratify nostalgic longings for childhood pleasures. In interactions that are comparable to make-believe enactments in creative symbolic play, *amae* recalls and transiently re-creates a derivative of the reassuring intimacy of the mother-infant relationship and the experiences of reunion and "refueling" of the separation-individuation process. Transient mutual regression in the service of the ego and emotional replenishment contribute to the progressive intrapsychic growth and development of both of the participants.

I will review some of the contributions made by seventeen psychoanalysts and social scientists who participated in a two-day conference on "*Amae* Reconsidered" in San Diego in May 1997. We hope you will join us in considering Western examples of wishing to be taken care of, to rely upon others, and to help and be helped, and creative intimate interactive regressions.

A DEVELOPMENTAL PERSPECTIVE ON *AMAE*

Dr. Takeo Doi first awakened the world's interest in *amae* when he wrote about it in 1956, 1962, and 1973. His conscious awareness of his own wish for *amae* was heightened by the experience of "culture shock" when he first came to the United States and found himself in the nonresponsive, non-*amae*-ing Western environment. What he missed in those around him was a sensitivity and receptivity to *amae* feelings. I vividly recall a corresponding, though more pleasant, state of surprise when my wife and I first visited Japan and found people to be so thoughtful, so considerate of our needs, and so sensitive in "looking after" us in ways that we would never have anticipated. Our crosscultural studies over many years had taught us to get to know people by wandering off on our own, "off the beaten track." In Japan, we repeatedly had a wonderful experience of people not only spontaneously seeking to help us but also often seeming to be loving in their warmth, and radiantly happy and glowing with enjoyment about having the opportunity to "look after" us—even without our being consciously aware of being in need of help! When we were not at all lost, for example, we might take out a map simply in order to decide which way we wanted to go next, and we would find ourselves warmly approached by someone we didn't know who was eager to help us and happy that they were able to do so. It was a wonderful experience to be treated so warmly and helped in this way when, as Westerners, we were anticipating needing to be autonomous and to handle things on our own. We too, in the West, have a deep responsiveness to being "looked after." But, as Dr. Nishizono later helped me to understand (1998), Western culture tends to encourage greater "severance" between individuals and "nomadism" in pursuit of individualism. Dr. Kaya (1997) and Dr. Kitayama (1997) explained to me that Western people often seem to be too "dry" whereas Japanese people enjoy exchanging warm feelings, savoring being close to each other, sharing intimacy, and nostalgia.

Innovators who try to formulate and to communicate new ideas, and those who attempt to translate ideas from one language or culture to another often face a challenge. There may not be preexisting words to adequately express the idea or accurately convey the author's meaning. If one borrows a preexisting term, it may have some connotations that inadvertently imply something different from the meaning that was intended. The potential for possible lack of clarity or misunderstanding may make it necessary to later refine or qualify such terms. Efforts to find appropriate English words to describe *amae* and to explain it in terms of psychoanalytic concepts have posed this kind of dilemma. A second semantic problem arose when Dr. Doi used the preexisting Japanese concept *amae* in a specialized way, selectively focusing his attention upon the intrapsychic experience of one of the two participants. At our "*Amae* Reconsidered" conference, he described his use of the term as "roughly" corresponding to "dependency" or "dependency need" within "a two-person relationship of an asymmetrical dependent type." He used the words "roughly corresponding" as he has become aware that there are problems when one attempts to translate *amae* using the words such as "dependency," "dependent," and "passivity," in that these words often may have a negative or pathological connotation (as, for example, when we speak of a "dependent personality disorder"). He described *amae* as "a nonverbal (good) feeling toward and seeking of another person who is supposed to take care of you." Dr. Doi has selectively focused not on the interaction as a whole but rather on the internal good feeling that the recipient seeks and experiences when taken care of. He suggested that this feeling originates early in infancy when a baby first "begins to recognize the mother and seek her."

Dr. Doi was interested in underlying motivational forces, wishes, positive feelings and appeal behaviors in the recipient of care and of dependent gratification. Other authors have pointed out that this differs from the traditional broader meaning of *amae* in three regards. *Amae* requires the participation of another person whose feelings and motivations need to be understood. Its interaction contrasts with customary social etiquette, involving transitions back and forth that need to be understood. And the appeal for *amae* may, in some cases, include not just positive elements but also coercive manipulative components which may impose an inappropriate obligation or burden on another person. Many authors have focused on *amae*'s interactional aspects (Johnson, 1993), using terms such as "interdependency," "attachment," "affiliation," and "intersubjectivity." *Amae* involves a reciprocity between partners who need each other. Dr. Taketomo has described how people negotiate through culturally structured nonverbal signaling prior to agreeing to suspend their usual way of interacting in order to enter the *amae* relationship (Taketomo 1986a, 1986b, 1988; Papp and Taketomo 1993). We will consider both intrapsychic and interactional aspects of normal *amae*.

Drs. Yamaguchi, Tezuka, and Freeman focused upon the bilateral give-and-take reciprocity in *amae*, and how this progressively evolves through the course of one's life. Although the original symbolic prototype for *amae* is the interaction between a benevolent parental "giver" of special indulgence and a dependent "recipient" of gratification, increasingly as one matures there are bilateral aspects to the interaction. An individual's role in the periodic giving-and-receiving relationship becomes increasingly compassionate as he or she matures and moves from infantile receptivity to becoming a giver of nurturance to others and to sharing in interdependent mutuality.

The motivations of the providers of *amae* were not included in the original theory. Dr. Yamaguchi presented a systematic study he had done of *amae* experiences in people of all ages. He found that in giving *amae* gratification, older, more mature people focus compassionately on the needs of the recipients rather than on their own needs. They value giving *amae* to others so much that they feel sad, lonely and distressed if they cannot fill this desire to give *amae*. Dr. Tezuka suggested that the caregiver's own *amae* needs are satisfied through projective identification with the recipient. Anna Freud (1936) described this in terms of altruistic relinquishment of one's own pleasure to a proxy, and vicarious participation in the proxy's experiences of gratification. Dr. Kitayama added that people are expected to be sensitive to each other's *amae* needs, and that a mature person feels compassionate empathic concern and offers a caretaking response upon merely seeing someone in need, even without their nonverbally appealing for help. Dr. Okano said that the genuineness of loving feelings is measured by how spontaneously and unconditionally each participant shows love, and a feeling that the relationship is not based on selfish demand but is mutually beneficial.

Dr. Doi based his original formulations upon psychoanalytic concepts available during the 1950s and 1960s. Since *amae* is related to the mother-child relationship of infancy and early childhood, we may find it helpful to consider some of our recent advances in understanding of early object relations and intrapsychic development (Freeman, 1993). Dr. Okano commented that although *amae* may be described as a search for the "primordial maternal cocoon," it is not a recapitulation of the actual maternal relationship. *Amae* is an attempt in later life to enact a derivative fantasy version of the original mother-child relationship. Dr. Taketomo has described this as an imaginative mimicking or feigning of the early mother-infant interaction comparable to enactments that occur in childhood play (1986a, 1986b). In Winnicott's terms, we may say that people periodically enter a shared make-believe world of transitional illusion and playful enactment of fantasy, in which they gradually creatively modify and reshape their memories and experiences of separation and reunion.

Drs. Ushijima and Kitayama discussed differences between the experience of *amae* and a young child's actual experiences in infancy. Dr. Kitayama noted that a young infant initially experiences himself as omnipotent rather than as "dependent." From the infant's perspective it appears that he or she initiates and controls his own gratification. The infant believes that it is he who is actively initiating a leap up into his mother's arms, rather than it being his mother who bends down to pick him up in response to his request. Dr. Kitayama suggested that instead of conceptualizing the infant's need as "a need for dependency" it might be more appropriate to define the infant's need as "a need to be met" (or, perhaps one might say, a need to be interacted with and responded to). Dr. Ushijima said that *amae* should not be considered equivalent to "congenital desire" or a newborn baby's feelings when he clings to his mother. He said, "it is necessary (for the infant) to have achieved some degree of development before the dependent attitude of the child might be called 'amae.'" The ability to participate in an *amae* experience arises once the child has established a stable internal image of mother, has a positive relationship with her, and can take a conscious active role in appealing for and initiating the interaction. It was suggested therefore that *amae* does not resemble the mother-infant interaction of the first months of life. During early attachment, the mother anticipates the infant's needs and responds to the infant's physiological reflex signals (including restlessness and crying), without consciously initiated active appeals on the young infant's part. Later, once the child differentiates an image of mother he develops object-directed "wishes" that are specifically linked to her (Akhtar, 1999). At this stage, a Japanese child starts to regulate socially disruptive reflex expressions of negative affect (such as crying), and starts to instead actively seek wish fulfillment by using more culturally acceptable forms of nonverbal *amaeru* appeal behaviors (Settlage et al., 1991; Okimoto, 1997). The child gradually becomes aware that mother and others have minds of their own and learns to "read" their facial expressions in order to, as Dr. Okonogi (1992) has described, anticipate whether or not the other person will be responsive. The child needs to learn what is "mutually comfortable" in terms of *amae*, which varies from one relationship to another (Maruta, 1992).

The word *amae* does not refer to a steady continuous drive or need. It connotes an intermittent yearning, from time to time, for reunion and regressive indulgent pleasure. It is a derivative of one side of the biphasic alternating back-and-forth separation-individuation experience called "ambitendency" (Mahler et al., 1975). The other side of the young child's back-and-forth experience is the active outwardly directed thrust to scrutinize, explore, discover, and gain mastery. The wish for *amae* is a derivative of feelings that are experienced in both Eastern and Western cultures when a child who has been curiously scrutinizing and exploring the surrounding world suddenly feels alone and feels an urge to check back and to reunite with mother. The child seeks, at these times, to return to sensuous intimacy in order to recreate the sweet illusion of shared omnipotence, to be emotionally nurtured and replenished, and to regenerate feelings of well-being, harmony, and safety. This emotional replenishment has been referred to metaphorically as "refueling" (Mahler et al., 1975). *Amae* is not so much about primordial attachment as it is about periodically revisiting the mother to whom one has an already-established attachment. Its goal is to achieve reassurance, to reaffirm and fortify one's established sense of basic trust, worth, and intactness. Drs. Okonogi (1992) and Tezuka (1997) add that in seeking *amae* refueling, the child also seeks forgiveness for autonomous aggressive impulses. The availability of mother when she is needed for emotional support and refueling (and, later, the availability of *amae* in other relationships) reinforces the sense of basic trust (Erikson, 1959). This contributes to the gradual development of stable internal symbolic representations of both of the reliable mother (object constancy) and of the refueling *amae* experience. As one matures, one comes to rely increasingly upon these stable internal representations, permitting progressive separation and autonomy (Freeman, Nishizono, Ushijima). Thus, reassuring *amae* experiences foster not dependency but rather gradual detachment from "dependent" reliance on the external actual object.

Appeals for *amae* may be used aggressively to manipulate responses from others. A recipient of *amae* is not helpless, but rather is in a position to potentially control the other person (Tezuka, 1997). Sometimes an appeal for *amae* indulgence may be inappropriate, coercively imposing a cultural obligation on the other person, presuming on and taking advantage of their generosity and benevolence (Taketomo, 1993). Dr. Okonogi has described a second kind of controlling relationship which may occasionally operate in the opposite direction (1992). A giver of *amae* may respond to someone who is needy in order to create a dependency from which the recipient finds it difficult to extricate or individualize himself, with the giver of *amae* thereby gaining control in the relationship. Dr. Nakakuki commented that Dr. Doi has selectively focused upon positive affectionate libidinal feelings and issues of separation and longing, but that he has not addressed issues of coercion and aggression.

The ego's role in regulating *amae* interactions was highlighted by Drs. Mizuta, Fujiyama, and Tezuka. Dr. Mizuta discussed how ego flexibility in mature individuals allows them to move back and forth between *amae*'s sense of oneness and unity at one moment and a recognition of separateness at other moments. In order for a smooth back-and-forth movement to be possible, both the denial of and the acceptance of separateness need to be held simultaneously in conscious awareness. Dr. Fujiyama discussed how this is based upon *jibun*, or reflective self-awareness, which leads to one's increasingly assuming responsibility and accountability rather than appealing to and depending upon others. Dr. Tezuka suggested that a key to distinguishing between healthy functional *amae* and unhealthy maladaptive *amae* can be found in how an individual expresses and manages his or her *amae* needs in interactions with others. She said that a person who has a socially appropriate "elasticity and flexibility in managing and expressing amae needs" and "a capacity to negotiate a good amae interaction" combines tenderness with ego strength, bounces back from the transient regressive experiences of *amae*, experiences a sense of agency, and can be considered to be functioning with ego autonomy. She quoted Prof. Takahashi, who has pointed out that "independence" is not equivalent to an absence of dependency. Rather, independence is built upon and supported by dependable relationships with a highly differentiated network of reliable attachment figures, upon whom one can fall back (in reality and in fantasy) when necessary.

The intermittent enactment of *amae* reunion followed by separation in which the participants reengage in their separate roles at a culturally defined proper distance is derived from the back-and-forth alternations of the separation-individuation process. Dr. Kitayama has noted that it is not only the coming together for an emotional experience of gratification that is important. Lingering in the transitions of the separations after the experiences of *amae,* and the resulting experiences of transience, are equally emotionally meaningful. Doctors Kitayama (1996, 1998) and Freeman (1993, 1994) have discussed how ego growth and reorganization, with gradual relinquishment of illusion and deidealization, occur in the course of these experiences of discontinuity. As a result, Japanese gradually become more tolerant of loss and separation. Dr. Kaya (1997) discussed experiences of separation in mourning and in the termination phase of therapy. He suggested that Japanese and Western experiences of separation may differ, in that Japanese separate with less of a sense of finality and with more of an anticipation of future reunion.

AMAE IN THE WEST

Some aspects of separation-individuation evolve more gradually in Japan than in the West. When Japanese scholars and clinicians look at Western culture, they comment upon the relative hastiness and abruptness, from a Japanese point of view, of our perhaps premature "severance" of ties with our mothers in childhood. This leads to what they refer to as our "personality of nomadism" (Nishizono 1998).

Japanese who are functioning in a healthy age-appropriate way are able to rely on the availability of *amae* refueling in their day-to-day interactions, as Japanese "daily life is made up of going into and out of this mindset" (Shiraishi 1997). They notice that we, in the West, seem to be more distant or isolated from one another as a result of our thrust toward individualism, and less comfortable appealing to others for special regressive indulgence. This has led to the suggestion that perhaps our greater distance from one another has contributed to our need to create formal affiliative affectionate "contracts" with one another—such as Western "romantic love"—in order to transcend our separateness and bridge the gap between us (Nishizono, 1998). In Western romantic love we also tend to concentrate or focus our yearnings for *amae*-like reunion and refueling onto a single idealized primary partner (described by Freud [1914] and Blos [1962] as a "narcissistic object choice," serving to complement and complete our sense of self). This is true both in our ideals of romance and in our spiritual focus on monotheism. In Japan, one may have a broader variety of healthy *amae* relationships, in different contexts.

In our discussion, we may wish to consider our tendency in the West to maintain affectionate contact with one another at a somewhat greater interpersonal distance. This begins in infancy when a Japanese mother seeks to be in direct physical contact with her baby as much as possible, while a Western mother tends to encourage the child to play or sleep on its own and often tends to maintain contact with the child through back-and-forth "baby talk" vocal interchanges at a distance (Caudill, 1972). In the West, concerns about loss of self and engulfment ("symbiotic anxiety") often contribute to conflicts about wishes for closeness and sensuous dependent intimacy, and may lead to a defensive attempts to maintain one's own "space" and boundaries. Discomfort about regressing and being looked after may contribute to defensive cultural taboos and rules of privacy which attempt to structure intimacy. In addition, Dr. Kitayama has added that we in the West may be less comfortable allowing ourselves to relax and participate in *amae* in a broad range of relationships because, "Western people may not like the sense of transience in *amae*" (personal communication, 1999). He has suggested that we are less acclimatized to the denouement phase of amae and thus perhaps less ready for the disillusionment and discontinuity.

People in both Eastern and Western cultures have needs for relaxation, refueling, gratification, and indulgence. But in the West there are fewer culturally structured mechanisms for periodic unwinding, regression, and regeneration within our day-to-day relationships. Dr. Shairashi suggested that, in the absence of opportunities to appeal for *amae* in our daily lives, Western culture created the church's confessional as a special formal spiritual "space" where one could experience an *amae*-like state in a solemn religious format. In this private, religiously structured space a worshipper may regress, admit to impulsivity and failings, and seek nurturance, indulgence, guidance, and forgiveness in relation to a divine spiritual parent. Regular weekly congregational worship services offer a similar opportunity to appeal for and receive *amae*-like nurturant refueling from a divine parent, but within a supportive group environment. The Judeo-Christian God gives *amae* to those who depend upon Him. People experience themselves as being like "sheep" who "return to the flock" to be nurtured and cared for in the arms of a "good shepherd." One then shares in divine omnipotence and beneficence within a transitional state of regressive merger and shared illusion, as individual boundaries, autonomy, and responsibility are suspended. We, as analysts, also provide our patients a special therapeutically structured opportunity to regress in the positive transference within the "holding environment" of psychoanalysis or psychotherapy.

6

Wa: Harmony and Sustenance of the Self in Japanese Life

Mark Moore

If fish are kindhearted, water is also kindhearted.

Japanese proverb

Living as a foreigner in Japan over a period of three years from 1995 to 1998, I often heard reference made to the importance of maintaining *wa* or harmony, often in the service of explaining an aspect of Japanese behavior that may have seemed particularly submissive, timid, or indirect to a Westernized *gaijin* (foreigner). The tone and manner in which my Japanese friends and colleagues spoke of *wa* seemed to indicate that it was a foundational component of the Japanese psyche. And yet it was seldom expounded upon and the term seemed to be used more as a stop-point in conversation than as a means of deepening any understanding of Japanese life. I began to suspect that *wa* was to the Japanese what water was to fish—something that one could sense as ever-present and influential, and yet so integral a part of daily experience that it was beyond most individuals' capacity to disengage from it and subject it to serious scrutiny or analysis. In approaching the writing of this chapter I experienced something similar—while books on Japanese culture are replete with references to concepts such as *amae, honne, tatemae,* and *wabi-sabi,* it is the rare book that makes reference to *wa* or harmony in its index, let alone as a title in its table of contents or as a central theme in a chapter.

Further limiting discussion of the concept of *wa* is the typically negative reaction it arouses in Westernized foreigners. It is associated with oblique behavior, rigid conformity, or a lack of assertion. The image most commonly connected with it is that of a hammer pounding down on a nail sticking out: compliance enforced with violent energy. However, an event that occurred toward the end of my second year in Japan, while I was working as a teacher in the northern province of Aomori, highlights both the seeming costs and more subtle benefits of maintaining *wa*, and illustrates the complexity of the concept.

THE EMOTIONAL ECONOMY OF MAINTAINING *WA*: A PERSONAL EXPERIENCE

As a state employee I was allotted twenty vacation days, all of which were to be used within a single academic year; unused vacation days could not be carried over. As the academic year came to a close I was acutely aware that I had five days remaining and accordingly I had planned to travel home to Ireland on a date that would allow me to use the five days of vacation from the ending year and several days from the new academic year. According to my contract, my academic year ended on July 31, which, in that year, fell on a Wednesday. I planned to leave on Thursday, July 25, thus using my five remaining vacation days to account for Thursday, Friday, Monday, Tuesday, and Wednesday. What I had failed to account for was our school festival, which fell on that intervening weekend.

When I discussed my travel plans with my supervisor, he communicated *kyoto-sensei*'s (the vice principal's) wish that I leave on Monday, July 29, so as to be able to attend the school festival. I appreciated his wish to have me attend and to aid the English club in their preparations and so I conditionally agreed. There was one obvious problem from my perspective: I did not think it was fair that I would have to use three additional vacation days from the upcoming academic year in order to accommodate the school. Surely *kyoto-sensei* would understand how I was making a compromise and so should not be made to lose vacation time? My supervisor agreed but the following day as he prefaced his conversation with the apologetic "*Gomen nasai, Maku-sensei, demo . . . (I'm sorry, Mark Teacher, but . . .)*" and as he painfully drew out the emphatically apologetic *demo*, I realized that the news would not be to my liking. He regretfully explained to me that I would have to use next year's vacation time if I intended to be present at the festival and then stay in Ireland for my planned two weeks. I looked at him quizzically and reexplained my dilemma. Did he and *kyoto-sensei* not understand that I was willing to accommodate them, but that I expected some degree of quid pro quo? I was certain that they simply misunderstood my dilemma. However, as I reiterated my point, my supervisor's face began to contort in a smiling mask of obvious embarrassment and awkwardness. He excused himself and explained that he would take up the matter again with the *kyoto-sensei*.

After several days my supervisor returned to explain that upon reviewing the situation, it had been decided that I could attend the festival and receive a weekday off in lieu of the Saturday I would be working, and that this would hopefully compensate for the extra days I would need to use from next year's allotted vacation time. Where before I was puzzled, now I was truly confused—what good would an extra day do me when it had to be taken before this academic year ended and as it stood I still had five vacation days that I was at risk of not being able to use?

I could recognize that my supervisor, while explaining himself with a smile on his face, was clearly feeling uncomfortable and self-conscious. Reminded of the poet Basho's well-known haiku ("Old pond, leap-splash—a frog"), it began to dawn on me that while he was desperately trying to maintain *wa* between all parties involved, keeping the pond of school politics calm, perhaps I was the frog splashing about with ungraceful force, oblivious to how turbulently I stirred the bureaucratic waters. While I felt strongly about not sacrificing vacation time, I began to feel sympathetic to my supervisor's dilemma, and I was also aware of how distinctly alien it was in the context of Japanese work culture to blithely use any vacation time, let alone argue for one's full allotment of days off. Indeed, many of my teaching colleagues would wait until retirement before planning any major vacations.

I valued my relationship with my supervisor, who had become a mentor and friend to me over the course of the past year—I had no wish to cause him further difficulty and I was sure that I was creating tension between him and *kyoto-sensei*. While my normal instinct was to stand my ground and demand some reasonable compromise, or simply refuse to attend the festival, I had no wish to leave him feeling responsible for a decision that would appear selfish and small-minded to his colleagues and superiors. I was approaching the problem the wrong way, but I was unsure what to do. For the first time since coming to Japan, I decided to place faith in my supervisor's empathy with the dilemma I was in, and to trust that he would manage to find some way to resolve the issue, provided I stepped out of his way. I explained that I was very eager to attend the festival and that while it was a dilemma because I would lose time with my family, I was sure something would be worked out. In effect, my approach was to resort to the Japanese practice of *amaeru*, or to passively depend on my superiors' willingness to indulge my "selfish" request without seeming to aggressively pursue my own agenda. I was also communicating that I had no wish to create conflict or disrupt the harmony of the relationship between my supervisor and *kyoto-sensei*, between me and my supervisor, and with my work colleagues.

Within a week, my supervisor called me aside while I was on the way to class and explained that a decision had been made. I would be expected to attend the school festival with the regrettable understanding that I would have to lose vacation time for the coming year if I wished to see my family for longer. He then advised me to officially inform the school that I would be taking a shortened vacation to Ireland in order to conserve holiday time for later that year. I began to explain that regardless of the loss of vacation days there was simply no way I would cut my holiday short—it had been too long since I saw my family and friends. My mentor quickly interrupted me and, with a look of mischief, explained that it was understood that I had every intention of visiting my family for only a short period and that this must be "sad" for me, but that it was also quite possible that I would become suddenly sick—"perhaps with allergies?"—and that I would have to delay my return to Japan. If such an "unforeseen" event should occur there was no need to inform the school as it was summertime and I was not expected to report in until the end of August!

The implications were clear: I was free to book my two weeks in Ireland as long as I attended the school festival and maintained the appearance of intending to stay in Ireland for shorter than two weeks. Yet more important than the three vacation days that had been saved was the relief I felt in having my request respected without damage to my relationships within the school. Furthermore, I felt that my needs, while recognized and met, were not indulged in a fashion that left me feeling petty, pampered, or the target of resentment. I could go home with the covert blessing of my coworkers and freely enjoy the experience of contributing to the school festival.

There are several ways to begin to understand this story and they include an emphasis on the conflict between my own individualistic desires and the needs of the group, the hierarchical structure of decision-making in Japan, the distinction between *tatemae* (the façade or truth of the tongue) and *honne* (genuine motives or truth of the heart) in how the dilemma was resolved, or the gaps in cultural and linguistic understanding. However, what most stands out in my memory of this experience was the profound discomfort I felt when my request was initially refused. It was not simply a sense of disappointment or frustration—rather, I felt the discomfort of discordance. I was out of tune with my supervisor, with the *kyoto-sensei,* and with the school, and they were out of tune with me. Resolution produced a shift from a state of discord to feeling in harmony again. This reinstatement of *wa* brought with it a sense of relief, purpose, and renewed vigor—all was right with the world.

LINGUISTIC, GEOGRAPHICAL, AND FAMILIAL UNDERPININGS

The Japanese term *wa* is most often translated as harmony but a closer examination of its root meanings reveals that the Japanese *kanji* (or character) for the term *wa* is composed of two characters. The first character is the symbol for a rice stalk and the second character is the symbol for a mouth, implying a meaning of "fat and happy, peaceful, placid, tranquil or harmonious" (Walsh, 1969, 75). It is also noteworthy that the term *daiwa*, literally translated as "great harmony," is also pronounced *Yamato*, which is the region considered by historians to be the birthplace of the Japanese state.

Davies and Ikeno (2002) refer to the theory of geographical determinism to explain the importance of harmony in Japanese culture. Japan is an island nation protected from invasion by dangerous and unpredictable seas and so its culture developed in relative isolation and safety. Eighty percent of the land is mountainous and thus uninhabitable, requiring people to "live close together in communities in which everyone was well acquainted with one another" (10). The concept of *wa* helped to "maintain relationships between members of close-knit communities" (10).

Japan's summer rainy season created by the monsoon winds arising from the ocean provides conditions for rice cultivation, and wet rice farming was established in western Japan circa 500 BC. The draining, leveling, and irrigation of valleys and coastal plains required intensive communal effort as did the planting, transplanting, and harvesting of the rice (Mason and Caiger, 1997, 21). From this need for cooperation, there developed a "kind of 'rule of the unanimous,' and people tended not to go against group wishes for fear that they would be excluded from the community (*murahachibu*, or ostracism)" (Davies and Ikeno, 2002, 10). A developed sensitivity to the maintenance of harmony was likely a consequence of needing to avoid ostracism.

A further possible factor in the importance of maintaining *wa* was the historical development of the concept of the "family system" during the Tokugawa period (1600–1868). During this period, a typical samurai family had only one source of income: the hereditary stipend paid by the shogun or daimyo to the recognized head of the family. This limited income placed great responsibility on the head of the family and encouraged a "hierarchical wholism" (Mason and Caiger, 1997, 250) in which the system's purpose was the ongoing welfare of the group as a whole, not the temporary aggrandizement of any member of it. The family head enjoyed authority and privileges proportionate to his responsibilities but also had an obligation to use it circumspectly and to ensure the welfare and dignity of his subordinates. Informal consultations marked much of the negotiation with such systems and it can be imagined that within such a system of well-defined proprieties and obligations that a premium was placed on consensus and the group's ultimate well-being. Disharmony or conflict could disrupt the delicate interplay of benevolent authority and loyal service upon which the family system rested. To that end, ambiguity (*aimai*) in the expression of ideas was valued.

Of use in understanding the impact of the family system in Japan and its role in self-experience is Roland's (1988) distinction between the *familial self* of the Japanese and the *individualized self* of Americans. He described the familial self as a psychological organization that facilitated the functioning of individuals within the "hierarchical intimacy relationships of the extended family, community and other groups" (7). Features of the familial self include symbiosis-reciprocity, narcissistic configurations of we-self regard, and a socially contextual ego-ideal. According to Roland (7–8), symbiosis-reciprocity entails intimate relationships marked by intense emotional connectedness and interdependence with permeable ego boundaries that allow for high levels of empathy and receptivity to others and a relational "we-self" sense of self. Self-esteem results from identification with the honor and standing of the family or one's group affiliations and is bolstered primarily by nonverbal mirroring. The ego-ideal associated with the familial self derives its form from traditional reciprocal obligations and the importance of observing etiquette in a variety of complex social contexts.

There are two other distinct features of the familial self: modes of communication that typically operate on two levels, and modes of cognition and ego functioning that are highly contextual. This contrasts with the modes of cognition and ego functioning characteristic of the individualized self that are "oriented towards rationalism, self-reflection, efficiency, mobility, and adaptability to extra-familial relationships" (9). Furthermore, the superego aspect of the familial self modulates aggression and sexuality in accord with the exigencies of the hierarchically structured family and group.

SOME DEVELOPMENTAL SPECULATIONS

An understanding of the roots of the intense emotional connectedness and the reciprocal nature of relationships associated with the familial self requires reference to the Japanese concept of *amae*. The concept of *amaeru* and its importance in Japanese society has been explicated by Doi (1973) in his book *The Anatomy of Dependence*. While *amae* can be translated as "to lean on a person's goodwill," Doi relates the root of the word *amae* to the "childish word *uma-uma*, indicating the child's request for the breast or food, which is the first word that almost all Japanese speak" (72). He notes that the prototype of *amae* is the infant's relationship with the mother, but that a child is not said to *amaeru* until the second half of its first year, while the infant can experience the mother and itself as independent beings. This awareness of separate selves brings with it the imagined threat of loss of the mother's love and care and so close contact is sought after or, in other words, the infant is motivated to *amaeru*.

A meaningful relationship between *amae* and *wa* is reflected in Doi's (1973) statement that the concept of *amae* "serves as a medium making it possible for the mother to understand the infant mind and to respond to its needs, so that mother and child can enjoy a sense of commingling and identity" (74). Just as Doi suggests that the psychological roots of *amae* lie in the child's dependent yearnings for the mother, I would argue that the desire for harmony in relations with others has its origins in the child enjoying the sense of "commingling and identity" with the mother.

The English term harmony originates in the Greek, meaning "joint, agreement, concord." Harmony as a musical term refers to any simultaneous combination of sounds, as opposed to melody, which is a succession of sounds (*Hutchinson Pocket Encyclopedia,* 1992). It typically denotes a pleasant sound, but the term can be applied to any combination of notes, whether consonant or dissonant. It is the dissonant components of harmony that are most typically highlighted when visitors to Japan comment on the issue of *wa,* stressing how it reinforces compliance and a disavowal of one's true wishes and feelings. Indeed, the example I described at the start of this chapter emphasized my own reluctance to "comply," and my initial unwillingness to value maintaining what seemed like a superficial "harmony" with my coworkers. However, the resolution, while appearing to be a bureaucratic sleight of hand, left all parties feeling that all was well with the world.

I do not pick my wording lightly in saying that all felt good *with* the world. Rather, I wish to reemphasize a fundamental characteristic of harmony—namely, a sense of gratifying commingling with the external environment. Balint (1959), in his discussion of object and subject, referred to a "fantasy of primal harmony . . . which was destroyed either through our own fault, through the machinations of others, or by cruel fate" (64). He noted that this form of harmony is a theme in religious beliefs and fairy tales and that the "striving for complete harmony between the subject and his environment may be approximated (a) in our sexual life . . . and (b) in all forms of ecstasy" (64). It has its origins in a period of development in which "there are as yet no objects, although there is already an individual, who is surrounded, almost floats, in substances without exact boundaries; the substances and the individual mutually penetrate each other; that is, they live in a harmonious mix-up" (67).

The primacy and power of this fantasy of a primal harmony in the Japanese psyche is reflected in Okonogi's (1978, 1979) emphasis on the concept of the Ajase complex as more central to an understanding of the Japanese individual than the Oedipus complex. The myth to which it refers tells the story of the prince Ajase who, after imprisoning his father, threatens to kill his mother when he learns that she is keeping his starving father fed with honey that she has rubbed onto her body. Ajase is struck by a guilt that exhibits itself in the form of a skin disease called *ruchu* that causes an odor, thus preventing others from approaching him. His mother tends to his illness and forgives him, at which point he reconciles with her.

In contrast to the Oedipus complex, where anger is directed to the father and desire toward the mother, here there is also a clear rage toward the mother in response to feelings of loss of their symbiotic tie. Ajase's anger toward his mother is triggered by her decision to feed her husband with honey rubbed on her body. While there are obvious erotic overtones in this action, there is also a suggested merger of boundaries in the meeting of mouth and skin and the transfer of nurturance in a manner reminiscent of a child taking milk from the mother's breast. It is also noteworthy that the consequence of Ajase's rage results not in an explicit fear of castration, but rather ostracism from others due to his odorous condition.

There is a risk, however, in focusing on the hypothesized developmental roots of harmony and Balint's emphasis on sex and ecstasy as the manifestations of that harmony found in adult life. To do so relegates the concept of harmony to extreme states of experience. It also overemphasizes merger and loss of the experience of oneself as separate. I would argue that the ability to feel that one is in step with the world and others, and the capacity to delight in such an experience, does not necessitate experiencing the subjective equivalent of an orgasm. The daily experience of harmony is neither as intense nor extreme as ecstasy, and involves a sense of feeling strengthened through recognition, and of being carried along with another's response rather than being lost in it. A simple example is the experience of clapping while part of an audience. Consider the nature of that experience: if one is among the first to clap, there is a brief moment of feeling alone and one's clap is hesitant as it probes out into the darkness for a congruent response. This brief flicker of doubt and vulnerability is often lost to conscious awareness, as past experience so bolsters the hope of a response that there is little differentiation of the moment between expectation and deliverance. In that pregnant moment while our ego holds on to hope as a defense against the experience of incongruence, we ignore our sense of hesitancy, of loneliness, and the weak sound of our tremulous hands. Hope holds its breath and time jumps to that instant of the joining response: the hall erupts and we are united in our response. In that moment, our clap is louder, stronger, and firmer. We are strengthened by the congruous sound reflected back to us and in another instant the rhythm of the audience feels as one. At this point, within the experience of the strengthened self, we can reach further into the dark and identify with others, no longer painfully aware of our own singular response but instead feeing that our clap is the clap of the many, feeling the roaring strength of the gathered response as if it were one's own.

Here the feeling of harmony with others does not necessitate a false experiencing of oneself, or a hiding of one's inner life. It need not be inextricably linked to ideas of rigid conformity or to the loss of a sense of self in subordination to the group. Instead, it emphasizes how pursuing an experience of harmony with others can lead to a strengthening of one's sense of self. It is the opposite of what Winnicott (1960) describes as the experience of someone in whom "there is a high degree of split between the True Self and the False Self which hides the True Self . . . one observes in such persons extreme restlessness, an inability to concentrate, and a need to collect impingements from external reality so that the living time of the individual can be filled by reactions to these impingements" (150). Such experiences of imposed conformity can be clearly differentiated from harmony. In harmonious experience with another, one's self is felt to be embraced and ego boundaries are strengthened rather than weakened, reinforced rather than threatened. Instead of a potential cause of a loss of one's sense of self, harmony may be the means by which one's "private self" is revealed and responded to in Japanese daily experience.

CONCLUDING REMARKS

In considering Japanese inner experience, Roland (1988) notes that as a result of the strong emotional enmeshment with one's family and involvement in hierarchical group relationships, a highly private self is a necessary component of the familial self. Complementing the permeable outer ego boundaries intrinsic to the familial self are strengthened inner ego boundaries that demarcate the private self. These inner boundaries are markedly less permeable and the individual has less awareness of his or her own wishes and feelings. Roland notes that the individual can feel extremely vulnerable in exposing this private self to a therapist. Persistent inquiry or interpretation from the analyst can be experienced as painfully intrusive. Expressions of the private self are communicated indirectly, under the cover of unspoken gestures and implied meaning and Roland describes how "as patients sense that the therapist is sufficiently empathic to pick up these innuendos and clues, they will reveal somewhat more of their inner world" (83). Another way to describe a therapist as being "sufficiently empathic" is to say that the therapist is engaged in a harmonious exchange with a patient, a simultaneous combination of expression met with understanding that provides the patient with an experience of integration rather than fragmentation. As harmonious therapeutic exchanges act to reduce the threat of disruptive intrusion and strengthen the patient's sense of self, more of the private self is revealed, and the analytic work deepens.

Such exchanges can be verbal and nonverbal, but one exchange that took place on my return flight from Japan exemplifies how *wa* is brought to life in our interactions with others. I found myself sitting beside an elderly and uncharacteristically effusive Japanese man with a sun-worn look that indicated many years spent outside and a wiry body that suggested a life perhaps of a farmer. He engaged me in conversation but spoke in a dialect that made it difficult for me to follow; yet his enthusiasm was such that an unspoken energy carried our talk along.

My sadness in leaving Japan at the end of my three years left me especially open to a final taste of what had endeared Japan to me so much: the warmth and openness of its people. And so I too made an equally eager effort to engage with my fellow passenger. Finally, after some time of lively back-and-forth, with a fierce smile and a reassuring pat on my arm, he pulled out a pen and piece of paper. He drew a *kanji* character and then its *romanji* form: *ishin deshin*. Pointing to his heart and then to mine, I knew immediately what he meant—our conversation had been an experience of *ishin deshin*—"from heart to heart." However, I cannot remember exactly what we spoke of. I am left only with impressions, warm and fond impressions—and gratitude for the kindness of this stranger who unknowingly provided me, as I was leaving Japan, not with a sense of singular isolation but with a profoundly harmonious sense of connection.

7

Psychoanalysis in the "Shame Culture" of Japan: A "Dramatic" Point of View

Osamu Kitayama

> When you know the masks as well as we do, they come to seem like the faces of real women.
>
> Fumiko Enchi (1958, 17)

Persona is a Latin word that signifies the mask that an actor puts on in classic drama. Discussion of *persona* tends to focus mainly on its exteriority. However, even with "sacrificial service," in which an individual blindly meets the demands of his or her environment by sacrificing his/her inner reality, clinical problems are likely to be connected to these inner realities. In other words, a persona incorporates various realities, both internal and external, and is an intermediate and ambivalent presence interposed between the inside and the outside. To consider the problem of personality, one takes into account the masklike elements on that "theatrical stage"—or, in other words, discusses life problems from a dramatic, or theatrical, point of view. This is indeed a classic activity.

In the first half of this paper, I will introduce the "dramatic" point of view of psychoanalysis, and discuss its significance in Japan. In the latter half, I wish to describe examples of clinical analysis and story analysis as seen from the "dramatic" point of view, while referring to my study on "The Prohibition of Don't Look." Furthermore, from the standpoint of dyadic psychology, I will discuss not only the problems of a drama's protagonist, or, in other words, the first party, but also the power of influence of the actor/actress playing opposite the protagonist, meaning the second party.

THE "DRAMATIC" POINT OF VIEW OF PSYCHOANALYSIS

"A Private Theater"

Psychoanalysis was initiated by physicians who dealt with hysterics who "played" a dramatic role. Patients who appeared in clinical lectures given at Paris University by professor of psychiatry Jean-Martin Charcot (1825–1893) were extremely theatrical. Charcot himself, who pointed this out, was said to have been "no doubt theatrical" and "far more than an actor" (Gay, 1998). Sigmund Freud, who attended Charcot's lectures, wrote, in a letter dated November 24, 1885, addressed to his future wife Martha Bernays, "Mein Gehirn ist gesättigt wie nach eimen Theaterabend (my brain is satisfied as if I had spent an evening at a theater)."

In Austria at the end of the nineteenth century, when Joseph Breuer was treating the patient Anna O., she referred to her daydream-like experiences as *Privattheater* (a private theater), and the "theater"-like aspect of psychoanalysis can be said to have begun here ("Studies on Hysteria"). Since then, there seems to have been a continuous line of individuals—from Freud to McDougall (1982), and more recently, those who advocate the concept of "enactment"—who regard psychoanalysis as something theatrical. One example of this is the concept of "acting-out" in psychoanalysis. Freud used this concept in a report on his treatment of Dora, a hysteric, as follows:

> In this way, the transference took me unawares, and, because of the unknown quality in me which reminded Dora of Herr K., she took her revenge on me as she wanted to take her revenge on him, and deserted me as she believed herself to have been deceived and deserted by him. Thus she acted out an essential part of her recollection and phantasies instead of producing it in the treatment. (Freud, 1905)

If I were to reexamine this "acting-out" concept, the German word *agieren*, as well as the English translation of the word, has two meanings: "to act in the sense of taking action," and "to act in the sense of performing or playing out a role." In Japanese, however, the latter meaning has never been translated, and there are no words in Japanese that show this double meaning. In the English phrase, "acting-out," that was used to describe actions outside the treatment room, emphasis was placed on the word "out," so this term came to signify undesirable behavior or myopic behavior. This has even led to the appearance of the phrase "acting in" (Zeligs, 1957) to reemphasize the message qualities and therapeutic significance of behaviors and acting performances directed toward the therapist.

Play Therapy in the Treatment of Children

In the past fifty years, moreover, analytic therapists of children, such as D. W. Winnicott, have made their appearance in psychoanalysis. In the play therapy that they carry out, "play" is a medium for understanding and analyzing a child subject. Since the word "play" can also signify "drama," they came to regard this dramatic element as entirely natural. The treatment records of adult patients written by these former child analysts spontaneously show that they equate treatment with play, meaning dramatic therapy. However, I believe it is safe to conclude that no word exists in the Japanese language that carries the double meaning of play and drama, such as the German word *Spiel* and the English word "play."

Moreover, based on the perspective of object relations theory, in which human beings repeat the relationship of objects and the self that was implanted during infancy, or, in other words, a specific object relation, the method of understanding therapeutic relationships (transference) that is the focus of interest in psychoanalysis, is now being reexamined. From the perspective of dyadic psychology, which was brought about by the object relations theory, the current therapeutic relation has become a forum for dramatizing object relations that are derived from the past. In the commentary of a treatment report titled "Piggle," Winnicott's wife Clare calls this process the "dramatization of transference." In other words, past object relations (a psychological script) are dramatized within the therapeutic relationship. Some insist that child analyst Melanie Klein is the originator of the dramatic point of view of psychoanalysis such as this. I personally feel that these points of view come from all child analysts who use play as the central material in their analyses.

In the psychoanalysis of children such as this, one of the analyst's jobs is to read a drama's scenario while taking part in the child's drama as an actor playing opposite the protagonist. Naturally, the analyst is liable to become involved in the drama as the child's costar, whether he likes it or not. According to the therapeutic theory that has prevailed recently in English-speaking countries, the part of the drama where the patients and analysts appear is called "enactment" and "reenactment" (for example, Joseph, 1988, and Renik, 2006). Concepts such as projective identification (Klein, 1946) and role-responsiveness (Sandler, 1976) are used to explain its mechanisms. These changes signify that the concept of acting-out, which was handled in a negative light by Freud, has now come to be utilized in a constructive fashion in treatment.

Summary

I will call this point of view "the dramatic point of view of psychoanalysis." To summarize things that are being discussed, using dramatic metaphors, the following may be said: (a) Human beings tend to repeat their "psychological script," which derives from the past, while playing opposite different characters; (b) when this "script" is also brought into therapy, then therapy becomes increasingly dramatized; (c) while appearing in a "drama," an analytical therapist will read the "script" as it is unveiled while agreeing to become an actor playing opposite the protagonist; and (d) emphasis will be placed on the significance of setting a therapeutic "stage" (or, in other words, an analytic setting).

Then, for what purpose does such "psychoanalysis as a drama" or "a dramatic point of view of psychoanalysis" exist? Therapeutic theories that follow the flow of psychoanalysis such as this aim to retell life stories that have been repeated. It is said, therefore, that there also are therapeutic aspects in reweaving one's life story and obtaining a better life story. This means that, although historical events that actually took place cannot be changed, retelling it may enable you to change your life story. It may also be possible to retell a tragedy as a neutral story or even a comedy. And the idea of "reweaving a life story that has been dramatized in analytic treatment" such as this contains not only views on treatment but also views on life in general, of "life as a drama," as described hereunder.

THE THEORY OF LIFE AS A DRAMA AND THE "CULTURE OF SHAME"

Life as a Drama

Needless to say, life is something you live, not perform. However, there are some elements in life that are "created" just like drama. A good example of this is the Japanese term *tsukuri-warai*, which means "a staged or a forced smile." (The literal translation is "to make a smile.") Of course, the view of seeing life as a drama has an extremely long history. As Shakespeare wrote in *As You Like It*, the view that "All the world's a stage, and all the men and women merely players" has now become more than a mere metaphor. That is to say, contemporary people have transformed themselves into "actors" who try to adapt themselves to meet external demands while suppressing their true personalities. We not only see the outside world from the inside, but also consider how we are being seen by the outside world. If one's eyes in the former case were to be regarded as "the eyes of the first person," the eyes from the outside in the latter case would be "the eyes of the second person," or, in other words, the eyes of the audience or the author of the play. To people who are like actors, the reflecting-back from the second person is important.

Moreover, as the Japanese term *uki-yo*, or "the floating world," shows, the Japanese share an awareness that, although "this life" is somewhat nonessential presence, it is a valuable and worthwhile reality which we human beings must live through sincerely and carefully in our own way (Yamazaki, 1971). There also is a theory of literature in our country that regards life as a drama. This indicates the characteristics of an "I" novel, or a novel that deals with the author's private life, that equates the novelist's life with the protagonist in the novel he or she writes. In the tradition of the "I" novels, both the novelist himself and the readers have the tendency to not differentiate the story of the novel's protagonist from that of the novelist's life. I believe that the dramatic point of view of trying to dramatically depict a case report in which a patient and a therapist appear has become extremely widespread, even in reports of contemporary psychoanalysis in Japan (Kitayama, 2007).

The Culture of Shame and the Treatment Room as "Backstage"

Individuals who have an especially strong awareness of shame regard life as a drama in which actors wear fragile masks. Anxieties about shame become stronger when their masks are stripped away and their real faces are exposed. As seen, understanding of life and clinical problems from the dramatic point of view allows shame-ridden individuals to talk about their own experiences in a rich and detailed fashion. The fact that a dramatic point of view is effective in clinical practice in the context of the "culture of shame" may be because the Japanese have a strong awareness of shame. In the psychology of the awareness of shame, as Kenichiro Okano (1998) states, it is easy to understand if we regard the self as carrying the duality of an "ideal self" and a "shameful self." It may be correct to differentiate the two by calling the former the adaptive self or the public self, and the latter the true self or the private self (Kitayama, 2004). This duality is repeatedly described in ordinary Japanese language, such as *omote* to *ura* (front and back), *honne* to *tatemae* (what one says and what one means), and *giri* to *ninjo* (duty and sentiment).

To use the metaphor of drama here, people who are ashamed continue to live by hiding their real vulnerable face or sinful self, all the while playing a respectable role in society. If we were to follow the dichotomy of the self that was advocated by British analyst Winnicott (1960), we may call them "the false self" and "the true self." According to him, moreover, the false self originates in a child's overadaptation to his parents and/or the external environment. In other words, a child sacrifices his true self to adapt to external demands or environmental failures. Many cases of adaptive failure are caused by failures of this duplexing. Here, we see the tragedy of an individual who cannot successfully live up to his parents' expectations, respond to his teacher's demands, or do what his friends expect him to do.

Seen from a dramatic point of view, moreover, a treatment room where the truth and depths of a patient's heart are opened up for analytic investigation has the potential to become "a backstage dressing room of life" of patients and clients who live their life as a drama, with the outside world as their "stage." The Japanese word *ura* has a dual meaning: "back" and "the heart," indicating that the Japanese people are aware that the heart is in the back. This is why, in the "backstage dressing room" known as the treatment room, a patient stops his exaggerated acting to think, "in the back," about what sort of a drama he is playing in the outside world. In so doing, a patient/client must return frequently to his true, natural self. In life's "backstage," a patient/client may confess, along with a feeling of guilt, a variety of repulsive feelings and aggressive thoughts toward his parents. A therapist listens to them but never discloses them to other people. In other words, the secrets of the heart are handled as an event that took place in the "backstage," that should never be brought out to the "stage." This is the fundamental rule. This is why a patient/client decides to begin talking about his mixed-up thoughts related to patricide (Freud) and matricide (Heisaku Kosawa) that are usually unconscious.

Shame and Resistance

However, people's hearts, especially those of Japanese people, tend to resist psychoanalytic approaches that use verbalization and self-expression as their methods. A patient undergoing an examination by a physician must strip their clothes off inside the treatment room; likewise, a patient undergoing treatment at a psychiatric treatment room for the mind must "strip" or reveal his or her heart in front of a psychiatrist. However, this is not easy to do. Inside the treatment room, a patient is expected to talk about himself who, as an actor in the outside world, is wearing a mask, or to gain an honest grasp of the true self that is behind the mask and think about it. This is not easy to do in actual treatment. What happens if a third person carelessly touches another person's heart? The fable, "The North Wind and the Sun" teaches us a lesson: if we try to forcibly remove a traveler's cloak, using a cold wind, we end up having the traveler put on even more clothes. The power that resists such act of "taking off one's clothes and removing makeup" or actions of that type, is called "resistance" in psychoanalysis. In terms of technique, the handling of this resistance becomes the top priority issue for us as psychoanalysts, rather than the content of a person's mind.

Psychoanalysis is currently divided into numerous groups concerning the handling of this resistance: it has become the point at issue for each school of thought to clearly "show its flag." In the context of "shame culture," moreover, resistance based on shame is a phenomenon that is anticipated to appear the most frequently when treating Japanese patients. Therefore, the issue of resistance seen where Japanese patients encounter psychoanalysis, which is sometimes referred to as the "uncovering method," as well as how to handle such resistance, deserve to be discussed more often. Resistance to self-expression in psychoanalysis will highlight the characteristics of Japan's psychoanalysis performed in the Japanese language, and understanding of the mind, in Japanese, will deepen through understanding this resistance.

The Second Eyes

The dramatic point of view takes such resistance fully into consideration, and verbally describes the way of life of human beings who live in a "shame culture." In this culture, moreover, experiences of a drama are often expressed as metaphors that describe life (Kitayama, 1987). This is why remarks made by Japanese actors are broadly welcomed and read as "a theory of art," and highly regarded as something that teaches people the art of living well and wisely. It is therefore no surprise to encounter a Japanese psychoanalyst who tries to use these theories of art in Japanese clinical psychology (Shigeharu Maeda, 2002).

Moreover, if a human being is regarded as gaining a lot by reading and weaving his life story, all the while living his life, it is important that he acquire an eye not only as an actor appearing in a drama but also the eye of a reader of life stories. And, as training for reading people's life stories in clinical practice, we read existing stories which are shared culturally, enabling us not only to take the point of view of the protagonist (the first person) but also see through the eyes, as well as understand the psychology, of the actors playing opposite the protagonist as well as the reader/narrator (second person). Mythologies and folktales are typical examples of people's life stories and are full of lessons. Tragedies in particular are very useful in clinical practice. I wish to discuss the points of view of reading about life tragedies, and the method of reading such stories, in the context of the recurrent "Prohibition of Don't Look" tragedy.

The Tragedy of the "Prohibition of Don't Look" as an Example of Learning from an Existing Drama

I have often discussed the general outline of the tale of a marriage between a human and a nonhuman being that is seen in the play *The Twilight of the Crane*, and the folktale "The Grateful Crane." In the contemporary version of the tale, the male protagonist rescues a wounded animal in the opening scene; however, this episode is not seen in the old version. First, an animal woman disguises her true self and visits a male human being. The two marry, and the beautiful wife weaves a piece of cloth and presents it to the man, who is able to sell it at a high price and becomes rich. He asks for more of this cloth. The woman prohibits her husband from looking at her while she weaves it, but the man violates the prohibition and peeks. What the man sees is the woman, who has become a crane, plucking her own feathers from her body to weave the cloth, and becoming wounded by this. The crane feels deeply ashamed that her true self has been revealed and leaves the man. The story characteristically ends with a separation, with the man losing his wife.

In many cases, the female protagonist is depicted as a maternal figure. A woman comes to marry a man in response to his passive object love (*amae*). The damage to the animal that was concealed by the "Prohibition of Don't Look" is the result of the self-sacrifice and production activities of the maternal woman who went beyond her limits to meet the protagonist's endless demands like those of a child (Kitayama, 1985). The crane-wife continues to weave cloth beyond her limit; in another folk story, a snake-wife submits her two eyes. The purpose of the "Prohibition of Don't Look" is to prevent sudden disillusionment caused by the exposure of the self as a wounded animal instead of a beautiful female image, and to avoid the shame that is experienced by the exposed woman who is being seen.

The story of "The Prohibition of Don't Look" also includes the Japanese myth featuring Izanaki and Izanami. In this mythology, the Mother Goddess, who died after giving birth to different countries and gods, ordered that no one look at her corpse. However, the Father God broke the rule and peeked at the Mother Goddess's corpse. Humiliated and furious, the Mother Goddess chases after the Father God. Even so, the goddess is fought off by the god, and the two end by divorcing. The Father God, who has seen something dirty, subsequently undergoes *misogi*, or a purification ceremony.

The Shame and Vulnerability of the First Person

In parallel to analyzing the stories such as above, I have thus far reported on the clinical cases of overadaptation of subjects, both men and women, who work hard like the heroines of "The Grateful Crane" and *The Twilight of the Crane*. The subjects' repeated failures to adapt overlap the images of the Mother Goddess in mythology who died after giving birth to numerous objects, and the wife who became injured by weaving cloth. I also occasionally encounter patients who strongly identify with these characters. The female protagonist is the drama's first person who is "being seen."

Here, I wish to present, from existing stories, a number of specific examples that show these female protagonists' wounds and death in the course of production that cannot be readily seen because of the "Prohibition of Don't Look." In the myth of Izanaki and Izanami, the Mother Goddess died while burning her genitalia in order to create a country. In the legend of Princess Toyotama, another myth, the protagonist princess writhes in agony while giving birth, and transforms herself into an alligator. In the folktale version of the crane-wife, the heroine becomes injured each time she did her weaving in response to her husband's request. In the folklore version that has been passed down over the years, the snake-wife submitted her eyeballs and became blind. In the folktale "*Uguisu no Sato* (The Bush Warbler's Home)," a bird flies away, lamenting that its egg was broken by a man. All these stories are essentially not about gods or birds, but about incidents that occur among human beings. However, the tragedies of mothers, the first persons, are none other than the pain to the hearts of the second persons who also experience these stories, as well as of third persons like ourselves who tell these tales. Therefore, the tragedies cannot be described overtly. This may be why the stories were created and told from a different perspective: that of a human being who was left behind, depicting the stories as incidents that had occurred with birds or gods.

The Sense of Guilt Experienced by the Second Person

Modern medicine insists that the injured crane should survive rather than fly away. Nevertheless, when I see patients who immediately begin to contemplate suicide once they are no longer useful to society, I can tell that a story that goes back more than one thousand years—of a protagonist who was humiliated and left the scene—is compelling vulnerable people to repeat this standardized life story, even today. However, if the ending of the story was to change, and if the crane-wife decides to stay and not leave her husband, the opposite player (the second person) must change as well. When he does, what things must he experience?

Many Japanese old tales end their story with a parting of the characters. Here, I see a sense of guilt on the part of the male protagonist in the background. From the Father God Izanaki, who appears in the Izanaki-Izanami myth, to male protagonists who appear in folktales, all the male characters break the "don't look prohibition" that their wives impose on them, and expose the wives' secrets that are death or injury. In "*Uguisu no Sato* (The Bush Warbler's Home)," the man who broke into the house drops eggs that he had picked up and breaks them. Seeing this, the woman cries and, transforming herself into a bush warbler, flies away. Overlapping these multiple tragic storylines shows that two issues are symbolically being repeated: the danger associated with a woman's childbirth and childrearing, and the issue of invasion and responsibility on the part of men who are the second persons. I feel that not only female protagonists who leave the scene, filled with shame, but also male protagonists, who are the second person, may also feel sinful and ashamed.

In mythological depictions, what we feel that the Father God Izanaki perceives in Izanami, who died after giving birth to this country and the gods, is his feeling of repulsion that her corpse is "dirty"; this "dirtiness" subsequently motivates Izanaki to cleanse himself through *misogi*, a purification ceremony. If this was a historical fact more than 1,500 years ago, this may be said to be Japan's first report of mysophobia, or pathological fear of contact with dirt. However, this Father God abandoned the corpse of Izanami, the Mother Goddess who died for our sake, and came home, never to return. In *Uguisu no Sato*, no feelings of regret on the part of the man who had dropped eggs are described; in "The Grateful Crane," too, the man just stands there, stunned, watching the crane fly away. No matter how we look at this, the task of the men left behind must be to work on their feelings of *sumanai*, or "I'm sorry," toward the maternal women who, although they were prolific producers, died or were deeply injured.

Clinical Vignette: 1

The patient was a competent female secretary, aged thirty, who came to me chiefly complaining of depression. Even during the interview, she was strongly self-reproachful, repeatedly accusing herself of being stupid. She told me about an episode when, still a young child, she had asked her mother to sew a costume for a school play. The mother worked throughout the night, and the following day, suffered a heart attack and collapsed. Since then, the patient has harbored anxieties that she might have done something terrible to her mother. Several years later, her mother actually passed away of heart disease. This compounded the patient's misery, strengthening her conviction that it was she who had killed her mother. Depressive feelings intensified as a result. It appears that people around her criticized her behavior and told her that she was to blame, and that this was also a contributing factor. So, in treatment, it became necessary for her to come to think that the responsibility for her mother's heart disease did not lie in the patient asking her to make a dress, but to consider its symbolic meaning. Just by thinking about it, though, the patient felt as if she was doing something bad or evil to her mother. It was extremely difficult for her to think about this because of her shame and guilt. This is resistance.

Through thinking about the reasons for this resistance and gaining an understanding of it, the patient gradually became able to think about a fantasy in which stupid things happened to her if she relied on other people. Once this became possible, she became able to discuss with me the image which she was the most anxious about—that, to bring her dead mother back to life, she may hug a woman, who is her mother substitute, and have a sexual relationship with her. The patient also understood the fact that her feeling of guilt that she had "killed" her mother was creating diverse sexual fantasies, and she shuddered with the notion that she might translate such fantasies into action. As she came to understand them, she settled down. In one interview, she shouted at the therapist, "I was not in the wrong!" Her final theme was her fear that the therapist, whom she was having even romantic feelings for by this time, might get disgusted with her and desert her. While discussing this fear with the therapist, however, she slowly and gradually accomplished her separation from him.

Clinical Vignette: 2

A man, a little past thirty-five years old, was a computer technician who came to the hospital with a variety of physical symptoms and social phobia. What the patient was good at, and enjoyed doing as a hobby, was repairing all sorts of things. His mother had a serious physical disease, and his father was often absent from home. Since he was the eldest son, he felt that he took the place of the parents. He was consistently obsessed with the notion that if he collapsed, the family would collapse as well. He therefore continued to repair his house. However, he ultimately experienced shortness of breath and could no longer go to work. Although he was good at taking care of other people, he could not take good care of himself. And, since he could not blame his difficulties on other people, he was constantly blaming himself. In treatment, I found the patient having a difficult time linking his overadaptation with his mother's illness and his father's absence. He said that, if he did, he felt guilty, as if he was saying bad things about someone behind their back. This is resistance.

At one of the treatment sessions, however, the patient was able to complain about the therapist's leadership and authoritarianism: that the therapist was trying to force the patient to say bad things about his parents. This proved to be the turning point in his treatment. One thought that came out from here that was very interesting to both the patient and the therapist was that the patient "killed" a Ptolemaic theory, of wanting to move the other person for one's own sake, and promptly carried out Copernican moves of simply going round and round around the other person, because he felt sorry for being taken care of by his sunlike parents. In other words, he felt guilty about criticizing his parents, who were like the sun to him, and was therefore afraid of being blamed by everyone else for it.

Clinical Vignette: 3

A female patient, who had just turned forty, worked at a bar. She also suffered depression and had a bedridden mother in her care. She compared her aesthetic principle to that of the female protagonist in *The Twilight of the Crane,* and said that she was willing to accept difficulties because this was what she was living for. An episode that symbolizes the relationship between her and her mother was described as an image of her mother trying to carry her baby but could not do it successfully because of her bad arm. The patient said that she resisted thinking about the negative aspects of childrearing she had received. When I pointed out to her that she, like a female protagonist in folktales, was trying to prohibit herself from showing the fact that she was hurt behind all the sacrificial caretaking, she agreed, smiling that what she had was a *jitensha-sogyo*, or shoestring operation, a metaphor for the way of life of a person who collapses unless she keeps on pedaling her bicycle hard. What had prompted her recovery, in this case also, was the expression of her anger toward her mother, and awareness of her feeling of guilt.

Clinical Vignette: 4

In the case of a young male patient (age twenty-one, compulsive neurosis) who was unable to attend school, simply hid himself in fear of a curse and repeatedly manifested praying-like seizures, his mother was also a sensitive, vulnerable individual. Soon after the patient began undergoing in-hospital treatment, his mother suffered a fracture. As I continued to discuss with the patient the causality of the incident, that the episode had nothing to do with the patient, he gradually felt a sense of anger toward an idealized mother rise inside him which he had thus far avoided seeing. His understanding further developed to the point that he recalled how, immediately after taking on the role of a chairman of a school cultural festival's organizing committee, he began suffering diarrhea, and that this prompted him to perceive a deep feeling of guilt unless he did what an authority figure told him to do. After he became aware that he actually did not want to go to school and that he wanted to rest at home, his diarrhea stopped. He also began to perceive anger toward the therapist, and became able to understand, through experience, that such fear leads to his anxiety of blaspheming against God, or, in other words, his fear of soiling something sacred, and, ultimately, to a sense of guilt. And, supported by a staff member, he finally became able to express himself toward the therapist, abandon his compulsive prayers, reflect on his mother's vulnerability and the "transience" of infinitely beautiful and fertile things (Kitayama, 1998), and "give up" his obsession with his parents and sacred objects. He has since become an outstanding scholar.

Clinical Vignette: 5

A thirty-year-old female patient with borderline personality disorder who came to me, chiefly complaining of insomnia, lived relatively successfully in society as an office worker. As I continued to interview her, I gradually discovered that she took good care of other people but never allowed others to take care of her, and that she engaged in self-harm, such as scratching all over her body with a peg or her fingernails. Her favorite line was "I'll die rather than rely on other people to live." When the therapist pointed out that the way she tried to hide her injured self reminded him of the "crane-wife," she agreed, saying, "Yes, that's right, I'm a crane-wife." She spoke of her wish to become a nursery school teacher and her compulsion to return whatever she had borrowed by multiplying it one-hundred-fold. While inflicting self-harm all over her body, she also said that it was better for her to die than have anyone else take care of her. Against this background was her experience of seeing her depressive mother attempting to commit suicide and she herself stopping that attempt. This gave me a glimpse into her conviction ("psychological script") that she had to rescue people, who, like her sick mother, tried to end their fleeting life and fade away. This was self-sacrifice on the patient's part, of repaying people several times more than what she had received from them. Still, her crane-wife-like ways of living that were accompanied by an entrenched aesthetic principle did not change very easily. She also spoke about her serious inner pathology—a fear that her body would melt if she took a bath. Her insomnia improved, at least on the surface, mainly with administration of drugs. In the end, however, she displayed a sense of distrust in me, saying, "I can't leave things to you any more," and abruptly ended the treatment without seeing it completed.

Discussion of the Cases

A selection of these cases shows patients who, at one time, were all productive. In the background of these prolific production activities, however, was an extremely strong and painful sense of guilt that resulted from their having, as a child, ordered the parents to make this and that. Their parents, especially their mothers, made many different things for them, including themselves, caretaking, food, warmth, and clothing. Specific items and episodes that appear in their illness history symbolize not only those things, but also the total sum of the love and devoted care they had received from their mothers. A major issue for these patients is a sense of guilt as individuals ("the second person") who look at their mothers ("the first person"). Their resistance of shame and a sense of guilt they experienced when they saw their wounded parents were the problems that were the most difficult to handle. Moreover, when these individuals became patients, it was the therapist who accepted their anger and aggression; it was imperative that the therapist handle the patients' crime and sin of "matricide" as purely psychological matters. Many patients dread the fact that, if they talk to a therapist, what they say will be leaked to the outside for everyone else to learn. However, this never occurs. These guilts remain in the background as something psychological, and an apologetic feeling of *sumanai* ("I'm sorry") is pondered on as something psychological, but is never allowed to be revealed. Of course, it is necessary for highly distrustful patients to discuss their fear of seeing their inner secrets leaked outside through the therapist, as well as the reasons for feeling this way. We as therapists do not tell them merely to "believe" or to "pray," like in a religion.

If psychoanalytic theory were to be applied here, these patients would be in a state of incomplete mourning. As Melanie Klein (1948) states in her object relations theory, when an infant who makes his mother produce milk with her breasts realizes that he is destroying someone he loves, with greed, he ponders on his sense of guilt. I personally feel that this sense of guilt corresponds to the feeling of apology (*sumanai*) stated above. This guilt exists where a desire for love encounters aggression, or, in other words, where a female image of production and fertility overlaps with an image of a woman who is hurt and dies because of our greed. This feeling remains somewhere in our minds and is never expunged. In treatment, moreover, even if a patient did not take out his/her psychological guilt to the outside, and acknowledged his/her impure[1] thought of *sumanai* inside the therapy room, if he/she is able to leave such feeling inside that room, then, in my view, that is accomplishment itself.

CONCLUDING REMARKS

Japanese people often do not use a subject in the sentences they speak or write. They prefer vague expressions; even in clinical situations, patients often tell me that they have no self or that they have no *watashi*, or "I." Therefore, Japanese people are liable to passively resist psychoanalysis, in the form of "erasing themselves." However, as far as seeing them from the outside is concerned, I am aware that these people "have no *watashi*, or I." It is true that the form which many Japanese people take with respect to *watashi*, or "I," may differ from the ego and sense of self of non-Japanese people. If I must generalize, my observation is that our *watashi* is mainly hidden in the back of the "stage," and that this *watashi* disappears when we are in public areas, where we dress up and act. In so doing, this *watashi*, or I, is intent on bridging people with people, the back with the front, and fantasy with reality. It is worn out and exhausted. *Watashi* is homonymous with the Japanese word for "bridging"—*watashi*—and *ningen*, a Japanese word signifying a human being, possesses the literal meaning of "between one person and another." As *watashi* fails to do things right, it feels a sense of responsibility and shame and dreads being reproached. A typical example of *watashi*'s thought such as this, put another way, is *sumanai* that one can do nothing about.

As our clinical experience teaches us, if misfortunes occur, especially in childhood, either in people around him or in himself, the child who is the weakest and the most vulnerable is liable to feel *sumanai* the most. There are many cases in which a woman blames herself for having been raped by her father, and, when many people come to recognize this sin after they grow up, they fear that everyone may learn about it and humiliate them. Treatment is about having a patient/client confront the anger and hatred of their "true selves," such as "I wanted to kill my father," and "My mother should have died—I don't even care," and not run away from the accompanying sense of guilt and shame; it is also about talking about these feelings with a therapist in the "backstage of life," weaving a life story, thinking about its meaning, and reliving the significant emotions but never being humiliated. Seen from a dramatic point of view, moreover, the basic rule of never taking these things out to the outside "stage"—although taken for granted—is extremely important.

NOTE

1. The Japanese word *sumanai,* although generally translated as "I'm sorry," can also homonymously signify "unfinished" or "impure."

8

The Butterfly Lovers: Psychodynamic Reflections on the Ancient Chinese Love Story "Liang-Zhu"

June Cai

> You are only moved by what excites your senses and indulge only in licentious desires, endangering your lives and natures.
>
> Tse Chan (500 BC, cited in Brown, 1938, 152)

Epic tales involving love, jealousy, and hate abound across the world. Such romantic stories include the Western Romeo-Juliet, the Middle Eastern Majnun-Laila, and the Indian Heer-Ranjha, to mention but a few. Insofar as these tales reflect the inescapable tragic consequences of erotic desire in conflict with reality, they are fundamentally alike. Yet every ethnicity has its own nuances of expression, originating from different cultural idioms and beliefs. Just as music and art of different historical stages depict life and culture of a given time, traditional romantic stories are paradigmatic of relational configurations (both real and wished-for) at the time they arose in a given culture.

Here, I will discuss a legendary romantic story of China, Liang-Zhu, and highlight the dynamic issues inherent in it.[1] The romance has touched millions of Chinese over hundreds of years. It was played out in Chinese opera in different dialects throughout years; among them, the most well known was the *Yue* opera using a dialect of Zhejiang, a province next to Shanghai, where the original story supposedly took place. The show was made into a popular movie and also inspired the production of a violin concerto in 1959. During the Chinese Cultural Revolution (1966–1976), the movie and show were banned. However, after the revolution, they were welcomed by everyone again. Despite the fact that the actors who played in the original movie were much aged, once they went back to the stage, they still attracted millions of fans. In 1994, it was rewritten as a conventional film, *Butterfly Lovers*. In recent years, Chinese producers have modified it into a martial arts film, a TV series, and a conventional movie. Although the producers have added or altered some details, the main theme and outcome of the story remain the same. What is described below is based on the popular original story as shown in the *Yue* opera (also called *Shaoxing* opera) since it is probably the version of the story that had the least influence from the Western culture learned by Chinese in recent decades. Through understanding this story and its evolution over the years, we can gain some appreciation of the Chinese mind-set.

THE STORY OF LIANG-ZHU

The story was set in Hangzhou, a picturesque scholarly town of southeast China during the Eastern Jin Dynasty (circa 1700). Liang-Zhu (known in the West as *The Butterfly Lovers*) is the abbreviation for the full names of Liang Shanbo and Zhu Yingtai—a teenage boy and girl, respectively. The sixteen-year-old Zhu Yingtai was the beautiful daughter of a rich official in a village near Hangzhou. She received a fine education at home but envied others who were able to leave home to study. Upon hearing from her maid that her father felt that he would let her go away for studies if she were a male child, Zhu cooked up a scheme. She told her maid to suggest to her father that he invite a fortune-teller to inquire about Zhu's unhappiness. When he agreed, the maid invited Zhu (dressed up as a young man and pretending to be a fortune-teller) to come in. The "fortune-teller" told Zhu's father that it would be good to let his daughter leave for Hangzhou to study. Seeing him taking the suggestion seriously, Zhu revealed the truth of her cross-dressing to her father and insisted on going away to study. He agreed on the condition that she dress up as a male and return home as soon as her course of study was over.

Accompanied by her maid, Zhu met Liang Shanbo, who was also on his way to the same school. When her maid heard that they were going to the same school, she ran to tell Zhu excitedly but slipped by calling her "Miss" in front of Liang. To avoid Liang's questioning, Zhu immediately took over the sentence and said, "She stayed at home. Why do you mention her?" Together, the two of them made up the story about a younger sister of Zhu's—"the little ninth sister"—who also wanted to come along and study in Hangzhou but couldn't leave due to their father's stubbornness with traditional rules. Though somewhat surprised by the idea of women going out to study, Liang was impressed by Zhu's sympathy toward women's rights to study. He said, "Yes, boys and girls should have the same rights to study and know what is happening in the world." Liang's open-mindedness surprised

Zhu as well. His fair attitude toward women made him stand out in Zhu's mind. Being the only child of the family, Liang recognized that Zhu could be his wise and close friend. Following the tradition of his time, Liang suggested that the two take an oath to be "honorary brothers" right away. Zhu accepted it happily. At the time, Liang was seventeen years old. Thus, Liang became the elder brother and Zhu the younger brother.

In school, they enjoyed studying together, playing together, and caring for each other. Time passed by quickly. Three years later, one day, Liang noticed an earring mark on Zhu's earlobe and questioned Zhu. Zhu had to make up another story about having to play Guan-Yin, a famous female Buddha, in the village festivals when young; she warned Liang not to make ridiculous guesses. Liang apologized and promised not to do so anymore. On that same day, Zhu received a letter from her father asking her to go home due to his illness; this was one among the many missives from him requesting her to return home. Zhu realized that she could not ignore her father's requests anymore. Feeling reluctant to leave Liang, she decided to reveal her true gender to her teacher's wife the night before she left and asked her to be a matchmaker for her and Liang. The teacher's wife expressed her approval of this match and happily accepted Zhu's promise gift, a white jade fan pedant shaped like a butterfly, to give to Liang.

Upon seeing her off, Liang walked Zhu back for a long distance. Along the way, a sentimental Zhu gave Liang numerous hints that she wished for them to be a couple. Yet Liang was unable to get the clues since he was convinced that Zhu was a male. Disappointed with Liang's seeming indifference, Zhu decided to make a match for her "little ninth sister" with Liang. After hearing that she was the twin of Zhu with similar character and appearance, Liang was happy to be considered. But he worried about their different family backgrounds. Zhu reassured him and invited Liang to visit Zhu's home and take the "little ninth sister" sooner than later. Zhu left for home on this note.

Liang missed Zhu and found himself having difficulty in concentrating on his study. He also worried about the differences of their family backgrounds. Around this time, the teacher's wife disclosed Zhu's true gender to Liang and gave him the promise gift left by Zhu. She advised Liang to go and visit Zhu's home. On his way there, he recalled everything Zhu cited and said. Regretful but also excited, he wished that he could be flying to her home.

Back at home, Zhu found herself missing Liang. One day, her maid interpreted a bird's singing on a tree as an omen of good news and said that Liang must be coming soon. Instead, Zhu's father came in telling her about a matchmaking deal that he was so excited about and just accepted for her: She was to marry Ma Wencai, the son of a more powerful official, who was also very rich. Stunned, Zhu said to her father that she did not think she was worthy of that man. When he confronted her, she stated that she did not want to get married and wanted to stay with her father all her life. He responded that "It is hard for me to let you go but grown women have to get married. I can't ruin your future." However, Zhu did not give in. Upon this, her father surmised that something happened while she was studying at school.

The father began to question Zhu's maid, who revealed Zhu's close relationship with Liang during those three years. She also told that, while leaving the school, Zhu had promised to match Liang with "the little ninth sister." Her father was outraged and declared that, according to the tradition, no woman could arrange a match for herself, even if it were done in a disguised manner. He emphasized that the proposal from Ma Wencai's family was formal; a matchmaker had arrived promising gifts from Ma's father. Liang, on the other hand, had not made any such overtures. This overcame Zhu's protest.

Soon, Liang arrived. He pretended that it was just a respectful visit to Zhu's father and wanted to meet his "honorary brother" again. Walking into the living room, Zhu excitedly called "Liang Xiong (i.e., brother)" only to encounter an angry father reproaching her that she belonged to Ma's family and shouldn't see Liang anymore. She argued that Liang came from far away and she had to meet him; in addition, she had not yet agreed to marry Ma. When her father insisted that the proposal from Ma's family could not be turned down, Zhu responded that the matchmaking her teacher's wife had done was equally formal. Her father pointed out that Ma's family was rich and powerful for generations; Zhu disputed that Liang's family was poor but morally clean. With anger, her father blamed her for breaking long-held traditions. However, he also realized that he himself had spoiled her over the years. Nevertheless, he said that marriage was not a game and his word to Ma's family was impossible to change. Seeing her sorrow and tears, her father finally gave her the permission to see her "honorary brother," Liang, once more but told her to persuade Liang to renounce the idea of marrying her.

Liang was ecstatic to see Zhu in woman's clothing for the first time. He teased Zhu whether he should regard them as brothers or brother and sister.[2] After formal explanation, she invited him to her own study. Though Liang was so thrilled, Zhu was more distressed than happy. She forced herself to smile and asked Liang's real reason for the visit. Liang again teased her and tried to get her to admit that she was that little "ninth sister" herself. He regarded their relationship as fated from a previous life. Facing his enthusiasm, Zhu felt heartbroken. She began to tell Liang about her father's arrangement for her marriage, but before she could finish, she had to run to another room and cry. Liang was puzzled and immediately wondered if she had another match. But then he consoled himself that she would not change her mind as she made their match herself. Unable to stand the uncertainty, he decided to find the answer from Zhu's maid, who was bringing in tea. Upon hearing about Ma, he was shocked and despondent. Zhu came back in to call him, and apologized for not being able to console him for his special visit. With pain, she asked him to have a drink prepared for him. But when they resumed talking, Liang complained, "I can't believe I just came to disturb you for a glass of wine!" Zhu recalled their three-year caring and loving relationship and divulged her love for him since then. She reminded him of the incident in which he found the earring mark on her earlobe that made her face red and awkward; she reminisced also about her attempts to get his attention before her departure, including asking him to see their images together from the well water as if a couple, asking him to pray in the temple that they passed by as if a couple, and the self-match with the request for him to come and fulfill the match early. With regret, she told Liang that by her father's drinking Ma's family's wine and accepting the promise gift, she couldn't be a couple with him anymore. In distress, she used the analogy of the loving couple of swans who had been beaten apart. Sorrowfully, Liang felt it was like the water lilies from the same root broken by strong wind. Realizing he couldn't marry Zhu ever, he was angry and sad. He became dizzy and fell down in the chair as he felt all his hopes became dust. Zhu blamed herself for hurting him. "I don't blame you at all," he said, "I really ran all the way here." He told how much he missed her that he couldn't dress up well or concentrate since she left. In reply, she told him that she couldn't taste food or tea from not seeing him. And they both expressed how they missed each other day and night.

Upon leaving, Liang returned her gift. She sadly accepted it. Worried about Liang's condition, Zhu asked if he was well enough to leave. Liang replied, "I can't die at your home." When asked if when he would be able to revisit her, he answered, "I'll come to visit you when I recover. But I'm afraid that I may die from my bad fate. If I die, my tombstone can be seen on that Hu Bridge Town." "Speaking of tombstone, please engrave my name in red and your name in black on your tombstone," Zhu requested. Breaking down into tears, she stated, "If we cannot become husband and wife in this life, we will be a couple after death." After Liang went home, he became very ill. Still later on his deathbed, Liang repeated what Zhu said about their being a couple after death to his parents.

When the news of Liang's death came, Zhu fainted. It was her wedding day. The carriage from Ma's family came over. Zhu was still mourning the loss of Liang. Zhu's father was trying to persuade her to get into the carriage on time and reminded her that Liang already died. Despite her protests, her father insisted on carrying on the ceremonies. Not being able to resist her father, Zhu put a condition: she asked that the carriage be decorated with white lamps in the front and followed with three thousand bills of paper money for the deceased. She also asked to be able to wear a white dress instead of red and stop by Liang's tomb for a last visit on her way to the wedding. Her father was angry but eventually gave in. He ordered that she should wear white over the red dress so that afterward she could continue on to her wedding.

Lamenting in front of Liang's tombstone, she again expressed her wish to be together with him after death. Suddenly, the thick clouds came over with strong wind blowing everything up and around. In the middle of this turbulence, the tomb magically opened. Without any hesitation, Zhu leaped in, and the tomb closed. Soon, the storm passed. In the bright sunlight, people saw a pair of beautiful butterflies happily chasing each other among the flowers, never separating again.

PSYCHODYNAMIC SPECULATIONS

From the Chinese cultural point of view, the two lovers were incredibly brave to pursue freedom to love. Their devotion to each other, especially since Zhu came from a highly affluent family and chose someone from a lower economic class, shows how pure and noble love can be. Their turning into butterflies, so to speak, symbolizes the wishful thinking and longing of freedom from the old societal rules. Underneath such cultural nuances lie matters of deeper psychological intrigue.

The omission of Zhu's mother strikes one as significant, to begin with. This absence is a negative visual icon of maternal deprivation. The effects of early maternal deprivation are myriad and long-lasting (Bowlby, 1958, 1963; Spitz, 1946; Mahler, 1961; Settlage, 2001). The feelings of hurt, anger, and entitlement displayed by Zhu are mostly likely derived from such an ontogenetic backdrop. Her intensified involvement with the father also seems to have similar roots. After all, it was very unusual for a father to keep giving in to a daughter on so many issues. It was virtually unheard of for a father to let a daughter go for more education outside of the home at that time. Although there were debates whether she was the only child or only daughter, it is insignificant here, in my opinion. What is important is that, apparently, Zhu and her father had a very close relationship. This can also be seen in the fact that she dared not only to disagree but also to tease her father in this old-fashioned family structure where women could hardly be heard or dared to "misbehave," not to mention doing so in front of a maid or servant. This powerful position in the family gave her the sense of being special in her father's eyes. Despite appearing forceful, Zhu's father was actually quite accommodating to her demands; it is as if he was trying to compensate for the missing mother.

Not surprisingly then, it was the unusual open-mindedness and sympathy toward women in Liang that Zhu found most attractive. He reflected the malleable and indulgent aspect of Zhu's father. This made him not only a highly desirable oedipal substitute but an improvement over the original object. The fact that Liang was easygoing and tolerant despite his intelligence and ambition made Zhu feel in control in this relationship. This too repeated the pattern of her dealings with her father. Liang's being from a lower socioeconomic class also rendered him a "forbidden" object and paradoxically fueled the underlying oedipal current of Zhu's choice.

Such erotic excitement needed the custom's inspection of the superego, however. And it was for this purpose that Zhu turned to her teacher's wife, literally called a *shi-mu* (teacher mother),[3] for help. By being a matchmaker for her and Liang, the teacher's wife served as a symbolic mother figure. Her permission and blessing was highly significant for Zhu; unconsciously, she needed a mother figure's permission to marry a man who greatly resembled her father. It was important for her to be absolved of any hint of committing an oedipal transgression.

Matters were hardly simple, though. On the one hand, Zhu obtained the developmentally appropriate maternal sanction for entry into adult femininity via romance and thoughts of marriage. On the other hand, she failed to reveal the role of her teacher's wife to her father until it was rather late. Overtly, this omission was attributed to the maid who told the father of Zhu's involvement with Liang without mentioning the teacher's wife's role in it. However, the maid was nothing but a split-off sector of Zhu's personality that was defiant and secretive. An intrapsychic conflict between choosing culturally proper (with oedipal resolution) and culturally improper (with the hints of oedipal defiance) pathways to love and marriage was thus played out.

When Liang arrived, he was confident and excited. However, he failed to reveal his true purpose for meeting Zhu's father and said that he was there to see his "brother." Since the teacher's wife had already revealed to him that Zhu was a woman, his approach might seem clever. However, given the cultural setting, his lack of formality in seeking Zhu's father's blessing first remains peculiar; this was a recipe for disaster. Could this "mistake" reflect the low self-esteem of someone from a lower-class background? Or could it reflect unconscious guilt at having chosen a girl in a manner that was unconventional? Either way, Liang's "mistake," coupled with Zhu's father's unshakable commitment to Ma, led him to lose his beloved Zhu. As an only boy in a Chinese family, Liang had felt entitled to his mother's adoration and father's blessing. But now he was powerless to do anything. Loss of the love object was thus compounded by narcissistic injury. He became depressed, succumbed to physical ailment, and died.

For Zhu, the subsequent wedding marked a double loss. It was a symbolic loss of her otherwise tolerant father and a real loss of the substitute figure, Liang, who resembled him. Having the loss of mother in her background, Zhu was unable to bear these losses. The wish for reunion with the lost objects (good father, lover, and, behind them, the early mother) now dominated her psyche. Her death at Liang's grave site accomplished such reunion(s). The two butterflies that fly out of the opened grave symbolize the playful romance of the lovers. The scene also serves as a "manic defense" (Klein, 1935; Winnicott, 1935) against the nearly intolerable depressive feelings aroused by the morbid end of their quest.

CONCLUDING REMARKS

Liang-Zhu is a story from ancient China. It depicts the powerful impact of a feudal, ritualistic, and sexually segregated society on burgeoning erotic desire in youth. More important perhaps, it demonstrates the tension between the necessity to follow traditions and the developmental imperative to seek self-fulfillment. Underneath its cultural cloak, one finds the complex vicissitudes of a girl's psychosexual development. Lacking maternal love, Zhu, the heroine of this story, develops an intense bond with her father; this bond has characteristically petulant oral undertones alongside the oedipally overstimulating aspects. In order to find gratification for the former and to renounce the latter, Zhu has to go away and seek a kind, older woman's guidance. Having received such blessing, she becomes more comfortable in her strivings for romantic intimacy and vis-à-vis her autonomy in general. However, as is typical of epic romantic tales, the protagonist's independence turns out to be no match for the weight of ancestral traditions. Freedom of such sort gets punished, often by death. One is left wondering though whether the punishment was for autonomy or for (female) sexuality per se. Does Zhu's father, for instance, find her blossoming into a grown-up sexual woman tolerable only if it is under his control (e.g., by arranging her marriage to a man chosen by him)? Is her choice of Liang intolerable because of his lower social class or because such autonomous choice underscores the existence of sexual desire in his daughter? Or is it only a matter of following traditions? It is this sophisticated blend of erotic, cross-generational, moral, and cultural themes that makes the saga of Liang-Zhu great. Its enormous popularity over centuries and the repeated appearance of new versions suggest that it has captured something of deep significance in Chinese emotional life. The more recent resurrections (in the form of movies and theater) of Liang-Zhu give the story a little westernized touch and thus resonate well with the younger generations who, as we know, have been undergoing a similar transformation themselves. Nonetheless, the powerful legacy of the past remains and the Chinese people, including today's youth, are vulnerable to clashes between their desires for erotic authenticity and their allegiance to culturally transmitted limits and prohibitions.

NOTES

1. The opinions expressed in this contribution are solely mine and do not reflect in any way on the positions of the Food and Drug Administration.
2. Of note, close relationship in China can be regarded as brothers and sisters. Often, it also indicates a love relationship, especially in villages.
3. The teacher or coach could be regarded as *shi-fu*—that is, teacher father. An old Chinese saying also states, "One day a teacher, forever a father." This tradition of respecting teachers has a long history among Chinese.

9

The Filial Piety Complex: Variations on the Oedipus Theme in Chinese Literature and Culture

Ming Dong Gu

> Water must be kept in by dikes; passions must be ruled by the law of propriety.
>
> Chinese maxim

The theory of the Oedipus complex has undergone significant changes since Freud (1900) first proposed it at the turn of the twentieth century (*Interpretation*, 294–99). Radical reconceptualizations by Klein (1946), Lacan (1966, 1973), Irigaray (1974), Deleuze and Quattari (1977), Chodorow (1978), and other theorists have enriched the classical concept in dimensions unforeseen by the father of psychoanalysis. Nevertheless, the core of the concept—the effects and affects of a child's early childhood relation with his or her parents in the formation of self and identity—has survived revolutionary reconceptualizations and continued to be the basis of what Freud called "the fate of all of us" (1900, 262). Since "Oedipus is part of our language in the West" and "From Homer to Aristotle to Freud, it is the old story," one noted scholar even suggests that Western humanism at large depends on it (Goodhart, 1978, 69–70). Nevertheless, "the Oedipus complex depends for its vindication less on empirical data than on the philosophical concept of the hermeneutic circle and on the literary power of Sophocles's tragedy" (Rudnytsky, 1987, 358–59). After all, although Freud's conception originated from his path-breaking self-analysis, well documented in his letters and writings on dreams, his fascination with oedipal themes in some masterpieces of Western literature, especially in Sophocles' *Oedipus Rex* and Shakespeare's *Hamlet*, gave him the inspiration and impetus to explore the mental complex, and the *Oedipus* drama provided him a most fitting metaphor for naming and discussing its theoretical implications.

ARE THERE OEDIPUSES IN CHINA?

Compared with the West, however, the centrality of the Oedipus complex to the Chinese culture is nonexistent. In contrast to other non-Western cultures (Johnson and Prince-Williams, 1996), the documented presence of oedipal themes in Chinese literature, both traditional and modern, is almost negligible. From the late 1970s to late 1980s, there was a so-called Freud fad in China—an explosion of interest (both pros and cons) in Freud's theory in particular and in psychoanalytic theory in general among scholars of different disciplines. Numerous articles and books were devoted to the study of Chinese literature using Freudian psychoanalytic theories (Yu, 1987; Wang, 1991). As part of the so-called cultural heat the interest in psychoanalysis continued to the early 1990s and remains strong in cultural circles nowadays. Oddly enough, in spite of the awesome amount of literary criticism produced, little has been reported about the existence of oedipal themes in the Chinese literary tradition. The only exceptions come from two studies, but both of them deal with modern literature. While one (Wang, 1992, 117–33) is a study of a modern drama by Cao Yu, *Thunderstorm* (1934), the other (Gu, 1993, 1–25) is a psychoanalysis of a modern novella by Yu Dafu, *Sinking* (1921). Both studies uncover oedipal structures comparable to those in Western literary works, but each unequivocally shows that the authors were influenced by Western writers and psychoanalytic theories. Cao Yu admits that his dramatic composition has been heavily influenced by classical Greek drama, especially the plays of Sophocles, and by the plays of Eugene O'Neill, a dramatist heavily influenced by Freud in his own turn. Scholars have also found a strong influence of psychoanalysis on Yu Dafu's literary composition and criticism. The locating of heavy influence seems to support a contra-Freud claim: the Oedipus complex is a theory derived from the European tradition and its universality is questionable in non-Western cultural traditions. At least, the absence of oedipal themes in premodern Chinese literature seems to reaffirm the value of Bronislaw Malinowski's (1929) skepticism and at least lend support to the counterstatement that the Oedipus complex is an alien theory imported into modern Chinese literature and criticism. This naturally leads us to ask: are there Oedipuses in Chinese literature and culture?

THE NATURE OF CHINESE FAMILY ROMANCE

The dust of the "Freud-fad" in China has settled down by now, but the Chinese case has considerable significance, because it seems to favor cultural relativism and cast doubt on the universality of the Oedipus complex. I, however, suggest that the seeming absence of the oedipal themes in Chinese literature, especially in premodern literature, only serves to highlight the differences between Chinese culture and its Western counterpart and confirms the greater emotional repression in Chinese culture founded on the deep-rooted Confucian moral system. "To say that the Oedipus complex is universal," notes one eminent analyst, "is to say that every human being is born of two progenitors, one of a sex identical to his own, the other of a different sex" (Green, 1969, 236). Since the Chinese child is born of a father and a mother like the Western child, and struggles through the early years of childhood to form his or her identity in relation to his or her parents, the psychological configuration cannot but be structured by what Freud calls the Oedipus complex in the mental dimensions. There is, however, a basic cultural reason for the seeming nonexistence of oedipal themes in Chinese literature. It is the precociousness of Chinese culture marked by the early systematization of ethics and moral codes.

In his three-volume study on the "experience of sexuality in Western society," Michel Foucault (1980, 1988, 1990) demonstrates that in the classical periods of the West, there was little prohibition on sexual pleasure, and sexual repression did not set in until a subtle but decisive break from the classical Greek vision of sexual pleasure occurred. In Chinese culture, the "secular advance of repression in the emotional life of mankind" (Freud, 1900, 264) occurred much earlier than in the West and became increasingly formidable until recently. Although Chinese and Western societies have both been patriarchal, family-centered societies through history, the dynamics of family structure for each culture is fundamentally different. While the Western family is an individual-based entity in which each member enjoys his or her individual freedom and independence while submitting to the family interest, the Chinese counterpart is heavily collectively centered with the expectation that every member is ready to sacrifice his or her own interest and even life for the interest of the family. Francis Hsu (1981), an anthropologist specializing in Chinese and American cultural studies, reduces the differences between Chinese and American ways of life to two sets of contrasts:

> First, in the American way of life the emphasis is placed upon the predilections of the individual, a characteristic we shall call *individual-centered*. This is in contrast to the emphasis the Chinese put upon an individual's appropriate place and behavior among his fellowmen, a characteristic we shall term *situation-centered*. The second fundamental contrast is the prominence of emotions in the American way of life as compared with the tendency of the Chinese to underplay all matters of the heart. (12)

If we replace "American" with "Western" in the above passage, Hsu's summarized contrasts would fit my study nicely. I argue that the Oedipus complex is a concept with universal significance, but the differences in family structures and ways of life give rise to different ways oedipal themes appear in literature. In ancient China, the dominance of the Confucian ethical system, which regarded any allusion to incestuous desires as strictly taboo and punished any manifestations relentlessly, made it impossible for oedipal themes to find overt expression in social life and literary works. Nevertheless, Oedipus does exist in Chinese literature, but it is an Oedipus disfigured. Because of moral repression, oedipal representation has been so distorted and so artfully disguised that it looks as though it did not exist.

In this article, I will explore the metamorphosis of the original oedipal configuration in some chosen Chinese literary works from the perspectives of the major characters in the Chinese family romance predicated on the dynamics of moral imperatives. Although I do not presume that a psychology of literary representations may pave a royal road to the inner life of the individual's mind, I do hope to find answers to these questions: (1) Do oedipal themes appear in traditional Chinese literary works before the coming of Western psychoanalytic theories? (2) If they do, what forms do they assume in traditional literary works? (3) Why do they assume the culture-specific forms in the Chinese tradition? (4) What implications do the culture-specific ways in which oedipal themes are expressed in Chinese literature have for the arguments for or against the universality of the Oedipus complex?

I suggest, under the crushing pressure of overwhelming repression in Chinese culture and society, the Oedipus complex in Chinese literature disintegrates and is transformed from a nuclear complex to a multiplicity of individual complexes: father complex, mother complex, son complex, and daughter complex. All of them, growing out of different individuals' responses to different family situations in a morally repressive culture, are the twisted manifestations of the original Oedipus complex. The fragmentation of the Oedipus complex is not unique to Chinese culture. Indeed, it is equally present in Western cultures. As early as the 1910s, Rank's (1912) study had already shown how the Oedipus complex disintegrates in Western cultures and how oedipal themes assume different forms in Western literary works. Compared with its Western counterpart, the fragmentation of the Oedipus complex occurs more drastically in Chinese culture. Indeed, the Oedipus complex in Chinese culture is so fragmentary that its literary representations are far more deeply hidden than in its Western counterpart. However fragmentary and however deeply concealed, oedipal themes in Chinese literature are still the twisted manifestations of the original Oedipus complex. In contrast to often overt representations in Judaic-Christian cultures, oedipal themes in Chinese literature are restructured on the dynamics of Confucian morality, which takes disguised forms of parental demands for filial piety and children's fulfillment of filial duties. For this reason, I may say that the Oedipus complex has been transformed into a "filial piety complex" in Chinese culture.

THE FATHER COMPLEX: FEAR OF PATRICIDE

In his *Creative Writers and Daydreaming*, Freud (1908) maintains that myths, legends, and fairy tales "are distorted vestiges of the wishful phantasies of whole nations, the secular dreams of youthful humanity" (442). The naming of the Oedipus complex originated from his analysis of the Greek dramatic form of a legend, *Oedipus Rex*. The Oedipus legend is not just about a son's killing his father and marrying his mother; it also tells of the father's wish to remove the son. In the original Oedipus myth, it is Laius, Oedipus's father, who first attempts to kill the infant and hence sets in motion the tragedy (Sophocles, 9–76). The attempted infanticide is instigated by a prophecy from an oracle that Oedipus would grow up to kill his father and marry his mother. In realistic terms, the prophecy is absurd because the anticipated patricide is not in the unborn infant's head at all. Psychologically, the prophecy is a grown man's refracted fantasy, whether it is cherished by Laius, the prophet, or the teller of the myth. It serves as an excuse for Laius's attempted infanticide based on projection: the father views the coming child as a rival for his wife's love and wants to kill it, but he rationalizes by thinking that the child, after growing up, would kill the father. The Oedipus legend dramatizes the father's unconscious wish to remove his son as a potential rival. Psychoanalytic research suggests that aggressive and libidinal oedipal fantasies may arise earlier and more powerfully in parents than in children, and especially in fathers rather than sons. Zilboorg (1973), for example, argues that the myth in Freud's *Totem and Taboo* demonstrated the primal father's narcissistic and sadistic motives for establishing sexual dominance over women and his anxiety over the ways the mother-child intimacy reduces his primacy. Children do not, at first, arouse feelings of tender paternality but feelings of resentment at intrusion because "there are the deep phylogenetic roots for that hostility which even the civilized father of today harbors against his own offspring. The unconscious hostility against one's own children is well nigh a universal clinical finding among men" (123). Thus, we may as well call a father's unconscious hostility and aggressivity toward his son a "father complex."

The Tale of Shun

The Chinese nation does not have an Oedipus legend. It has one legend, however, which reveals in what manner the Chinese Oedipus complex differs from its counterpart in Western literature. In the *Shiji* or *Records of the Grand Historian* by Sima Qian (c. 145–c. 85 BC) of the Han dynasty, there is a legend about Shun, a legendary forefather of the Chinese civilization. Shun was a very filial son of a blind man. His mother died when he was still small. His father later remarried another woman who became his stepmother and gave birth to another child named Xiang. Xiang was arrogant and selfish by nature. He conspired with his mother to ill-treat Shun. They often spoke ill of Shun before the blind father, who, out of his infatuation for his second wife, wanted to kill Shun. They plotted several times to kill Shun but each time Shun escaped. After each murder attempt, Shun became even more filial and obedient, serving his father and stepmother with even greater care. Still, the father wanted to get rid of him (Sima Qian, 32–34). This legend sets the pattern for the Chinese representation of oedipal desires: through mechanisms of repression and distortion, patricidal and incestuous desires are transformed into a hidden fear of patricide or sublimated into a blind demand for filial piety. It anticipated a rule in the relationship between father and son in ancient Chinese society: "The father is the ruler of the son" and "If a father orders a son to die, the son has to die." The fear of patricide on the father's part constitutes what may be termed "father complex," a constellation of unconscious desires to remove the son as revealed in the Oedipus legend. Shun was a filial and obedient son. There was no reason for his father to dispose of him. It seems the father had the same "father complex" as that of Laius in the Oedipus legend. The father was blind, which might suggest a symbolic loss of male potency. He was so set on killing his own son for no reason at all, perhaps because he secretly nursed the fear that his eldest son, already a married person with two wives, might take his second wife.

A Dream of the Red Chamber

If the oedipal motif of the "father complex" in the legend of Shun is only vaguely presented, it has been more fully narrated in a classic Chinese novel, *A Dream of the Red Chamber* (c. 1760), also known as *The Story of the Stone* (1973) in David Hawkes's famous translation. Acknowledged as the peak of premodern Chinese fiction, it shatters all the traditional ways of thinking and writing in Chinese literature (Lu Xun, 1930, 128). One aspect of the novel's breakthrough is the author's untraditional way of depicting the father-son relationship. Confucian filial piety stipulates that a son must respect and obey his father even if the father is not respectable. The father controls everything the son has, even his life. As a result, premodern Chinese literature is a gallery of filial sons and daughters; literary works centering on father-son conflict hardly exist. *A Dream of the Red Chamber* is a rare exception. This classic novel, which narrates the motif of a father-son conflict, is a rare specimen that affords us an insight into the Chinese mode of the "father-complex."

Bao-yu, the male protagonist, is born into an aristocratic family. His father, Jia Zheng, is a Confucian scholar, the epitome of Confucian morality. Like any other Chinese son of his time, Bao-yu lives anxiously in the shadow of his father. He is nevertheless pampered by his mother and grandmother, who are devout Buddhists. Tyrannized by his father, who forces him to pursue the Confucian way of life, Bao-yu can always evade his oppressive father by turning to his grandmother for help. Brought up by his mother and grandmother in the midst of female cousins and maidservants, he grows up to be an unconventional person with a rebellious heart. Naturally, he comes into conflict with his father, who also clashes with his wife and mother over their adoration of Bao-yu. Overall, the novel is structured on a triangular love relationship between Bao-yu and his two female cousins. On one level, it narrates another conflict involving the son, the father, the mother, and grandmother that reveals a hidden oedipal theme. If Bao-yu's love relationship with his two female cousins constitutes the major theme of the novel, the triangular conflict forms the background and determines the development of the major theme.

In the novel, the father's attitude toward Bao-yu is characterized by conscious infanticidal desires. From the time of Bao-yu's birth, Jia Zheng has ill feelings toward the infant, as he himself confesses: "Bao-yu came into the world with his jade, and there was always something strange about it. I knew it for an ill omen. But because his grandmother doted on him so, we nurtured him and brought him up until now" (Cao, 5: 360). His words imply that had the grandmother not taken to the infant, Jia Zheng would have disposed of his son in some way long ago. Because of this confession, we have reason to believe that from the day of Bao-yu's birth, the father nursed the secret desire to remove him in the same way Laius felt toward Oedipus. Thus, from the very beginning, the father-son relationship is characterized by a hidden oedipal antagonism. At the first birthday celebration, Jia Zheng wants to test his son's disposition. He puts many objects in front of Baoyu and observes which the infant would pick up. The child is only interested in women's things, completely ignoring all the other objects: "Sir Zheng was displeased. He said he would grow up to be a rake, and ever since then he hasn't felt much affection for the child" (Cao, 1: 76). As Bao-yu grows old enough to understand human relationships, he instinctively feels that his father dislikes him. So, he tries, as much as he can, to stay out of his way. When his father's presence cannot be avoided, Bao-yu is always filled with anxiety and trepidation.

The father-son conflict comes to a head in a climactic episode in which Jia Zheng literally almost kills his son. There are several precipitating incidents leading to the incident. The major factor, which infuriates Jia Zheng, is the misinformation that Bao-yu attempted to rape his mother's body maid. The maidservant reportedly resisted and Bao-yu gave her a beating. Humiliated, the maidservant committed suicide by drowning herself. The fact is that Bao-yu has nothing to do with the girl's death. Without any investigation of the report, Jia Zheng flies into a rage and orders his son to be beaten to death. It seems that he has at last found an opportunity to dispose of him. Fearing any interference with his aim from his mother and wife, he makes sure that the door is locked and no one is to disclose the order. What infuriates Jia Zheng most seems to be Bao-yu's alleged attempt to rape his mother's maidservant. His rage betrays an oedipal fear shared by Laius toward Oedipus. Jia Zheng must have suspected that Bao-yu chose his object by a way of displacement. Since the mother is a fond impossibility, the maidservant who is close to the mother is a good substitute for that which he fears to have. It is perhaps this unconscious fantasy in Jia Zheng's mind that throws him into an uncontrollable rage and makes his mind up to dispose of his son. Otherwise, it is rather unthinkable for Jia Zheng, a cool-headed, calculating Confucian scholar, to believe in unproved gossip without going into any investigation.

Throwing away his usual benevolent demeanor of a Confucian scholar, Jia Zheng, not satisfied with the executor of his order, who, he thinks, does not hit hard enough, kicks the servant impatiently aside, wrests the bamboo from his hands, and, gritting his teeth, strikes his son with the "utmost savagery." When his literary colleague tries to intervene, he responds by saying that he cannot wait until his son "commits patricide, or worse." The word "patricide" reveals the real nature of Jia Zheng's unconscious fear. It is not any different from Laius's fear. The worst he fears may allude to the boy's incestuous desires, which find support in Jia Zheng's strong reaction to his wife's appearance and pleading: "Her entry provoked Jia Zheng to fresh transports of fury. Faster and harder fell the bamboo on the prostrate form of Bao-yu, which by now appeared to be unconscious" (Cao, 1: 149). The beating with renewed savagery may have been prompted by his recollection of his wife's pampering of his son. But it may also have been provoked by his oedipal jealousy. Jia Zheng is very angry at his wife's interference with his purpose. Up to now, the narration bears a close resemblance to Laius's attempted infanticide. The difference is that Laius wants to kill Oedipus in his infancy, whereas Jia Zheng nurses the idea at Bao-yu's birth and wants to kill the boy in his adolescence. It is worth noting that all in the family agree that Jia Zheng has overdone his disciplinary job as a father. Even if Bao-yu had done something wrong, even if he had raped the maidservant, he should not have incurred such a savage beating, still less a threat on his life. After all, who among the male members of this official family is not a rake indulging in sensual pleasure? Jia Zheng's overreaction to an alleged rape only testifies to his oedipal hostility toward his son.

THE MOTHER COMPLEX: INSANE JEALOUSY

In critiquing Freud's theory of the Oedipus complex, feminist theorists have argued that the Freudian model is based on findings solely from the male perspective and leaves the female perspective almost untouched. This is certainly true. Scholars have yet to fully appreciate the implications of Sophocles' play from Jocasta's perspective. In my view, her hasty marriage to Oedipus is determined not so much by the latter's success in solving the Sphinx's riddle as by her need to fill the emotional and spiritual vacuum left by the dual disappearance of her son and husband. In psychoanalytic terms, Chodorow (1978) addresses this need:

> That women turn to children to fulfill emotional and even erotic desires unmet by men or other women means that a mother expects from infants what only another adult should be expected to give. These tendencies take different forms with sons and daughters. Sons may become substitutes for husbands, and must engage in defensive assertion of ego boundaries and repression of emotional needs. (211–12)

The need may develop into instinctual antipathy to her son's wife and conscious or unconscious strivings to remove his wife so as to repossess the son. This is a common theme in Chinese literature, and bears a striking similarity to a motif in D. H. Lawrence's (1913) *Sons and Lovers*. Anyone who has read the English novel must have an indelible impression of Mrs. Morel as an excessively possessive mother. The possessive motherhood Lawrence described with insight and thoroughness has long been a subject matter in Chinese literature, and again, it asserts its right on the demand of filial piety.

"The Peacock Southeast Flew" and the Story of Lu You

As early as the early third century AD there was a long poem called "The Peacock Southeast Flew," one of the most famous Chinese poems. The poem narrates a tragic story of how a jealous mother compels his son to divorce his wife and drives both of them to death (Mair, 1994, 462–72). The long poem was said to be based on a real tragedy and thus has a special significance for understanding ancient Chinese family relations. Previously, critics' attention has been solely focused on the poem's social significance. No one seems to have examined the poem more deeply than its manifest content. It seems to me that the poem touches on the same theme of possessive motherhood so profoundly depicted in Lawrence's novel. The poem does not tell us much about the male protagonist's father. Instead, the family is completely under the control of the mother, who regards her authority as unassailable. The young man and his wife are devoted to each other, and their marriage is happy in every sense of the word. The daughter-in-law is beautiful, virtuous, and diligent, and tries as hard as she can to please the mother-in-law. But the latter is simply dissatisfied with her, deliberately finding fault for nothing. Unable to bear the abominable treatment, the daughter-in-law asks to be divorced. In ancient China, it is a great disgrace for both the woman and her family if a daughter is to be divorced and sent home. Many a woman would rather endure ill treatment and even torture than be sent home. But in this poem, the woman, fully realizing the grave consequence of her action, insists on being sent home. This seems to suggest that she must have realized the impossibility of coexisting with her possessive mother-in-law. The son begs his mother not to drive his wife away, threatening to remain single all his life. The mother becomes angry and resorts to filial piety to overcome his resistance: "My son, have you no respect?/ How dare you speak in your wife's defense!/ I have lost all feeling for you,/ On no account will I let you disobey me!" (464). Finally, the son commits suicide. Perhaps his action is an indication of his awareness that even if he gets another wife, as his mother promises, his married life would end in tragedy because of his mother's insane possessiveness.

About nine hundred years later, the tragedy of "The Peacock Southeast Flew" was repeated in similar details. Chinese literary history has it that in the twelfth century AD, Lu You (1125–1120), a famous poet in the Southern Song dynasty, literally went through the tragic experience described in the ancient poem. At the age of twenty, he married his cousin. Like Lu's family, the cousin's family was also famous and prosperous. She was beautiful and virtuous like the wife in "The Peacock Southeast Flew," and moreover, intelligent, a poetess herself. Being a relative and daughter from an official family, she was an ideal choice for the poet in terms of tradition and compatibility. The marriage was indeed a perfect match, for the couple loved each other with devotion. But due to interference from the poet's mother, he had to divorce his wife and marry another woman. The divorced wife later died of a broken heart, thus reenacting the tragedy of "The Peacock Southeast Flew." Since the marriage was a perfect match, Chinese scholars have kept wondering why it should meet disapproval from the poet's mother. One reason, according to a contemporary poet, is that the mother feared that the wife's love would distract her son from his study (Qi, 15). This has not convinced scholars because Lu You had been a diligent scholar since childhood. His newly wedded wife should in no way distract him from his study. On the contrary, as she was a poetess well versed in Chinese classics, she would be a help rather than a hindrance (15). After their divorce, they happened to meet each other while touring a garden. The poet was so grieved that he wrote a poem on the wall, in which he blamed his mother for the separation. His ex-wife soon died of grief after this chance meeting. After her death, the poet was immensely grieved. The tragedy remained an unhealed scar in his heart. In his later life, he wrote many poems in memory of their short-lived married life and secretly condemned his mother's tyrannical meddling. One of his poems bears a striking similarity to "The Peacock Southeast Flew" in the description of the wife's diligence, virtue, filial piety, and eagerness to please the mother-in-law, and in her ultimate fate of being sent home in disgrace (Liu, 1988, 378–79). In the poem, the poet explicitly expressed his protest against the mother's tyranny through the mouth of a waterbird: "Madam Is Cruel!"

The Golden Cangue

If the two mothers in the above discussion heavily disguise their intention to possess their sons under the pretext of filial piety, another mother in a novelette *The Golden Cangue* by Eileen Chang (1942) scarcely attempts to cover up her possessiveness. This novella is a sophisticated exploration of feminine psychology and comes closer to Lawrence's *Sons and Lovers* in the characterization of possessive motherhood. Ch'i-ch'iao, the mother in the story, motivated by insane jealousy, persecutes her two daughters-in-law to death. She does not think of finding her son a wife until he begins to frequent brothels. She adopts a hostile attitude toward her son's wife from the first day of their marriage. At the wedding, she scarcely covers up her jealousy of her daughter-in-law: "I can't say much in front of young ladies—just hope our Master Pai won't die in her hands" (Chang, 1942, 548). These remarks carry an undertone of sexual possessiveness, implying that she is forced to give up her son. From that point on, she begins to work methodically and ingeniously to get rid of her daughter-in-law so as to wrest her son back. She acts like the two mothers discussed above, trying to carp at the daughter-in-law for nothing. She humiliates her by making allusions in public to her daughter-in-law's supposed indulgence in sex: "Our new young mistress may look innocent—but as soon as she sees Master Pai she has to go and sit on the nightstool. Really! It sounds unbelievable, doesn't it?" (549). These remarks show how abnormally concerned she is with her son's sex life. Moreover, she induces her son by taunts and exhortations of filial piety to leave his wife's bed. She forces her son to accompany her on the opium couch all night long, extricating secrets about her daughter-in-law's sex life. In the daytime, she would make known to her relatives, including the girl's mother, those personal secrets, always adding some touches of her own imagination. To further humiliate her, she gives her son a concubine. All this is done for the sole purpose of removing her rival. As time goes by, both wife and concubine break down under her unbearable mistreatment. One dies of a broken heart; the other commits suicide. Her son does not dare to marry again, knowing full well that his mother would not tolerate it. He goes whoring from time to time.

My brief analysis of the woman shows that she is not just a malevolent woman out of her mind. Her insane jealousy of her son's wife and concubine is not just a manifestation of her inability to abide normal sexual life around her due to her own frustration. It is a disguised move to repossess her son sexually as an emotional compensation for her lack of a sex life. In one episode, she forces her son to leave his wife one night and to accompany her on the opium couch all night. While smoking opium together, she recalls: "All these years he had been the only man in her life. Only with him there was no danger of his being after her money—it was his anyway. But as her son, he amounted to less than half a man. And even the half she could not keep now that he was married." And she puts a foot on his shoulder and keeps giving him light kicks on the neck, whispering, "Unfilial slave, I'll fix you! When did you get to be so unfilial?" (549) The flirtatious gestures, the coquettish banter, the recollection of her sexual frustration in early life, and the mother and son spending the whole night together on the opium couch—all these details carry a sexual undertone, which is difficult to discount. Of course, her attempt to possess her son sexually is covered up under the smoke screen of filial piety. This is a central point, which differentiates Ch'i-ch'iao from Mrs. Morel, and distinguishes the mother complex in Chinese literature from that in Western literature.

THE SON COMPLEX: FULFILLMENT OF FILIAL DUTIES

In ancient Chinese society, a father's conscious desire to dispose of his son might be justified by the Confucian requirement of filial piety, whereas a son's desire, even unconscious striving, to remove the father and possess the mother was viewed with absolute horror. Hence, in Chinese literature, a son's oedipal feeling is channeled to other avenues and assumes the form of profound longing for a woman who has a mother stature or is a surrogate mother or an aunt.

The Novella *Fuxi Fuxi* and the Film *Ju Dou*

If patricide appears in a literary work, it is committed either because of mistaken identity or because of social or moral imperative. There are quite a few cases in modern and contemporary Chinese literature. A notable one is found in a novella by Liu Heng, *Fuxi Fuxi* [*The Obsessed*], later adapted by the internationally renowned film director Zhang Yimou into a film, *Ju Dou* (1990), which received Oscar nominations for Best Foreign Film in 1991 and won a handful of international film awards. In the novella, Yang Jinshan is an old man in his late fifties. Impotent and childless, he raises his nephew as his farmhand. His nephew, Yang Tianqing, is a young man in his early twenties. He falls in love with his aunt, Wang Ju Dou, a woman in her mid-twenties, and they lead a secret love life. His uncle becomes the obstacle to their love. A couple of times, he wants to kill his uncle, but each time, his sense of filial piety stops him short. Their secret love gives birth to a male child, Tianbai, who grows up to find their secret life. Tianbai hates his natural father and refuses to accept him even after he comes to know his true origin because he feels duty-bound to his father in name. He beats his real father and attempts to kill him, but he does not follow his patricidal thoughts. Unable to bear social pressures and mental sufferings, Tianqing commits suicide. Only after his death, his son seems to show a sign of remorse and reconciliation (Liu Heng, 16–125). There is certainly an oedipal motif in the novella, but it does not develop into a full-blown oedipal conflict.

In the film, however, the oedipal theme is intensified into a full oedipal conflict that consumes the lives of three generations. In the end, Tianqing's illegitimate son born of his secret love relation with his aunt commits a double patricide. He kills both his biological father and his father in name. Rew Chow (1995) correctly observes that

> "Zhang introduces a significant number of changes in the Judou story in order to enhance the Oedipalist focus on femininity." Thus, the adaptation "makes full use of the modernist conceptual method that many have called, after Freud, Oedipalization." (147–48)

The intensified oedipalization may have been due to the impact of the "Freud fad" upon contemporary Chinese literature and cinema. But even in this modern film, filial piety shapes the development and outcome of the oedipal conflicts. Tianqing and his aunt at first lead a secret love life and give birth to a male child. They begin to live like man and wife after his uncle becomes a cripple. While the child is growing up, Tianqing attempts to get rid of his uncle several times, but each time he stops short of killing the latter because of his filial scruples. Ironically, his natural son grows up to be a filial son to his father in name. The crippled uncle wants to kill his illegitimate son while he is still small. He tries a couple of times in vain but never gives up. One day, he again attempts to push the child into a water tank. But the child, who cannot speak since birth, suddenly opens his mouth and calls him "Dad." Now the old man finds in filial piety his most effective weapon to fight back. He asserts his right as the father to the child and uses the child to make life miserable for the young couple. Under his tutelage, the child grows up to hate his biological father and starts to persecute the latter as soon as he is capable of doing so. In the end, even after the mother discloses in unequivocal terms who his real father is, the child coolheadedly kills his biological father amid the frenzied pleading of his mother. Distraught, the mother sets fire to the place and burns herself to death in the fire. The film ends in total destruction and tragedy.

The film does not tell us clearly why the child persecutes his biological father and eventually kills the latter even after he learns about the identity of his victim. A little psychoanalysis may throw light on the cause and show how intricately an individual's emotional life is enmeshed in the social fabric of family honor and filial piety. When the child is about five years old, the film shows that he starts to resent his mother's liaison with his biological father. There is one episode in which when his real father is having a tryst with his mother in a room, he throws stones at their door, thereby disrupting the young couple's tryst. At this time, the child is still too young to understand the concept of filial piety, but he has reached the oedipal stage of childhood development. His hatred for his real father and resentment of his mother's liaison with his real father seems to be determined by his oedipal feelings. After the old man makes deliberate efforts to inculcate in the child the idea that he is the latter's father, the oedipal hostility becomes enmeshed in the social dynamics of filial piety. Now the child can justify his persecution of his real father under the pretext of filial duties. In the film, there is an episode in which the child chases a young man in the village and is determined to kill him because the latter gossips about his mother having an affair with his biological father. He nearly commits murder in defense of the family honor. This episode adds a social dimension to the already complicated picture of the oedipal conflict and determines that the real father and son will never be able to reconcile. After the old man dies, Tianqing is no longer permitted to live in the same premises. The film shows how each evening, when Tianqing finishes his day's work at the house, his son callously drives him away. The image of the son who locks the door against his real father implicitly hints at an oedipal jealousy that motivates the child to guard the mother against the father. Tianqing tries to endear himself to the child, but each time he is coldly rebuffed. When the child grows into an adolescent having enough physical strength, he knocks his real father to the ground on one occasion when the latter tries to soothe the son's wounded finger. In my opinion, he kills his real father partly in the name of fulfilling his filial duty as a son to his nominal father and partly because of his hidden oedipal hostility.

Ju Dou is a rare artistic representation of oedipal conflict in Chinese culture, which reveals the complexity of oedipal configurations. It dramatizes two oedipal triangles among three generations with two cases of patricide. While one patricide is perpetrated unconsciously and unintentionally, the other is committed consciously and deliberately. A close analysis of the two patricides will reveal something interesting. In both cases, the two fathers die in the hands of the child and in the family's dyeing pool. In the first patricide, the child is about five years old and accidentally trips his nominal father into the pool, causing him to drown. In the second patricide, the child, now an adolescent, throws his fainted father into the same pool. When his father comes to life and holds onto a pole for his life, the adolescent ferociously hits his father with a big stick, causing him to drown. The child's attitudes toward the two deaths are portrayed differently. In the first case, when the child sees the old man struggling for life in the pool, the child jumps up for joy and claps his hands as though he were watching something funny. A commonsense explanation would be that the child does not know what he is doing and what consequences would come out of his accident. But a psychoanalytic reading may interpret the child's joy at the death of the old man as a representation of the child's unconscious wish for the removal of the father. In the second case, the adolescent clearly knows that he is committing a patricide. While he goes about killing his father, his face shows no expression. The lack of facial expression may suggest that he is committing a patricide quite against his will but in conformity with his filial duties to his nominal father. In both cases, the cinematographic use of the dyeing pool as the death scene is not simply made for visual effects. The red-colored water splashing turbulently in the pool when the dying man struggles for life not only symbolizes an uncontrollable eruption of oedipal hatred but also hints at the bloody, violent nature of oedipal conflict.

Surrogate Mother Motif

In traditional Chinese literature, rarely do we find violent, full-blown oedipal conflicts in a literary work, still less oedipal patricides. As a rule, one dimension of the Oedipus complex—the hatred of the father—disappears while the other dimension—the love for the mother, or a surrogate mother—is intensified. Bao-yu, the male protagonist in the already discussed traditional Chinese novel, is a case in point. According to psychoanalytic theory, a successful resolution of the Oedipus complex should enable a male person to transfer his love for the mother to a different person of the opposite sex out of the family, thus bringing about the confluence of the affectionate and sensual currents in the psyche. The affectionate current is formed on the basis of the self-preservative instinct and is directed to the members of the family and those who look after the child. From the outset, it carries along with it contributions from the sexual instinct—components of erotic interest. It corresponds to the child's primary object choice. It persists throughout childhood and throughout life. Then at the age of puberty it is joined by the powerful sensual current, which has as its aim genital contact. Normal people are able to find another person of the opposite sex with whom the affectionate and sensual currents can be united, but in Bao-yu's case his upbringing turns him into an abnormal person. A child is nursed usually by one caretaker, his mother. But several female persons nursed Bao-yu. His biological mother, Madame Wang, who does not attend to Bao-yu's nursing and upbringing personally, is not as closely related to him as the other female figures. To a great extent, these female figures assume the maternal role of Madame Wang. Above all, his eldest sister Yuan-chun assumes the role of a mother. As the novel tells us: "Although they were brother and sister, *their relationship was more like that of a mother and son*" (Cao, 1: 358, italics mine).

This pseudo mother-son relationship is further corroborated by Yuan-chun's letter home. The tone of her letter is one of motherly love rather than sisterly love. When Bao-yu is led to her presence on her visit home, Yuan-chun, "stretching out her arms, drew him to her bosom where she held him in a close embrace, stroking his hair and fondling the back of his neck" (1:363). Pleased to hear that Bao-yu can compose verses, she asks him to write an octet for each of the four places in the garden that she likes best. In the first poem, the whole tenor is one of waiting, expecting, and longing, which characterize the feelings of anxiety lest the slumberer's dream might be disrupted by violent intrusion. In the second poem, there is a literary allusion. The mention of "grass at spring" (*san chun cao*) alludes to the Tang poet Meng Jiao's (751–814) "A Departing Son's Lament": "Who would say that a small grass's longing/ could requite the radiance of spring." Meng Jiao's poem describes a son's profound gratitude to his mother and his inability to repay her kindness. Bao-yu's use of the allusion betrays the surrogate mother stature of his sister in his mind. Of the four poems, three are composed by Bao-yu and the fourth by Dai-yu. Bao-yu's poem contrasts with Dai-yu's poem in tone and mood: the former is dominated by melancholic depression and anxious expectancy, while the latter is characterized by a joyful jubilance and carefree nonchalance. Perhaps Bao-yu expresses his unconscious desire to repay his sister for the kindness of nursing and upbringing. Thus, Bao-yu's emotional complex is also connected to the dynamics of filial piety.

THE DAUGHTER COMPLEX: BLIND LOYALTY TO FATHER

"Autumn"

In Chinese literature, the female counterpart of the Oedipus complex often takes the form of a daughter's profound longing for her father or a blind loyalty to his image. A typical example is to be found in Yeh Shao-chun's story "Autumn" (1932). It has a hidden oedipal motif similar to that in Faulkner's "A Rose for Emily" (1954). Miss Emily is an old spinster whose oedipal attachment to her father turns her into an odd person capable of what are normally considered human follies and perversions. In Yeh Shaochun's story, we also encounter a spinster whose unconventional behavior is considered odd by her relatives and contemporaries. Like Miss Emily, she is a daughter of an old, once prosperous family. Her father died when she was twenty-one, leaving behind a large home-estate for his several children to share among themselves. As it is the traditional Chinese way for grown-up children to live in an extended family under one roof, the home-estate provides a spiritual and emotional haven for the female protagonist. Unlike Miss Emily, she is a modern woman who seems to come under the sway of women's liberation. She chooses to study obstetrics and becomes a midwife in Shanghai. Hers is a difficult job and she faces strong competition from quacks. Though she realizes this, she sticks to her profession and decides to remain single for life.

The story opens with her returning home to attend the annual family reunion on the occasion of sweeping her parents' graves. She lies in bed in her own room, overhearing two maidservants talking disparagingly about her and her profession. Imagining the servants' contempt on their faces, the protagonist does not feel angry at all, for the old maidservants only render in words the disparagement she has often encountered. But their conjecture about her age makes her feel somewhat upset, for she is nearly forty. In ten years' time, she will no longer be fit to do her job. She is worried about her future as a spinster. Her sister-in-law seizes the opportunity to persuade her to accept a proposal of marriage, a match quite ideal in the conventional sense. But the effort is unwelcome and made in vain. Her refusal is puzzling not only to her relatives but also to the reader. A superficial reason is offered: having seen the travail of childbirth endured by so many women, she does not want to experience the same ordeal, especially at her age. This explanation, however, is self-defeating. We are told that the man meant for her is a widower who does not wish to have any more children, because his children have all reached adulthood. She has strong maternal instinct, for her thoughts about being a mother "made her feel as warm inside, as if she had drunk some wine or heard herself respectfully addressed as 'Madam' or 'Mistress.'" She is not an asexual female with no interest in marriage. When matchmakers come with proposed marriages, she ostensibly adopts the perspective of a disinterested bystander, but in her heart, there is "a bubbling cauldron in which satisfaction and jealousy were churning in a turbulent mix" (119). Her nonchalance and disinterestedness are only feigned. The image of a "bubbling cauldron" indicates that there is an intense internal conflict within her deep psyche. She is even willing to ask probing questions about the proposed marriage. This betrays her desire for married life. She feels satisfied because the talk about matrimony enables her to imagine the fulfillment of her desires; yet she feels jealous because marriage is something beyond her reach because of some unknown inhibition. She has to be content with this kind of talk in the same way a sexually starved person has to make do with sexual talk

The ambivalence in the story makes it difficult to pin down its central theme. C. T. Hsia (1961) suggests that the story is a "study in loneliness" (67–68). This perhaps accounts for one aspect of the story but is certainly unable to explain why the woman refuses to marry. My close reading of the story convinces me that it has a similar oedipal theme to Faulkner's "A Rose for Emily": it is the woman's unconscious wish to be loyal to her father that incapacitates her for love or even contemplation of marriage. What is her inhibition against matrimony? The story provides us with a casual hint which, examined in terms of the Oedipus complex, offers an explanation: "When she was twenty-seven or twenty-eight, she decided not to marry, since her father's will stipulated that any daughter who remained a spinster should receive twenty *mou* of land" (118). An unsuspecting reader would interpret the father's will as a measure of precaution against a rainy day. But there are two possible hidden motives. Either her father had realized that his daughter had an inhibition against marriage, or he was unconsciously encouraging his daughter to remain single. Either is plausible. In any case, his daughter takes the terms in the will literally as a reason for not considering matrimonial matters. By observing her father's will literally, she proves herself to be a filial daughter. To her, the estate left by her father has a symbolic stature, and is in many ways a symbol of her father's existence. So long as it is intact, she can always come home for spiritual sustenance and be reinvigorated by her father's legacy despite her psychological and physical frustrations. This explains why she feels so devastated by and antagonistic to the idea of selling the family property.

With regard to the way to cope with her psychological conflict, the story shows a different feature from "A Rose for Emily." In Faulkner's (1954) story, Miss Emily manages to solve her problem by murdering her lover and placing him in her bed so that she can sleep with him in the same bed while still remaining faithful to her father. In the Chinese story, the woman has the normal desire for motherhood, which cannot be fulfilled unless she consents to marriage. She succeeds in solving her dilemma by a process of transformation and an act of sublimation. Due to her inhibition against marriage, she cannot perform the maternal function. She chooses the study of obstetrics quite late. It is reasonable to believe that her belated decision is a way to transform her repressed maternal desires. The profession of obstetrician was not a highly regarded job for a woman at that time: it is "disgusting," "low-class," and "embarrassing" for a woman to face the world. In this sense she has made a big sacrifice. Her repressed desire for motherhood is sublimated through her choice of her profession. The job is particularly satisfying to her for psychological reasons. Otherwise, we cannot understand how she can make such a "sacrifice" and stick to it in spite of all the odds against it. The hidden satisfaction seems to be: if she can not perform the maternal function, she would like to help other women perform it. Delivering children into this world becomes equivalent to having children by herself. Since she cannot have the conflicting options, she has to be content with a compromise solution.

THE FILIAL PIETY COMPLEX

In his study of the Oedipus complex, Fenichel (1931) acknowledges the assumption that the complex might have a phylogenetic root and even children who are not brought up in any family have their Oedipus complex because they are not free from family influence in society. He, nevertheless, emphasizes the impact of culture, especially family structure, upon the specific forms of the complex. In his opinion, the forms of the complex will change in accordance with the changing conditions of family structure (219–20). My study confirms his observations and insights. Both China and the West have been patriarchal, family-centered societies. The difference in emphasis on the role of the family determines the different forms of the complex in Chinese and Western societies. The Confucian moral system produced perhaps the most systematic moral codes in the world concerning the family and an individual's behavior within it. In a traditional Chinese family, the Confucian moral codes ensure an early identification of children with their social roles. From early childhood, Chinese children learn their proper places in the family and society and act accordingly. In terms of the classical psychoanalytic theory, the resolution of the Oedipus complex occurs in a more thoroughgoing manner than in the West. Nowadays, most psychoanalysts no longer expect the Oedipus complex to be fully resolved in childhood development but believe that it does not adversely affect a healthy adult life. In terms of this view, if oedipal feelings in some Chinese children remain strong until their adulthood, they are rigorously suppressed by a strong sense of horror into the deepest recess of the mind.

My study has shown that in contrast to Western literature, oedipal conflicts with a complete paraphernalia of Sophocles' drama are rare in Chinese literature. Still rarer is the representation of overt erotic attachment to a parent of the opposite sex. My analysis of the Chinese works shows that oedipal feelings are always displaced on to objects having similar qualities or disguised as manifestations of unusual behavior. For this reason, we may call the Oedipus complex in Chinese culture a "muted complex." To make the situation more complicated, this muted complex is fragmented. A classic oedipal situation constitutes a triangular relationship involving father, mother, and son. In a muted oedipal situation, the oedipal relationship may be a conflict between father and son, a triangular conflict involving mother, son, and son's wife, a son's insatiable longing for maternal love, a daughter's incomprehensible inhibition against love and marriage, or a male person's erotic love for an aunt, or mother's sister, stepmother, or even mother's close maid. In this sense, Harry Guntrip's (1961) term "family complex" may be an appropriate epithet for the Chinese form of the Oedipus complex.

In his study of cultural manifestations in Western literary texts, Jameson (1986) identifies "a radical split between the private and the public, between the poetic and the political, between what we have come to think of as the domain of sexuality and the unconscious and that of the public world of classes, of the economic, and of secular political power" (69). He simplifies this split into one between Freud and Marx or between the private and public spheres. In my study of the oedipal themes in Chinese literature, that split does not seem to exist. Instead of the split observed by Jameson, my analysis demonstrates how the private is intricately implicated in the public, libido is inseparably attached to morality, personal fulfillment is bound with family interest. The film *Ju Dou*, in particular, is a profound representation of how an individual's oedipal feelings are intricately enmeshed in the public manifestations of love, loyalty, family honor, and filial piety. In all the Chinese works that I have analyzed, oedipal desires are always related to parental demands for filial piety or children's fulfillment of filial duties. Since the moral dynamics of filial piety has exerted such a profound shaping impact on oedipal themes in Chinese literature, we may as well call the Oedipus complex in Chinese culture a "filial piety complex."

CONCLUDING REMARKS

I hope that my study may provide a convincing case against the contra-Freudian view that because the Oedipus complex is unique to Western culture, its theory is ethnocentric and cannot be considered universal to human experience. My uncovering of oedipal wishes and structures in premodern literary work untouched by the introduction of psychoanalytic theories from the West warrants me to observe that Western psychoanalytic theories may have contributed to the advent of more open representations of oedipal themes in modern Chinese literature, but these representations do not lend support to the claim that all oedipal themes in Chinese literature arise from the importation of Western theories. A careful reader of this chapter may notice that in spite of the dazzling variety of oedipal themes in Chinese literary works, there is hardly any positive Oedipus in Sophocles' dramatic representation. This observation necessitates a follow-up and some afterthoughts from a conceptual perspective.

The manifested oedipal themes in the literary works that I have analyzed are less abstract, less general, and less inferential than, but more colorful and more multifaceted than the original Oedipus legend in Sophocles' Oedipus drama. This seems to suggest that the Oedipus complex might not be an inflexible, abstract, general concept but may be an inclusive organizing principle that arises from the inevitability of any child's coming into and growing in a world where there are differences in gender and generation. Thus, it may comprise a series of organizing schemata with which children consciously or unconsciously structure their emotional life and construct their self-identity in a family setting in relation to the moral codes of a society. On the conceptual level, we may view oedipal structure as a generalized principle that has universal applicability, but what we deal with in real life and literary works is always its particular and unique expressions in individual cases. At a descriptive level, the expression of underlying oedipal conflicts is specific to each individual and to each culture. In a particular culture, certain aspects of the oedipal conflicts as observed by Freud and other theorists in the West may be suppressed into the deep unconscious, or displaced onto seemingly innocuous materials, or distorted into forms that we normally do not associate with the original Oedipus complex. For example, in my study of Yu Tafu's[1] (1921) *Sinking*, "A Chinese Oedipus in Exile," the male protagonist's love for the mother is transformed into erotic desires for older women (12) and a profound love for Mother Nature and his motherland (6–9, 16–18).

Zhang Yimou's adaptation of Liu Heng's novella into the film *Ju Dou* is a good example to illustrate what motifs are forbidden subjects that must be avoided in an oedipal representation. In an interview about his film production, Zhang vigorously denies a film critic's comment that *Ju Dou* is a film about incest. According to him, in the original novella, Yang Tianqing was Yang Jinshan's biological nephew, but in Zhang's adaptation, he deliberately changed Tianqing's identity to the old man's adopted nephew so as to distance his film from the theme of blood incest. He accepts the interviewer's observation that Judou does not start to have an affair with Tianqing until after she finds out that he has no blood relation with her husband (Ye, 1999). His consent points to an insight that I have observed in my previous analysis: erotic desires for a parent of the opposite sex constitute a taboo and horror for men as well as women. Ironically, after his adaptation, the faint oedipal motif in the novella is intensified into a full oedipal conflict with a double patricide.

Cao Yu's play *Thunderstorm* (1934, 1978), which I mentioned in the opening of this chapter, is another good example to illustrate the taboo in oedipal representation. Among Chinese dramatic works, this play may be the one that comes closest to Sophocles' *Oedipus* in oedipal structure and elements: abandonment, mistaken identity, father-son conflict, attempted patricide, mother-son incest, sibling incest, and deaths arising therefrom. Nevertheless, there is one fundamental difference: the mother-son incest is not between biological mother and son. The male protagonist has an erotic relationship not with his natural mother but with his stepmother. This difference characterizes all literary works with oedipal themes that I have read. And almost without exception, the outcome of oedipal development is determined by the moral dynamics of filial piety or social responsibility. The overdetermination of oedipal themes by the cultural imperative of filial piety leads to the most important insight that my study has uncovered: the abhorrence for and the defenses against oedipal wishes will invariably determine culture-specific ways in which oedipal themes are expressed in the literature of a given culture. This insight may help us better understand the complexity of the Oedipus complex that has fascinated and will continue to fascinate scholars and analysts for generations to come.

NOTES

*I wish to thank three anonymous reviewers and the editor of the Psychoanalytic Quarterly for their perceptive comments and suggestions for revision. I also take this opportunity to acknowledge my indebtedness to Professor Peter Rudnytsky, editor of *American Imago,* for his comments on an early version of the present chapter.

1. Although the name under which *Sinking* was originally published was Yu Tafu, today this name is more commonly translated as Yu Dafu, according to the pinyin notation system.

10

Transformation of Korean Women: From Tradition to Modernity

Mikyum Kim

> For one chrysanthemum to bloom
> a nightingale has sobbed since spring, perhaps.
>
> Midang So Chong-ju (1946, 17)

Beginning with the decline of the Choson Dynasty (1392–1910), Korea experienced intense social, cultural, political, and economic changes. This period of Korean history has been characterized by many tragic events and traumas from which Korea has been recovering for the last half-century. The Choson Dynasty, which had lasted for more than five centuries, ended when Japan annexed Korea in 1910. Korea was under Japanese rule for thirty-five years, a time when Korean society began a transformation from traditional Confucian society to modernity. No sooner had Korea begun to emerge from the trauma of Japanese imperial rule than the country found itself caught up in the ideological conflicts of the Cold War. This conflict between communism and democracy led to war in 1950, a war that ended in the creation of two separate Korean states: North and South Korea. The Korean War had tragic consequences for the Korean people. During this chaotic period, few Korean families survived without the loss of family members. Needless to say, the loss of homes and industrial capacity were also profound. The Korean War accelerated a cultural transformation from traditional Confucian society to modernity.

In this chapter, I will examine the transformation in the lives of Korean women through observation of a fictional character in a Korean novel and through case material provided by the analysis of a Korean-born woman who emigrated to the United States in her late twenties. The lives of each woman span two different generations. The fictional character is about twenty years older than my patient and lived through this cultural transformation. The analysand (whom I will call Betty), not only experienced a transformation in Korean culture but also a transformation from Eastern to Western culture.

HISTORICAL BACKGROUND

Koreans traditionally claim that their culture is a half million years old. However, written history began in the "Three Kingdoms" (57 BC–AD 668) period where the Goguryeo, Baekje, and Silla Kingdoms coexisted on the Korean peninsula. In AD 668 the three kingdoms were unified under Silla hegemony, an arrangement which lasted until AD 935. While Silla was declining, a new Koryo dynasty had risen and come to power in AD 918.

Buddhism was first introduced to the Korean peninsula in AD 372, and gradually spread from Goguryeo to Backje to Silla. Buddhism had heavily influenced "the Unified Silla Kingdom" politically and culturally, and it had continued to have strong effects during the Koryo Dynasty. In the culturally rich, Buddhist-dominated Koryo period, Korean women enjoyed high status both at home and in society. The Koryo family was matrilocal: in every social class, the new husband moved into the bride's house, where the children and grandchildren were born and raised. As a result, women were economically independent, and they controlled the upbringing and education of their children (Deuchler, 1977).

While internally united, Korea had been externally dominated by the Mongols for almost a century. In the last decades of the Koryo period there were efforts to revitalize the country and to eliminate the socioeconomic exploitation for which the Buddhists were considered responsible. At this point, a neo-Confucian philosophy was introduced into Korea (Deucher, 1992). This exerted a profound influence on East Asian political culture, as well as on East Asian spiritual life. Confucianism is a worldview, a social ethic, a political ideology, a scholarly tradition, and a way of life. It is not an organized religion (Wei-Ming, 1998). Confucian ethics are based on three social bonds: the authority of the ruler over the minister, the father over the son, and the husband over the wife. The idea of the three bonds in ancient China (Han Dynasty, 220–206 BC) was an integral part of the Chinese curriculum for moral education. In that society the three bonds were used as a mechanism of control and for the promotion of social stability. These three bonds were based on dominance and subservience; their primary intent was not the well-being of individual persons but a particular pattern of social stability resulting from the rigidly prescribed rules of conduct (Deuchler, 1977; Wei-Ming, 1998).

After AD 1392, the political elite of the Choson Dynasty adopted Confucianism to consolidate their own power in Korea. They expelled the previously powerful Buddhist elite and monopolized political power on the basis of Confucian teaching. The reorganization of Korean society thus reached a scope and depth of control that was rarely attained by social organization anywhere else in Asia that adopted Confucian social ethics (Deuchler, 1977). Confucianism was once a more dynamic philosophy, but it became dogmatized and used as a means of obtaining power during severe periods of political strife. In the process, Korean society became extremely rigid. From the seventeenth century forward, Confucian practice in Korea became pervasive and widely accepted as a way of life. Confucian teachings became the major principles upon which the nation was based, and Confucianism became accepted as the basic form of religious life even though it is not an organized religion. An individual's conduct was judged in terms of the Confucian ultimate value (Deuchler, 1977, 1992).

PHILOSOPHY OF CONFUCIANISM

Confucianism is a philosophy of patriarchy, that is, relations through the male line, even though all human relations are rooted in the union between a man and a woman. This male relation is regarded as the foundation of human morality and the mainspring of the socialization process that extends from the relation between father and son to that of ruler and subject. In cosmological terms, Heaven (yang—male) dominates Earth (yin—female), and, correspondingly, male has precedence over female. The clear hierarchical order between sexes is cosmologically sanctioned and is thought to be imperative for the proper functioning of the human order (Deuchler, 1977; Wei-Ming, 1998).

Confucians drew a sharp distinction between the woman's "inner," or domestic sphere, and the man's "outer," or public sphere. This asymmetry of the sexes was believed necessary to restrain sexual indulgence and selfishness, which would lead to social disorder, and to establish different social functions for husband and wife. In the Confucian view, the law of nature thus accorded the woman an inferior position from birth. Consequently, women fell into subservient roles. They had to obey their fathers before marriage, their husbands after marriage, and their sons when they were widowed. Before the marriage, girls were not only instructed in Confucian ideology, but also in its practical consequences. After the age of seven, girls could no longer associate with boys or men. They were more and more confined to the inner quarters of the house, where they received instructions in domestic duties from mothers and grandmothers. The girls' cultural training was focused entirely on becoming able to fill the role of a married woman serving the man and his family. It was important to prepare girls for their future function as moral guardians of the domestic sphere and as providers for the needs of their families (Deuchler, 1977, 1992).

Marriage was the precondition for adulthood, and to remain unmarried was socially unacceptable. For a woman, the wedding signified a rite of passage from childhood to adulthood, in order that she might become a full member of society. Once she was married, the mother-in-law was the most important individual in the life of the young bride: her mother-in-law stood at the apex of female social prestige and authority while the young bride was at the lowest level. The filial daughter-in-law was to strive to follow the mother-in-law's orders precisely, and she was taught to avoid situations that might give rise to scolding. The young daughter-in-law, sometimes facing inhuman treatment from her husband's family (especially from her mother-in-law), had no place to turn for relief from her bonds of obedience. She had only one choice: she had to endure and survive within her husband's family.

TRADITIONAL KOREAN WOMEN AND THE LIFE CYCLE

The life cycle of the traditional Korean woman can be seen as consisting of two stages. In the first stage, a young woman is helpless, innocent, at the mercy of her family of origin and later her husband's family. This fate is not the outcome of her own intrapsychic development but rather the culturally determined role imposed upon her by society. In psychoanalytic terms she is defined as lacking a penis in a patriarchal culture. We might ask what effect this has on the development of a young woman's psyche. In the west, a Freudian theory that defines females as, essentially, castrated males, envious of the penis, emphasizes the psychopathology of castration. However, in the traditional context, *Namjon Yobi* (the principle that men are superior to women), a woman's feelings of inferiority and her desire to gain power and identity through males are considered not only normal but also virtuous.

In the second stage of adult life, a woman gains identity as a person by producing a son who will grow up and take a wife of his own. A woman then assumes the position of mother-in-law, essentially becoming the very person who tormented her in the years before she added a male heir to the patriarchal line. Thus a sadomasochistic relationship (a relationship of dominance and submission) comes full circle, with the new daughter-in-law playing the role of the tormented victim. For the new mother-in-law, the son becomes her identity and her repository of worth, as well as her source of social and economic power: he becomes her phallus. As mother and son become closely intertwined for life, the son also comes to represent a narcissistic object choice for the mother. Reich (1953) wrote of this dynamic:

> In many cases, the phallic level is never relinquished and the fantasy of possessing a penis persists. Numerous women continue to have masculine longings which find expression in many ways, frequently in the form of inferiority feelings and of specific, unrealizable ambitions and ideals. Solution to such conflicts is some times reached through a specific choice of a love object representing what these girls originally wanted to be, and which they can love on this basis. An object that is different from the self, but which has qualities they once desired for themselves, indeed represents a narcissistic object choice. (22)

It is unclear whether or not this traditional sadomasochistic cycle will continue now that many Korean women appear to be adopting a more modern or westernized view of their own value and position in society. Clearly these modern women find that the traditional expectations placed on them as wives and daughters-in-law are no longer realistic. It remains to be seen whether the lingering *Namjon Yobi,* abetted by the seductive power of a narcissistic object choice, is still strong enough to lead these women to inflict the same pain on their own daughters-in-law.

Men in this culture are witnesses to the subjugation of women who are seen as lacking a penis. Such men are thus acutely aware of the power of the penis and the fear of castration. Filial piety appears to offset that fear somewhat, since the son gains protection as being a phallus for the mother. Yet paradoxically, that transfer of phallic power to the mother is also experienced as a form of castration. At the same time, the principle of *Namjon Yobi* is a result of the fear of castration; it is also a reaction formation against that fear. Terrified of being rendered helpless as a female, the male appears to revert to the opposite, which in this culture traditionally means a man who treats women (other than his mother and grandmother) as inferior beings. In this context, true oedipal issues do not appear to apply. While the tight mother-son bond certainly involves feelings that could be called oedipal, this unchallenged duality also obviates the triangulation that usually gives rise to the Oedipus conflict. In the traditional Oedipus paradigm, the young son's romantic longings for his mother are effectively spurned by her and strongly opposed by the father. The boy comes to accept that his mother prefers the father to him. In traditional Korean society, however, the mother-son bond is a joint endeavor, with the mother apparently desiring the son as much as he covets her. In this way, traditional Korean society approves of the idealized mother-son bond, lauding the male participant as a good son.

THE PROCESS OF WOMEN'S MODERNIZATION

During the Japanese colonial era (1910–1945) and the Korean War (1950), many families were pulled apart when men emigrated as voluntary or involuntary laborers, joined independent resistance movements, or joined the army while women became the heads of the family with heavy responsibilities. For women who lived through this troubled time, the patrilineal principle was maintained as a cultural ideal even though women were the center of the family, taking care of everything from supporting the family to educating the children.

A socialist, Cho Hae Jong (2002), argues that for postcolonial Korean women, the first transition from traditional patriarchy to modern patriarchy began in the 1960s and extended through the 1980s. During these years, the most visible transition in Korea was from the extended family to the urban nuclear family. In this generation, with economic growth and rapid urbanization, large numbers of young men could pursue secure and well-paying jobs in the modern sector, and their young wives would manage their husband's income and children's education. As the nuclear family system became firmly established in a rapidly urbanizing society, the wife's role gained in importance compared to the role of mother or "mother-in-law" or both. Young husbands suffered from divided loyalties and came to refer to themselves as the "sandwich generation"; they were torn between mother and wife. For many women of this generation, marriage was simply a fact of life. They formed families with their children and often lacked intimate connections with their husbands. Other issues surrounding a woman's femininity were relegated to a place of unimportance.

The second transition occurred in the 1980s and the 1990s. In this period, a majority of girls lived in urban settings, grew up in nuclear families, and indulged in the arts and music. They struggled through intense competitions for the university entrance examinations. In the 1980s, many female college students joined and sympathized with student activists. They became the brave partners of patriotic men engaged in this activism. The Korean woman's liberation movement was also launched at this time. In this period of modernization, economic production was strongly emphasized, giving way to a postmodern period in which consumerism became the central focus of sociocultural production. Korean women in the postmodern era desired to be "charming" and "sexy." Advertising and the mass media appeared to accelerate the movement toward consumerism. Young women in this generation, for the first time, began to use cosmetic surgery to improve their appearance. College students in the mid-1990s became very fashion-conscious, unlike the young women of the 1980s, who were urged to be patriotic and intellectual. In current Korean society, there are several coexisting generations, in which changes in society regarding family structure and social and cultural transformation are highly visible. It is less clear how deeply these changes have penetrated in the psychic lives of Korean women.

At this point I would like to focus my discussion on the lives of two particular women: one is a fictional character who lived through the Japanese colonial era and the Korean war as a young woman, and the other is an analysand of mine who went through the war as a very young girl and lived through the difficult period of Korean modernization, and then emigrated to the United States in the 1970s.

A FICTIONAL CHARACTER

The Late 1950s Novel *Pyo Ryu Do*

The character I have selected, Kang Hyun Hoi, is from the novel, *Pyo Ryu Do* ("A Floating Island"), written by a woman, Park Kyung Lee (1926–2008), in 1959. During the Korean War, the author (who was then in her mid-twenties) became a widow and the sole breadwinner for her family. She worked at various odd jobs until she was able to earn enough money to support her family through her writing. In her mid-thirties, she published the novel *Pyo Ryu Do*. Since then, Ms. Park has become one of the most prolific writers in Korean history. I have chosen this novel, in part, because it was a very important book to my analysand, Betty, during her adolescence. The main character in the novel, Ms. Kang Hyun Hoi, had become almost a real person for Betty. The character's trauma during the war and the many losses she had experienced in early life seemed to be a reflection of Betty's own life. "Looking back on my life, I dare say that through the novel, *Pyo Ryu Do*," said Betty, "I had my very first psychotherapy."

The novel *Pyo Ryu Do* (A Floating Island) is the story of Kang Hyun Hoi, who is a madam in a tea-salon. She is a single mother of a five-year-old daughter, born out of wedlock. In 1950, in the midst of the Korean War, Kang's fiance, Chan Soo, a newly graduated medical doctor, was killed by his classmate, a Communist. For economic reasons, Kang Hyun Hoi and Chan Soo had been living together. Kang Hyun Hoi was pregnant when Chan Soo was killed. Having become a single woman in her late twenties, Kang Hyun Hoi became the breadwinner of a family comprised of her widowed mother, her half-brother whose mother was the father's mistress, and an illegitimate daughter. To support her extended family, Kang became the madam of a tea-salon, called Madonna. Unlike the usual madam of a tea-salon in that period, Kang Hyun Hoi came from an elite class, and was a college graduate with a degree in history.

Kang Hyun Hoi struggled to survive postwar Korea. Because so many men had disappeared or were killed, women were forced to carry the economic burden of the family. In this way, the traditional belief system was keeping pace with the external reality. At that time, a tea-salon madam was viewed as a prostitute; her job was to serve men who used her. Kang Hyun Hoi was different; she was intelligent and highly esteemed. She refused to compromise her belief system and maintained her ideals. When she was not on duty, she translated foreign books into Korean. She maintained her intellectual curiosity and demanded from society the respect she believed she deserved.

Kang Hyun Hoi was an only child. Her father was a womanizer. He had been wandering the northern part of Korea and Manchuria participating in the Korean liberation movement. Her mother was a beautiful woman, but was somehow unattractive to her husband. When Korea became independent from Japan in 1945, Kang Hyun Hoi's father returned home with his concubine, and he began a new life with his new woman in the same village where his wife and daughter were living. It angered Kang Hyun Hoi so much that she refused to talk to her father again. She sarcastically stated that her only inheritance was her father's illegitimate son, Hyun Kyu.

The mother had been abandoned by her husband and deprived of his love. She often turned to her daughter for the love and affection missing in her life. Kang resented her mother's demands for love and tried to keep her mother at a distance. Kang had been angry with her mother and looked down on her mother's helplessness; the mother was forced to depend on a husband who did not love her. Mother and daughter often quarreled over the daughter's insistence on privacy and maintaining boundaries.

Kang Hyun Hoi fell in love with a customer in the tea-salon, Lee Sang Hyun. He was a journalist working at a reputable newspaper. He was also a married man. Their illicit love affair caused anguish, sadness, and grief in Kang Hyun Hoi. Even though she was deeply in love with Sang Hyun, she did not trust him and she did not trust society in general. Though she described him as a humanist, she was cynical toward his love for her, and she interpreted his love and kindness as merely pity for the poor. For her there was a big gap between inner desire and outer societal prohibition. This inner struggle was as deep as the disparity between them in terms of social class.

Lee proposed to her even though he was still married, and he knew that breaking his marriage contract would not be an easy task. He was very much in love with Kang Hyun Hoi and was jealous over other customers' attraction to her. He urged her to give up her business but she insisted that he should not be in control of her life. The more she desired to be with him and spend her life with him, the stronger her suppression and repression of her own desire: "When it comes time, we should separate from each other and go live our own lives, otherwise our love will become ugly." She seemed to accept that it was inevitable their love would end; there were too many barriers for them to overcome. She also refused to succumb to social prejudice. Her pride and self-respect did not allow her to accept any help either from a male friend from her college days—a publisher, Kim—nor her lover, Lee.

Madonna, the tea-salon, had been started with a private loan from a childhood friend, Kae Young, who had become newly rich. The high interest charged by her friend was humiliating to Kang. It was very difficult for her to depend on the rich friend whose money came from her father's illegal business allied with the Japanese government officers during the colonial era. She looked down on the lender-friend as much as the lender-friend looked down on her. One day, when she was able to sell her business, she visited her lender, Kae Young. She intended to pay back the remaining principal. Kae Young informed her that Mr. Lee had returned from a month-long business trip to America. The lender, Kae Young, was a friend of Mr. Lee's wife, and the Lees resided next door to Kae Young. Kae Young claimed that Lee's wife was alarmed at her husband's love affair with Kang and decided not to accept his request for divorce. Kang came back to the tea-salon in a state of shock. The day after his return from America, she had still not heard from him. From Kae Young's house she was able to see Lee sitting with a woman, presumably his wife (in fact, it was his sister who was visiting from America) in their living room. What she saw appeared to her to be a scene of domestic bliss. She felt betrayed by Lee. Perhaps she was momentarily insane with jealousy. She returned to the tea-salon and sat down at the counter. Her mind was detached from reality. There were many familiar faces in the tea-salon. Professor Choi was one of them, with his foreign guest Mr. Smith. She felt that Mr. Smith was staring at her, and he seemed to be very interested in her, but she did not seem to care because her mind was preoccupied with thoughts of her former lover. Professor Choi had been a frequent customer at Madonna and was interested sexually in Kang. He was an opportunist who used people to manipulate the system to get what he wanted. She looked down on Professor Choi, who had tried to show off his rather shallow knowledge of economics and political philosophy. She despised what he represented. He was no gentleman.

Kang overheard a dialogue between Professor Choi and Mr. Smith in which Choi claimed to Mr. Smith that Kang belonged to him, and if Smith helped him to gain power professionally and financially, he was willing to give Kang up because she had become too expensive to maintain. He told Smith that: "A woman like her, a madam in a tea-salon, is not a lady, so it is easy to get her without concern for any responsibility." At this point, Kang completely lost control. Her heart, her brain, her sight, and her entire body were on fire with rage. She grabbed a bronze vase on the counter and threw it toward Professor Choi's head. She lost consciousness and when she woke up, she realized she that had become a murderer.

In Kang's trial, the prosecutor confronted her motivation for murdering Professor Choi. "Why did you kill him? What was the motivation to kill him? Did you have a relationship with him, a sexual relationship?"

"He tried to sell me to a foreigner," she said. "Even if I am the mother of an illegitimate child and a madam in a tea-salon, I am not a prostitute."

The prosecutor responded: "You indulged in sex without marriage, and consequently you had a child. Your job as a madam in a tea-salon is to serve men, why was it such a big deal to be humiliated by your customer? You are not a virgin, nor are you a housewife."

The prosecutor was not convinced that the motivation for killing Professor Choi was her anger toward him in trying to bargain with a foreigner for her. Her pride and self-worth were deeply hurt. In her trial, she gave up her right to be treated as a respectable human in spite of the fact of her being a madam in a tea-salon and having a child out of wedlock. With her lawyer's advice, she declared that she was temporarily insane when she overheard the conversation between Professor Choi and Mr. Smith.

After a year and a half of incarceration, Kang was freed. Upon her return home, she had to face another tragedy: her daughter's death in an automobile accident. While undergoing unbearable pain, she was confronted by Kim, a practical man. Mr. Kim urged her to marry Lee Sang Hyun, who now was divorced from his wife. She vehemently rejected Kim's advice: "I loved Lee, and then I had to suppress my desires bitterly, and now I do not want him. My rational judgment does not allow me to marry him." Mr. Kim replied:

> Don't take it seriously. We are going to die sooner or later. Right now we are alive, and each of us is a floating island in the ocean. We are all lonely. The destiny of any human relationship is determined by the distance between islands. There is nothing that belongs to us. One day, an island next to you is sunk and disappears from sight. Your island, regardless of the circumstances, should continue to float until it drowns. Don't take life seriously. Accept losses without resistance. Once you lose someone, it means that the island next to you has disappeared. Row your island toward another. In order to stay afloat, you need to be rational, calculating and realistic.

Kang refused Lee's proposal.

She had had three men: Chan Soo, a man of intellect; Lee Sang Hyun, a man representing emotion and romanticism; and Kim, a man of determination, willing to overcome any obstacles in life including love, work or even death—a realist. At the end, she chose to marry Mr. Kim. In doing so she succumbed to the social reality of traditional Korean society.

Psychoanalytic Reflections

Kang Hyun Hoi is a woman in her late twenties, the child of a Korean couple during the period when Korea was occupied by Japan. Her father abandoned the family by participating in the independence movement. Her father was a wanderer, and he had many affairs while he traveled around the country.

During the Choson Dynasty, women were not allowed to have an official education. Women's responsibilities were to serve their husbands, to procreate, especially sons, and to sacrifice their lives for their in-laws' well-being. As discussed earlier, women had few if any rights, and eventually they were confined to the inner rooms of the house. The government, however, set up a special institute for girls in order to educate them how to serve and entertain men, especially government officers, foreign ambassadors, and even kings: these girls were named *Kisang*. The institute was the only official place of education for young women, who were underprivileged or unfortunate. They were taught art, music, calligraphy, poetry, and Oriental philosophy. However, they were not allowed to have their own lives. They were the lowest class in society even though they were the most intelligent and well-educated women. Their highest achievement was to be chosen by an established upper-class man and become his concubine.

It is not surprising to me that Kang had an affair with a married man. Her yearning for her father could have been an unconscious motivation for having an affair with an unavailable man. It might also be an unconscious recreation of her desired father. Apparently, she is a very intelligent woman who had the freedom to have higher education. Unlike a traditional Confucian woman, she fell in love with her college classmate, and she became pregnant before she was married. Then her fiancé, Chan Soo, was killed by his friend, a leftist. Hence, she became a mother to an illegitimate daughter. Pursuing her sexual desires led to unfavorable consequences, and crossing forbidden barriers led to tragedy. The barriers derived from the Confucian tradition in which female sexuality is prohibited and indeed not even recognized. These barriers are also her own inner prohibition: the incest taboo.

Subsequently, she became the head of a family comprised of her widowed mother, her illegitimate daughter, and her half-brother—her father's illegitimate son. She owned a tea-salon called Madonna. Each of the four family members were, in some important sense, outside the norm of traditional Korean society. Certainly, she is not a typical woman from that period of Korean history, even if we grant that in that period Korea was in the process of modernizing. Kang did not respect her father or depend on him as unmarried daughters were supposed to in the traditional society. She not only had a premarital sexual relationship with a man but also had a child as a result. It was unthinkable for an unmarried woman to have sex in such a society. In a devastated postwar Korea, she became a "madam" of a tea-salon to support her family, and she demanded to be respected by society in spite of the society's view of a madam of a tea-salon as a prostitute or *Kisang*. She tried to survive, but she also rebelled and protested against traditional beliefs, which was not an easy task. Her confrontation with the old established society was vigorous. Rage against the establishment led to the murder of Professor Choi. However, she was opposed by forces too powerful for her to defeat. In the process of fighting against the old established society, she was going through inner turmoil, in which her desires and prohibitions were fighting against each other intensely. Finally, she emerged from her inner world, a world that contained too many desires and barriers, and entered reality as represented by her marriage to the realist, Mr. Kim.

AN ANALYTIC PATIENT

Clinical Background

Betty is a professional woman in her early forties who emigrated from Korea in her late twenties. She came for a consultation a few months after her grandmother passed away in Korea. She said that her grandmother had been the most important person in her life, but since her death, Betty had been feeling numb rather than sad. She wanted to understand what was going on. She had been in psychoanalytical psychotherapy for many years with an American male psychoanalyst, and she claimed that it had been very helpful to her.

Betty was the first of two children in a family in which her father was a high-ranking engineer working for the Korean government, and her mother was a housewife with some college education. She grew up as an only child in Seoul. Her younger sister was born when Betty was two. She had no recollection of her sister's birth. The sister died just before her first birthday. Betty was told by her grandmother that her father wept when her sister was born because he had another daughter. Whenever she heard about this, she wondered how he felt when she herself was born: "Was I my father's disappointment because I was not a son?" she asked. The Korean War started when Betty was six years old. During the war her father was accused of being a Communist and put in jail by the South Korean government. He received a death sentence, and was subsequently executed.

Betty wondered "Was he a real Communist? And what does it mean that he was a Communist? He was an engineer and not a politician. What sort of crime had he ever committed?" The family had never been informed that the father was executed during the South Korean government's evacuation of the capital when the North Koreans, with China's help, renewed their attack on the South. They later learned that the execution must have occurred on January 4, 1951, when the South Korean government ordered the evacuation of Seoul. Since the jailers also had to be evacuated, it was decided that, depending upon the weight of their crime, some prisoners, who had light sentences, were transferred to another jail in the south. Other prisoners who had heavy sentences, like Betty's father, were executed. For many years, the family could not accept that the father had been executed. While they waited, still hoping the father would return, another tragedy occurred. Betty's mother suddenly abandoned the family after her small business failed. The mother had owed money to the members of *gye* (voluntary associations for mutual aid) and she had been cheated by a crook. It was very common in that period that naïve women, the heads of households, were preyed on by dishonest thieves. Her mother abandoned her daughter and Betty's maternal grandmother became her guardian. Betty recalled that her childhood had been filled with longing for her lost parents. She never saw her mother again. She was twelve years old.

After her mother disappeared, Betty waited for her with an intense yearning—feelings that ultimately turned to anger. She told me that she was ashamed of missing her mother. "After all, how could I miss her? She abandoned me, and I was not important enough for her to take to her next life. Is there any worse situation than being abandoned by one's own mother?" Acute feelings of helplessness compounded with sadness, anguish, and anger settled on her like an enormous weight. She was left with a feeling of numbness and a heavy heart. She described feeling as though she were in the middle of a dense fog. Dull headaches invaded her brain, and it was as if nothing in her life had any importance. Apparently, she was suffering from depression.

A few years after Betty's mother left, a rumor started in the family that her mother had met a man with whom she had a child. Betty remembers the day she received the news as one of the saddest of her life. She decided that from that day forward her mother was dead. Her grandmother unofficially adopted her granddaughter. Betty's grandmother was herself an illegitimate child. Betty's great-grandmother had given her illegitimate daughter up for adoption. When Betty's great-grandfather died, his daughter was only thirteen years old. The widowed mother enrolled her daughter in an institute of *Kisang*. When Betty's grandmother was fifteen years old, she became pregnant by Betty's grandfather, an aristocrat, who was married and already had two children. Betty's grandmother, as a concubine, gave birth to three children: a daughter and two sons. Betty's grandfather did not want his children to be illegitimate, so he registered their birth certificates with his original family. Thus, legally, Betty's grandmother did not have a home or children of her own. Betty's grandmother was barely thirty-five years old when Betty's grandfather died. She, as a concubine or unofficial wife, became a widow.

Betty's father was also an orphan and his family also belonged to the aristocratic class. His father was a high-ranking government officer. His mother died when he was two years old while giving birth to his younger sister. He was the middle child of three siblings, having both an older and a younger sister. The children were raised by their stepmother. His father died when he was fourteen years old, and his stepmother became the children's legal guardian. Betty's maternal grandfather had known Betty's father since he was young. The grandfather was impressed by her father's intelligence and his determination to succeed. Her grandfather kept an eye on him throughout his adolescence, and eventually Betty's father became a son-in-law to Betty's grandfather. Within a year of his marriage to Betty's mother, the grandfather died unexpectedly; a minor infection had progressed to blood poisoning. He died a few weeks later. Thus Betty's father became an orphan again. Betty believed that she was also fated to become an orphan. She believed she had received the genes for being an orphan from both sides of her family.

Betty's grandmother expected Betty to be a good student. She admired people who had good brains and achieved academically. She was very proud of her sons' intelligence and high academic achievements. However, the grandmother did not respect Betty's mother's intelligence. She often said that Betty's mother was not intelligent and was more interested in playing than studying. She also respected Betty's father's intelligence and his academic achievement. Based on her grandmother's views, Betty came to idealize her father and during her adolescence had fantasies of her father tutoring her in English. Betty's grandmother had always treated her like a grown-up person. She shared her anguish with Betty about not being able to have an opportunity to study, to become a professional person.

"If I were a man," she said, "I could have been a very successful person. In our culture, men have been given opportunities to work and earn money; women have no opportunity unless they become professionals. To become a professional woman is more important than becoming a housewife who must depend on her husband and later on her children." Thus, Betty became an excellent student and attended the most prestigious schools in Korea from junior high school through graduate school. Betty chose chemistry as her major in college and was one of the few female students in her class. During college she was totally immersed in her studies. She vigorously suppressed any temptation to date. For her, falling in love would lead to marriage, and marriage would lead to tragedy and even death. She did not care about her appearance. Her focus was on competing with male students academically rather than having personal relationships with them.

Betty began graduate school in Korea but soon realized that she could not have a fair chance at success because she was a woman. She wanted to be in a place where she would be accepted on merit, not on gender or connections. She was eventually accepted at a university in a Midwestern city in the United States. Upon arrival here, she found life to be stressful. Her difficulties with the English language accentuated her sense of inferiority and insecurity. She claimed that she could not express her ideas freely in the new language. Back home in Korea, she did not have to verbalize what she knew. She was understood to be intelligent whether she spoke up or not. Moreover, women were discouraged from displaying their knowledge. In her upbringing, intellectual capacity was highly admired, and she was determined to challenge the cultural value of male superiority. In the United States, she felt intellectually inferior and it took a long time for her to adapt to the new culture. Nevertheless, she earned a Ph.D. in biochemistry and moved to a prestigious university in the northeast where she accepted a postdoctoral fellowship at a cancer research center. Eventually, she got a job in a university as a researcher.

Betty was well aware that her life was unbalanced. Her life had been absorbed by work and study. She wanted more out of life and decided to seek professional help. She had undergone psychoanalytical psychotherapy with an American male analyst for few years prior to coming to see me.

Deeper Understanding

In her lifetime, Betty had experienced great losses. Even though these losses were traumatic, real mourning followed by a meaningful resolution had never taken place. This was so in part because her parents had disappeared from her life rather than dying a natural death in her presence. Lack of mourning had very serious consequences and she suffered from melancholia. It might seem that Betty's many losses were circumstantial, but if we examine them on a deeper level, these losses appear to have been unconsciously determined. Her melancholia was also determined by a lifelong sense of inferiority.

From the standpoint of traditional Korean society, being a female destined one to a place of inferiority. From Betty's grandmother's point of view, being a female destined one to tragedy. To be free from that destiny meant becoming a professional woman and becoming financially independent. The grandmother's inferiority, on a deeper level, stemmed from being an illegitimate child who had been abandoned by her mother. Becoming a *Kisang* and subsequently becoming a concubine to a rich aristocrat was automatically to be an inferior being. Legally she could not claim the status of mother or wife. Her grandmother's deep sense of inferiority, as well as her ego-ideal of emancipation through becoming a professional, were transmitted to Betty. Betty had also been abandoned by her mother just as her grandmother before her. Thus, she and her grandmother came to mirror each other's sorrow and inferiority. Betty's mother was an illegitimate child like her own mother and was legally adopted by her father's legitimate family. Grandmother, mother, and daughter were all officially or unofficially adopted by other families.

Betty's emigration to the United States was another form of an adoption, and it stirred up a deeply rooted sense of inferiority and personal anguish. Betty's father was abandoned by his parents through their early deaths, when he was left in the care of his stepmother at the age of fourteen. Betty's grandmother's ego-ideal was transmitted to Betty's psyche, and as a result she overemphasized intellectual capacity and development while denying femininity and repressing her sexual desires. Intellectual achievements for Betty were a means to gaining phallic power, and she tried to win men over by her achievements.

Betty was told that her father wept when his second daughter was born. On a superficial level, these tears might have been about failing to produce a son to fulfill his duty to his ancestors. On a deeper level, the tears were a reenactment of his mother's death as a consequence of his younger sister's birth; he suffered from his unconscious guilt. During his adolescence, he lost his father, which may have precipitated a sense of oedipal victory. Perhaps a death sentence was imposed by his inner tribunal even before the South Korean government executed him. In Betty's memory, her grandmother had strong negative reactions when each granddaughter was born although in telling this to me, she excluded herself from the description. The grandmother had three other granddaughters from her two sons. Betty's grandmother seemed to be projecting herself onto her granddaughters and, in so doing, predicting that their lives would also be tragic. The grandmother treated each of them as though they were second-class citizens like herself. Betty felt as if she had a different grandmother than her female cousins. Her grandmother silently discouraged Betty from becoming a feminine girl. She emphasized that it is not an admirable life for a woman to be married and dependent on her husband or on her children.

As her grandmother's ideal mirror image, Betty pursued her professional life aggressively and succeeded in a predominantly male profession. In spite of her success, she had endlessly questioned whether or not she was as capable as the men in her field. In addition, her sense of her inferiority might relate to her dead sister. Her grandmother had often brought up the idea that if her dead sister were still alive, she would have turned out to be a real beauty. The grandmother had said, "She was really beautiful even in her infancy," and Betty experienced a pang of jealousy each time she heard this. The grandmother's feelings of guilt over her granddaughter's death might have led to an idealization of the dead. In any case, Betty could not compete with this "perfect angel," her dead sister. "I have been inferior to the male sex, and to the female sex as well," she said. "It seems to me that my inferiority is also my destiny. I can't win, can I?"

Emigrating to the United States accentuated her sense of inferiority; her inability to speak the new language made her feel stupid and coming from an impoverished native country further diminished her self-worth. In her childhood, intellectual capacity was much admired, and it became her way of challenging the cultural value of male superiority. Yet, in the United States, she could no longer feel that she was an intellectually superior person because of her language difficulties. Her ideal self-image was shattered, and her narcissism was deeply wounded.

Betty's grandmother had been known as a stoic, rigid, overly rational, obsessive, and often paranoid person. She was certainly not fun or playful, rather a very critical person with high expectations from life. Contrary to her grandmother, Betty's mother was playful with lots of humor. Her temperament seemed to be emotional and impulsive, qualities that her grandmother could not accept. When her mother's business failed, the grandmother blamed the daughter, seeing impulsivity and emotionality as the cause of her failure. Betty had tried not to be emotional even though her true nature, she believes, is both emotional and often impulsive. She wondered how her grandmother had been able to attract her grandfather with such a stoic and rigid posture. It was unthinkable that her grandmother was once a *Kisang*, whose job was to attract men and to entertain them.

Kang Hyun Hoi, at the tea-salon Madonna, in the novel, was treated by society, especially by Professor Choi, as if she were an ordinary prostitute. Betty identified with Ms. Kang's rage against a society that looked down on her. When Professor Choi referred to her as if she were a prostitute, her rage caused her to kill him. Betty's rage against her parents and society was in many ways comparable to Ms. Kang's, and as a result, she found an outlet for her bottled-up anger through her identification with Ms. Kang, who killed Professor Choi. Even Ms. Kang's lover, Mr. Lee, expressed his uneasy feelings about Kang's job. He advised her to work at a more socially acceptable job as a college graduate. She replied, "When you are hungry, your priority is to eat to fill your stomach; everything else is less important."

Kang protested against Lee and the Korean social hierarchy: "I am thinking about closing the tea-salon, not because of your advice, but because of the poor business." She thus proclaimed that she was not the kind of person to follow anyone's orders or even advice. Betty experienced her own emotional catharsis through Kang's protest against the established society. Betty had absorbed her grandmother's wishes like a sponge absorbing water. Her grandmother's repressed femininity, repressed sexual desires, and emphasis on academic achievement had been successfully transmitted, and she in turn had repressed her sexuality and denied her femininity.

Femininity meant being helpless, dependent, stupid, and even dangerous. From her point of view, her mother's tragic life was the result of helpless femininity and uncontrollable sexual desire. This brought disgrace on the entire family, making her child an orphan. Betty's only focus had been her intellectual pursuits. She believed that she could compete with men intellectually and thereby win them over. It compelled her to study the sciences, and ultimately she earned a doctorate in her field.

One of Betty's dreams reflected this issue.

> In the dream I was standing at the edge of the cliff. I had to cross the river to go to the other side. There was no means to cross the river. A willow tree stood near me. My grandmother suddenly appeared, and she took a branch of the willow tree and flew over the river like Tarzan. I took the branch of the tree, like my grandmother before me, and flew across the river.

She painted her grandmother not only as if she were a male, but also as though she were a very masculine mythical figure. The dream expressed very well her identification with her grandmother.

The Course of Treatment

Betty was a pleasant-looking woman in her forties of medium height and weight who appeared to be younger than her stated age. She wore very little makeup. Her hair was short and she wore a navy blue pantsuit. Overall, she looked professional. The reason she gave for the consultation was that her grandmother had passed away a few months earlier, and she was worried about her reaction to her grandmother's death, that is, her lack of feelings of loss. She claimed that her grandmother had been the most important person in her life. She wanted to understand what was going on inside her mind. After three consultations, she decided to go enter psychoanalytical therapy, and I began seeing her in three-times-a-week psychoanalysis, a treatment that lasted for seven years.

No sooner had she decided to undergo analysis with me than she expressed a concern: "I wish that this experience will be like my past one with a Korean male psychiatrist. I saw Dr. C only three times for consultation. It was a very painful experience. I could not talk about my family history because I was very ashamed of my background. I felt that he would look down on me." When I asked her what aspect of her history made her feel so ashamed, she replied, "My mother had many debts to members of *gye*. Those members used to accuse me of being the daughter of a thief. My mother disgraced the family by having another life with a man. That was unacceptable to my family. As matter of fact, it was a big family secret. No one talked about her, her man and her two children with him. When any one of my friends asked me about my mother, I told them that she was dead. It was very uneasy for me to lie like that. It angered me that she put me in the position of being a daughter of a disgraced woman and a thief. After all, I was an abandoned child. I could not go back to Dr. C."

After the first consultation with Dr. C, she went to an American male psychoanalyst, Dr. N, with whom she started twice-weekly psychoanalytic psychotherapy, and later three-times-weekly psychoanalysis. In her own words: "It was easier to talk about my story. I did not feel ashamed about my background. I didn't feel he looked down on me no matter what I said about my shameful stuff, my family history. It was a good experience for me." The following passage by Krapf (1955) elegantly captures the essence of this situation:

> The superego that corresponds to the first language is so prohibited that it allows no access to the id impulses it opposes and one must approach the neurosis through the second language, which has more permissive "new superego" if one is to bring about discharge of repressed traumatic neurosis. In other words, the use of second language must not necessarily be regarded as an undesirable resistance, but is occasionally a good (useful) transference phenomenon. (345)

During her analysis with Dr. N, Betty began to have relationships with men. She had a very passionate love affair with a married man. That secret love affair lasted two years until he relocated to another city. When this happened, Betty nearly had a breakdown. From the beginning, she had been very sure the relationship would go nowhere, and she had no intention of breaking up his marriage. But when he moved away from her, her heart totally crumbled, and she collapsed and took to her bed. Her relationship with the married man seemed to mirror that of Ms. Kang's affair with Mr. Lee in the novel, and in her real life she identified with her grandmother's experience. Betty was torn between her inner desires and Korean cultural prohibitions. Her experience of love crossed all boundaries of illicitness including the most basic of all: oedipal love. She compared the delicious feeling of love in the book with her own experience. In both cases, there was an intense love in spite of equally intense prohibition.

In the early period of the treatment, toward the end of the first year, which happened to be in December, Betty started to talk about her life during the Korean War. She said that it had not been easy to talk about her childhood with her previous analyst: "When I have talked about it, somehow, it did not seem to reach my heart. I used to talk about it from my head. I knew there was something more to deal with. It was about my father. It was not real for me to believe he was dead, or that he was executed. I have walked with him so many times from his jail cell to the place where he would be executed. I have tried to feel what he would feel when he was walking the corridor with the jail keeper." At this point, Betty was in tears, saying: "I feel numb, my body is running away from me."

She recalled North Korean soldiers and South Korean soldiers shooting at each other across the valley where she and her mother were hiding in a cousin's basement. By that point, she was numbed by bullets flying around the front yard, the sounds of bombing, the sound of sirens, and the midday silence. In between sirens, she rushed out to the front yard to her playhouse. She cooked passionately with very colorful summer flowers. Apparently, she was hungry, very hungry. In the midst of war, most Koreans were suffering from starvation. Hunger is long remembered as one of life's most painful experiences.

Back to the novel, Ms. Kang had fallen in love with Mr. Lee, a married man, just like the man Betty had found. She and I had worked on this issue over many sessions. I had come to understand that her love affairs with married men, and her longings for unavailable men, were her way of keeping her father alive. Mourning for her father had never been completed. Perhaps it had not even begun at the time she first came to see me.

Betty usually spoke Korean in the sessions. But at times she spoke in English, especially when she was angry. She felt intense anger and contempt toward Korean people, especially Korean men: "They are all castrated by their mothers. They seem to have power and high self-esteem, but it is just what is given to them by the patriarchal society. It is disgusting to accept that you are a woman, so you are inferior to men. I was very rebellious to that idea. I could not simply accept it. With my intelligence, my ability, and my achievement, I wanted to have a fair competition with men. For me, having a penis does not make a man superior to a woman. Korean women, or more likely Korean mothers, own their sons, so they possess the power of men. Korean mothers are more powerful than men." This statement and others like it reveal that Betty had identity issues. Her grandmother's unhappy life has deeply influenced Betty's sense of herself. She seems to have been competing with men on merit rather than on gender difference.

I have already discussed how in traditional Korean society, the male gender is superior. Betty has violently fought against that belief system, and as a result she had to leave her country for Western society. She later realized that women in American society were also struggling to achieve equality. She has often had the experience that they were less liberated than she herself was. She said: "I was very surprised that women in America were not as independent as I thought they were. They claimed equality without being ready to be fully responsible. Well, in some way they still want to be taken care of." She has worked through this issue and as her treatment progressed, she became much softer, gentler, and more feminine, maintaining her strength and independence in her own way. As her self-esteem has grown, her anger toward Korean men has diminished.

In the transference, she has progressed through several phases. In the initial period, I became the grandmother whom she both respected and feared, the grandmother she tried to please and whose expectations she tried to meet. Within the first few weeks of treatment, she reported a dream: "The dream occurred out of space. It was dark, a pitch black dark. A section of a floating bridge was hanging in the air, and I was crossing the bridge. But a very strong wind was blowing, and as a result, the bridge was shaking violently. I was scared to death. Suddenly my grandmother's face appeared. So I became courageous and started to walk toward the other side of the bridge, but it was almost impossible to step forward." Her grandmother seemed to have been her life force. Any change for Betty was influenced by her. She claimed that I was trying to mold her like her grandmother had. She often accused me of violating her freedom. She manifested rage against me. She did not think I was doing my job. She questioned my ability as an analyst. "Dr. N has never made me feel this way," she claimed.

Following a session in which she expressed violent anger, she typically became quite depressed: "I was afraid of coming here today, it reminded me that I used to be very worried and hesitant to come home after I made my grandmother upset over something. She had a tendency to misinterpret my intentions. She insisted I was thinking in a certain way. She often surprised me with this. She was totally paranoid, wasn't she?"

Another aspect of transference was that she was skeptical about my ability as an analyst, whether I was as good as an American analyst or a male analyst. Even if she was angry with the traditional Korean belief system, the concept of male superiority was deeply ingrained in her unconscious. I pointed out to her that she seemed to project her own insecurity as a woman onto me and to devalue me. She also projected her devalued mother onto me. She insisted that I was too feminine and too concerned with my appearance to be a truly intellectual woman: "It made me mistrust you." Femininity for her did not coexist with intelligence. The traditional Korean society seemed to have completely occupied her inner world. Her striving to be free and independent seemed to be fighting against her ideals and Korean traditionalism.

She experienced me as a mistrusting, unworthy person. She often expressed her skepticism as to whether she could work with me or not. Her deep-seated anger and mistrust toward her mother was transferred onto me, and she has frequently expressed her doubt concerning her therapy. "Are you really a certified analyst?" she asked. Her skepticism about my ability seemed to be a projection of a deep-rooted traditional Korean woman's devalued self. Her transference had vacillated between the intelligent, independent, powerful, but sexually repressed grandmother and the emotional, impulsive, helpless, dependent mother. She claimed that in life her goal had been not to become like her mother. However, by the time analysis ended, she was able to see her mother positively: her femininity, her sexual freedom in spite of traditional values, and her courage, even though it seemed to be based on ignorance.

It took a very long time for her to be free from traditional Confucian values. She reported a dream: "In the dream, my grandmother and I were sitting next to each other. My grandmother was wearing a very traditional Korean wedding gown." Her grandmother's status was finally elevated as a respectable Korean woman who had gained her own identity. Betty's grandmother had been her mirror, and so her own self-worth as a woman was elevated as well.

By the time analysis terminated, she was involved with a man. He was an available man, but she was determined not to marry him even though he was very compatible with her. "I will not have a conventional life. I have worked very hard all my life to have freedom. I just want to have a good relationship, and I have one now," she said.

CONCLUDING REMARKS

I have discussed two individuals that exemplify the transformation of Korean women from traditional Confucian society to modern Korea. These two individuals, a fictional character and my patient, lived in two different generations. Kang Hyun Hoi lived through the beginning of the Korean modernization during the Japanese colonial period and the Korean War. She confronted traditional Korean values vehemently, but ultimately her pursuit waned. The current of the culture in which she lived was too strong to prevail against. She was exhausted. She gave up fighting and succumbed to the reality of traditional Korean values. Betty lived through the period in which Korean society was actively modernizing: politically, economically, and culturally. It was not unusual for women to receive a higher education during this period. In a sense, Betty's striving for academic achievement and professional ambition was a reflection of a modernizing Korean society. Perhaps from another perspective, Betty's striving and ambition were heavily motivated by her desire to be free from traditional values. Betty is not only a product of these traditional values in which she was inferior; she was also a granddaughter, or the unofficial daughter, of a concubine who was a *Kisang*, the lowest class in the traditional Korean hierarchy. Her grandmother's ideal was reflected in Betty's psyche. She had been striving to achieve this ideal, and thus, her life did not seem to be her own. Her purpose in life was in liberating her grandmother from Korean tradition. She was merely her grandmother's shadow until she began to gain her own identity through her analysis.

It was also in her analysis that she was able to see her mother objectively, not just through her grandmother's eyes. Her mother's femininity and her pursuit of her own desires, which Betty had originally despised, had come to have a very different meaning. While her masculine protest faded, her feminine self evolved. Simultaneously, as her idealization of Western culture became more objective, she started seeing Korean culture in a different light. Ultimately, Betty was able to separate from her grandmother as well as being able to free herself from traditional values. As she became psychologically free from her, she was able to mourn her beloved grandmother.

11

The Food-Sex Equation: Psychoanalytic Reflections on Three Sizzling Movies from the Far East

Salman Akhtar and Monisha Nayar

Anything that walks, swims, crawls, or flies with its back to heaven is edible.

Chinese proverb

A major characteristic of the primary process that dominates the system Unconscious (Freud, 1900) is its fluidity. One object can readily come to represent another and part becomes equated with the whole. Such lability of cathexis allows for condensation and telescoping not only of thought content but also of developmental conflicts from different phases and libidinal excitements emanating from different erotogenic zones. Myriad illustrations of this exist but none catches the clinician's attention with greater force than the unconscious equation of eating with having sex. The fusion of the two gives rise to juicy celebration of sensuality under fortunate circumstances. Sucking and aromatic pleasures associated with food and sex coalesce and enhance each other. Oral sex gains greater cathectic investment and comes to serve diverse instinctual aims. A penis in mouth allows one to draw oral supplies from father and performing cunnilingus ("eating") permits devouring of the mother while simultaneously giving her pleasure from the very organ (mouth) that had been the beneficiary of her indulgent breast early in life. Zonal blurring leads to mouth-vagina and penis-nipple symbolism. Oral impregnation fantasies (Freud, 1908), instead of mobilizing anxiety and defenses, become a source of playful exchange between the partners. In the context of a deep object relationship, all this contributes to the lover's body turning into a "geography of personal meanings" (Kernberg, 1991).

When things go awry, however, the proximity of food and sex in the mind can get diabolically aggressivized. Ingestion of food then becomes tantamount to violation of one's boundaries and therefore leads to its rejection by self-induced or reflexive vomiting. Hostile intrusiveness finds expression through what Salman Rushdie (1989) has called "pitiless hospitality" toward others. The biting component of eating gets highly cathected and a secret idealization of vampirism prevails. Transgression of the incest boundary now surfaces as the breaking of all religious and societal taboos on what is edible and what is not. Gluttony replaces the orgy of genital sex and the mind becomes crowded with cannibalistic fantasies.

In this chapter we seek to highlight such libidinal and aggressive fusion of eating and sexuality and the various psychostructural and dynamic constellations that result from it. With the help of one movie each from China, Japan, and Korea, we will flesh out the developmental origins of such condensation and its unconscious uses. While conceptualization of this sort is inevitably linked to the "drive psychology of psychoanalysis" (Pine, 1988), our effort would be to locate such mental goings-on in their proper relational context whether they belong to early childhood of the protagonists in these movies or to their current life.

SOME CAVEATS

First and foremost, we must acknowledge the inevitable element of personal bias in the selection of the three movies discussed in this contribution. As cinephiles ("movie buffs," in North American colloquialism), we were familiar with a large number of movies from China, Japan, and Korea, but we selected *Tampopo* (Japan, 1985), *Dumplings* (China, 2004), and *301/302* (Korea, 1996) for their evocative qualities, plot, and deft use of cinematic techniques. That in making a judgment of this sort of subjective factors play a role goes without saying.

Second, we are psychoanalysts and not social anthropologists with specialization in Far Eastern cultures. Our emphasis in discussing these movies is therefore essentially psychoanalytic. Though our own, admittedly limited, knowledge of their cultural matrix and our consultations with colleagues and friends from the countries involved has helped us, the possibility that we might have missed some finer cultural nuances certainly exists.

Third, we do not possess knowledge about the personal backgrounds of the writers and directors of these movies. On the one hand, we are aware that a movie is different from a poem or painting in being a final creative product to which many, many individuals (including those with predominantly financial interests) have contributed and therefore lacking knowledge of its writers' and directors' background histories might not diminish an interpretive effort to any significant degree. On the other hand, factors of a personal nature do play a role, especially if there is a trajectory of movies the writer and/or the director have made with similar themes. Keeping their professional and developmental background in mind can illuminate matters in their instances.

Finally, in focusing upon psychodynamics of the characters in these movies, we might initially appear to give short shift to the political undertones of the plot. Being firm believers in the "principle of multiple function" (Waelder, 1936), we do bring this dimension in toward the end of the chapter and thus urge the reader to bear with us until then. It is with these caveats that our discussion of these three movies should be approached.

TABLE MANNERS, FOOD, AND SEXUAL BLOSSOMING: *TAMPOPO* FROM JAPAN

Directed by Juzo Itami, this lark of a movie bustles with hilarity even when it deals with the serious matters of rivalry, love, and coming of age. *Tampopo* (New Century Productions, 1985) is the eponymous story of a young Japanese widow trying to break through in the highly competitive market of Japanese-style noodle shops (hybrid between a diner and a fast-food joint). The movie deals with the intricacies and intrigues of this cutthroat business while also slyly smuggling in how, in the course of such adventure, Tampopo (literally, dandelion in Japanese) finds romance and love.

The movie uses food, cooking, and eating as symbols of varied psychic contents and as conveyers of traditions from one generation to the next. Built as a collage, the movie weaves different strands together into a composite whole of meaning and excitement. The first four scenes, though seemingly disjointed from each other, set the groundwork for the gestalt that emerges with the unfolding of the movie. The opening scene shows a flamboyantly dressed, mob-connected man coming to see a movie with his moll on his arms. As he takes his seat on the very front row of the theater, two waiters set up a table in front of him covered with white linen. Soon they bring champagne and hors d'oeuvres for him and his lady friend to enjoy. As he lifts his glass, though, he hears the crunching of potato chips by a man sitting a couple of rows behind him. Livid with rage, the mobster grabs the man by his neck and threatens to cut his head off if he makes any noise eating potato chips while the movie is on. There is no mistaking at this point that we are in for a lot of fun!

The second scene shows an old man painstakingly instructing a hurried youngster in the art of eating noodles: "First observe the entire bowl, next caress its contents with chopsticks, then gently pick up the pork slices and dip them in the soup on the other end of the bowl, finally apologize to the pork before eating it, and so on." Handled in this manner, eating becomes a sacred dance expressing wonder, humility, and gratitude for the offerings of the material world. Being taught how to eat in a way that will enhance and deepen the sensual pleasure of the activity, the young man becomes the recipient of what Blos (1985) has called the "father's blessing": the door to erotic mysteries is now open to his generation.

In the scene that soon follows, we encounter a similar "teaching session" vis-à-vis the art of serving food. A handsome young man, Goro, is seen explaining to Tampopo the steps essential for being a good hostess. Tampopo's goal is to be an outstanding noodle-maker but Goro insists that cooking well is not enough. One also has to know how to serve the customers well. He tells her to cast a loving glance at the food that she is bringing on the tray and, as she is placing the food down on the counter, to shift her eyes to look at the customer whom she is serving. Since she cannot touch her customers, her glance becomes the caress that highlights the maternal aspect of her nourishing gesture and subliminally kindles the unconscious "infant-at-breast" memories in the customer's mind.

The fourth "opening scene" is set in an upscale restaurant where society women are shown taking pride in eating quietly. They are shocked to encounter a man who slurps his noodles with all imaginable sorts of grunts and noises. Close-ups of noodles sliding noiselessly in an eel-like manner underscore the feminine defense against the public display of sensual (oral) pleasure, while simultaneously nudging the audience to think of them as performing fellatio. Yet another sojourn into irony is evident when a newly recruited office intern upstages the senior management by displaying a far superior knowledge while ordering food at a gourmet French restaurant. A generational "game" is present here, too, except with the reversal of the young and the old.

Following such forays in the values of knowledge and etiquette of eating and serving food, the next logical step is to move into the art of cooking, per se. Here we see Tampopo struggling, visiting other noodle shops to sample their dishes, and, in a funny, if a bit transparent, scene, "stealing" recipes from an unsuspecting garrulous chef.

This trident of cooking, serving, and eating turns into the Cupid's arrow as Pikusen, a traveling truck driver with a penchant for interior decoration of all things, steps into the drama. Unlike Goro, who instructs Tampopo in the art of serving food and memorizing the orders of various customers, Pikusen puts greater emphasis upon the appearance of Tampopo's noodle shop. This sparks rivalry between the two men, who end up in a street brawl. Soon, however, they become friends and begin to cooperate in helping Tampopo. As this is happening, the camera cuts back to the mobster and his moll. Now, for the first time in the movie, we openly see the confluence of food and sex. These include highly erotic depictions of licking whipped cream off nipples, passing the yolk of a half-fried egg back and forth between their mouths while kissing, and stimulating their buttocks with a live fish and then cooking it. The ground is thus set for the coming synthesis of love (Goro) and sex (the mobster) on the masculine end of the equation. And we do see Goro look with charmed eyes at Tampopo for the first time.

As its feminine counterpart, Tampopo is also shown to blossom. Her business is booming. She can effortlessly rattle off the menu and the orders placed by her customers. More importantly, she is dressed up in the formal attire of a hostess; paradoxically, her covered body heightens the awareness of what is hidden by these clothes. The noodle shop is now decorated and named after her. The dandelion has finally turned into a rose.

ETERNAL YOUTH, FOOD, AND OEDIPAL JEALOUSY: *DUMPLINGS* FROM CHINA

The movie *Dumplings* (directed by Fruit Chan, Fortissimo Films, 2004) was originally the part of a trilogy of short films called *Three Extremes* (2002). It was later expanded to feature length and in that form has been a widely recognized phenomenon. Before going into the formal cinematic devices used in it for underscoring its dynamic content, it is useful to lay out its "story" in some detail. Essentially, this revolves around Ching Li, a fading Hong Kong television starlet in her early forties married to a philandering businessman. Mrs. Li, as she is frequently referred to in the movie, seems very concerned about her diminishing attractiveness and wishes to reclaim her husband's attention by increasing the youthfulness of her looks. She dresses impeccably in the appealing colors of orange and red and her clothes are always formfitting. Still worried, she turns to Aunt Mei, who prepares dumplings that are known for their skin-enhancing properties. Curiously named "Aunt," Mei is only thirty years old, or at least that is what she claims to be her age. Living in a small apartment in the poor section of town, Mei comes across as carefree, confident, and comfortable with her body eroticism.

There is tension between Mrs. Li and Mei from the very first time they meet. Mrs. Li arrives at the shabby tenement building and appears strikingly distinct in social class from the surroundings. Mei's apartment is cluttered and unclean. Upon Mrs. Li's request, Mei serves her celebrated dumplings but not without revealing their main ingredient: aborted fetuses obtained from a hospital in mainland China, across the border. Mrs. Li is shocked and runs out of the apartment. However, driven by her desire to enhance her beauty, she soon returns and agrees to sample one of the unusual offerings. We see her eat it gingerly, so to speak, but then gradually pick up pace and become increasingly comfortable with the culinary adventure.

Meanwhile, Mrs. Li's husband continues with his dalliances. He too resorts to consuming fertilized chicken eggs, with ill-formed though live fetuses, in order to bolster his departing youth and virility. Sexual "quickies" with maids and masseuses keep him amused and occupied. Nonetheless, Mrs. Li is desperate to arouse his erotic interest. She seeks ever stronger potions to rejuvenate her fading youth. She finds a willing partner in Mei, who informs her that a more "advanced" fetus would be a more potent ingredient in the beauty enhancing dumplings. Setting aside her usual trips to the mainland, Mei reluctantly decides to resume her earlier profession as an underground abortionist. An opportunity soon arises when a pregnant teenager arrives at Mei's threshold, accompanied by her mother. Mei performs the abortion and obtains a fetus that she preserves carefully and later serves to Mrs. Li in a new batch of dumplings. Mrs. Li, who is initially overjoyed with this new concoction, and the aesthetic fruit it soon bears, is alarmed by finding a foul-smelling rash on her body. We are told that this might be due to the fact that the fetus she consumed had resulted from an incestuous father-daughter relationship. The dumpling was further cursed, it seems, by the fact that the girl died of excessive bleeding following the abortion conducted by Mei.

Meanwhile, Mr. Li has continued his extramarital affairs. He not only has had a voluptuous one-night stand with Mei, of all people, but has been carrying on a sustained affair with his young secretary, who becomes pregnant. When Mrs. Li learns of this, she is enraged. She turns to Mei for advice but finds to her chagrin that Mei has vanished without a trace. An incensed and vengeful Mrs. Li now decides to take matters into her own hands. She approaches the young secretary to undergo an abortion. She offers a substantial amount of money for the fetus. The unsuspecting young girl agrees and we see the bloody abortion take place under the diligent and watchful eye of Mrs. Li. And, just as the movie reaches its last scene, we see Mrs. Li carve out the young fetus to prepare her own special dumplings!

While the movie is not for the soft-hearted and can make one feel queasy, it never descends to being merely gory or shocking. The mindless chomping of the dumplings containing human fetuses—hardly a topic of dinner-table conversation—is mostly depicted in an ironic manner. It is intended to convey the extent to which Mrs. Li (and others like her) are willing to go in the search of eternal youth. It is as if one can do anything to maintain one's physical appearance. Behind such surface narcissism is the deeper issue of the human desire to reverse the flow of time. Childhood can thus be relived, youth rediscovered, bodily changes denied, and impending death repudiated. The search for potions and recipes that would make one youthful forever is universal; it serves as a defense against the helplessness in face of aging and becoming older, a defense that can acquire grotesque qualities in the setting of pathological narcissism (Kernberg, 1980). All this is clearly evident in *Dumplings*. Mr. Li eats raw egg fetuses to stay virile. Mrs. Li devours human fetuses to stay attractive. And the swift-footed Mei hardly appears to be the "aunt" that she is supposed to be.

The pressure to stop the passage of time and even reverse it serves more than a narcissistic agenda, however. There are oedipal issues lurking here as well. Here it might not be out of place to cite Chasseguet-Smirgel's (1984) proposal that the Oedipus complex is essentially a tragedy of time. In other words, parents are born before the child and choose each other as romantic and sexual partners; the child is simply born too late. This temporal lag is the essence of the oedipal trauma and there is no way around it except to politely bear it and wait for one's own erotic life to begin in actuality. When this developmental step is not taken, hatred of time persists and generational differences cannot be accepted. The taboo against cross-generational sexuality is then readily defied. In *Dumplings*, the married Mr. Li's sexual peccadilloes with his young employees and with "Aunt" Mei both bear the stamp of such incestuous transgression. Mrs. Li's asking help from an "aunt" to enhance her sexual life with her husband constitutes another triangle with oedipal overtones. The vindictive act of her arranging the abortion of Mr. Li's baby in his young secretary's womb depicts sexual jealousy across generations, so to speak. Her sexual aggressiveness with her husband after eating a male fetus betrays phallic and negative oedipal aspirations. The fact that some hanky-panky is going on throughout the movie is well captured in Mei's encounter with the custom officers (the superego) while she is secretly bringing aborted fetuses from the mainland China into Hong Kong.

Fascinatingly, in this movie replete with images of aborted fetuses, the two main characters (Mrs. Li and Aunt Mei) are both childless. One wonders if they are trying to remain "girls" instead of becoming "women." The question about the unconscious envy of childbearing women in their minds also comes up. The fact that Mrs. Li gets enraged when Mr. Li impregnates his secretary lends support to this line of thinking. Besides fueling such oedipal jealousy, the destructive envy extends in a more fundamental direction: a malignant reversal of the role of parents and children. Ordinarily, it is parents who provide literal and metaphorical nourishment to their offspring. In *Dumplings*, however, it is parents who are living off their (yet to be viable) "children"; the younger generation has literally become the fodder for the older generation's ruthless appetite for narcissism and sexuality.

The narcissistic, temporal, oedipal, and existential conundrums in this elixir-of-youth fable are also evident in the manner in which the movie is shot. The camera angles are often uneven and the frames erratic. Often the characters do not stand in the center of the shot and, at times, even walk out of the frame leaving the screen rather like a womb that has prematurely lost its inhabitant. On the other hand, the scenes of Mrs. Li in the shower behind a glass door and in a bathtub bring the images of a fetus in a womb to the mind. And yet, a sense of incompleteness, embodied by the house being remodeled with plastic tarps all over the place, pervades the movie. There is, as a result, a peculiar tension between claustrophobia and emptiness in the movie.

SEXUAL ABUSE, FOOD, AND SADOMASOCHISM: *301/302* FROM KOREA

Chul-Soo Park's outrageous *301/302* (Arrow Release New Line Presentation, 1996) depicts the story of two women living across the hallway from each other in a high rise building. The movie is titled after the two apartments in which they live. One of them, Yoon-Hee Kim, is a fledgling writer who pens advice columns for women's magazines on sex and food. The other, Song-Hee Kang, who, at the opening of the film, moves in the apartment across the hallway, is a self-designated food expert. Their differences are, however, not limited to their vocations. Yoon-Hee is intensely shy and reclusive to the extent of being schizoid. Song-Hee, on the other hand, is effervescent, talkative to the point of intrusiveness, and, in her choice of words, crude. Yoon-Hee lives on little sips of water, avoiding food. Song-Hee is not only a consummate cook but also relishes eating and feeding others. Yoon-Hee has never been married. Song-Hee is recently divorced and claims to have a lively sexual appetite. Their apartments reflect their passions. Yoon-Hee's décor is spartan and the living space is filled with books. Song-Hee's apartment is a recently remodeled space that resembles a restaurant kitchen with a supersize refrigerator and stove with a larger counter for eating and serving food. The movie tells the story of their evolving and complex relationship, which ends in a surprising and disturbing manner. With the help of carefully placed flashbacks, it also tells a story of the two women's lives before they meet each other.

Yoon-Hee, we learn, has grown up in a butcher shop owned by her stepfather and mother. A congenial merchant who is popular in the neighborhood, the stepfather undergoes a transformation every night. His nightly nefarious activities include the unwelcome intrusion into his teenage stepdaughter's bedroom, where she is repeatedly raped and sodomized. As often happens (Escoll, 1999), Yoon-Hee's mother acts unaware of her daughter's anguish and does not rescue her; she is forever preoccupied with money. We see her repeatedly counting the day's income and running to the bank. Yoon-Hee's countenance reveals her inner pain and torment but seems to draw little attention from the mother. Yoon-Hee's only solace comes from her school studies and from playing a game of "hide-and-seek" with a younger neighborhood girl. The latter provides a turning point in Yoon-Hee's life that changes things forever. However, before describing this further, let us turn to Song-Hee for a moment.

Song-Hee's background is less fleshed out. At the very beginning of the movie, however, we learn of young Song-Hee, bragging about how her mother cooks fresh food for her each day despite all sorts of food items stored in the family's refrigerator. Food, as an important reality and metaphor in her background, is thus established. Her parents are never shown in the movie though there is a voice-over from the mother later in the course of the movie, and, to be sure, it pertains to food. We are privy to more information about Song Hee's adult life. She is married to a business executive, is sexually active, and enjoys cooking for her husband. She takes great efforts and puts a lot of thought in preparing sumptuous dishes and desperately longs for praise from him. He, however, becomes increasingly indifferent to her culinary overtures as the story unfolds. To their dog, Fluffy, however, he remains ever attentive, to the growing resentment of his wife. Her initial reaction to his growing indifference is to turn to food and we see her consume large quantities, thereby gaining weight and losing her shapely figure. But then something happens that changes the course of her life.

The turning points in Yoon-Hee and Song-Hee's lives involve death. For Yoon-Hee, the life-changing event occurs one night when an attempt to escape from her stepfather's sexual advances is mistaken by her young friend to be a game of hide-and-seek; this, in turn, leads the little girl to be locked up in the meat locker and freeze to death. When her body is discovered, the stepfather forces Yoon-Hee to chop the young friend's body up in little pieces. The gory scene adds to the violent and perverse undertone of the constant display of meat being cleaved and sold in the shop. The exact trajectory of Yoon-Hee's life from this mayhem to her life in apartment 302 is not shown in the movie. At the same time, her terrified and rigid countenance leaves little doubt about the lingering effects of this trauma. Yoon-Hee is a bundle of "no entry defenses" (Williams, 1997); she receives no visitors, refuses to pick up the phone when it rings, and is given to throwing up the little food she eats.

For Song-Hee, the life-changing event is constituted by the discovery of her husband's infidelity. Feeling already compromised in the marriage, she retaliates by killing the family dog and serving the canine stew to her unsuspecting husband. Not satisfied with this silent sadism, Song-Hee mockingly reveals to her husband that the stew contains his "most favorite thing" as the main ingredient. All hell then breaks loose and we see them undergoing a rather bloody divorce.

This brings the two protagonists to their respective apartments—namely, 301 and 302. Now their lives begin to coalesce in a sadomasochistic brew of bizarre compassion and benevolent violence. Song-Hee's antidote to her recently dissolved marriage is to renovate her apartment to a culinary hilt. She passes her days and nights cooking and eating until one day, in response to her encounter with the svelte and skinny Yoon-Hee, she decides to lose weight. Simultaneously, she begins to cook delicious meals and, following the usual custom, brings them to Yoon-Hee's apartment as a welcoming gift. However, Yoon-Hee throws the food away secretly. When Song-Hee finds this out, she is enraged. Now she takes it upon herself to "force-feed" Yoon-Hee to fatten her up and spoil her figure. In the process, Yoon-Hee reveals her shameful history, leading Song-Hee to acquire a much more sympathetic attitude toward her. This, too, not surprisingly, is expressed via food. Song-Hee decides to cook "soothing and comforting foods" for her newfound friend. Unfortunately, Yoon-Hee is unable to tolerate even this. She cannot allow anything to enter her. In fact, she herself wants to disappear from this world. Meanwhile, Song-Hee grows frustrated, as she finds herself running out of recipes and ingredients to offer Yoon-Hee. Both are at their rope's end.

In a final and macabre twist to their moving saga, Yoon-Hee comes up with a way out of the helplessness both face. She offers herself to be killed and cooked by Song-Hee who, in an act that combines mercy with cruelty, agrees. As the local police investigate Yoon-Hee's "disappearance," we see Song-Hee sitting down to a meal of meat stew.

It is at the juncture of such cannibalistic merger of the two main characters that their psychodynamic similarities and existential agendas become evident. It turns out that both Yoon-Hee and Song-Hee have suffered maternal neglect: Yoon-Hee's mother failed to note the sexual transgressions of her daughter's body. Song-Hee's mother often left her alone until late at night; the fact that a young Song-Hee is shown dressed only in her underwear while preparing food and waiting for her mother in the first scene of the movie speaks volumes to the maternal neglect she has suffered. Both Yoon-Hee and Song-Hee lacked biological fathers. Both came to a decisive moment in their lives around a "murder." In Yoon-Hee's case it was the accidental death of her young friend, followed by the hacking into pieces of her body. In Song-Hee's case, it was the ruthless killing of the family dog. While Song-Hee had been married before, the fact is that when they came together, they encountered each other as single women living alone.

The major areas of psychic conflict for the two women pertain to food and sex. Yoon-Hee is averse to food while Song-Hee is preoccupied with cooking and eating. For Yoon-Hee, inability to eat is the last-ditch effort to protect the boundaries of her violated self. For Song-Hee, feeding and even force-feeding is the result of a massive "identification with the aggressor"

(A. Freud, 1936). Yoon-Hee's reflexive vomiting is mirrored in Song-Hee's unstoppable ingestion of food.

Sex is also difficult for both of them. Yoon-Hee, the victim of childhood sexual abuse, is unable to be intimate and experiences no sexual desire. Song-Hee, on the other hand, has substituted prior sexuality with regressive orality. Yoon-Hee writes a column giving sexual advice and Song-Hee talks about sex, but neither of them have heterosexual partners.

Conflicts about sex and food are condensed into each other for both. Thus, eating becomes equated by being violently penetrated for Yoon-Hee and feeding becomes synonymous with erotic love for Song-Hee. Though aggression is more marked in the inner world of Yoon-Hee, there is unmistakable sadism to Song-Hee's hospitality as well. Yet another overlap is in the form of anally regressed emphasis both characters show upon precision. The neat arrangement of books in Yoon-Hee's apartment is a counterpart to the impeccably clean kitchen in that of Song-Hee. More important than such phenomenological mirrors is the dynamic complementarity between the two women. As the story unfolds, they become closer and each begins to serve as a "container" (Bion, 1962) for each other's repudiated aspects. Yoon-Hee embodies Song-Hee's thwarted autonomy and Song-Hee represents Yoon-Hee's dissociated sexuality. This is true on the positive side of the libido-aggression economy. On the hostile dimension, Yoon-Hee becomes the child who Song-Hee (in identification with her mother) can force-feed and Song-Hee becomes the intrusive parent (the stepfather) whom Yoon-Hee can reject. With the progress of this ambivalent dance, more regressive efforts at merging the aggressive and libidinal agendas come to the surface. Yoon-Hee offers herself to be killed and devoured in an attempt to undo the remorse at her having contributed to the young girl's death in the meat freezer long ago. Song-Hee takes Yoon-Hee up on this offer to reverse the sadistic killing of the dog, since killing Yoon-Hee appears to be an act of kindness. It will release Yoon-Hee from her lifelong suffering and make her wish to disappear come true.[1] Thus while concurring on a mutual agenda, the two women come very close indeed. There is even a tinge of homosexual excitement there. Yoon-Hee has finally allowed herself to be "appetizing" to another and thus accepted the innocent and natural eroticism of her body. Song-Hee has turned her oral hunger into a means of service to a friend. Thus, in a folie à deux of cannibalism, both Yoon-Hee and Song-Hee find redemption through convoluted means.

CONCLUDING REMARKS

Being willing "prisoners" of psychoanalytic thought and remaining loyal to the title of our chapter, we have focused on intrapsychic issues while discussing these three movies. We have elucidated the condensations and mutual replacements between oral, anal, and phallic-oedipal drive derivatives in these scenarios. We have also sought to explore how the psychic elaboration of childhood trauma as well as phase-specific fantasies impact upon the current life functioning of the various protagonists. The unconscious overlap between food and sex in these movies has "confirmed" what seems ubiquitous in our clinical experience—namely, the outcome of the condensation depends upon the balance between libido and aggression in the psychic economy. In other words, when love predominates over aggression (e.g., *Tampopo*) the food-sex equation can result in "delicious" phenomenology ranging from culinary exhibitionism to mutually gratifying oral sex. However, when aggression dominates the psyche (e.g., *301/302*) the same symbolic condensation can lead to bitter outcomes of gluttony and cannibalism. Moreover, the food-sex condensation seems to be more frequent and more intense in women; this clinical observation is paralleled by the fact that the main characters in all three movies discussed here are female. Archetypes of our mammalian heritage coupled with the actual nourishing of the infant by the mother lay the foundation of food-sensuality link; the vaginal receptivity is subsequently merged in a "downward displacement" with the oral pleasure of eating.

Such psychoanalytic emphasis in our conceptualization does not mean that we overlook the cinematic devices employed to underscore the messages of these movies. In *Tampopo*, the gawky coming-of-age angle is emphasized by the comic exaggeration of otherwise serious rituals, by the characters beginning to talk directly to the audience from time to time, and the strict separation of eating etiquette (pre-genitality) from sexuality, which gets undone only toward the very end of the movie. In *Dumplings*, the juxtaposition of the shabby naturalism of Aunt Mei's surroundings and the synthetic radiance of Mrs. Li's makeup and attire is an ironic ploy to remind the audience that natural grace outweighs cosmetically enhanced beauty. It also emphasizes that the acceptance of one's age and appearance comes from inner confidence and, in a feedback loop, enhances that confidence. The fact that the camera angles are often tilted and do not frame the characters well and the characters, at times, walk out of the frame while talking conveys the precariousness of youth and slipperiness of passing time. In *301/302*, the location of the two apartments at the blind end of the hallway underlines the claustrophobic nature of the main psychological issues (e.g., sexual abuse, anorexic inability to eat, force-feeding) in the movie. The oversized kitchen in the apartment 301 betrays the manic quality of idealizing food and cooking above everything else. The jarringly alternate depiction of eye-catching and mouthwatering dishes with scenes of cutting gleefully with huge and sharp knives, spurts of blood, and evisceration of animals being prepared for cooking serves to highlight the erotic and sadistic oral substrate of it all.

There are hints of political irony in these movies as well. The seeming hilarity and oedipal overtones of the Japanese *Tampopo* can barely hide the mocking identification with the Hollywood "westerns," a taunt that is perhaps aimed at United States (and its conduct toward Japan) in general. The emphasis upon one generation teaching the next to eat and cook properly betrays the concern about the survival of old Japanese traditions in the cell phone/fast food culture of today's Tokyo. In the Chinese movie *Dumplings*, "Mei's cool-headed border hopping enterprise is a case study in market pragmatism serving the requirements of the Hong Kong vanity industry with the waste products of the Chinese birth control policy" (Walters, 2006, 12). There is also the potential of seeing this movie as a wry commentary on the mutual dependency of a poor nation and a small affluent enclave of it—who will eat whom up remains an open question here. The edgy mistrust and threat of violent breakthrough between neighbors in the Korean *301/302* similarly kindle the memory of tensions between North and South Koreas.

Besides such ontogenetic, psychodynamic, cinematographic, and sociopolitical strands, there exists finer cultural mythopoeisis idiosyncratic and specific to each of these movies and their historical context. At the same time, it should not be overlooked that the themes these movies explore are ultimately human in nature and hence ubiquitous. Thus it is not surprising to find libidinally as well as aggressively dominant food-sex movies from the Western countries. *Babette's Feast* (Danish Film Institute, 1987) and *Chocolat* (David Brown Productions, 2000) represent the first trend, and *Eating Raoul* (Paul Bartel, 1982) and *Sweeney Todd* (DreamWorks Pictures, 2007) exemplify the second. That such similarities of deep psychological kind in human beings exist despite the formal differences owing to their cultural surround is a reassuring thought. To extend the metaphor at the heart of our essay, this gives one much food for thought, some of which is hot and spicy indeed.

NOTE

1. One is instantly reminded of the last scene from Clint Eastwood's *Million Dollar Baby* (Warner Brothers, 2004) in which committing a murder is similarly redemptive to both parties concerned.

12

Zen, Martial Arts, and Psychoanalysis in Training the Mind of the Psychotherapist

Stuart Twemlow

> Words, words, words—fluttering drizzle and snow.
> Silence, silence, silence—a roaring thunderbolt.
>
> Shigematsu Osho (cited in Johnson and Paulenich, 1991, 3)

Traditionally, Buddhism is regarded as a nonpsychopathologically oriented system (Engler, 1983; Walsh, 1988). Expert practitioners of Asian psychologies (e.g., Kenneth Cohen, personal communication, April 17, 1991) indicate that many of these systems, although purporting to encompass psychological functioning in the broader sense, are remarkably unpsychological when compared with what is usually considered psychological in Western science, i.e., focusing on subjective experience. Cohen found that psychological prescriptions by "therapists" in Asian systems tend to be mostly somatic (e.g., herbs, acupuncture, and various prescriptions for exercise and correction of thinking with little emphasis on human relationships and feelings). Modern medical anthropologists sometimes seem to consider this phenomenon to be an idiosyncrasy of the Communist revolution, when Chinese life was altered by Marxist political philosophy with its emphasis on the somatic expression of mental states (Twemlow, 1995). However, in an examination of ancient Taoist texts, one is struck by the somatic orientation to management of difficulties with the path.

ZEN BUDDHISM

Zen Buddhism is a system that is particularly suited to psychotherapy (Fromm et al., 1960). In its purest state, it eschews religion and even Buddhism, in certain ways (Wood, 1951). For example, the Zen purist has no theory of the afterlife (Deshimaru, 1982, 1983, 1985). From this point of view Zen is seen fundamentally as a method of coping with day-to-day life. Some pundits consider that Zen is a "path toward liberation." Liberation here is used in the Buddhist sense of liberation from *dukkha* (suffering) (Rahula, 1959). Zen mostly avoids metaphysics, merely theorizing that one's experience in the mind is one's experience in the moment and that theory of any sort does not necessarily enhance the impact of personal meaning of that experience, and may even detract from it by distracting one's attention from the present to abstract conceptualizing or worrying. Thus, the experience can become decolorized and often confused by the abstract idea of thinking itself, but more of that complicated issue later.

These Eastern disciplines are in many ways the opposite of the plodding path prescribed by the modern-day psychotherapist who tends to emphasize systematically facing hard reality, not expecting magical transformations, and learning to live with less-than-ideal states. In fact it has been said that true enlightenment and wholeness arise when we are without anxiety about perfection. In that sense, then, disciplines that emphasize special transcendent experience, including the satori of Zen, are the antitheses of what psychotherapists might consider achievable. Whereas the writings of Zen and other disciplines do emphasize these special and dramatic forms of insight, the actual practice of Zen much more emphasizes the mundane daily lived-through experience. I myself will address my comments mainly to the day-to-day practice of Zen as it can assist in the training of the mind and body of the psychotherapist.

It is the proposition of Zen practitioners that attention to mundane daily matters will assist in the efficient and effective living of one's life, rather than preoccupying oneself with things that have happened (the past) or might happen (the future), although such a temporal depiction is an oversimplification of the idea of the here-and-now, as I will discuss later. Writers such as Kapleau (1965) consider that training in such mundaneness changes pathological character patterns. It requires little stretch of the imagination to see how this might be. For example, historically, Zen became part of Japanese life in a typically highly practical fashion (Addis and Hurst, 1983). Practitioners of Zen Buddhism emigrated from China to Japan only to find a complicated esoteric form of Buddhism already popular among the Japanese aristocracy. Zen practitioners adapted the precepts of Zen to weaponry—initially archery—and used these means as a way of teaching for the samurai class (the soldiers). The samurai quickly adapted Zen in preference to more complicated and less practical forms of Buddhism. Zen taught value and ritual-free techniques applicable to the exigencies of the life of the soldiers facing death every day.

Zen was chosen for this training model as opposed to Buddhism, in general, because Zen tends to give attention to the essential facts of life that are manifest in day-to-day behavior, which is, of course, the primary impetus that motivates a patient to visit a therapist. Practitioners of Zen traditionally require three personal qualities for their work: great faith, great doubt, and great perseverance, all of which are also required by modern-day psychotherapists, especially when dealing with difficult and needy patients.

Using as special cases near-death experiences and "UFO abduction" experiences, I have outlined an integrated psychodynamic view of reality based on the difficulties inherent in establishing the validity of an improbable or incredible event (Twemlow, 1994). I concluded that such phenomena, and even "ordinary reality," have no meaning when considered separately from the experiences of one's state of mind, belief system, personal investment in whatever paradigm is chosen, the state of consciousness, or the explanatory usefulness of any particular paradigm. These factors operate in the context of a set of basic assumptions for the psychodynamically informed psychotherapist: that all human behavior is meaningful; that the past influences the present and thus can be useful in understanding the present; that cause and effect are not simple, linear concepts, but that principles of multiple causation and overdetermination operate in all reality; and that health is a relativistic concept (i.e., that there are no absolute criteria for health versus illness). I considered these psychodynamic precepts to be necessary, implicit, basic presuppositions, or what can be called "values," that modify and affect how a therapist processes and deals with the relationship with the patient. A positivist view, common today with an increased focus of medicating the patient in psychiatry, proposes a return to scientific materialism: The patient becomes an object to manipulate and instruct, however benign that active role is. Once this medical model position is assumed consciously or unconsciously, the therapist is then automatically mainly responsible for the "cure"—indeed, an unenviable and undesirable position.

The idea of "values" here does not imply a judgmental position on what is right and wrong or good and bad in human behavior. Beyond these basic values derived from psychoanalytic psychology there are several additional concepts derived from Zen that I have found very helpful in the training of the therapist's mind:

1. The core concept of emptiness and its relation to self, identity, nonattachment, and the principle of unity vs. duality;
2. The idea of nonattachment as a central experience necessary for the full understanding of the true nature of emptiness. Once nonattachment has been achieved, greedy possessiveness of an idea or an object ceases, and suffering (anxiety) is thus relieved. Far from being a

schizoid withdrawal, nonattachment is letting alone of the phenomenon so that it can manifest itself as it is. It is felt that possessive holding on distorts the phenomenon;

3. The training and modulation of attention and how this impacts on the individual's perception of reality, including how attending enhances the quality of existence in the moment (here and now);
4. The principle of impermanence concerning the idea that attempting to establish a secure and predictable world is doomed to failure and itself creates insecurity;
5. The centrality of paradox to a realistic view of heath and illness. This is an extension of the idea of the double-bind to situations of health as well as illness. Paradox is an essential and basic part of all life, and transcending paradox rather than resolving it is an essential part of being healthy;
6. The principle of compassion. Compassion is unconditional regard for all sentient beings, and even nonliving things. Reverence is combined with *saddha* (like faith but with understanding, conviction, and enthusiasm) and unselfish attention to the needs of others before one's own (altruism). Compassionate acts should occur in the everyday life of healthy people. In such acts, altruism outweighs egoism.

A BRIEF DIGRESSION INTO MARTIAL ARTS

Hand-to-hand combat has been part of the military history of humankind from the beginning of time. It would be natural that it would be systematized into sets of more or less useful techniques and named usually after the inventors of the system. No one knows how martial arts originated, but it can be said for certain that every culture has some form of fighting art, even if only institutionalized in a special forces military and for close-quarter combat. Much of martial arts history is oral and as such is quite unreliable, just like the tale told at the beginning of a line is usually radically different at the end of even a short line. The oral tradition of martial arts has been written, rewritten asserted with dignity, without dignity, and even with a great deal of combat and nastiness. Martial artists are not psychologically sophisticated in the main and they tend to be what they call "ego-bound"—what in the West would be called narcissistically self-absorbed and particularly loyal to their teachers. Many martial arts are thus taught through obedience and mimicry. These ways of teaching, while effective in producing rote learning, have become problematic because they also tend to inhibit creativity and original thinking, and are not well adapted to Western models of learning. One such oral version of martial arts history that I have been taught was what they originated in India as the folk martial art system

Kalaripayatti, a tough form of fighting in quite brutal conditions and using multiple weapons including sticks. Kalaripayatti is practiced today largely in southern India, in the province of Kerala. The story goes that the prince of southern India took the system to China and introduced it there along with some of the drills to keep the monks from Mount Shaolin awake during their deep prolonged meditative practice. Kalaripayatti may have evolved from Pankration—the hand-to-hand combat method of Alexander the Great, who was at war in India.

Traditionally, martial arts have been connected with meditative and spiritual practice, and traditional schools reflect that influence to this day. Draeger and Smith (1980) list Asian fighting arts as evolving from China, Japan, Korea, India, Pakistan, Burma, Thailand, Indonesia, and the Philippines. Combat arts in the West were always restricted to military activity, but throughout most of Asia this did not happen as mentioned. Early on, martial arts became imbued with religious and philosophical ideals but also because in the long Japanese wars, settling the mind down, a basic principle of meditation, of course would be enormously helpful when fighting a war and dealing with the threat of death. Practical techniques using weapons to illustrate principles were welcomed. Teaching the samurai ways of managing anxiety was often dressed up in phrases like learning to transcend the fear of birth and death by minimizing their importance in life in the present moment. D. T. Suzuki (1973), an experienced Zen practitioner, has three chapters in his book on Zen and the samurai and Zen and swordsmanship. He points out that the spirit of the samurai "deeply breathing Zen into itself" (85) is a letting go and focusing on the pressing moment and is of course is how a warrior must fight: 100 percent committed. The focus and target must be clear in the mind and accompanied by *Isagi-Yoku* (no regrets), clear conscience, and no reluctance at all. Suzuki noted that the ancient warriors and even the modern Japanese hate meeting death irresolutely; their desire is to be blown away like cherries before the wind. The early fighters were very well-educated individuals occupying a samurai class that had high status, just below that of royalty. At the end of the wars in the 1600s many of them retired and became priests and political leaders because of their capacity to inspire and their education. Starting in the 1600s the tradition of the Japanese samurai evolved along more intellectual, less combative lines; much samurai poetry and brush painting is classical and highly regarded in Asia these days. To my knowledge there are no active samurai families currently in Asia but there are families that carry the tradition forward from the 1600s.

Part of the division of these fighting skills into thirty-six varieties, with fifty-two variations at a minimum, largely grew out of the desire to teach martial arts in peaceful times with a light sprinkling of Zen and meditative philosophy. Within the Asian traditions, China evolved softer styles like kung fu that tend to use continuous circular movements with combat techniques largely coming through surprise, that is paradoxically appearing in an apparently soft flowing move. Chinese martial arts is highly focused on family traditions, so there are as many variations in the schools of kung fu as there are families that value martial arts. Chinese martial arts has embodied Qigong, a use of martial arts "energy" in the service of medical conditions like cancer and are being used to this day for that purpose. Most of the Japanese systems involve straightforward block counterattack techniques that are quite out front and easy to see. While brute force is by no means the entire methodology of the hard systems, extremely fast block counterattack actions are the hallmark of Japanese and Korean martial arts. Tae kwon do, a very popular Korean martial art in the United States, is one such example. Another way of looking at the softer styles like kung fu in China and aikido in Japan is that the block counterattack method is replaced with a blend and redirect method in these styles, including avoiding (blocking) the technique and using the power of the attacker to complete the strike where it would naturally end without resistance (i.e., on the ground). *Karate* means empty hand, the term coined by Gichen Funakoshi in the early twentieth century, becoming the main medium by which martial arts spread into elementary schools from Okinawa, under the sponsorship of the emperor of Japan. Many of the techniques were made less harmful for teaching to children. Colored (*kyu*) and black (*dan*) ranking systems were adapted into martial arts from the Japanese game of Go. Beginning in the 1900s, martial artists were unable to reach any collaborative agreement between masters and instead decided to divide themselves into a set of styles based on what were seen as the primary techniques within the system, so, for example, kicking and punching routines became karate. Judo became a primary sport of Japan and emphasized throwing techniques. Jujutsu emphasizes choke holds, grappling techniques including ground technique, and has evolved in modern times into submission fighting. Aikido presents itself as a recent martial art emphasizing sweeps and joint locks.

Martial arts was introduced into the United States in the 1950s and found its place as a sport, evolving into such traditions as pit fighting and the cage fighting now very popular on American television. The whole idea of tournaments, and winning trophies and prizes, became a major part of what martial arts was in the United States. In contrast, traditional schools in Asia and the United States do not do very well financially since the road is long and hard and includes meditative practice and readings, as well as very strenuous and demanding martial arts practice. Student numbers are small. The United States probably has fewer than ten fully established traditional martial arts schools that do not emphasize fighting but instead personal development. Over the years martial artists would become often very absorbed in the art because it had helped them so much personally. These enthusiastic teachers have introduced martial arts into various forms of psychotherapeutic and physical help, in a wide range of conditions that we have summarized in Twemlow, Sacco, and Fonagy (2008). Modern research (Trulson, 1986) has shown that if martial arts are taught traditionally (i.e., with the philosophical ideals and code of conduct relating to harmfulness), it reduces aggressiveness and antisocial tendencies as measured by the MMPI. However, if introduced primarily as a method of winning a fight, it increases antisocial and violent tendencies.

Bringing martial arts to the doorsteps of psychoanalysis, although counterintuitive at first, has been aided and assisted greatly by the recent surge of effort in attachment theory. Many like myself who have trained in martial arts in a very serious way and have been connected with it for decades have become aware that disturbed young people, when in martial arts schools, become excellent students and their unruly behavior often settles remarkably rapidly. Frankly, it was easier for me to find teachers for juvenile delinquents referred to us for training than it was to find teachers for children from private schools who were verbal, intelligent, unruly, and not inherently interested in martial arts at all—that is, those children whose parents made them come. It was as if violent and disturbed young people had an intuitive knowledge that something within the martial arts would speak directly to their problems. We called this "embodying the mind" (Twemlow, Sacco and Fonagy, 2008). Winnicott (1963) indicated that the core of the true self in all of us is a segment that must remain incommunicado. Winnicott's idea was that there is a difference between a subjective object that is the infant as a projection of the mother and the objective object that is the infant partially created by the mother and partially by attunement to external reality. Winnicott implied that this piece of the true self was independent of external reality and reminiscent of embryonic stages of the mother-infant bond that should never be analyzed and was an essential part of the true self. Kurtz (1984) and Olinick (1982) elaborated this idea: Olinick with the idea of pathic speech (i.e., speech in the service of not transmission of information but the forging of a contact), and Kurtz with silence as protection of the true self. He points out that if the true self does not meet with the maternal response required to confirm its subjective reality it may split off and become hidden and embryonic (i.e., not desirable). Kurtz felt the endless task for the therapist was to enable its emergence by empathically containing the patient's situation offering a safe haven and we would add allowing communication through nonverbal techniques as suggested by Stern et al. (1998). Gaddini (1982) theorizes that there are "primitive mental experiences of the body which are made up of particular sensations connected to a particular function (originally that of feeding)" (379). The use of the reflective mind evolves from this set of primarily sensation-oriented experiences beginning in the womb. He further points out that the womb is a physical experience alive with sensation. The always-present contact with the internal world of the mother is terminated at birth and the need to have physical contact with the mother becomes primary. If the caregiver fails in this key element of soothing the baby, then the baby can experience the world as a dangerous place filled with dread and enemies, a projection of the unsoothed internal state. Violence can thus become "hard-wired" into the infant.

In this conceptualization the baby relies on the repetitive physical contact with the mother to help develop a sense of safety. This model uses the idea of a "body-mind-body circuit" to explain "body fantasies" or stored memories of preverbal experiences. Violence may enter a baby's world through this mechanism and remain insulated from the impact of psychotherapy exclusively reliant on verbal strategies and the capacity to understand abstract ideas. His research from our attachment perspective illustrates that this narcissistic absorption, rather than protection, needs communication and management. A caregiver/therapist who does not resonate with this part of the true self causes the individual to feel less soothed, and, as Gaddini says, the world can thus become experienced as dangerous. Fonagy has added the concept of "mentalization" to spell out and explain the importance of making what Freud called the body ego, i.e., a fully metabolized and explicable aspect of the individual sense of self. He asked the question: How is the infant to decide soon after birth which is more likely to be productive in the sense of assuring survival, one of violence or one without it? He feels that evidently what is required is some kind of signaling system, a way the infant can learn about the social environment that he is likely to face as he matures. Thus children who stay on the violent track from infancy to adolescence are far more likely to have received hostile ineffective parenting in early childhood. This leads us to a clear connection between the action of a martial arts dojo with a traditionally trained instructor who can address, by the ambience of the whole school and even the meditative mysticism of martial arts, a comprehensive and secure attachment experience for a child. Such children not only become highly attached to the art itself, often adopting Asian identities, but also easily learn the language and carry martial arts skills and explanations into their day-to-day existence. Without going into the details of this life as a whole philosophy as reflected in karate-do, a Zen life, is focused on the here-and-now experience, the practical value of managing anxiety by the process of letting go and the mastering of the fear of both life and death with a form of nondismissive, effortless dismissals of the importance of both. Thus, when embodying the mind, the violent individual learns that the part of their mind that may feel persecuted and in danger becomes much safer, with embodiment.

In summary, the role of the body in Zen and martial arts has always been central in the way it is taught through actions of various sorts, so the idea of embodiment involves gaining a true awareness of who one is, including the deeper reaches of one's self. Our researches with violent individuals have suggested that Zen can be connected in the context of martial arts with a very effective way of making contact with a fragile embryonic form of the true self that remains latent and reaching for expression in a world of danger and persecution if it cannot be attached in a secure relationship beyond language. For many such children, that secure relationship does not exist in the home but, as our experiences have suggested, the martial arts school can become in many ways a surrogate home for such children. At least several children have wanted to actually live in the karate school that we have had for some twenty years ironically titled School of Martial and Meditative Arts.

ZEN-GEIST: FURTHER REFLECTIONS

Zen teaches that ignorance leads to a delusional misperception of reality. Unlike Buddhists, Zen practitioners have no position on the afterlife. Zen teachers such as Deshimaru (1982, 1983, 1985) consider such preoccupation a distraction from the work of the moment, leading to a decrease in the quality of the lived experience. In addition, such preoccupations promote unanswerable questions and encourage delusional thinking in the following sense: if you have to deal with overwhelming terror (angst) about matters of survival after death and so on, and tussle with unanswerable questions, there develops a frustration that encourages something akin to unconscious lying or self-deception. As one psychoanalytic author, Wheelis (1980), wrote: "people deal with existential anxieties by creating an ongoing dialectic between the way things are and the schemes of things." The "way things are" may be unacceptable and anxiety provoking, for example, leading an individual to varnish the painful reality of meaningless death with "schemes of things," i.e., a more acceptable notion of survival in the afterlife. The Zen practitioner believes that it is possible to look at the way things are without schemes and without overwhelming and distracting anxiety. Alan Watts once called the worldview of Zen "an accident" that keeps happening, highlighting in literary metaphor the importance of spontaneous moment by moment creation of life from a Zen point of view. Deshimaru (1982) responded to the question "What survives the body after death?" by arguing that when the body dies it decays and recycles, so that following the law of conservation and of energy, the atoms in the body are spread all over the universe. Deshimaru implied that an atom of your dead body might be an atom in the brain of the next Aristotle! Thus, such a teaching may end with a challenge that, what more could you want to bolster your self-esteem and activate your omnipotence! You never die, you are just recycled! I have used this paradoxical idea in teaching students of martial and meditative arts and in teaching therapists. On one occasion the idea stimulated an experience of satori in a medical professional who was in the middle of divorce and wrestling with the problem of dissolution of his marriage and loss of his family. This example illustrates a Zen-like attention to what is known while not giving up the quality of the numinous self, often lost in modern agnostic cosmologies. Zen admonishes the individual to live each day, in the words of a samurai, "as though a fire is raging in your hair," and to which was added by a psychoanalytic scholar, "And as if you are going to live forever" (Ishak Ramzy, personal communication, June 5, 1992).

The constant re-creation of each moment, as if it were the rebirth of the universe, does not involve loss of memory of prior experience; it is merely that prior experience is integrated into the present. Seeing things as they are is central in Zen. Needs created by defenses against overwhelming anxiety creates self-deception. As most of us know, if you lie enough times, you begin to believe it. It is this self-deception that is the "cardinal sin" of Zen.

The central metaphysic of Zen is that the idea of a Cartesian duality is only one half of knowable reality. By rough analogy, the two sides of a coin represent duality, but the coin itself as a whole is undividable. This central unity is depicted in Zen painting as a circle (*enzo*) that describes the unthinkable unity; the inexperiential experience, "the mere experience." These paradoxes can only outline the general field since language itself is a dualistic mechanism.

When I began working with dying people, especially very old people, most of whose relatives and friends had died before them, I noticed that they were often focused on severe pain or other aspects of physical deterioration. I found that it was insufficient, even irrelevant, to focus attention on the process of mourning and acceptance of one's death. There is much in the immediate present to be done for oneself. It is work with such patients that led me to introspection about why it is that a world without a future place to go is so depressing and meaningless when seen from a traditional Western viewpoint. I became acutely aware that as I gave up the wish to create "schemes of things" in Wheelis's (1980) sense, and instead dealt with my own anxiety about a meaningless life, I did not feel depressed about a meaningless life; paradoxically, I felt relieved. One patient helped me understand this choice by his confrontation of such a paradox. This gentleman was a college professor who had been hospitalized, suicidally depressed. He came to me one day asking that I write an order so that he did not need to go to occupational therapy, where, along with all other patients, he had to make wallets. He thought that this was beneath him and that he would profit more from individual therapy with me. I noted that he had two basic choices—either to leave the hospital or to stay. If he stayed, he had to make wallets since everybody made wallets on his ward. He said, "You leave me no choice, I need to be here; I guess I will just have to make wallets." I further pointed out to him that there was yet another choice: He could be a happy wallet-maker or a miserable wallet-maker! This apparently frivolous example highlights the possibility of the freedom from having to lie to oneself; having to create a varnished reality to avoid dealing with the way things are. Freedom from the burden of self-deception is like a weight off one's shoulder. But Zen does not leave it there. Self-deception is replaced by a perception of one's place in the whole, a small part of an extraordinary puzzle. Being part of that puzzle makes the universe far from depressing.

From a more clinical and less metaphysical point of view, this Zen-geist implies that attention to object relationships is what makes life bearable and pleasurable. These relationships, however, are not limited to humans and animals, but to life in its totality. Thus, reality need not be varnished with self-deception and man need not be the center of the universe nor to struggle to prove that he is special. There is a knowledge that, by being part of the puzzle, one is also special, as anybody knows who has ever lost one piece from a complicated jigsaw puzzle! Obviously, such a Zen-geist, if achieved by the therapist, would be synonymous with significant freedom from pathological narcissism. There is a Zen a phrase for this: *Kenshogodo*—looking into your own nature directly and finding it to be the same as the ultimate nature of the universe (Wood, 1951). Thus, the grandiose infant is dissolved into the universe, egocentricity is lessened, and the fruitless search for the nonexistent self is abandoned. In the original-face koan, a famous Zen patriarch asked: "Before your father and mother were born, what was your original face?" It poses the challenge that ignorance and craving must be transcended before our original unfettered nature is realized.

CORE VALUE PRESUPPOSITIONS FOR THE ZEN-TRAINED THERAPIST

The Emptiness of the Concept of Self

Zen psychology is a form of mental microscopy, and at heart, a phenomenology. It requires a fine and detailed examination of the nature of everyday experience from moment to moment, at times appearing almost obsessive in its detail orientation, ultimately allowing the experienced affect and idea, as well as a capacity to grasp the broad, basic whole. Introspective data collected by Zen practitioners on the concept of self and identity is radically different from most extant Western psychologies. A psychoanalytically trained psychiatrist who also practices meditation once commented that our whole concept of self and others is a verbal concept (Samuel Bradshaw Jr., personal communication, December 23, 1992). For centuries, philosophers have attempted to search for mind, which, like the self, is often referred to by philosophers as the search for "the ghost in the machine" (Gabbard and Twemlow, 1984). The search for this self has a certain pointlessness and emptiness. Within psychoanalysis, there are various conceptualizations of self, including the supra-ordinate self of Kohut as totality of mental functioning. However, in a recent review, Kirshner (1991) concluded that a self, even a sense of self, is not intrinsic but requires intersubjective experience. It is built up out of interactions with others. The appearance of self as a supra-ordinate structure, Kirshner refers to as a kind of fantasy, or wish-fulfilling belief. The idea that the self is intersubjective is credited to Hegel (1807), the phenomenologist, who theorized that the consciousness of self requires an encounter with another subject. Psychodynamic theorists like Winnicott, Klein, and Stern have arrived at similar conclusions by studying the relationship between babies and mothers. Contributions to the concept of self as a verbal construct, rather than a reality in itself, has also been assisted by the research of Lacan (1964), who pointed out that word "signifiers" will mediate the individual's exchanges with the world, and that those exchanges are what constructs the subject as a whole human being. This position was pioneered in depth by the philosopher Hume (1787). For Hume, identity was seen as an illusory product of the mind's capacity to remember and to infer causes. He called it the chain of causes and effects that constitutes our self or person. Twentieth-century philosophers, including Sartre, have also followed this line. Kirshner suggests that perhaps a good working modern philosophical and psychological definition of self might be: The emotional and intellectual expression of an experience of otherness in the present. Following this definition for many thoughtful Western psychologists and philosophers, there is little argument with the Buddhist theory that the self is empty of meaning separate from experience of what is called inherent existence in Buddhist philosophy. The Dalai Lama (1984, 149) gives an insightful and simple clarification of the idea of emptiness. He points out that the position of the observer defines the content and form of the experience. For example, a tired individual will see a chair as a place to sit, whereas a microphysicist will additionally see it as a conglomeration of atoms. Thus, searching on a finer and finer microscopic level for the basic building blocks of existence shows that all things reduce to atoms and space, and that the arrangement of these atoms and space is what constitutes the apparent surface form for what is called in Buddhism "dependent existence," i.e., dependent on other conditions. Emptiness, then, refers to emptiness of its own inherent power and dependent means, being dependent on other conditions. Thus, according to the Dalai Lama (1984, 150), dependent arising refers to the mind, self-consciousness, and identity, all existing as a result of the interaction of the five aggregates of Buddhism, akin to the actual body and its psychophysiology. Consciousness, then, is seen as not having substance unless there is an object for it. This essentialist view is an abstract conceptualization of the way the whole being functions when called upon to act. According to the Dalai Lama, nothing has inherent existence. He calls this "the nonexistence of an independent 'I' under its own power call the selflessness of the 'I'" (163). Thus, in some ways Zen redefines the self dialectically.

Now, what practical importance does this have for the psychotherapist's daily work? First, such a conceptualization allows the therapist to realize that people are more the same than different. It also evokes empathy, especially with those whose values are very different from, even contradictory to, one's own. Realization of basic, shared human structures allows a more tolerant view of the errant, aberrant, and perverse patient, a less judgmental attitude. In addition, the actual observation of events of the mind that proceeds from Zen and martial arts training reveals a very important insight upon which this concept of emptiness is grounded: experience shows that what appears to be on the surface, a relatively stable and consistent entity (e.g., the self) is, in fact, in constant flux and quite transient. Events are constantly being built up and being deconstructed. The idea of self-representation in object relations theory is compatible with this revised idea of self. The self-representation is changing from moment to moment. It is truly a dynamic image. Not only does input from day-to-day experience modify that self-representation, but also so does thinking about it internally (unconscious fantasy). This idea allows the individual to experience two different subjective senses of their own being. First of all, the idea that one's self can be changed because it is constantly changing is especially important in many pathological conditions, giving greater hope and ease for that possibility, and secondly, a greater sense of oneness with others leads to a more compassionate mental posture. The exploration of these psychologies indicates that all human beings are capable of transcending the self with intellectualization. An empty self allows the individual paradoxically to maintain more distance from highly charged, affective states that can blur boundaries and result in impulsive action and impaired judgment. For example, Walsh (1988) points out the thought "I am scared" in the presence of a dangerous situation is inherently fraught with possible danger to the individual. If it can be seen from a transcendent position, a position of self-observation, then adaptive responses have a greater likelihood of succeeding. It is from this position of selflessness, sometimes called egolessness in Buddhism, that enlightenment proceeds. Enlightenment akin to waking up (the adjectival definition of the word Buddha) can be sudden or gradual, but unfortunately such drama has become tainted with elitism and distance from possibilities for the average individual. Gradual change, like the mutative interpretation, is also possible from this perspective. The Zen-trained therapist comes to these states without having to pathologize them. Wilber (1980) has argued that there is a psychology that he calls a "pre-transfallacy." He points out, I believe correctly, that pathologizing interpretations of these experiences as regressive forms of narcissistic self-absorption derive from a fallacy that the individual is at heart an infant, incapable of self-object differentiation. In fact, infant research shows the opposite to be largely true (Stern, 1985). Wilber (1980) also points out that the capacity for self-transcendence comes from a developed, mature subject who *can* step beyond subject/object duality while remaining clearly aware of this conventional duality. It is not a loss of boundaries that occurs instead; it is an establishment of expanded boundaries.

In many respects, the Buddhist idea of codependent origination (i.e., that nothing is self-originating) is similar to modern psychoanalytic views, particularly the interpersonal theories of Sullivan (1953), and the object relational theories of Greenberg and Mitchell (1983). The original enlightened mind of Zen, *Honshin*, is similar to the healthy "psychoanalytic mind," free from pathological narcissism and essentially relational in functioning. The dynamic qualities of the dialectic are central to this concept: Its ever-changing self-negotiation in creation of new entities and careless integration avoids the static and fixed rigidity of mechanical concepts often present in classical psychoanalytic ego psychology and in the doctrines of modern religious systems. This can be represented as Zen self-experience in dialectical relationship with the body. The body defines the self from this perspective and vice versa: Similarly, in a more general way, individuals can be depicted as in a dialectical relationship with other individuals.

Thus, the self does not exist until it is interacting and the individual does not exist from this point of view until he/she is interacting with the world around. Fundamentally, this idea breeds a freedom from self-consciousness and thus releases a capacity to immerse oneself in work. Basho (1991) once said, "While working, work; while resting, rest," and "Learn the rules well, and then forget them." Such learning is more efficient and is not self-conscious. Knowledge is learned and then becomes automatic, so that living can become smooth and fluid rather than turbulent, which is created by worry about remembering each action. However, of course, the conscious mind can stray.

The Impermanence Principle

In an interesting paper, Parsons (1992) indicates that there is an act of personal engagement required with theoretical concepts rather than the pseudo-objective application of what had been taken for fact. To make reality more real requires not only an abandonment of the static concept of self or "I-ness," as we have already discussed, but is also a new way of looking at what is present. The open secret of Zen states that the most obvious thing of all is often the hardest to see. We are often better at finding things that are more obscurely hidden than seeing the obvious. By deconstructing concepts that are not useful and that distort perception, Zen allows the individual to see things as they actually are. The realities of life are most truly seen in everyday things and actions, but to believe that to be fact requires a deconstruction. Parsons says of psychoanalysis that we serve the truth not only by seeing it and pointing it out to the patient, but by embodying it in our relationship to the patient and to our theory, and in that way we may help the patient also to become the embodiment of his own truth. This Zen-like statement implies an action in the here-and-now that is critical to psychotherapeutic results. Modern object relations theory indirectly recognizes this by postulating *actualization* and *reenactment* in the transference, wherein the immediate here-and-now relationship with the patient is played out in the drama of moment-by-moment transference/countertransference enactments.

Zen challenges an idea inherent in our current psychologies that attempts to feel secure and free from anxiety require the establishing of control and predictability over self and the environment. The search for security becomes a wild goose chase that is doomed to failure because the universe is *not* like that reality; security and changelessness are considered to be fabricated by the *control-oriented* mind and do not exist in nature. To accept insecurity is to commit oneself to the unknown, creating a "relaxing faith" in the universe. A therapist who can roll with the punches is more likely to be a useful role model for the patient as a means of handling day-to-day reality. Thus, there is nowhere else to be, other than fully present with gusto and a relaxing faith! Embodiment of this impermanence principle can lead to increased flexibility and decreased possessiveness, envy, and greed.

The Concept of Paradox

Life can be seen as paradox, and humor an essential part of learning to live with that paradox. Individuals, such as patients with borderline personality disorder, who shift from one extreme to the other, want a world that is both predictable and homogeneous and thus, will tend to be frustrated (ill). The humor is more like C. S. Lewis's "joy"—not a belly laugh, but a constant, gentle wonderment. Psychotherapists frequently use paradox as a vehicle for interpretations. The paradoxical nature of the human mind was recognized by Freud in his dichotomous love/hate theory of ambivalence. Zen employs paradox in a deliberate and unique way to illuminate the nature of the mind and of growth. Wittgenstein (1956) was the first to attempt to explore the philosophical function of paradox; however, its behavioral implications were first explored by Gregory Bateson (Bateson et al., 1956), an anthropologist, who proposed the double-bind theory of the etiology of schizophrenia, later elaborated into a system of psychotherapeutic interventions called paradoxing, which has become an inherent part of some forms of psychotherapy and hypnosis (Weeks and L'Abate, 1982).

It is likely that the double-bind is, in fact, a universal given of the human condition. The double-bind provokes anxiety because whatever the person does is wrong, including no response at all, i.e., there is no logical way out! Consider the notion: Have you stopped beating your wife/husband yet? Sluzki and Veron (1971) indicate that there are two basic core sources of conflict: the universal conflict stemming from the dependence/independence dilemma, the need for the individual to grow up and separate and, at the same time, in pathogenic situations—the efforts that parents and others make to prevent that separation from occurring, including unconscious pathology in those individuals. These general needs come into conflict with the individual, idiosyncratic effects of the family constellation that creates illness, a repetitive behavioral stereotypy. True as this may be in pathology, it is also very much true of life, for example, the need for emotional intimacy requires that the individual maintain optimal distance. Hatefulness allows an increased figure-ground contrast for love.

Zen training has placed great emphasis on "understanding" paradox through the didactic role of the koan, an exercise for the mind that is beyond thought. The koan violates basic postulates of logic—it cannot be solved by the application of reason. Over 1,700 koans are alluded to in the Zen literature. Essentially they are teaching devices to bring students to an understanding of reality (enlightenment). These exercises can be of great training value to the psychotherapist to increase both empathy for patients and/or to highlight the possibilities for transcendence to health. Therapists such as Rothenberg (1976) have demonstrated such ideas with his concept of homospatial and Janusian thinking. Therapists in general probably underemphasize how putting contradictions together helps the patient to transcend the problem without necessarily needing to resolve it. The critical issue for the koan is not that there is a logical answer, but that in dealing with the question, a *transcendent answer* becomes obvious—that is, beyond the koan—and an experiential state in which both/and can exist as well as either/or. Transcendent knowledge reveals that, for example, regressed components of the personality can coexist with and even enhance more mature elements; one does not preclude the other. This concept is similar to the notion that the capacity for whole object relatedness requires the acceptance of both good and bad in the same individual. The "correctly" answered koan does not lead, then, to a dismissal or decoloration of the question in an "answer," but is more a revivification of the experience of the question and its implications. With this approach, there is maintained an aliveness, immediacy, and an excitement with the question rather than a "now it is finally solved, and I can go on to something else" attitude. Kapleau (1965) puts it in most dramatic language. He describes the koan *mu*, probably the most famous of all koans. In response to the question; "Has a dog Buddha nature nor not?" the Chinese Zen master Joshu, retorted *mu*, which means essentially "nothing." Kapleau says

> *mu* holds itself coldly aloof from both the intellect and imagination. Try as it might, reasoning cannot gain even a toe-hold on *mu;* in fact, trying to solve *mu* rationally, we are told by the masters, is like trying to smash one's fist through an iron wall because *mu* is utterly impervious to logic and reason and in addition, is easy to voice. It has proven itself an exceptionally wieldy scalpel for extirpating from the deepest unconscious the malignant growth of "I" and "not I" which poisons the mind's inherent purity and impairs its fundamental wholeness. (69)

Preachy, perhaps, but he vividly captures why the koan is useful, and what its goal is—that is, to enlighten the individual to the fundamental understanding of the true nature of the empty self.

A koan can be useful for psychotherapists in their own training and thinking about the human condition but not necessarily for direct use with patients. The important role of the koan as a teaching device is illustrated by the famous story of the young student who, while vainly staring at herself in the mirror, found that her head disappeared (an optical phenomenon). She rushed to various individuals wanting reassurance. Her teacher could not reassure her by instruction, her psychotherapist could not treat her, and her friends could not reassure her. Finally she visited a Zen Roshi, continuing to assert that she could not find her head. The Roshi said nothing but gave her a peculiar look, lifted a stick, and hit her gently on the head, at which point she grasped her head, her face lit up, and she said, "Ah, my head." Do not hit patients, but let teachers hit your mind with a koan! The koan is a means of bypassing the distractible mind that will grasp detail and irrelevancy and go off on a tangent without continuing to focus on the core question. Because these tangents lead nowhere, the individual may spend long periods of time following exhausting byways and dead-end streets. By thus subverting the distractibility of the mind with its tendency to intellectualize and theorize, the koan functions as a form of direct learning that, by its nature, highlights the natural distractibility of the mind and which can thus be of use to psychotherapists in their own growth and understanding of the difficulties patients have in grasping concepts (insight).

An intriguing essay by DeMartino (1960) titled "The Human Situation and Zen Buddhism" comments on the human situation as seen by the practitioner of Zen. He points out that the ego requires an object to be a subject, and thus can never gain complete fulfillment in or through an object.

Despite the actual abundance of life, the ego is left unfulfilled. DeMartino states that there is "one fundamental longing of the ego" (151): to "find and fulfill," to "really know," to "come home," and to "fully be and have itself in and with its world." This is what he considers to be the "existential beginning and the final end of Zen Buddhism" (152). Furthermore, he says,

> The koan in its double function may therefore be considered a deliberate and calculated attempt to secure a result previously obtained naturally and without contrivance . . . the koan does not permit itself to be fitted into any dualistic, subject/object scheme of the ego . . . it cannot be solved if it remains an object external to the ego as subject. (157)

Twemlow (2001) offers a detailed discussion of the remaining four aspects of attributes of mind that have emerged from a study of Zen and the martial arts. In brief summary these attributes include the fine-tuning of attention—listening and hearing skills. The mind is considered to be a sixth sense along with vision, hearing, and so on, and has as its food "thoughts" (mind-objects), according to Rahula (1959). How one attends to these thoughts as they flow, both letting them go and hearing and listening to them, is central to the concept of being fully present. A wealth of experimental studies has shown that even the resting unoccupied human mind entertains many different thoughts each minute. In Buddhism, these distractions are seen as attending to the wrong thing. It should be noted that the naturally functioning mind is capable of modulated attention. In his classic paper on technique, Freud (1912) perhaps erroneously dismisses the training of the thinking of the analyst as simple. He says: "The technique (of thinking of the analyst) however is a very simple one" (324). Freud felt that all that was needed was to simply make no effort to concentrate the attention on anything in particular, and to maintain a regard for all that one hears with the same measure of calm, quiet, and attentiveness of evenly hovering attention. This of course is very hard to do. The purpose for which Freud postulated this mode of attending was partially practical—to avoid the strain of concentrating for hours at a time and to reduce the selectivity of attention to a particular type of material, thus leading to scotomatizing other material. Freud conceived of evenly hovering attention as the corollary of the golden rule of analysis, which demands that the patient communicate everything that occurs to him without criticism or selection (324). Freud then considered the golden rule for the analyst to be: All conscious exertion is to be withheld from the capacity for attention and one's unconscious memory is to be given full play; to express it in terms of technique, one has simply to listen and not to trouble to keep in mind anything in particular. He then goes on to say that listening in this way will be "sufficient for all requirements during the treatment"; however, that statement is not correct. Many different states of attention are necessary during treatment. Freud was probably referring primarily to the "data gathering" phase of psychoanalytic treatment. He admonishes the analyst to "take as a model for the psychoanalytic treatment the surgeon who puts aside all of his own feelings, including that of human sympathy, and concentrates his mind on one single purpose, that of performing the operation as skillfully as possible" (327). Here he introduces the concept of countertransference, although rather than implying a cold, inhumane therapist, he is merely using analogy to describe how important it is to not let one's own conflicts interfere with the process of listening, or, as he said, "If he does not, he will find himself in consequence helpless against certain oft he patient's resistances" (327). He says in the same article (328): "It is justifiable requisition that he (the analyst) should further submit himself to a psychoanalytic purification and become aware of these complexes in himself which would be apt to affect his comprehension of the patient's disclosures." Later on, he says that "too intimate an attitude on the part of the doctor interferes with the treatment and that the physician should be impenetrable to the patient and like a mirror, reflect nothing but what is shown to him." (Perhaps the mind mirror of Zen!)

Generations of psychoanalysts since Freud have echoed these comments, perhaps idealistically described by the well-known historical figure in psychoanalysis, Max Eitingon, the founder of the first formal school of psychoanalysis in Berlin in 1920. He used to enjoin his student analysts that every new patient must be treated as if he had come directly from Mars: as no one has met a Martian, everything about each patient must be considered as utterly unknown (Ishak Ramzy, personal communication, June 5, 1992). It is known that the human mind does not function randomly; even when it is hovering evenly and apparently being nonselective, it is likely to be highly selective in the way it operates because it operates according to certain conscious and unconscious assumptions. Thus, it is necessary to train this mind to achieve the sorts of fine distinctions and personal understanding necessary to engage in attending to the patient.

People often pride themselves in being able to do several mental things at once. Research in meditation has shown this not to be possible, and more recently, so has work from experimental psychology. In reviewing the literature on doing two things at the same time, technically called parallel processing, Pashler (1993) considers that certain mental operations are bottlenecks that require exclusive use of some cognitive resources and therefore cannot be done concurrently. These include even the most trivial forms of decision-making and memory retrieval. Processes that require less effort may be partially done at the same time, although meditators say that for greater mental sharpness, doing one thing at a time is most efficient. Thus, decision-making and memory retrieval, two operations that are constantly involved in the day-to-day activities of the psychotherapist, will interfere with the listening and hearing process as we have defined it. Bion (1983) described the ideal therapeutic listening posture as a disciplined attitude in which tolerance of the unknown is paired with confidence that something will evolve in the emotional contact with the patient and that this something will be possible to put in words, thus generating the possibility for change in the mind of the patient. Bion considered quite emphatically that any wish to cure and the remembering of things interfere with the process of listening and hearing as I describe it. He says of the listening posture of the analyst that it needs to be without memory or desire. Zen defines seven thought patterns that vary from logical thinking through scanning, automatic thinking, selfless concentration, one-pointed concentration, and enlightened awareness.

"Here and Now," and Temporal Experience

This idea in Zen as opposed to the psychobabble version of it popular in the 1960s implies the blending of past and future to enrich the concept of the present, not to distract from it. Thus the concept of now by no means ignores the past or future but is instead blending into a harmonious and balanced whole with action only being possible in the immediate present.

Nonattachment embodies the principles outlined in the four noble truths of Buddha. A healthy nonattached individual is fully involved with the relationship and is not distant and withdrawn. This full involvement is possible *because* the suffering created by attachment, a form of thirst and greed, is observed and abandoned. Thus the object of attachment can be itself and the individual does not have to defensively control or possess the object of attachment.

In the four noble truths of Buddha life is considered to be fundamentally filled with suffering (*dukkha*) for which there is a cause and a cure. The suffering is seen to have come from thirst (*tanha*). Thirst is sometimes seen as a rather subtle form of dissatisfaction or clinging and at other times as a specific and intense form of possessiveness and greed. The Buddhist position as depicted in the four noble truths considers that this thirst fuels attachment that creates suffering by overinvolvement. When the object of attachment is no longer responding, the individual experiences are suffering. Psychobabble and psychopathological forms of nonattachment are forms of defensive distancing. By contrast, healthy nonattachment frees the individual from having to be possessive and controlling of a person or object. At the same time, this nonattachment allows the object of greediness or possessiveness of the other. In one sense the relationship between attachment and nonattachment is a dialectical balance never completed and is not a pure or ideal state. The concept is useful especially for the unique form of distancing required for the listening posture of the psychotherapist where there has to be a meld of distance and involvement in a delicate dialectical balance.

The "Umbrella" of Compassion

Without the more saintly versions of compassion in the service of the human race and peacefulness embodied in the actions of the selfless saints. On a less saintly level, Ella Cara Deloria (1988) writing in *Waterlily* an account of family life in the Dakota Indian culture indicates the need for generosity, and the constant giving of gifts. It is felt, according to the ancient ones of this tribe, that if everyone gives, then everyone gets, and so "old men and women preach continually to be hospitable, to be generous. Nothing is too good for giving away" (52). Generosity of the heart, and altruistic concern for others, may seem idealistic, yet recent research reviewed by Shapiro and Gabbard (1994) and applied by Twemlow and Sacco (1996) indicates that altruism may well be a fundamental attribute of the human condition, and the task of the therapist is to appeal to it.

CONCLUDING REMARKS

Clearly a teacher of psychotherapy oriented in this manner must embody what h/she teaches. Although freedom from all blemishes is obviously neither required nor desirable, an understanding of these "truths" requires regular practice of meditation and the meditative (including martial) arts, which could be fairly easily incorporated into training curricula for psychotherapists and psychoanalysts. A psychologically healthy, technically well-trained psychotherapist is not yet sufficiently prepared for the awesome and demanding task of helping patients psychotherapeutically. I hope I have convinced the reader that the mind itself must also be trained.

NOTE

*Parts of this chapter are derived from two papers previously published in the *American Journal of Psychotherapy* titled "Training Psychotherapists in Attributes of 'Mind' from Zen and Psychoanalytic Perspectives, Parts 1 and 2," vol. 55, no. 1 (2001): 1–39.

III

TRANSPOSITIONS AND TECHNIQUES

13

The Chinese American Family: Some Psychoanalytic Speculations

June Y. Chu

> The old should treat the young with loving kindness, and the young should treat the old with respect. What a shame when the young do not respect the old.
>
> Confucius (circa 500 BC)

This chapter is an inquiry extrapolating from our understanding of the Chinese psyche by considering the immigration experience and its impact on the emerging second generation of Chinese Americans, typically referred to as "ABCs"—American-born Chinese. The Chinese American family can choose three distinct paths: first, to assimilate into American society, adopting Western cultural constructs of independence and shedding the behaviors and beliefs associated with the native culture.[1] Second, to forgo assimilation and acculturation processes, choosing perhaps to live within ethnic enclaves and associating solely with Chinese immigrants; and third, to attempt to be bicultural, not assimilating but rather going through an acculturation process that attempts to integrate aspects of both Western and Eastern cultures. All three methods of development have their challenges and this chapter focuses upon this last group.

Bicultural youth face many challenges but within these challenges, strengths can readily emerge. By integrating the best of both worlds, many opportunities present themselves for these youth to restructure their identity in a diverse world. Here we will examine the Chinese American family, considering the importance of using a cultural lens to interpret behaviors and roles found within these families. We shall consider the historical context first, sketching out the immigration patterns of the Chinese, and move on to aspects of Chinese culture,[2] including parent-child relationships and children's roles within their family. From here, the discussion delves into the work in clinical psychology to consider the label "parentification" in light of the cultural norms found in Chinese families. The chapter attempts to integrate culture with Freudian theory and opens up the possibility of future explorations with the Chinese American mind.

HISTORICAL BACKGROUND

The Chinese first began their migration from China to the islands of Hawaii in the early 1800s, where many replaced native Hawaiian laborers on the sugar plantations that were being established. Beginning in the 1840s, the Chinese began their immigration to the mainland of the United States as laborers in search of fortune. For many of these laborers, this journey was merely seen as a temporary one—lasting three to five years—to work in a foreign country and return home to support their families. Shortly after the annexation of California in 1848, American policymakers submitted a plan to Congress to facilitate the importation of Chinese laborers to the United States. Approximately 380,000 arrived onto the U.S. mainland between 1849 and 1930, with immigration first begun as a result of the California gold rush. In addition to seeking fortune in the United States, there were a myriad of other reasons for emigration from China. Some sought sanctuary from internal conflicts within China, others for financial hardships as a result of corrupt imperialist rule, and still others from poverty and hunger due to flood and famine. America, christened *mei guo* ("Beautiful Country") by the Chinese, seemed to be the ideal solution for the younger men in search of escape from harsh conditions in China. Lured by the stories of the *gam saan* ("Golden Hills") and the gold to be mined, America seemed the perfect solution for all the problems in China.

At first, the Chinese immigrants were greeted hospitably for a number of reasons.[3] Not only were the Chinese "cheap labor" to be had, but factory owners were able to keep wages for whites down by threatening to strictly use the imported Chinese laborers instead. Chinese workers were hired in 1865 to lay the tracks for the transcontinental railroad; within two years, over twelve thousand Chinese were employed by the Central Pacific Railroad. These immigrants were employed in numerous other capacities as well, from the garment industry to factory labor, as well as in development of California agriculture. However, with the rapid influx of the Chinese, people began to voice concerns about this immigrant group. Anti-Chinese sentiment also led to the burgeoning ethnic enclaves, communities where the Chinese were able to create their own organizations, celebrate their own holidays, and, in essence, reclaim their native heritage while on foreign soil.

Hawaii and the mainland of the United States developed very different policies regarding the immigration of the Chinese—whereas Hawaiian quotas exempted women and children, the mainland actively sought to keep out Chinese women with their immigration laws. In 1852, of the 11,794 Chinese in California, only seven were women. Restrictions on the entry of women as wives to the mainland United States led to single women entering as prostitutes; in fact, most of the Chinese women entering California before 1875 were prostitutes. Fear of being overrun by Chinese immigrants and with the U.S. workforce feeling threatened by the Chinese, government enacted the 1882 Chinese Exclusionary Law, which forbid laborers from coming to the United States.

In 1906, earthquakes hitting San Francisco led to the destruction of citizenship records, and those in the United States were able to claim U.S. citizenship since there were no records to refute such claims. The U.S. government resorted to detaining these new immigrants on Angel Island, reserving the right to deport any individual unable to correctly answer questions about relationships to their U.S. relative (most often, their "father"[4]). With U.S. law allowing citizenship to the children of those living in America (even if the children were born abroad), enclaves not only developed but also thrived. These enclaves rapidly became tourist destinations in the 1930s and 1940s, viewed as strange places for tourists but home and community for the Chinese. Chinese children were often told that although they were American by birth, they would not be accepted based upon the way that they looked. This second generation of children was told early on that they would be the "perpetual foreigners" on this land—while born here and deserving of constitutional rights just as any other American, they would never be seen as anything other than foreign on U.S. soil. In the 1940s Chinese Americans were again seen favorably by the United States given their support of World War II (with the Chinese and Americans fighting against the Japanese, Germans, and Italians) and with the sudden open arms of mainstream society, the Chinese found that employment opportunities outside ethnic enclaves became a possibility—and, in fact, a reality.

Often the Chinese took on employment that others would not—for instance, as laundry owners. Whereas laundry was viewed as "women's work" by the whites, Chinese laundries were abundant from Los Angeles to Chicago and New York. Additionally, open immigration post-1965 allowed for a second influx of Chinese immigrants. These immigrants, rather than seeking a quick fortune on the streets thought to be "paved with gold" in the United States arrived seeking educational opportunities as a means of obtaining upward mobility. The children of these immigrants, the second-generation Chinese Americans, are the main focus of this chapter given their status as "children of two worlds" whose very existence brings to the forefront notions of internal and external conflict.

PARENT-CHILD RELATIONSHIP

Qualitative research with Chinese and Chinese American families has shown that sex roles are rigidly defined within families (Chu, 2004). Confucian principles of filial piety lead to an expectation by Chinese parents that children will repay in kind their efforts to raise children—while it may be that these expectations are not explicitly communicated, the indirect communication[5] patterns found in Asian American households make this a reality for many second-generation Chinese Americans. Numerous studies illustrate the interdependent nature of Chinese families. These studies have noted how many Chinese families within the United States continue to retain and value an emphasis on filial duty (Fuligni, Tseng, and Lam, 1999; Fuligni, Yip, and Tseng, 2002; Uba, 1994). Triandis found that the Asian self depends more on the values of the group when compared to the Caucasian self, and family obligatory systems in the Asian family structure are believed to maintain family solidarity (Chao, 1995). Chinese cultures also tend to promote autonomous behaviors at a later age in life when compared to parents from Western cultures (Juang, Lerner, McKinney, and von Eye, 1999; Uba, 1994).

Early studies in the development of Chinese American children were born of the "model minority myth."[6] The model minority myth led to curiosity surrounding the stellar achievements seen within the Asian American racial group, and thus studies began to examine the influence of family on this phenomenon. Studies revealed Chinese parents to be "authoritarian"—those parents who have rigid, inflexible demands of their children (cf. Dornbusch, Ritter, Leiderman, Roberts, and Fraleigh, 1987). This method of parenting came under scrutiny when researchers noticed that these supposedly "cold" parents were raising high-achieving students. These early studies led ethnic minority psychologists to question the dynamism of culture, bringing into consideration indigenous concepts to assist in describing the Chinese American family.

Ruth Chao (1994) furthered the inquiry of parenting styles by introducing cultural variables to the discussion. The authoritarian label, according to Chao's argument, has its roots in the Puritanical tradition, where the rigidity of the parental role was necessary to "stamp out evil" and free will in children. In the case of the Chinese American family, argues Chao, indigenous concepts of *jiao shun* and *guan* are more applicable in defining family structures. The maternal role, rather than being a cold and removed one, needs to be defined and examined through a cultural lens. In doing this, Chao revealed the Chinese mother-child relationship to be ill-captured by the Western mind, for in actuality, these notions of *jiao shun* and *guan* reflect a loving method of training children—with the training of children being the most important responsibility for Chinese mothers.

As elucidated in this chapter, the parent-child relationship in the Chinese American family is qualitatively different from those typical in the Western world. Additionally, expectations that parents have for their children are quite different. Childhood in the traditional Chinese sense is not a time for learning independence and exploration. Children are not indulged in ways that would allow "children to be children" but, rather, they are trained for the future responsibilities that they will have as adults. Chinese American boys and girls have well-defined roles in the family, with the primary goal of each to be responsible toward the family upkeep (Chu, 2004). Male children are expected to take on chores that are physically demanding—e.g., moving, yard work, working with their hands. Female children's responsibility lies in the domain of the home—taking care of siblings, cooking, cleaning. In addition, children—most often the older children but not always—are expected to do the translation work for the family. This translation work not only involves parent-teacher notices, but may also involve complex legal documents that children as young as age twelve are expected to comprehend, interpret, and respond to on behalf of their parents. To a clinician who is not versed in cultural psychology, Chinese American children, because they take on so many of these tasks that are not expected of host culture children, may appear to be highly "parentified" given their naïve notions of what contributes to well-being.

PARENTIFICATION

In Western culture, when children appear to bear the burden of family responsibilities and assume roles traditionally reserved for adults, the clinical label applied to these children is "parentified." In Western culture children are encouraged to "be children" and there are definitive roles that are considered the realm of parents and those that fall within the domain of childhood. When discussing the responsibilities of immigrant children, we need to recognize that cultural norms are different, keeping in mind Triandis's (1996) definition of culture and the cautionary tale that he issues, reminding us that culture is an important aspect of understanding individuals.

Parentification has been described as an atypical relationship between parents and children (Jurkovic, 1998). Chase (1999) describes household tasks that included preparing meals, taking care of siblings, household chores, earning money for the family, managing the family budget, serving as a parent's confidante, family peacemaker, and mediator as those that are the responsibility of parents. Qualitative research with Chinese American adult children (Chu, 2004) found that these tasks are often delegated to children. The question that follows, then, is whether or not the label of parentified is aptly used in such cases when this apparent "role reversal" is the norm.

Research findings in Western culture have pathologized the child who must take on a great deal of filial duties. The bulk of findings have pointed to the negative outcomes in adulthood resultant of duties that may have been incongruent with developmental level, or remained unacknowledged by parental units. In mainstream cultures, where individuation is a goal in life, this comes as no surprise. The self is not defined in relation to others and therefore these demands that are placed upon a child are not congruent with early experiences (for why else does the child need to separate from the mother and be autonomous so early in childhood?).

As Anderson (1999) argues, parentification is a social construct. Such a label, therefore, is not reliably used unless accurately applied to the culture which we are studying. Chu's (2004) qualitative study established that what are considered "everyday tasks" include all those that would characterize a child raised in the United States as parentified, assuming we did not consider cultural norms. However, as taking on family responsibilities—however burdensome they may be—is nothing out of the ordinary, many Chinese American children undertake these responsibilities with little questioning of whether or not these roles are of the "norm." As they age, however, and compare themselves to non-Asians around them, they recognize that there are differences that exist. In starting to compare oneself to others, the realization of a bicultural duality begins to occur, leading to distinct new challenges as the individual must integrate these parts of the self—parts taken from the native culture and parts taken from the host culture. This duality, these differing self-representations, presents itself in a way that may align with some concepts from psychoanalysis.

This discussion of parentification serves to illustrate how families must be viewed within the cultural context. Based upon this argument of different ways of being, some may argue: Chinese American families differ from mainstream Western families in what is considered typical, so how can we presume to use a Western-based form of therapy with Chinese American groups?

THE CHINESE AMERICAN MIND

In psychological studies conducted with Asian Americans, cognitive behavioral therapy (CBT) has been shown to be the most "effective" form of treatment (Zane, Morton, Chu, and Lin, 2004). The appeal of CBT rests on the cultural group's belief in personal will and the ability of the self to overcome mental obstacles. For example, studies in the area of Asian American achievement have shown that Chinese Americans are more likely to endorse personal effort rather than displacing accomplishments onto biological factors[7] (cf. Chao, 1995).

Psychoanalysis, therefore, has not been a focal point of research in the relatively "young" field of Asian American psychology, whose research tradition only came to fruition in the mid- to late 1970s, having been led by the African American civil rights movement. The field of Asian American psychology itself continues to rely upon methods of inquiry[8] that preclude a detailed understanding of how Chinese American clients may fare under the guidance of a psychoanalytic clinician. Thus from here, this chapter will attempt to integrate what is known about the Chinese American family and Chinese views of psychoanalysis, including the possibility of using such a methodology with this group.

As early as 1935, psychoanalytic thought was introduced in China by Bingham Dai (1899–1996) a Chinese native who studied at the University of Chicago under the tutelage of Harry Stack Sullivan and Karen Horney (Blowers, 2004). Dai's interest in psychoanalysis was related to his interest in introducing students to various schools of philosophy—including psychoanalysis—and allowing the students he trained at Peking Union Medical College to make their own decisions on effective therapeutic action for patients. At this time in China, the strong desire for social change facilitated more eclectic approaches and Dai's own theoretical views in adapting psychoanalysis to the Chinese population not only took into account cultural ideology but also called attention to the dynamism of this new inquiry. Dai's work incorporated an understanding of emphases on filial piety and brotherly respect, as well as social situations that reflected the turmoil in society—including loss of family, sexual tensions resultant of concubinage, and premarital sex difficulties (Bowers, 2004). Dai's approach to psychoanalysis within the Chinese cultural group emphasized interpersonal relations and his interest in psychoanalysis was due to his philosophy that it was "more urgent to help their patients tackle the problems of being human" (Blowers, 2004).

What then, of the applicability of psychoanalysis to the Chinese American mind? Can psychoanalytic concepts as developed by Freud in a European context—one that is based on cultural tenets that are antithetical to the Eastern value system—be used and applied in a similar fashion? What of Freud's concern that incompatible identities (and what we have is exactly this as the bicultural Chinese American develops) will lead to pathological outcomes? Freudian theory, with its emphasis on individuation, may not readily appear to be applicable, then, given the conflicting foundations of Western and Eastern parenting beliefs. However, as is evident with Dai's work in China, perhaps there are pieces of psychoanalytic theory that can be considered as a means to treating Chinese Americans, particularly if we must consider a multitude of options for treatment before settling on just one.

Gu (2006) offers us a way in which we might consider psychoanalysis for the Chinese. In Western literature, oedipal themes can be found in various forms. However, Gu noticed that this was not the case in Chinese literature. This, Gu claims, highlights the differences that do exist between Chinese and Western culture—differences that have been addressed in this chapter. This difference in the themes led him to suggest a manifestation of internal conflicts that results in what he terms the "filial piety complex." Cultural values such as emotional repression that are a direct consequence of the Confucian moral system lead to sexual repression at earlier ages in the Chinese culture as compared to in Western culture. This in turn leads to a distortion of oedipal representations—in the form of filial piety. Unlike in Western culture where there exists an individual complex, the interdependent nature of Chinese families lead to a multiplicity of complexes: the father complex, the mother complex, the son complex, and the daughter complex (Gu, 2006). This explanation that Gu offers allows us to reconsider psychoanalysis as a means of working with Chinese Americans because it takes into account the cultural variations that exist and gives us a framework that is not merely based on assumptions of individualism. This is perhaps one of the most critical steps in applying Freudian theory to Chinese Americans for it integrates an understanding of cultural differences while also understanding conflicts that arise.

Having established that there might indeed be a way in which psychoanalysis—when culturally reconstructed—can be used with Chinese American clients, we might be better able to integrate the key obstacles for this population with Freudian ideas. Thus, let us also consider biculturalism along with immigration processes, which may give us a glimpse into the relationship between the Chinese mind and psychoanalysis.

BICULTURALISM

In the discussion on biculturalism, we will take as a starting point Freud's conception that man is divided against himself. While this idea is based upon European intellectual movements of the Romantic and Enlightenment period thinkers, it can allow for some speculation on how Freudian ideas might be played out within the Chinese American household. For Chinese American children, the most apparent division of the self is due to reconciling the bicultural identity. With the bicultural identity are the specific behaviors associated with the native culture—the ones that we have discussed herein being the filial responsibilities that children have throughout their life span that are remnants of their immigrant parent's native culture.

As discussed, the bicultural individual exists in a world of duality, constantly needing to reconcile the Chinese side of the self with the American side of the self. The psychoanalyst working with a bicultural Chinese American must keep in mind their own prejudices when working with such a client. While a mainstream psychoanalyst may assume the path to psychological health is one where individuation occurs (and thus, there is a desire for autonomy as dictated by mainstream cultural ideology), for the bicultural individual, a balance between these two selves is likely necessary for optimal health. Theoretical models of cultural orientation point to an integrated identity as one that is most often associated with optimal well-being (cf. Tsai, Chentsova-Dutton, and Wong, 2002). Whereas traditional psychoanalytic thought may have one think that these two incompatible identities will result in pathology, the research on Asian Americans seems to indicate that when these disparate identities are reconciled, therein lies an achieved self. Perhaps what it means to "be human" (as Dai states) is different as a function of individualistic versus collectivistic cultures.

FAMILIAL TIES

The Chinese American family stands in contrast to the Western family, promoting autonomy at later ages. There exists a "we-self," whereby the self is not necessarily defined in isolation but rather in context. Thus, independence is not a core value; rather, what we might find in Chinese American families is "interdependent independence"—a situation where independence can occur but it remains defined in a relational way[9] (Russell, Chu, Crockett, and Lee, under review). What we have concluded thus far about Chinese American families has led us these assertions: one, interdependence as a value in Chinese American families; two, rigid sex roles are found in children's responsibilities to the home; three, children have numerous filial responsibilities that continue to and through adulthood; and four, labels such as parentified and authoritarian cannot be applied without consideration of the cultural norms and ideology behind these acts.

The psychodynamic approach presupposes that human acts are an outer expression of motives and desires derived from early childhood experiences. The psychoanalyst can make many different interpretations when working with the Chinese American client in light of childhood experiences. The psychoanalyst may assume that childhood experiences for this client arise from a culture where filial duty is the norm. This would require the analyst take one approach in working with this client, for the individual may actually experience no conflict between these actions of duty and what they have learned from early childhood. Perhaps this is the most unlikely scenario though, because such individuals would therefore not experience any conflict (or resulting neuroses) that would necessitate a visit to the psychoanalyst.

However, the psychoanalyst may see these acts of filial piety as derived from psychological forces that potentially divide an individual against himself and this is why the patient has ventured to seek help. The division of self may be due to a clash of Western and Eastern ideology, of collectivism versus individualism. The question one must ask then, is: are these acts purely altruistic or rather, are these acts a sublimation of clashing aggressive forces that are not allowed to manifest themselves in an Eastern-based culture that places an enormity of value on outward appearances and expectations of filial piety?

Here, the approach a psychoanalyst may take would assume that the individual desires autonomy from the pressures of these responsibilities that are due to a curtailed attempt to individuate. Regardless of the approach taken, the family and parental influence play a strong, if not stronger, role in establishment of any sense of self for the Chinese American and, therefore, psychoanalysis can shed some light on this cultural group. Gu's (2006) proposal that the Oedipus complex is transformed in Chinese families makes sense if we agree that an Oedipus complex is individually oriented. This would fall in line with Western individualism. However, with Chinese families, collectivism is the more typical norm and thus the idea of multiple complexes—as individuals can only be defined within the context of others—makes the most sense in incorporating family members to the understanding of the complexes, and conflicts, which arise due to cultural differences.

Case 1

> J.H. is a twenty-one-year-old Chinese American woman attending an elite university. In middle school and high school, she exemplified the role of "good daughter," with stellar achievements in high school, both academically and physically. Her father was proud of her athletic and fitness achievements. As the good daughter, she strove to maintain this image, rapidly developing body image issues, leading to the development of anorexia, bulimia, and exercise bulimia as a means of maintaining her role as the "good daughter" given her implicit understanding that her father's main concern with her was how she looked. As she moved out of her family home to attend college and overcame her eating disorders, she put on some weight. In doing so, her father's attitude toward her changed—in her own words, her father "stopped caring" after her weight gain, as she no longer "looked" attractive. In college, J.H. seeks out parental figures and substitute mothers in her friends, as her own parents do not fulfill this role for her.

Parental practices reflect parental belief systems (Gallimore, Goldenberg, and Weisner, 1993) and thus we must consider the relationship of Chinese

American children and their parents as the foundation on which future relationships with others are based. Here, J.H.'s father clearly believes that the appearance of being athletic and attractive is of utmost importance. Manifestations of J.H.'s desire to satisfy her father have included purchasing clothing that he wants her to wear, as well as cosmetics to make herself more attractive. Her father's distancing of himself from her as a result of her weight gain has created a prototype for her in the relationships she now has with others—being thin, in her mind, is equated with being accepted and liked. When seeing thin women, J.H.'s immediate thought is "I bet they have a lot of friends."

Although J.H.'s relationship with her father is one that is fraught with negative interactions, her development within an interdependent culture continues to affect her in her relationships with others. Rather than seek complete autonomy from others, she instead seeks out parental figures within her environment, which would perhaps allow her to ease the conflictual feelings she has about her own familial relationships. Her understanding of what is desirable about women ("thinness") stems from her relationship with her father and his acceptance of her only if she is athletic and thin. Because of the interdependent nature of Chinese families, such pressures can become exacerbated because the need to remain connected exponentially increases the potential for conflict and detrimental behavior as a means of ameliorating the conflict.

Case 2

> A.V. is a twenty-year-old Chinese American man attending community college part time while working full time. He arrives to discuss issues of feeling "overwhelmed" and unable to concentrate in his schoolwork. Because he is unable to concentrate, he becomes anxious, which then perpetuates the inability to focus. After discussing issues relating to schoolwork, it is revealed that A.V. is living at home with his parents, and every paycheck earned is signed over to his parents. Additionally, his father has not only used his name to secure a second mortgage on the home but also routinely places checks in front of A.V. for him to sign (for accounts that A.V. did not open himself). A.V.'s father often speaks of the financial burden in helping to pay for A.V.'s college tuition, which only serves to add to A.V.'s anxiety because it is likely he will not do well in school given his inability to concentrate. A.V.'s parents call him at least four times a day to see what he is doing and to make sure he is either at school or at work. In addition, A.V. is currently dating a female who is not Chinese American, but rather African American. His family does not know of this relationship because A.V. fears they will disown him.

In this case, we see A.V.'s conflicting feelings about the familial relationship manifesting itself in a psychological form. At an age where those around A.V. are moving out of the family home and gaining autonomy, A.V.

continues to be beholden to his father. While his father does not directly address the need for A.V. to excel in school, the indirect communication about the financial burden of college costs clearly weighs heavily on A.V., leading to a greater inability to concentrate. The anxiety that we see is exacerbated by his current dating situation. A.V. expressed the high likelihood that his father will disown him if he were to reveal he was dating an African American, given his family's prejudiced attitude toward other racial minority groups.

With A.V., we see a number of clashing forces that stem from the bicultural identity. Attempts to individuate are stymied, given A.V.'s living situation and his inability to manage his own finances. Furthermore, his father's strict control and handling of finances that A.V. is unaware of poses a unique dilemma for A.V. because any attempt to individuate may lead to financial repercussions (since he remains ignorant of all finances that are held in his name). In short, if A.V. were to attempt to disentangle himself from the family, there would be real-world liabilities on his end, as well as on his family's.

Case 3

> J.L., age eighteen, is a second-generation Chinese American male in his senior year of high school. He arrives because he has been referred for conduct issue problems at school. Although reticent at first, he gradually begins to reveal a history of physical abuse within his family. His father physically abuses J.L.'s mother, and has done so since he was a small child. J.L.'s father is the patriarch of the family, going so far as to refuse to seek medical care for his wife when she had taken ill and was unable to move. A year ago, J.L. again witnessed another scene where his father attacked his mother. Rather than be silent, J.L. ran to shield his mother from the blows, which resulted in his father turning to beat J.L instead. As his father hit him, J.L.—for the first time in his life—verbalized his anger toward his father before he ran from the house, telling him he was the "worst father" in the world and that he wished he [his father] was dead. J.L. had never "talked back" to his father before. Although they continue to live under the same roof, J.L. has not spoken more than perfunctory sentences to his father since that time.

J.L.'s case is interesting in that it may have direct implications of internal conflicts that can be revealed through psychoanalysis. Here, we see a situation reminiscent of the classical Oedipus complex—not only has J.L. vocalized a desire to see his father dead, but his assertion came as a result of protecting his mother from harm. This situation is slightly in contradiction to how Gu (2006) would propose complexes arise in the Chinese family, but there remains evidence of links to familial issues and, consequently, leaves room for the possibility that there are both oedipal and filial themes in this case.

Here, J.L. has been referred for situations relating to conduct problems, which we can see have arisen from issues with his father and their fight. Chinese families being largely patriarchal (much more so than Western families), the control exerted by his father places a stronger hold on J.L. and is likely to have aroused greater than usual levels of conflict between father and son. Additionally, this is a case where J.L.'s concern was with the *protection* of his mother. Thus, there is a relational aspect to this encounter—one that brings with it an inherent conflict in cultural tenets. J.L.'s position as the son in a patriarchal culture has clashed with his position as a son within a family unit where he has relationships with both the abuser and the victim. The importance of filial piety as a cultural construct exacerbates the conflicts experienced by J.L. because in protecting one family member, he turns his back against another. This case herein is not one that Gu would consider a son complex, but, rather, there is a potential for us to witness the father complex.[10]

The J.L. case has been placed last because it illustrates the challenge in working with Chinese Americans. It is not only the case that Western concepts (i.e., oedipal themes) might apply but, additionally, culturally nuanced psychodynamic themes as well (i.e., filial piety complex). The interplay of two differing cultures calls for analysis at many different levels and a psychoanalyst must carefully construct an understanding of the conflicts affecting the individual by assessing levels of acculturation and assimilation in order to accurately choose which orientation to take when working with a bicultural individual.

CONCLUDING REMARKS

It is clear that Chinese Americans, especially the second generation, live life in two divergent worlds. These worlds often stand in direct opposition to one another with individualism battling collectivism at the very core. These opposing forces that the bicultural individual must reckon with only serve to add to conflicts that already exist within the individual. Thus, for the Chinese American, organizing conflicts are both interpersonal and intrapersonal in nature. In other words, conflicts occur at many levels: within the individual, between the individual and those in his family, between the individual and native culture, and between the individual and mainstream culture. While it can be said that those who are not Chinese American also live their lives within such contexts, what relegates the Chinese American to the periphery of historical understandings of psychoanalytic thought is the relational concepts that are omnipresent in Chinese culture. In other words, psychoanalysis has predicated itself purely on an individualistic platform, therefore making it seem an ineffectual way in which to work with those from a collectivistic orientation.

The cases that have been presented in this chapter demonstrate the complexity of the issues that affect second-generation Chinese Americans whose status as Americans are also tempered by their status as children of immigrants whose values are dissimilar to mainstream America. While this chapter has not focused on the minority status of the Chinese, psychoanalysts must also recognize the long history of the Chinese in the United States and that it is one mostly marred by the inherent hostilities associated with their "perpetual foreigner" status. This dates back to their first steps onto the mainland and continue to affect Chinese Americans today. Thus, to fully embrace mainstream culture might also include conflicts for some[11] that might be recognized on both conscious and unconscious levels.[12]

These individuals, the ABCs, are thus placed in a position where they are required to reconcile divergent concepts that not only include parent-child interactions and relationships but also the uniqueness of such dynamics in a Western world where they remain a minority. In traditional Freudian psychology derived from European history, the individual wrestles with libidinal urges and conflicts with the same-sex parent. In this form, there exists the need for conflicts to be negotiated as the goal is for the person to individuate. However, in the Chinese culture where individuation is not the norm nor is it the expectancy, critics of the psychodynamic model would surely find fault with using this method of analysis.

Redefining psychoanalytic approaches, as demonstrated by Dai's early proposal and Gu's (2006) contemporary stance, brings to the forefront a recognition that there might be culturally appropriate ways in which to utilize psychoanalysis with Chinese Americans. Because Chinese Americans do encounter mainstream American ideals, the use of such methods is not entirely foreign—as Chinese Americans are aware and cognizant of individualistic culture based on exposure to mainstream friends, colleagues, and peers. Consequently, perhaps there is validity in the use of psychoanalysis with bicultural Chinese Americans, given their greater familiarity with notions of autonomy and individuation. Furthermore, because psychodynamic thought is predicated on notions of conflict, there are aspects that might be directly applicable to the Chinese American psyche as this chapter has illustrated how a bicultural existence is fraught with conflicts that need to be reconciled.

In summary, what we have discussed in this chapter points to differences that exist between Chinese Americans and white Americans. As a bicultural person, the Chinese American can potentially become a marginalized individual because of the cultural forces that clash. Recognizing the existence of conflicts in the Chinese American's life, however, allows us to consider the use of psychoanalysis with such individuals since much of the premise of psychoanalysis is to alleviate conflicts. However, rather than seeing conflict relief as necessary because the goal of humans is to *individuate*, to apply psychoanalysis to Chinese Americans would require a reinterpretation of this type of therapy in light of the cultural differences that exist. Finally, because Chinese Americans are bicultural (and thus are possibly acquainted with Western ideology), it might also be the case that such therapy would also take on significance as Chinese Americans acculturate and eventually assimilate to Western culture.

NOTES

1. Native culture refers to Chinese culture, whereas the host/mainstream culture herein refers to U.S. culture.

2. Culture being defined as a shared set of attitudes, beliefs, norms, roles, and self-definitions (Triandis, 1996).

3. Important to note is that the Chinese immigrated voluntarily, which affects the psychological state of such immigrants as they had the choice to come to the United States.

4. I use quotations around "father" to reiterate the point that many of these immigrants were in fact not blood relations to men in the United States. Instead, they were the "paper sons/daughters"—those who purchased a claim to a relation in the United States as a means of immigrating.

5. Asian cultures are considered high context, with situational cues and indirect communication as integral to the balance of the group harmony.

6. The belief of mainstream culture that all Asian Americans were high-achieving students, a "model minority" group with little difficulty.

7. In stressing personal effort, a participant may state, "I worked hard," whereas in displacement to an external factor, one may state, "The test was easy."

8. Sue, S. (1999). Science, ethnicity and bias: Where have we gone wrong? *American Psychologist, 54*(12): 1070–77.

9. For example, an adolescent might say, "I'm allowed to decide when I am supposed to be home at night. But I make sure to call my parents to let them know."

10. In the father complex, we would witness a father's unconscious hostility and aggression toward the son, whereas in the son complex, a son's oedipal feelings are channeled into other avenues and assume the form of longing for a woman who has mother stature (Gu, 2006).

11. Especially those who are highly ethnically identified because these individuals are likely to be the most aware of the cultural differences that exist and most attuned to experiences of their minority status.

12. This recognition can be transmitted across generations as well as within.

14

Second-Generation Korean Americans

Lois Choi-Kain

> There aren't any bands like Kim in Chicago, let alone in America. So I don't expect the masses to comprehend that. Yes, women rock and, yes, Asian American women also rock, and we rock hard, dammit!
>
> Mia Park (2001, 269)

In the last two decades of the twentieth century, Korean Americans have burst forth into the American cultural landscape, breaking out of their former "invisible minority" or "model minority" mold (Wang, 1997; Kibria, 2002). Previously trapped under the glass ceiling of scientific professions, Koreans in America had achieved success but not visibility in the public eye. However, in the recent years, Korean Americans have expanded their cultural influence in this country as award-winning novelists (Chang Rae Lee), award-winning fashion designers (DooRi Chung), professional athletes (Michelle Wie), high-profile fashion models (Hye Kim), comedians (Margaret Cho), actors (Sandra Oh, Daniel Dae Kim, John Cho), and even rock stars (Joseph Hahn of Linkin Park). Koreans have begun to occupy visible positions in a broad range of professional, community, and artistic realms in the American world.

It is also in this period of time that Korean Americans have earned notoriety. The largest massacre committed by single gunman in American history was perpetrated at Virginia Tech in 2007 by a deeply troubled Korean American student named Seung-Hui Cho. At universities, a number of other Korean American young adults have made headlines for suicides. A particularly high-profile case of suicide at Cornell University involved the murder of nineteen-year-old Young Hee Suh and her roommate, Erin

Nieswand, by a young Korean American man, Su Yong Kim, who attempted suicide unsuccessfully in the aftermath of this event. In 2000, Elizabeth Shin committed suicide at MIT by overdose and burning, leading her parents to file a highly public lawsuit against the university. In their breaking out of the model minority myth, Korean Americans have become associated with domestic violence, psychological instability, and gang-related criminal activity (Kim and Sung, 2000; Shimtuh, 2000; McGarvey, 2002).

Most of these (in)famous Korean Americans are either 1.5 or second-generation immigrants (from now I will refer to both groups as second-generation Korean Americans or SGKAs), born in America to Korean-born parents or alternatively, having immigrated to the United States in early childhood. These two poles of Korean American fame and notoriety reflect both the strengths and the vulnerabilities of this generation of immigrants. Very little has been written about this group of Asian Americans in both the psychiatric and psychoanalytic literature. Most of the literature that has been written to date on this Asian American immigrant group describes Asian Americans in general, oftentimes describing them as a monolithic group. Upon searching the term "Korean" in the Psychoanalytic Electronic Publishing (PEP version 7) Archives, forty-five papers appear. Of these, twenty-one refer to Korean events or objects, not people, most often referencing the Korean War. Twenty-three of these references mention Korean issues or patients briefly, generally, or hypothetically. Thirteen papers describe cases of Korean or half-Korean individuals in treatment. Only one paper exclusively on Koreans appears in this literature search, which focuses on the applicability of the Oedipus complex to father-son relationships in Korea (Moser-Ha, 1999). No papers have been written to date on SGKAs in the psychoanalytic literature.

This chapter seeks to elucidate unique features of the SGKA experience.[1] To start, I will review factors which have contributed to both the prosperity of Koreans in America as well as the consolidation of a visible culture in America. Then, I will outline some developmental dilemmas that occur for SGKA in the context of these factors that influence their trajectory toward both incorporation as well as marginalization in America. Lastly, I will review some clinical considerations for SGKAs in psychoanalytic treatment.

FROM IMMIGRATION TO ASSIMILATION: FACTORS CONTRIBUTING TO KOREAN AMERICAN INTEGRATION INTO THE AMERICAN MAINSTREAM

In order to understand the development of Korean American culture, it is critical to recognize the history of immigration that brought this group of

Asians to America. Korean immigration to America has occurred in three waves (Hurh, 1998; Kang, 2002; Kim, Kim, and Kelly, 2006). The first wave of Korean immigration (1903–1905) consisted of the entry of approximately seven thousand Korean men entering Hawaii as plantation laborers. Contiguous to this wave of immigration was the entry of Korean women who came to join these laborers as their "picture brides." These Korean plantation laborers and their picture brides formed the first Korean American families in the United States, settling mostly in Hawaii and parts of the West Coast.

The Korean War precipitated the most significant waves of Korean immigration to the United States. With the Korean War came a massive influx of American culture to South Korea. A number of American servicemen married Korean women while stationed in Korea, bringing them back to the United States, forming the second phase of Korean immigration to America. This wave also included the entry of a number of Korean War orphans adopted into American families. Following this phase of immigration, the third wave began after the passage of the Immigration Act of 1965, which stipulated preference for professionals in the engineering and medical fields. These professionals had good reason to leave South Korea, which was plagued by the "cumulative consequences of military dictatorship" (Kang, 2002, 48). The process of postwar industrialization in Korea led to enormous economic stratification, political oppression, and "career frustration of a large proportion of white collar workers" (Hurh, 1998, 41). Korean doctors saw the opportunity to study and train in the United States appealing, as the medical system in Korea was behind, beginning the trend of Korean immigration driven by desires for education and professional advancement. While this last wave of immigration has expanded to include Koreans who are not doctors or engineers, education and professional opportunity remains the primary impetus for immigration. A sample of U.S. visa applicants from Seoul interviewed in 1986 stated the four main reasons for leaving Korea for the United States: (1) higher wages, (2) reward for hard work and ability, (3) a more benign political environment, and (4) educational opportunities for their children (Kitano and Daniels, 1995; Kang, 2002). This last wave of immigration has brought most of the current Korean American families in the United States here.

The 2000 U.S. Census reported that currently over one million people living in the United States claim Korean ancestry (U.S. Census Bureau, 2001), which is 10.5 percent of the Asian population and 0.4 percent of the total population. In general, Asian Americans have been among the most economically and academically successful minorities, claiming the highest median household income as well as the lowest poverty rate of all racial groups (white race included) (Kim, 2006). While Asians comprise only four percent of the U.S. population, they make up 6 percent of college enrollees and

20 percent of students at Ivy League universities (Zhou and Gatewood, 2000).

What has contributed to the progress of Korean Americans in the United States? While the focus on education and occupational success for Korean in immigration provides an obvious rationale for these outcomes, the conscious intent and self-reported motivations of Koreans in coming to America is not an adequate explanation for this phenomenon. Other immigrant groups also come to America for the same reasons. I will argue that several unique factors bridging dimensions of the culture and values of Koreans to important dimensions of life in American have eased Koreans into the American fold in mostly beneficial but also problematic ways. These bridging factors include (1) the early prevalence of intermarriage and adoption of Koreans, (2) the absence of significant political conflicts between South Korea and the United States, (3) the centrality of Protestant churches in the Korean American community, and (4) core Korean cultural values that suppress open expression of negative affects.

Korean Immigration into American Families

From the beginning of Korean immigration into the North American mainland, Korean-born women and children became part of American families. The second wave of Korean immigration involved the Korean brides of American servicemen as well as Korean adoptees. In the aftermath of the Korean War, Bertha and Henry Holt adopted eight Korean orphans in a highly public process, involving the passage of special laws in Congress for international adoption. In fact, South Korea has the world's oldest international adoption program. Since the Holts' adoption in the 1950s, over two hundred thousand Korean orphans have been adopted in America (www.adoptivefamilies.com) and Korea ranks fifth among the countries involved in the most international adoptions (behind China, Guatemala, Russia, and Ethiopia). From 2003 to 2007, between 939 and 1,817 Korean orphans immigrated to the United States (travel.state.gov). About five times as many children are adopted from China, but considering that the population of China is approximately twenty times that of the population of South Korea, the rate of Korean adoption in comparison to its total population exceeds such statistics in China.

Consequently, the inclusion of Koreans into American families has been a significant part of the Korean immigration story from almost the beginning of Korean American history. Because of this, Koreans have favorably infiltrated American family life as insiders as well as outsiders. However, this source of integration of Koreans in American family life is tinged with associations to what would be called a shameful history by Korean standards. Korean women have been sexually appealing to American men since the Korean War, where they interfaced with American military servicemen in the "camptowns" or entertainment districts surrounding U.S. military bases in Korea (Yuh, 2002). While these women enjoyed the social, economic, and geographical mobility that came with marriage to American servicemen, they become ignominiously associated with prostitution and sacrifice of their Korean identities. *Yanggalbo* (Western whore) and *Yanggonju* (Western princess), the two Korean names for these camptown prostitutes, signify the split between the tendency to degrade and value these women. The prostitution of Korean women to U.S. soldiers during the Korean War was regulated and supported by both the Korean and American governments as a means to maintain "friendly relations." This may explain in part the relatively low rate of intermarriage among Korean Americans (compared to Chinese and Japanese) and Americans (Kitano, Yeung, Chai, and Hatanaka, 1984) since this second wave of Korean immigrants. Similarly, adoptees from Korea have traditionally been orphaned initially by ravages of war, but more recently by the situation of single motherhood in Korea, which is rarer than in America and less socially accepted. These hidden sources of scandal or shame in the second wave of Korean American immigration that underlie the predominantly positive association of Koreans transplanted into American families may be an important source of hidden or subtle conflict about assimilation into American culture.

The Absence of Significant Political Conflicts Between United States and South Korea

The political relations between South Korea and the United States have been primarily favorable since, in fact, it is the United States that was most instrumental in the formation of South Korea. In 1938, it was the United States that set the 38th parallel in Korea, dividing the Soviet-occupied North from the American-occupied South. The Korean War started on June 25, 1950, when North Korean military forces invaded the South Korean border. The United States fought on the UN-supported South Korean side of the war under the leadership of the famed General Douglas MacArthur. Interestingly, the United States continued to refer to this war as the "Korean Conflict" rather than war to avoid the need to formally declare war through Congress. In contrast to the Vietnam War, American involvement in the Korean War was largely welcomed by South Koreans. At its height, the approval of U.S. presence in South Korea by its natives reached 94 percent. One of the most popular television shows in American history, *M*A*S*H*, broadcast real-life stories of American doctors and medical personnel serving in the Korean War. Its final episode in 1983 still holds the distinction as the most-watched television finale in U.S. history (television.aol.com).

Since the Korean War, the United States and South Korea have remained allied against North Korea. It is with both significant military and economic aid from the United States that the Republic of Korea has enjoyed the extent of modernization and industrialization that it experienced during the latter half of the twentieth century, making it one of the world's fastest-growing economies (Oliver, 1986; Smith, 1993). South Koreans and Americans have remained on the same side of the Cold War (unlike the Chinese) and are not plagued by a history of opposition in World War II (unlike Japan). In fact, South Korea has been largely dependent on the United States for political, military, and economic support as a small and less powerful country located in close proximity to Russia, Japan, and China. For these reasons, Koreans in America are not plagued by associations with political difficulties or opposition against Americans, have not been targeted by any formal segregation policies, and, for the most part, have not been perceived as threatening to the American public. This history may form the basis of the idealization of the United States in the minds of Koreans that may contribute to deference to American authorities. While anti-American sentiments have always existed among Koreans and had been on the rise at the turn of the twenty-first century with trade relations becoming increasingly strained, scholars indicate that this trend is getting worse (Larson et al., 2004).

The Centrality of the Protestant Church in the Korean American Community

In South Korea, compared to other Asian countries, Christianity is strikingly widespread. The CIA "World Factbook" states that almost 27 percent of the South Korean population is Christian—that is, 20 percent Protestant and 7 percent Roman Catholic—compared to 23.2 percent Buddhist. This fact suggests that Western religion is more dominant in South Korea than Asian religions. Seoul is the home of the largest Christian congregation in the world, Yoido Full Gospel Church (Cox, 1996). South Korea is second only to the United States in its missionary efforts internationally. It has been argued that the growth of Christianity in South Korea was facilitated by native monotheistic Korean religious tradition. The predominance of polytheistic models in Japan and China and the lack of religious freedom in China impeded the relative growth of Christianity in those settings. In addition, identifications with Christianity by Koreans have historically been an important source of distinction from, resistance against, and persecution by the Japanese during their occupation of Korea from 1905 to 1945 (Cho, 1984). Thus, Christianity has been an important source of Korean national identity in the twentieth century.

In America, the most important source of homoethnic community for Koreans is in the church (Kang, 2002; Kim, 2006; Kim, 2006). An estimated 70 percent of Korean Americans belong to ethnic Korean churches (Hurh, 1998). First-generation Korean Americans formed churches that served both social and religious functions (Kim, 2004; Jeung, 2005). These churches provided Korean-born Americans with an important source of *intramural refueling* (Akhtar, 1999) as well as opportunities for social status within a structured hierarchy. Korean American Christianity also serves as an important vehicle for the social visibility of Koreans, both among other Christian groups and the community at large. In a book entitled "God's New Whiz Kids? Korean American Evangelicals on Campus," Rebecca Kim (2006) seeks to answer the question of why SGKAs, most of whom speak English (and sometimes not Korean) and come from ethnically diverse neighborhoods, disproportionately choose exclusively Korean churches and campus religious groups over multiracial and white ministries. Contrary to popular belief, these SGKAs are not just remaining loyal to their parents' churches, but rather forming new SGKA churches that are distinctively different from the churches in which they grew up. In Kim's study of SGKAs' religious involvements, she reported that SGKAs distinguish their church organizations as "democratic, egalitarian, and dynamic" as opposed to the "hierarchical, patriarchal, and static" nature of first-generation Korean congregations (Kim, 43). Kim quotes an SGKA pastor to make this point:

> The first-generation is into distinctions, they are title-oriented . . . for example, *gip san nim* [the Korean word for deacon] means servant, but the Korean interpretation of that is like a higher stage of being religious, more reverential, more honorific. But the second generation do not view it that way, once you are done serving, you discard the title; being a deacon is more functional. (43)

Kim points out other important differences including the presence of women higher in the church organization hierarchies in SGKA churches as well as the open expression of emotions that are more characteristic of SGKA churches as opposed to its first-generation counterparts. Interestingly, SGKA churches identify themselves as having more "religious authenticity" (46). SGKAs witnessed a great deal of "splitting" in their parents' churches, due not to religious ideas or problems, but more to political, financial, and social issues. SGKAs saw their parents' religious commitments as secondary to professional or academic commitments. One student reported a tendency of first-generation Koreans to discourage too much religious devotion: "It is like they drop me off at Sunday school to pick up good values, but did not really take [my religion] seriously, so when I wanted to be a missionary . . . they were like whoa . . . No way, you are going to med school" (47).

The church, a central source of Korean identity in America, provides an important bridge and container of Korean influences within the context of its host culture. As explicated by R. Y. Kim (2006), the church and campus exclusive ethnic Christian fellowships has been a focal locus of an emergent second-generation Korean identity that has developed in a form of quiet and nonviolent contrast, rebellion, and rejection of its parents' religious/social traditions with the influences of facets of American culture such as egalitarianism and emotional expressivity. This second-generation phenomenon also provides SGKAs with a source of cultural contact and intramural fueling of cultural identity (as opposed to Akhtar's notion of *re*fueling). The Korean American church is a visible and solid source of Korean community in America that comes complete with moral values and purpose, not just geographical concentration, businesses, and cuisine that organizes the communities in many ethnic enclaves.

Perhaps, what is most significant about this form of cultural identification for Koreans in America is that it is distinctly *American* at its basis. What is more American than Protestantism (Weber, 1930; Kirschner, 1996; Kim, 2006)? In his landmark sociologic text *The Protestant Ethic and Spirit of Capitalism*, Max Weber (1930) outlined the way in which central developments in religious tenets within the emerging Lutheran and Calvinist doctrines spurred the growth of nascent capitalism in America. In contrast to Catholicism, where salvation is mediated through church officiants and figureheads, the Protestants disbelieve that any religious authority can determine whether or not an individual has been chosen for salvation. Rather, the Protestant ethic involves a challenge to look for signs of salvation, which included worldly occupational success, driving intense commitment to vocational activities and investment of moneys into increasing one's productivity. Weber referred to the ideas of founding father Benjamin Franklin, who, though not strongly religiously affiliated, wrote of the values of hard work, thrift, and frugality, which were in line with the new Protestant ethic.

The strong ties between Koreans in America and Protestantism may be the single greatest factor for Koreans assimilating to mainstream culture since Korean values founded in Protestant beliefs neatly converge with the religious basis of American culture and economy. First-generation Korean Americans who came to this country for opportunity became well-known for their work ethic and business success. Because of their Protestant roots, Koreans in America not only worked hard to earn money, they eschewed spending such money on luxurious items or status symbols, but rather invested that money, primarily into the education of SGKAs.

In summary, the involvement of Korean Americans in the Protestant church is among the most critical features of the Korean cultural experience and identity in America. Worldwide, Koreans have a long-standing and impressive history of religious activity within the Protestant world. At the core of Korean nationalism is its differentiation from its neighbors by their religious affiliations. In America, the first wave of immigrants established churches for both religious and social purposes. The SGKAs have developed as an original visible and vibrant cultural force that combines important aspects of its native culture and its newly adopted American culture. Lastly, the core of Korean religious life in Protestantism provides a substantial bridge to shared cultural values between Korean immigrants and its new American cultural context.

While these religious factors have eased Koreans into acculturation in America, they have also been the source of negative strains of racial exclusivity and unforeseen intrapsychic pressures. More so than other Asian ethnic groups, Korean Americans are perceived as more ethnically exclusive in their religious practices, which converges with more general impressions of Koreans as racist. This Korean American racism has been played out most publicly in the long-standing tensions between Korean shopkeepers and minority Americans as reflected most pointedly in the Los Angeles riots following the Rodney King verdict, in which 2,500 Korean businesses were looted and vandalized. While the legacy of economic and personal self-sacrifice among first-generation Korean Americans has helped this generation to break the barriers of the invisible minority myth, it may also serve as an important source of pressure, constraint, and guilt among the SGKAs as they confront freedom and egalitarianism in the United States.

Core Korean Values of *Haan*: Identifications and Disidentifications with Aggression

Korea is plagued by a long history of invasions, occupations, and territorial conflicts with its aggressive and more powerful neighbors China, Japan, and the Soviet Union. Its geographical position between these countries has made it politically and economically appealing, thus making it a constant target for invasion with constant threats to its independence. Irene Kim (2006), a psychologist at University of Notre Dame, has written one of the only comprehensive articles on cultural competence in working with Korean immigrants in which she succinctly defines the term:

> *Haan* is a multifaceted indigenous and cultural construct, rich with symbolism and emotion-laden. *Haan* refers to suppressed anger, unexpressed grievances, resentment, indignation, despair, or holding a grudge. According to traditional Korean society, individuals were discouraged from overt expressions of emotion, particularly anger. Instead, individuals suppressed their anger, and over time this anger accumulated, the suppressed anger eventually transforming into feelings of *haan*. (152)

Kim explains that *haan* carries both positive and negative potentials. One expression of *haan* is a fierce capacity to sustain motivation and persevere until "justice" is achieved. Kim quotes a Korean phrase, "I will show you who will eventually win" (152), as a reflection of the way that this Korean notion of *haan* fuels "endurance of hardship, determination, and even heroic deeds" (152). Primarily, *haan* captures the more passive and suffering side of anger, rather than its active and destructive forms. Another term, according to Kim, captures this dimension of anger, called *o-ki*, which is used to describe anger mobilized into purposeful action, like in student demonstrations against the government. This concept is less idealized in the Korean context.

Both constructions of anger, *haan* and *o-ki*, frame anger as reactive to injustice and righteous, reflecting the deep valuation of goal-orientation and a repudiation of more basic instinctual forms of anger in Korean mores. This public containment within the Korean value system has contributed to the notion that Koreans in America are largely nonaggressive and nonthreatening. However, while this dominant nonthreatening Korean America persona has allowed Koreans to be easily assimilated in the United States, the explosive transformations of *haan* into *o-ki* have more recently plagued the Korean American image. In general, domestic violence is becoming increasingly associated with the Korean American population, as are ethnic gangs (Kim and Sung, 2000; Shimtuh, 2000; McGarvey, 2002). Both the 1992 slaying of an African American girl by a Korean grocer in Los Angeles (*New York Times*, November 6, 1992) and the Virginia Tech massacre of 2007 are more high-profile incidents reflecting the explosive potential of Koreans who feel unjustly victimized or attacked. These violent outbursts perpetrated by Korean Americans have catalyzed the expression of intense anti-Korean sentiments.

The grocer event involved a female Korean shopkeeper who believed a fifteen-year-old African American girl was trying to shoplift a bottle of orange juice. Video from the store's security cameras show the victim punching Mrs. Du several times before Mrs. Du reached for the handgun under the counter and shot this young girl to death. In court, Judge Joyce A. Karlins sentenced Mrs. Du to probation for the charge of voluntary manslaughter, inciting fervent protest by the African American community. The murder occurred close to one year before the unrest and violent protest staged by the African American community in response to the acquittal of four white LAPD officers on the charge of beating an African American man named Rodney King. The Rodney King riots left fifty-three people dead and approximately one billion dollars in damages in the Korean American business community. It is probable that the outrage incited in the Du case fueled the targeting of Korean businesses as a statement of backlash against maltreatment of African Americans.

There is an interesting dynamic evident in these unfortunate events involving Korean merchants and African Americans in the community. Kang (2002) has written that the position of Korean immigrants as the "middleman minority," who supply goods produced by the dominant class to underclass minorities, thereby putting themselves in the position of being scapegoated for the economic deprivation and political marginalization experienced by African Americans. However, as depicted in Spike Lee's movie *Do the Right Thing*, the Korean shopkeeper has empathy for what it means to be black in America—that is, not being a privileged white person and having to struggle to make economic progress (Cooper, 1999). Here, what gets set up is a situation of double victimization for Korean business owners, both by whites in America as excluded and relegated to work in ghettoes and by the minorities within those ghettoes for their position as the middleman, representing and serving the privileged white class. This situation enforces the notion of *haan* in racial conflicts between Koreans and other Americans, where Koreans are targeted and victimized, and their angry responses as justified. Needless to say, these dynamics do not improve Korean and African American race relations.

Seung-Hui Cho perpetrated the largest massacre by a single gunman in United States driven by what appears to be a sense of *haan* transformed into *ok-i*. In the manifesto Cho mailed to NBC prior to the shootings, he made statements such as "You forced me into a corner and gave me only one option. The decision was yours. Now you have blood on your hands that will never wash off" (NBC, 2007). In this manifesto, Cho expressed self-righteous criticism of the "debauchery" and "hedonistic needs" of his wealthy mostly white classmates. Here, evidence of a sense of long suffering, resentment, and suppressed anger consistent with the Korean notion of *haan*. Also evident in Cho's rantings is a disturbing notion that "I will show you who will eventually win."

In both tragic events described here, violent acts perpetrated by Koreans are communicated in the framework of victimization, righteousness, and reactivity to threat. These constructions illustrate the tendency of Koreans to repudiate their internal sources of anger and aggression. This denial of innate aggressive drives results in both a paranoid/schizoid phenomenon where the aggression is projected externally and justly reacted against with violence. A possible explanation of this cultural repudiation of aggression may be that Koreans have needed to differentiate themselves from other Asian nationalities, specifically China and Japan, in their nonaggressive nature or only-aggressive-when-victimized stance. Unfortunately, this leaves Koreans without any cultural channels for healthy expressions of aggression or metabolization and mentalization of angry affects. This emotional cultural lacunae leaves Koreans most vulnerable to explosive anger, while also making them appear, for the most part, nonthreatening.

Summary of Factors That Bridge and Complicate Korean Assimilation into the American Mainstream

To review, there are four factors that have primarily facilitated but also complicated the integration of Koreans into the American mainstream: (1) the contribution of intermarriage and adoption to the second wave of Korean American immigration, (2) the absence of political conflicts in South Korea–U.S. relations, (3) the central role of Protestantism in Korean culture both in South Korea and in the United States, and (4) the Korean value of *haan* and the repudiation of native aggression. These factors have created relatively open channels for contact between Korean immigrants and Americans both in the sense that Koreans have experienced early entry into American families through marriage and adoption and seem to share deeply held common Protestant values, without appearing outwardly anti-American or threatening. Koreans have immigrated to America with many of the psychosocial variables that favorably affect the transition to a new country (Akhtar, 1999), including favorable circumstances and reasons for migration, access to refueling both intramurally and extramurally, mostly positive reception by host community, and experiences of efficacy in the new culture.

The Limits of Assimilation in America

While these factors I have outlined have facilitated the success of Koreans in America, they have also provided an important nidus of vulnerability and marginalization among SGKAs particularly. In some ways, Korean Americans have benefited from their associated stereotypes as nerdy, self-sacrificing, docile, and nonaggressive people since this nonthreatening image of Korean Americans has made way for access to opportunities in the United States. The other side of the model minority myth that shapes predominant stereotypes of Asian Americans generally is the "yellow peril" myth, which paints Asians generally as an insidious uncontainable force characterized as sneaky, corrupt, greedy, and opportunistic (Kim, 1986; Lee, 1996; Kawai, 2005). Both sides of this "model minority–yellow peril dialectic" (Kawai, 2005) define a group that is competitive force that is threatening by virtue of their potential to displace and edge out Americans in terms of opportunities for work and education (Mathews, 2008). Additionally, the two sides of the Asian American stereotype coin have provided a basis for what Korean American political scientist Claire Jean Kim (1999) has called "racial triangulation." According to Kim, the presence of Asian Americans has transformed the black-white race dichotomy in America into a triangle, where Asians, as the "model minority," rank above the status of blacks, but still inferior to whites. On the one hand, the white end of the racial hierarchy "valorizes" Asians to both distinguish them from the bottom of the racial hierarchy at the black end, while the whites also distinguish themselves from Asians through what Kim calls "civic ostracism." This civic ostracism involves the perpetuation of the notion of Asian-ness as statically foreign, with limits to the extent to which they can be considered "insiders." The two sides of the "model minority–yellow peril dialectic" (Kawai, 2005) thus represent both the valorization of Asians alongside with their characterization as essential outsiders.

While the racial triangulation of Asian Americans generally serves as a marginalizing force for SGKAs, this particular group of Asian Americans maintains "strong co-ethnic networks" particularly associated with campus evangelical groups and other church-related organizations (Lew, 2004; Kim, 2006). This tendency to maintain exclusively homoethnic organizations has provided important means of maintaining cultural identity, but also tends to cast Koreans as racist (Lee, 1996). The tendency to exclusively socialize with others within their ethnic group is compounded by the dynamics of racial triangulation whereby Asians seek to differentiate themselves from the other "inferior" minorities, which ultimately isolates SGKAs at the same time it provides for a consolidation of an available, visible, and vibrant SGKA community.

Consequently, while SGKAs have been predominantly associated with success and integration into the American mainstream, there are also strains of exclusivity, difficulty, and marginalization in the SGKA experience. In the section that follows, I will outline the way in which these factors pose particular developmental dilemmas for the SGKA.

DEVELOPMENTAL DILEMMAS OF SGKAS: FROM THE INVISIBLE MINORITY TO FAME AND NOTORIETY

Perhaps the most important distinction between first- and second-generation Korean Americans lies in difference in acceptance of and attainment of visibility, expressiveness, and individuality. While first-generation Korean Americans faced adulthood in a period where Korean culture was relatively unfamiliar to the American public and where Korean figures were relatively absent from the cultural and political landscape, the SGKAs are now facing adulthood in the context of Americans being more aware of Koreans in a variety of contexts, both positive and negative, because of the changes in Korean American attitudes toward self-definition and self-expression. In the next section, I will frame these conflicts that SGKAs face as they stand on the edge of integration and separation with the American mainstream. These include conflicts of invisibility versus fame/notoriety and fulfillment of stereotypes versus creativity. Lastly, I will also examine the effects of the first generation's immigration that continue to ripple into the course of the SGKAs' lives.

Invisibility vs. Fame/Notoriety

In a poignantly written collection of personal narratives by Asian American college students called *Balancing Two Worlds: Asian American College Students Tell Their Life Stories* (Garrod and Kilkenny, 2007), Patrick S. writes of the dilemmas of membership in the invisible or silent minority:

> I didn't want to be different, but because I couldn't do anything about it, I avoided calling attention to myself. If people didn't notice me, then maybe they wouldn't notice my differentness. If people didn't notice my differentness, maybe I wouldn't feel it either. I suppose that is how I explain to myself how I got to be a "quiet" person. But, I did wish that more people knew me somehow. For all my desire to not be noticed, I still resented the fact that people saw me as "quiet"—and not much else. . . . I did well academically, and people seemed to know that. But being labeled "smart" was never much satisfaction to me. . . . It was just another label. . . . And that's how people would talk about me. If only people knew me, I thought to myself, they would see me not just as a quiet (but smart) person but as a regular three-dimensional individual. The paradox, though, was that although I didn't want to be known only for being unnoticeable, I didn't want to be different from everybody else. (38)

The sentiments that Patrick is able to articulate here are deeply resonant with the experience of many "smart" SGKAs, who can comfortably achieve recognition for academic performance but little else. While the first generation of Koreans strove to be successful, fueled by both a Protestant ethic against flashy lavishness and toward constant hard work with an emphasis on functionality rather than personality, SGKAs, influenced by American dictates of individuality, are painfully caught between the desire to be recognized and a fear of being "too different" or not fitting in. Social options for SGKAs seem largely constrained, as Steinberg reports; Asian American students are "permitted to join intellectual crowds, like the 'brains,' but not the more socially oriented crowds—the 'populars,' 'jocks', and 'partyers'" (Steinberg, 1996). This leaves SGKAs with the options of colluding with the silent stereotype and achieving respectable but ordinary levels of academic achievement, achieving notoriety through academic failure, or achieving fame by exceptional levels of accomplishment. Clearly, none of these options are without propensities toward masochism, self-deprivation, guilt, shame, and feelings of inadequacy since the options seem to be decent achievement, extraordinary achievement, or abject failure. This dilemma also closely relates to the next conflict of creativity versus fulfillment of stereotypes that SKGAs face, since the other option in this constraining system of choices within the silent invisibility versus notoriety or fame dilemma is the option of creativity in forming one's young adult path.

Fulfillment of Stereotypes vs. Creativity and Self-Determination

As noted above, Asian American young adults in general are much freer to take on "nerd" or "brain" identities than "jock" or "popular" ones in American social networks. When SGKAs specifically, and Asian Americans generally, leave home for college, access to social choices widens and provides more possibilities for intellectual interests and extracurricular activities. While in some communities with large concentrations of Koreans, some high school student bodies have enough Korean Americans to form homoethnic groups, it is more commonly in college that SGKAs encounter this option to affiliate with exclusively Korean American social networks. There exist greater differentiation of current Korean American subcultures in young adulthood, including but not limited to those who conform to positive stereotypes like campus evangelicals, premeds and other science "nerds," or take up allegiances with groups aligned against such stereotypes like "slackers," partyers, and gangsters. Alternatively, some SGKAs become more primarily identified as American, leaving their Korean-ness behind altogether. With more choices comes more creativity within existing categories and options to create or move into new categories of Korean American identity. Unlike their parents' generation, who closely guarded and remained tied to the Korean cultural ideals (that is, those that remain static in their minds as the culture in South Korea actually became radically modernized) while quietly conforming to American expectations nonoffensively, SGKAs are engaged in a process of collectively forging emergent Korean American identities that not only contain more options but also are in themselves dynamic, mixing influences from its two cultural sources to widely varying degrees at different times and in different settings.

Since the SGKA identity is in tremendous flux, there are remnants of former stereotypes that still shape the expectations of SGKAs as they become adults and also against which they tend to rebel to claim their own individuality. Like all children in America, the SGKAs tend to be more socially and politically liberal than their parents and also want to create their own paths in the expressly American proverbial process of leaving home In his study of narratives by SGKA young adults, Steven Kang notes that contrary to stereotypes that Korean American children always listen to their parents, SGKAs emphasized valuing developing (1) careers of their choice often outside medicine and engineering, (2) financial and geographical independence from their parents, and (3) lifestyles of their own preferences (153). More SGKAs are entering college with intentions to become doctors, lawyers, or scientists, and through a process of individuation, increased self-awareness, and increased opportunity leave as artists, writers, philosophers, sociologists, teachers, and even therapists (Kang, 2002; Garrod and Kilkenny, 2007).

One important Korean American stereotype that SGKAs view with significant ambivalence is competitiveness. First, while academic success is both strongly emphasized by first-generation Koreans and provides an important channel toward social mobility when other options are constrained (Steinberg, 1996), the stereotype of academic competitiveness also results in SGKAs being targets of peer envy and hostility. Siu's review (1996) of Asian American students at risk reveals that many Asian American students report feeling that their image as a model minority incites discrimination and anti-Asian sentiments. Jenny Tsai, a Harvard College graduate, wrote her senior thesis in the social studies department on the notion of "Too Many Asians at this School," a sentiment articulated at elite public magnet schools. Tsai developed the idea of taking on this intellectual investigation after hearing people in her own school community decrying the influx of Asians who were thought to "threaten the culture of Hunter College High School . . . [which] prided itself on being a school that fostered student leadership though a plethora of student clubs, sports teams, and artistic groups." Tsai continued to recount: "Students attested that the growing Asian student population had detracted from the creativity and independence that had defined HCHS's activity scene as Asian students focused primarily on their academic studies. Those Asian students who were active in extracurricular activities were perceived to be disingenuous" (Matthews, 2008). Generally speaking, this academically competitive Asian stereotype is loaded with conflicts between opportunity for success and visibility at the expense of being perceived as passionless, calculating, and "disingenuous."

More specifically for Koreans, competitiveness is problematic because of the cultural needs to dis-identify with innate aggressive drives. Being overtly competitive invites envy and scorn for being aggressive and even greedy, two personality traits that are not acceptable in Korean culture as they are internally associated with Korea's invaders, China and Japan. In addition, being lumped into uniformly Asian stereotypes with other Asians is also naturally demeaning, even when there is some reality that enforces these stereotypes. Many Koreans have sought as the solution to this competitive stereotype trap going into fields which are not competitive and not highly populated by Asians. This move to escape the academically competitive stereotype has broadened the range of occupational activities in which Koreans are involved.

Leaving Home Part II: The Impact of Immigration on the Second Generation

Most of the current generation of Korean American individuals in young and middle adulthood witnessed the complex psychosocial process of their parents' leaving their native land and adjusting to a foreign one. As described thoroughly by Akhtar (1999), the process of immigration is full of pain, losses, anxiety, and mourning. As this generation of Korean Americans step into the phase of their lives that they saw their parents live through with such pain and sacrifice, SGKAs may come into adulthood with expectations and preparation for similar degrees of deprivation and marginalization. This may be an expectation that has in fact facilitated the entry of SGKAs into realms of American life that they are the first Koreans to be a part of—for example, those SGKAs who have broken into the arts and athletics.

However, it also seems to have fueled more generally a phenomenon of SGKAs navigating the American developmental milestone of leaving home in dramatic ways. Kang's study of SGKAs revealed that most SGKA young adults choose not to move back home after college unless a family tragedy occurs and they are needed for supporting afflicted family members. The immigrant values of the first generation were to provide opportunities for their children that they did not have. Koreans have done this fairly successfully, leading their children to in fact have greater opportunity to leave them for schooling and jobs. More recently, more SGKAs appear to be attending both secondary school and university away from home and taking jobs overseas after obtaining degrees or traveling overseas for missionary work. In geographical, emotional, and professional directions, SGKAs choose paths that create great distances between themselves and their parents, causing their process of "leaving home" to be even more dramatic and painfully experienced by their parents. While SGKAs do make significant efforts to reconnect and maintain contacts with parents, there remains a distance between the first and second generations' lives and cultural identities. Despite the fact the SGKAs have not always left the country where their parents live in a geographical sense, in their emotional, professional, cultural life, and personal life they often do. However, it is difficult for SGKAs to openly express feelings about these differences both because of knowledge of major sacrifices and losses endured by parents for their future and also because of the devaluation of open aggression or assertiveness in Korean culture.

CONCLUDING REMARKS

Technical guidelines applicable to working with immigrant populations more generally have been developed and described elsewhere (Akhtar, 1999). This specific exploration of SGKAs provides more specific recommendations for working with SGKAs in psychotherapy. First, considering that the cultural identity of this group of individuals is emergent, varied, and in flux, assuming too much about an SGKA's cultural experience and values is a dubious endeavor. Being mistaken as either Japanese or Chinese is a painful experience, especially given the historically problematic relations of China and Japan with Korea. Moreover, the immigration history of this group is quite different from those of Chinese and Japanese Americans, with the shared cultural stake in Protestantism being a primary point of harmony between Korean immigrants and Americans. In the spirit of "cultural sensitivity," understanding SGKAs using prevalent Asian stereotypes of competitiveness, deferential tendencies, and "filial piety" (Gu, 2006) may endanger, not foster, the therapeutic alliance as SGKAs may experience varying degrees of conflict about these aspects of their identity.

Second, because of the witnessed sacrifices, losses, and vulnerabilities their parents faced as immigrants, SGKAs may be very protective of their parents and not willing to openly criticize them in a therapy situation when a therapist's best intention may involve validating the newly emergent parts of the SGKA's self not mirrored or supported by his/her parents. While the forces of acculturation may widen the generation gap between first- and second-generation Korean Americans, the intense bonds experienced between parents and children may be difficult to detect or appreciate as aspects of this relationship might have been internalized in known verbal forms. As Irene Kim (2006) points out, "in Western cultures, clear, direct, and explicitly verbal communication is highly valued but in Korean culture communication is less clear, more subtle, indirect, implicit, and non-verbal" (153).

In general, SGKAs may not only be reluctant to openly discuss sexual or aggressive impulses or fantasies. Regarding sex and aggression, the intrapsychic life of SGKAs may be shaped in a way that such drives are less often openly expressed, partly due to native cultural values but also because in American culture Korean aggression and sexuality are not prominently represented. Korean or Asian female sexuality is often fetishized and objectified in representations such as geisha girls, mail-order brides, and concubines. The terms "Asian fetish" and "yellow fever" refer to sexual engagement between Asian women and Caucasian men in derogatory terms. While Asian female sexuality is largely cast as subjugated and fetishized, Asian male sexuality is simply unrepresented. As Joan Kee (1998) has written: "Asian American male sexuality has long entailed a discourse of nothingness." The combination of more conservative sexual mores in Korean native culture and these narrow, pejorative, and underdeveloped representations of Asian sexuality generally in American culture may constrain the ways SGKAs can mentalize and express their sexuality. Similarly, SGKAs may have inhibitions about open and free expressions of aggression, both in part because of the way Korean native culture frames angry affects in terms of *haan* and now in the current climate because of painful associations and deep guilt within the Korean community about the Virginia Tech massacre (Nordboe et al., 2007).

Ultimately, SGKAs are a diverse group of individuals with dynamically shifting and emerging identities, in flux because of age-appropriate developmental processes as well as larger processes relevant to the formation of a dynamic hybrid cultural identity influenced by both Korean and American cultures. While it is important to understand this group as distinct, with unique features that necessitate flexible adaptation of traditional psychoanalytic frameworks, it is equally important to acknowledge the ways in which this group is essentially American as well.

NOTE

**Acknowledgments: Dedicated to my Korean parents for making the space for my second-generation Korean American identity to emerge.

15

An American-Japanese Transcultural Psychoanalysis and the Issue of Teacher Transference

Yasuhiko Taketomo

> "You've changed." The professor's voice was warm with a relative's affection. "A childish name like Bird doesn't suit you anymore."
>
> Kenzaburo Oe (1964, 132)

This report deals with the work done by a psychoanalyst from an "American" background and an analysand from a "Japanese" background.[1] It is a highly personal disclosure, so it may cause some discomfort to my professional colleagues. I wish to make it clear, however, that my interest is in a full and candid scientific discussion of the issues of transcultural analysis raised in this report. In this regard, I should point out that, in referring to a "Japanese" background (or an "American" one), I am not considering Japanese culture as a monolithic entity; it would be wrong to speak of *the* Japanese background or *the* Japanese character.

Despite Freud's theoretical stance, which is generally opposed to that of the "culturalists," his interest in culture began in childhood and pervaded this lifetime work—even if at times his interest seemed submerged by his absorption in his neurological studies and later in psychodynamics and structure of the mind (Freud, 1935). As is well known, Freud's psychoanalytic theories stimulated new ideas and critical scrutiny by outstanding scientific thinkers from the boundaries of psychoanalysis and cultural anthropology. Out of these endeavors, the so-called culture and personality school emerged. Born, raised, and educated in Japan, I began my psychoanalytic training in the United States at the age of thirty—at the height of the influence of the culture and personality school. From the outset I felt resistance to the direction this school was taking, although I readily acknowledge its valuable contributions. In particular, I was skeptical about applying general cultural descriptions to an individual coming out of a modern technological state such as Japan. Japanese society has been actively changing, differentiating into increasingly complex cultural subgroups, so that it is no longer possible for Japanese politicians to appeal to a homogeneous racial identity. In this regard my criticism of the culture and personality school is similar to the views expressed by John Spiegel (1971), when he wrote:

> In any society . . . the culture does not present itself as a unified, monolithic whole. It appears as a system of beliefs and value orientations which are patterned variably for the different parts of the social system and which are constantly subject to change. Nor is the individual directly related to the society's stock of cultural beliefs and orientations. The relationship is obtained systematically through his participation in the family and in other small groups in shared activities. It is these activities which are patterned in accordance with variation in cultural orientations for the part of the social system in which they occur. This orderly variation makes room for the inevitable variation in personality types—a variation which receives contributions from both the somatic and psychological systems of the individual. (64)

In this present paper dealing with the teacher transference, the school, though not mentioned by Spiegel, looms large as the representative of the "small groups." I further wish to emphasize historic situations as important moments that subject the constituents of a society to change in various ways, especially the situations confronting a society regarding its mode of adaptation to foreign cultural input.

The issues I wish to address here concern the way the influence of culture can emerge in the search for *individual* personal meaning. The analyst must meet the analysand without stereotyping, without the encumbrance of any propagandistic cultural therapy. Culture is not to be ignored, but it must be looked at through the individual's experience. Indeed, in a strict sense, one might say that every psychoanalytic psychotherapy is transcultural. In any case, the approach I am advocating involves a shift from earlier field studies to an exploration of the dyads of the psychoanalytic interchange. And it is with the hope of furthering this exploration that I have decided to discuss my own analysis.

A PRECONSCIOUS TEACHER TRANSFERENCE

The impetus for this chapter came when I was invited to participate on a panel titled "Through a Stranger's Eyes: The Experience of Being Psychoanalyzed for Analysts from Different Cultural Backgrounds." My immediate response was that my relationship to my analyst was hardly a relationship between strangers. True, we had not met each other before we began, and certainly we were from different parts of the world. But it seemed out of tune with my sense of our relationship to describe ourselves as strangers. The theme I would propose is more one of "not necessarily strangers."

On reflecting further on my relationship to my analyst, I realized that there was a special dynamic at play—what I propose to call the "teacher transference." From almost the beginning of our analytic work, I was aware that I was relating to my analyst as my "teacher." By this I do not mean that my attitude was determined by the fact that my analyst was also a faculty member of the analytic institute. Nor am I referring to a simple variant of the father or mother transference. Rather, my "teacher transference" derived from my particular Japanese schooling; it also reflected the particular historical period and my family background.

From the age of eight or nine, I had formed an intense relationship of affectionate respect to a teacher at each stage of my schooling: primary school (age six to twelve), secondary school (thirteen to seventeen), college (eighteen to twenty), and medical school (twenty-one to twenty-four). It began with the teacher assigned to my third-grade class, who carried us through to graduation from primary school. This remarkable teacher immediately gained the respect of the forty-two notoriously mischievous boys in my class. My family regarded him as sincerity incarnate. With him, I entered into my first relationship with a mentor, other than my parents.

In light of Erikson's (1959) epigenetic timetable, this dawning of the apprentice age at eight or nine may sound a bit precocious. I should add, however, that around this time I was thrown not only into the life space of the school, outside the family boundary, but also into a taste of some historical reality. During this period there was an escalation in the power of the ultranationalistic leaders in steering the Japanese empire. It was the time of the Manchurian incident, withdrawal from the League of Nations, and group assassinations of some leaders resisting the ultranationalism by army extremists. Even at their young age, my classmates were affected by the increasingly right-wing ideology rampant in the nation. For me, result was a sense of alienation. I happened to be perhaps the only student from a Christian family, and my father—quite unlike my classmates' fathers—earned his living by teaching English literature. Moreover, I was miserably unathletic and clearly overprotected, often being specially dressed for my health. One sign of my classmates' disfavor was that I was "demoted" from the class presidency. I also felt an increasing cognitive dissonance in the class discussions. Classes in Japanese history, particularly of such events as the early Catholic converts' revolt against the Tokugawa Shogunate (leading to two hundred years of closure for the country) were lonely periods to endure.

The year following my graduation from this primary school, the Ministry of Education issued a communiqué on religious education. Referring to a previous order from 1899, which prohibited public schools from teaching the doctrine of any specific religious sect, it indicated that there had—"regrettably"—been "cases of improper practice of the said order" (Editorial Committee of the Historical Sources of Educational Institutions, 1956, 336–67). "Education in the school," it reemphasized, "should maintain its neutral position in relation to any of the religious sects or churches." Specifically, "It is important not to injure the religious spirit cultivated at home or in society, but to be attentive to the religious desire stemming from within the pupil's heart. One must absolutely avoid belittling or despising this religious spirit or religious desire."

This document suggests that my experience was not uncommon at the time in that the ministry itself was concerned about this issue. In all fairness, however, my teacher was exemplary in his handling of religious references—even before this communiqué was issued. In all this, however, I sensed that my teacher empathized with my experience of alienation and my efforts to cope with a serious narcissistic wound in the face of my declining popularity. Even though he never involved himself directly in my struggles, I never doubted his personal concern for my welfare. I had a persistent sense that he was proud of me, despite my repeated failures to be reinstated as class president or vice president. And I wanted to be worthy of his care and trust. Indeed, after graduation I continued to visit him until his death some thirty years later.

My next teacher was in charge of my class for five years, until my graduation from secondary school. During this period, when I was sixteen, I experienced the first symptoms of a career-identity problem. I began to feel that a career in science, to which I had dedicated myself, might not be suitable. Instead, I felt drawn to some areas of philosophy. It deeply impressed me when my teacher, after a heart-to-heart conversation with me, stood staunchly by my side and even visited my parents to persuade them to approve of my career change. His attempt, however, failed. I ended by submitting my application to the science curriculum of the college and embarking on a long course of career-identity confusion (which was only resolved later, with my psychoanalysis). As with my first teacher, I continued to want to be worthy of this teacher's care and trust.

During college I chose to become the disciple of a teacher who taught my class for only a semester, presenting a course on jurisprudence for science students. This man, a scholar on Kant and St. Augustine, had a small following of Protestant students, who met periodically with him. To my regret he died shortly after my graduation, but today in my study—fifty years later—I still have a brief letter from him, his portrait, and a set of his complete works. He taught by living up to his beliefs.

My "teacher" in medical school was the professor of biochemistry. The year before I entered medical school, he had met me through a chance happening and learned of my unsettled career identity. After I began medical school, he encouraged me to work in his laboratory. Much later, after I had already graduated with a Ph.D., he encouraged me to transfer to the department of neuropsychiatry. This recommendation was based on his intimate observation of my continued struggle with my career identity. He was a most thoughtful man, interested in my growth—an unusual *Menschenkenner*. In my analysis, when the memories of these days came up, my analyst remarked, "Some people have deep insight without specialized training."

Thus, in each phase of my education, I found a teacher who served as a mentor in my maturation. It should come as no surprise, then, that I developed a similar teacher transference in relation to my analyst. I wanted to be worthy of his care and trust, and this feeling continued in our relationship after the termination of my analysis until his death in 1976. As far as I am concerned, the primary preconscious context of my positive transference to my analyst was this teacher transference. My concern over how he regarded me, my respect for him, my attachment to him, as well as the caring concern I could not help but experience for him: all this must be understood primarily in this context.

My analyst was John A. P. Millet, whom I shall call Jack here, as he preferred to be called. Admittedly, Jack probably had some difficulty in understanding the extent of my teacher transference, and how this determined some of my behavior toward him, even after termination. To start with, it was very difficult for me to call him Jack. Instead, I called him Dr. Millet. For his part, he called me Freddie, after finding out how I invented my name, out of transcultural necessity.

Coming from the authoritarian atmosphere of a Japanese medical school, I found the democratic footing of relationships within American medical schools a surprise. I was particularly impressed by the custom of calling people by their first names; even superiors seemed to prefer this informality from their subordinates. It was a custom that appealed to me, and I wanted to reciprocate by offering my first name. But to offer my Japanese first name was problematic, because I had never been called by my first name, except when I was scolded at home. My Japanese first name thus made me acutely aware of a difference in authoritarian status, undermining the idea of democratic relating.

I therefore decided to use a Western name with some meaningful connection to my Japanese first name: Yasuhiko. The ending *hiko* refers to a man, while *Yasu* primarily means "peace." I associated this to the German *Friede* and thought of the name Friedrich. But Friedrich the Great had never been personally significant to me. So I tried the French version: Frédéric. Of course, I thought: Frédéric François Chopin—my favorite composer. Then, mentally crossing the Channel, I recalled Frederick Hopkins, the Cambridge biochemist who discovered tryptophan, an amino acid that held a lot of personal importance from my biochemistry days. I decided to adopt the name Fred as first name.

The appellation Freddie had a further significance. When I grew up in Japan, friends usually used the family name plus a suffix, either *san* or *kun*, indicating courtesy or friendly feeling respectively. Within the family circle, a nickname or the first name plus a diminutive, such as *chan*, was often used.

Jack was truly generous whenever I sought his guidance after the termination of my analysis. Most often the difficulty pertained to a political impasse or clash of personalities in my professional life, which then threatened my family's security and my personal integrity as head of my family. Whatever unfairness might be attributed to my adversary in these situations, the experience was also one of my maladaption. It was as if I had a culturally conditioned scotoma in this area. I wanted to learn how to handle these situations from Jack, who had known me so deeply at the cultural interface. But for an American at my age to seek guidance on such matters might have been taken as a sign of overdependency. After repeated experiences of this nature, I took the initiative and tried another approach to the problem. I decided to receive personal tutoring from a specialist in administrative communication—which by then, I had bitterly realized, was totally different from personal communication (i.e., I had to learn at least two kinds of American English). Perhaps, for the first time in my life in New York, I began to understand the culture of negotiation and power.

Jack may well have wondered whether I was overdependent. I clearly remember an occasion when I inadvertently transgressed his sense of independence as a result of my teacher transference. One day, after the termination of analysis, we happened to meet at La Guardia Airport, on our way to different meetings in Washington, D.C. I was happy about that circumstance. "Possibly he may perceive how active I have become in my professional life. He may perhaps be proud of his disciple," I thought. The line started to move for us to board. Without thought, I extended my hand to pick up his luggage. It was the natural act of respectful care for my teacher. In the next moment he abruptly grabbed the luggage away from my hand. I have never seen such anger in his face, either before or after that time. Never have I felt more acutely the value of independence in his cultural backbone and how this clashed with my own cultural value of respectful care for my teacher.

DISTINCTION FROM THE FATHER TRANSFERENCE

One may wonder if my teacher transference was not simply a father transference, particularly as the teachers I have mentioned were all male, and my father himself was a professor for as long as I could recall. Although I agree that there are similarities, the teacher transference is on a different level, closer to consciousness, than the father transference. I believe it must be differentiated.

To start with, my father and my teachers stood in mutually exclusive domains of my life space, for there was a rigid boundary delineating home (*Iye*) from the space of encounters with significant others outside the family. To form a strong, affectionate bond with a person beyond this boundary represented psychological growth, and may even have contributed to the resolution of my Oedipus complex (discussed later). My father, during my student years, more than once complained with a grim smile: "You regard your teacher as more deserving of respect than I."[2]

With regard to my teacher transference to Jack—it was quite active from the beginning of my acquaintance with him (giving rise to my sense that Jack was not necessarily a stranger). It could even be said to have been activated in anticipation of my meeting my analyst. In contrast, what is usually discussed as transference in therapy is what emerges through the process of analyzing deeper layers of the mind. Looking back, I can see clearly how my father transference emerged in this sense.

With the benefit of hindsight, however, I can also say that the first inklings of my father transference to Jack arose in our very first meeting, before my analysis. On an April morning in 1952, I was interviewed by three members of the faculty for admission to the Columbia University Psychoanalytic clinic for training and research: Sandor Rado, Henrietta Klein, and Jack Millet. When I first shook hands with this tall gentleman, I somehow thought of Ralph Waldo Emerson. After World War II Emerson became my father's favorite writer. It was with a sense of mission that he interrupted his major work in translating *La Divina Commedia* (The Divine Comedy) to translate Emerson's essay "Self-Reliance." His aim was to inspire his defeated and disheartened compatriots.

When the twenty-minute interview was over, Jack again shook my hand, saying, "Good luck, my son!" I could not believe my ears. Something that had been amorphously forming in my mind during that interview suddenly took shape, growing into a positive father transference. This feeling also contributed to the sense that our relationship was not necessarily one of strangers. The phrase "Good luck, my son!" had come so spontaneously from Jack's lips. It was unforgettable. A colleague who heard this story was skeptical and asked, "Did you really hear that?"—implying that I might have wishfully imagined the remark or that my memory might have been somewhat distorted. I have to say that my memory is quite clear on this account, but, to avoid any misunderstanding, I must add that we were not in an analytic relationship at the time.

That expression lingered in my ears when about two months later, upon receiving my acceptance letter from Columbia, I wrote to Jack, asking if he would consider becoming my training analyst. He promptly replied with a courteously phrased "yes." I was particularly impressed by his signature. Even today I feel that his is the most elegant penmanship I have ever seen. Perhaps, unknown to himself, he was, at that moment, revealing to me that we shared an area of aesthetic value: the joy of calligraphy.

I should note that, for me, the respect for calligraphy was couched in the warm memory of my relationship to my grandfather. This grandfather was overprotective of his firstborn "inner" grandson (the phrase used in Japanese to indicate direct lineage). But he proved to be quite a disciplinarian in my early education in Japanese calligraphy. He would ask me to try to write four letters on a sheet of rice paper with brush and ink. He would then praise or criticize my efforts and ask me to try again. We repeated this process until my writing became somehow satisfactory in his eyes—both in terms of the forms and in the expressed control and freedom of the brushmarks. The women in the household used to whisper about how spartan my grandfather was in this particular area, and they remarked on how I silently persevered under his training. Sixty years later, I reflect with gratitude on the values he implanted in me. Throughout my life I have developed a deep enjoyment of fine calligraphy. This appreciation was extended to fine penmanship as I learned English.

And penmanship in fact came up at the very beginning of my analysis. Before we used the couch, Jack asked me to present a simple chronology of my life, including my medical history. I prepared a handwritten account. Upon looking at it, Jack turned to me with a smile and pronounced: "Spencerian."

But I wish to return to the father transference. Relatively early in my analysis I had a dream: Jack was in the driver's seat; I was sitting behind. The car was going along a winding mountain road across the Izu Peninsula. I felt that he was driving too fast.

Of course, the meaning of the dream is transparent. But I want to add that I had a specific memory of driving along that mountain road, although from the opposite direction. (Was this a retraction of the past?) It was during the last summer vacation of my primary school years, when my father took us on a tour of the lakes around Mt. Fuji. At the end of the trip, before boarding the train at Atami for our return to Tokyo, he hired a car to show us the beauty of the historic peninsula landscape. We children proceeded to fall asleep during the drive. My father was quite annoyed to see his thoughtful plan disrupted in this way. With this dream, then, my positive but problematic relation to my father had begun to surface in the transference.

My relationship with my father was at the core of my psychological problems, and—somewhat to my surprise—my free associations frequently revolved around him rather than my mother. Before starting my analysis at age thirty, I had already become more aware of how my identity had been prevented from solidifying in the shadow of my affectionate relationship with him. In part the difficulty was prompted by my gradual recognition of his weakness. My father was a devoted scholar and talented poet, a decent man of refined aesthetic sensitivity. In my early teens, however, I could not fail to notice a weakness in his spirited way of life—a difficulty in stepping outside his subjective world. The problem may, in retrospect, have arisen from a combination of factors: (1) a professional hazard, for his studies encouraged a subjective stance; (2) an overconfidence in his own *Weltanschauung* over that of his family members (a problem shared by other Japanese gentlemen of his generation); and (3) his own personality.

In his subjectivity, my father was always well-intentioned, but his stance often seemed dangerous since his views were not necessarily in accord with the reality I saw. At that age, arrogant as it must sound, I felt I had to do my best to protect him. To carry out this mission I became a self-appointed, loyal devil's advocate, whose candor he deserved and needed—or so I thought. At the same time I tried as much as possible to make his dreams come true. But, unfortunately, this was in part at the sacrifice of my identity solidification.

This conflict in my relationship with my father came to the fore when I applied to the Columbia University psychoanalytic clinic in the second half of the second year of my life in the United States. It was also at this time I learned of my father's precipitously failing health in faraway Japan. The decision to remain in the United States and embark on years of analytic training was one of the most difficult decisions in my life. But I decided, and the didactic analysis began.

My body, in competition with the analytic process, started to show signs of the urgency of my dilemma, of the pull between my need for identity solidification and my caring for my father. After about a month of analysis I bled profusely in the stomach. In light of Alexander's (1950) psychosomatic theory, which was popular at the time, professional acquaintances might well have diagnosed my ulcer as a dependency conflict triggered by the analysis. I myself felt that the conflict was not precisely between the urge for independence (and defiant anger) and overdependency, but rather between the urge for independence (and defiant anger) and the love for my father (and my mission to care for him).

Almost, it seemed to me, the bleeding was a necessary price to pay for surmounting my conflict. I had already become increasingly aware of the presence of defiant anger during the half-year before my analysis. But there was a strong resistance to this awareness. What was important was that in beginning my analysis with Jack, I was able to recognize my anger in the presence of this teacher with whom I was searching for myself.

In view of the intensity of emerging anger, one may wonder whether my relationship to Jack also reflected a negative father transference. While I cannot cite a proper dream example, the following experience comes to mind. When, for the first time, Jack pointed to the couch and asked me to lie down, a thought crossed my mind, "Just like selling my soul to Mephistopheles." I then heard him, above and behind, unseen by me, succinctly explaining the basic rules. Free association began. I believe I told him that too many thoughts were coming to my mind and that made it difficult for me to hold on to one, but I also mentioned the passing thought about Mephistopheles as I lay down on the couch. Certainly I did not identify myself with Faust, an aging sage, disappointed after all his scholarly pursuits. But I was struck by my spontaneous identification of Jack as Mephistopheles, a fundamentally sinister figure. A totally benevolent personage had suddenly changed into someone unfathomable and uncanny the moment our postural relation changed. It there were any moment that could be described as meeting a stranger, it perhaps was this moment. Here I mean "stranger," not in the sense of a non-Japanese foreigner, but in the sense of an established citizen of yet unknown psychoanalytic culture.

Amid all these reactions, there was also a hope, an anticipation that Jack would liberate me from a lifelong conflict that Christianity, I had learned, could not. Indeed, how psychoanalysis stands in relation to faith has become a theme of ongoing interest to me. My perspective has certainly changed since that moment at the beginning of my analysis, partly through my reading of such thinkers as Pfister (1928, 1963), Tillich (1967), Ricoeur (1970), Siirala (1969), Küng (1979), and Meissner (1984). Psychoanalysis now more clearly delineates the meaning of faith to me.

Anyway, I somehow feel that this experience set the stage for the following occurrence. Not long after my return to analysis after recuperating from my ulcer Jack tried to finish a session with an interpretive remark. To my regret I do not recall what he said. The only thing I do recall is that he said something pertaining to Christianity. Raising myself up from the couch, I voiced my blunt refusal to accept his interpretation; it was untenable. I was surprised at the intensity of my own verbal expression, which approached an angry protest. Jack calmly looked at me. In retrospect, I can recall many heated arguments with my father about such issues as Christianity. My self-appointed mission to be his loyal critic allowed me to be intense in this kind of limited defiance of my father.

I think I should also add a comment on the significance of the couch here. I often wondered why my father, who readily accepted the Western-style of breakfast, never introduced the bed into our household. We slept on futons (which have recently gained some popularity among the American people). The only occasion, besides staying at a hotel, when I used a bed was when I was hospitalized. A couch, to me, was a derivative of a bed—and so was an operating table, behind the Mephistopheles experience. (And Mephistopheles was an agent of the disintegration of the soul.) But this was the only moment I can remember when the competitive relation with my analyst (/father) might have deflected into castration fear.

I have long believed that somehow Japanese culture resisted the idea of castration in its literal sense. Despite the active importation and assimilation of Chinese culture throughout the centuries, the Japanese never adopted the Chinese policy of castrating criminals (see Mitamura, 1963). Moreover, as Mitamura points out, there were never any eunuchs with special social functions. My own initial formation of an image of castration, in the sense of penile amputation, came through weekly exposure to a life-size model of a male body, which was on display in a cabinet in the science room of my primary school. The model's penis was sectioned to reveal structural details. I cannot recall that castration was ever referred to in the jokes or fantasies of my classmates. Nor do I recall any dreams even symbolically reflective of that aspect of the Oedipus complex.

I should perhaps add that I once had a dream of penile amputation after living in the United States for twenty-five years. This dream, however, was directly tied to the day residue—an experience connected with my sense of impotence in maintaining my integrity. Moreover, it was an experience tied to the feeling of being confronted by someone from a totally alien culture, where there was no common sense and where I had no control.

To conclude my discussions of the father transference, let me cite another dream about Jack, which I had sometime later in the analysis. He was standing in front of the blackboard of our classroom in the Psychiatric Institute, and I became increasingly worried whether he could cope with the sharp questions of my classmates. This transference dream vividly portrayed my need to protect my father, my care for him. It was also a clever synthesis of my father transference and teacher transference.

THOUGHTS ON THE MOTHER TRANSFERENCE

To clarify the analytic relationship and the transferences involved, I also wish to examine how my relation to my mother could have been transferred to Jack. I was the first child, in a culture imbued with male chauvinism, born when my mother was twenty-one. At my birth we lived in an extended family of considerable complexity.

My paternal grandparents were still quite active. There was also a woman they had adopted as a child, who remained a loyal, unmarried family member until her death. She supervised a few maids and a male helper. One or two young relatives from both sides of the family used to board with us, mostly to pursue higher education in Tokyo. In addition, my house was connected by bridge structure to that of my father's younger sister, who had two sons, five and two years older than I. Although life for my young mother must have been complicated, she was staunchly available to me, as well as, later on, to my young siblings. As children, we often bathed with our mother. And she was almost always there at bedtime.

The births at home of my two brothers and a sister, when I was four, five, and seven, were significant events for me, both in terms of a temporary disruption of my closeness with my mother and in terms of the mystery of birth. I had never heard of a stork, nor had I any access to the ribald, if childish, tales of street kids, as it was before the time that I crossed the strict boundary of the home to enter school. The maids must have been told to conform with the Victorian atmosphere of the household as far as avoiding any disclosure of sexual reality to children. (I assume that my father and my grandmother, a devoted church member, were at the center of this Victorian attitude.) In any case, the sexual reality was mystified by the knowing smiles of the adults around me. Just before the delivery of my first brother, I remember being caught trying to get a glimpse of my mother in bed through a narrow slit I made in the sliding door. I must have been four then. Jack suggested that this may have been the germ of my later intellectual curiosity.

Despite the baths with my mother, I did not have a realistic image of female genitalia and thus could not form an image of the coital process as I passed through the chronological age of the Oedipus complex. I had an amorphous sense that the process of reproduction was somehow connected with the pleasure I began to experience in my body. But the nature of that connection was not clear. I envied the reproductive capacity of my mother, and I started relating to my teddy bear as my child. I named this teddy Yasuko, a female version of my name, although I related to the image of my mother. As I reported to Jack, when I was about eight, I dreamed that, while walking through a passage in a field, I met a well-bred girl. She smiled and said that she was Princess of the First Harvest (Hatsuho, literally "the first ear of rice"). Then we parted, leaving me with a feeling of blissful joy. In school I had learned of the national ritual of offering the first crop, first to the imperial ancestry deity and a month later to the emperor himself. But, in line with the common tendency to symbolize one's own parents as king and queen, the dream may have symbolized my wish for a girl in my life I could relate to, somehow duplicating the mysterious intimacy I fantasized as existing between my parents. It is of interest that in the dream I did not long to be united with the queen, but with the princess.

To return to my memories of my mother, my most salient early memory of her involved the death of my second brother around Christmastime, shortly after his birth. I vividly recall that a golden folding screen containing a cosmological quotation[3] in Chinese calligraphy—a favorite conversation piece between my grandfather and me at the time—was placed upside down, in accordance with a cultural ritual in honor of the dead. In front of it my mother and grandmother sobbed brokenheartedly. My father tried to console them both, patting their shoulders. This was my first experience of how desperately unhappy my mother could become, showing an emotion so different from her usual smiling face. The sense of death as an irrevocable separation came through to me. I do not recall whether I cried at this sight.

A few years later I was taken by my family to a performance of Hans Christian Andersen's stories. I recall seeing, in the middle of the stage, a mother dozing while holding an infant. Then Death came on stage and stole the infant, without the mother's being aware of it. At that moment I could not control myself; I burst into tears and cried so intensely that I had to be taken away by a maid. I recall quite clearly that I did not identify with the infant being separated from the mother, but with the mother. I was overwhelmed by tears in anticipating how heartbroken the mother would be when she realized that her infant was gone forever. For me, this experience contains more than a crucial memory of my mother; it suggests a seed for my irresistible temptation to care for others.

Throughout my childhood my mother was always available to me, offering both encouragement and consolation. She was there to help me with my homework, at least until around the middle of grammar school, when her attention had to turn to my siblings. She made her high expectations of me quite clear. The day I told her I had been made president of my class, she rewarded me with unexpected praise. In a deeply felt voice she told me how proud and happy she was to see me receive such an honor at probably the best school in the nation. This blissful conversation took place while we were alone, taking a bath together. Yet in this solid, affectionate bonding, one can also see some seeds for my later status anxiety.

While my mother may be prototypical of the "education Mama" of contemporary Japan, she was quite liberal in terms of the direction of my development. Certainly she did not try to keep me within her reach. To the contrary, I think she encouraged my fantasy and my originality (I hated, for example, to draw or make things in accordance with a given model). In recent years she has told me that she dreamed of my career as a diplomat or a musical conductor, but she never imposed her choice on me—except that she used to echo, literally echo, my father's stance in discouraging philosophy as a career.

Tracing back my relationship with my mother in terms of mutual trust, affection, and mutual care, I cannot but think that both my teacher transference to Jack and its prototypes in my relations to earlier teachers were based on the feeling that prevailed between my mother and myself. Admittedly, I was not conscious of this at the time, nor can I recall a convincing dream regarding this matter. I did, however, have a memory emerge during my analysis that seems relevant to this issue. I recalled an experience at bedtime when I was seven or so. My mother was sitting at my bedside while I was crying. The reason for my outburst was that the clock indicated it was past 8:00 p.m. and I was supposed to be asleep by then. It was what I had promised my teacher. My mother consoled me, saying that my teacher would understand and would be proud of me for being so faithful to my promise.

In this memory my mother and my teacher were in harmony in their pride, care, and understanding of me. I felt I could trust them, even in the face of the ruthless passage of time. Some twenty-five years later, the passage of time and the recumbent position were part of the external structure of the process Jack and I were involved in.

THE CONTRIBUTION OF MY GRANDFATHER

In searching for the early foundations of my teacher transference, I discovered another important precedent—my relationship with my grandfather. Before I began school, he and I had frequent conversations regarding that cosmological quotation on the golden folding screen. Following a classical education that emphasized rote memory without interpretation, he taught me how to read the passage. He was proud of my memory. For my part, I found his lessons amusing because of the "funny" shapes of the characters—a portion of the character for "existence," for example, looked a lot like a pair of scissors.

In addition to instructing me in calligraphy, as I mentioned earlier, he attempted to teach me a few Chinese classics, including the *Analects of Confucius* and a Japanese history written in classical Chinese. Again, the emphasis was on rote memory. He must have tried to duplicate his own experience of learning such classics in childhood at a private school (*juku*), before the establishment of the modern Japanese school system. I think he was convinced of the benefit he had received from such an education and wanted to pass this on to me.

My progress was slow, and the teaching was relatively short-lived, as I became too busy with other activities. But my experience was of his concern and pride in me, a prototype for the feeling I had from my teachers. My grandfather was my first teacher, and his participation in my life in this way made an important contribution to my resolution of the Oedipus complex.

REFLECTIONS ON JACK'S BACKGROUND

Despite Jack's stance as a neutral analyst, I began to get to know him as a person and picked up clues to his personal background. This process continued after the analysis and has continued even after his death until today.

Quite early in the analysis I learned that Jack's father had once been an ambassador extraordinary to Japan. A portrait of his father, dressed in the uniform of a war correspondent during the Russo-Turkish War, overlooked the analytic couch. Talented both in writing and in painting, and interested in architecture, his father was instrumental in establishing the American Academy in Rome and contributed to the cultural bridge between the United States and Italy (see Sharpey-Schafer, 1984). To me, there was a parallel to my father, part of whose life's work was the translation of Dante into Japanese.

Although born to a New England family, Jack had been brought up in Worcestershire, near Stratford-on-Avon. There his parents lived among such artistic talents as John Singer Sargent, Henry James, and Edmund Gosse, who summered there (see Ratcliff, 1982). Again, there was a parallel, for Stratford-on-Avon and Edmund Gosse were inseparable from my father's ambience. Moreover, I found out that Jack had been a classmate of a granddaughter of the physicist Michael Faraday (my boyhood idol).

Jack returned to the States to attend Harvard and later faithfully attended his class reunions. I can readily identify with his feeling for a cherished alma mater. And I should note that Jack was pleased to see my sons attend his school and specialize in two fields he once considered: banking and architecture.

I have already mentioned Jack's penmanship and its meaning to me. For me, there is another tie in the coincidence of the ways we lost our fathers. I lost my father just after crossing the International Dateline in the Pacific, while bringing my family here on a cargo ship. He lost his father in the Atlantic, during the tragedy of the *Titanic*.

All these coincidences endorsed my initial impressions of Jack as somebody close to me, despite the differences in our backgrounds. His office, with its heirloom silver plates hanging on the wall, was a cozy and personally appealing place. I used to feel that my father would have liked to occupy such a study. The fact that I was a foreigner did not make us strangers.

A CONTINUING RELATIONSHIP

My narrative regarding my transcultural analytic relationship with Jack began the day I first met him, about five months before the formal beginning of my analysis. My relationship with him has continued not only after the termination of analysis, but in a sense even after his death.

Throughout the years I have continued to build on what was started in my analysis. In this process my teacher transference has continued to play an important role, and there are similarities to my grateful memories of what was set in motion by my contacts with my other earlier teachers. A comparison could be made to the way one continues to learn new meanings, throughout life, from the teachings of spiritual leaders. Of course, there is a difference, in that Jack did not exactly give me a doctrine. Instead, he showed me a method, through which I can rediscover myself in the different adaptations of life.

At this point, to complete the picture of my transcultural analysis, it seems necessary to go beyond the strictly analytic relation and reflect on some of my life situations. As I thought about how to do this and how to convey an ongoing rhythm, I associated to three pieces of poetry, connected in my mind with three phases of my analysis: the beginning phase, the middle phase, and the post-termination phase.

When I started analysis, I paid the fee with my salary as a research psychiatrist at the Rockland State Hospital Research Facility. I was also trying to save money to bring my family to this country. Owning a car was just beyond my budget. Jack lived at the bottom of the Palisades, at Sneden Landing. I used to get up early to catch the first bus that passed the grounds of Rockland State Hospital, where I lived in the staff house. This bus left me at Tappan, and I then walked for an hour to reach Jack's home, passing through a wooded area. Often I experienced the lifting of the morning fog. A poem by Hermann Hesse that I had learned in college came to mind:

> Seltsam, im Nebel zu wandern!
> Einsam ist jeder Busch und Stein.
> (It is wondrous to wonder in the fog
> Each bush and stone is solitary—my translation)

It was my first experience of fog lifting, and the memory of these lines from Hesse's *Musik des Einsamen* (1915) seemed appropriate. For it was at this time that I was starting on my solitary path to my individuality.

After my father's death, in the middle phase of my analysis, I mentioned to Jack in a session that I was surprise that I seemed free of any crippling sense of mourning. Half a year after my father's death, I received a telegram from my old medical school in Japan, stating that the professor of psychiatry had suddenly passed away. A week previously, I had received a letter from him telling me that he had proposed a course in psychoanalysis to the Ministry of Education with the idea of obtaining an appointment for me. Because of his death, this plan did not materialize.

My thoughts went to my father's poem, titled "Requiem" (Taketomo, 1916), written in Japanese upon hearing of *his* professor's death, here in New York some forty years earlier. This professor was *the* teacher in my father's life. In this poem my father implored the wind to carry, to the shores of Japan, the scent of the flowers he was offering in memory of this teacher.

He wrote on to recall his student days in Kyoto with this teacher, and to recall the teacher's enjoining him, in his search for the essence of European aesthetics, to cherish his memory of Japanese pines in the rain and the aroma and color of the white chrysanthemum.

Much later, some fifteen years after termination of my analysis, I learned of the death of Mark Van Doren, whose brother Carl was one of my father's favorite teachers at Columbia. At the time I was moved by a poem I read titled "Report on a Memorial Service: A Letter to Mark Van Doren" (Claire, 1975). That poem, with its sensitive portrayal of the New England countryside in mourning, became connected in my mind with a trip I made two years late with Jack. We drove to New Canaan, Connecticut, for a meeting at the Silver Hill Foundation, which he had founded. During the drive he told me one after another of his recollections of his life, from happy moments to tragedies. After we left the meeting he invited me to lunch at a nearby restaurant, an old New England establishment. Then he took me to visit a relative of his, a young woman living in that area. As I walked with Jack in this New England village and felt the warmth between us, I somehow thought of the poem for Mark Van Doren. That day was the last day I saw Jack.

In February of the following year Jack passed away. The memorial service, with a Beethoven quartet played by students of the Manhattan School of Music, and attended by the professional community of Rockland County, seemed quite fitting. For Jack had contributed much to the school and the county. On that day, and on and off since then, I have felt like reporting to Jack that I am free of any crippling mourning.

CONCLUDING REMARKS

Plato's "Phaedo" starts with a conversation between two of Socrates' disciples: Echecrates, who was not with Socrates on the day he died, and Phaedo, who stayed with him. Echecrates asks Phaedo to tell him what happened and describe how Socrates was on his last day. Phaedo responds willingly and adds, "It is always my greatest pleasure to be reminded of Socrates whether by speaking of him myself, or by listening to someone else" (Plato, 1971, 205). This passage seemed so fitting to me that when I lost the college teacher I mentioned earlier I wrote a paper in his memory beginning with this quotation.

Looking back, I am struck by how I have been affected by similar impressions of significant teacher-student relationships from other cultures. I found, for example, that the Chinese classic by Confucius that my grandfather tried to teach me began, "The master said . . ." Although my exposure to Buddhism has been limited, I have been deeply impressed by how

Shinran, the founder of the Jōdo-Shin-Shū sect, trusted his teacher Honen (see Kanedo, 1931). In Zen Buddhism there seems to be an intense relationship between the teacher and his student, mediated by the koan. In this light I have long wondered about the meaning of a passage from Rinzairoku, a Zen classic: "If you encounter Buddha, you should kill him,/If you encounter your teacher, you should kill him" (Asahina, 1966, 88). Recently, however, I learned from scholars in this area that this passage can be interpreted: "A true convert to Zen Buddhism (or a truly enlightened person) pursues his way even beyond Buddha or beyond the founder of his sect."

The importance of the teacher-student relationship to me can be seen in a problem that arose for me during my adolescence when I read the Bible. In speaking to his disciples about their relationship, Jesus stated: "No one who prefers father or mother to me is worthy of me" (Matthew 10:37). Yet elsewhere he endorsed the Mosaic command to respect one's parents. For me, there was also a contradiction between this teaching and my personal feeling of care, as well as the Confucian ethic, which advances the supremacy of filial devotion. Much later I learned of a similar teaching in the Talmud: if one faces a crisis in which only one's father or one's teacher can be rescued, but not both, one should rescue the teacher.

The precise Talmudic text reads:

> If a man's own lost property and the lost property of his father [require attention], his own has precedence; his own lost property and his teacher's lost property, his own comes first; his father's lost property and the lost property of his teacher, that of his teacher has first place, because his father brought him into this world, but who teacher, who taught him wisdom brings him thereby into the world to come; if, however, his father were also a sage (equal to his teacher), that of his father has precedence. If his father and his teacher were each carrying his own burden, he must relieve his teacher first and then he relieves his father. If his father and his teacher were . . . captivity, he must ransom his teacher first and then he ransoms his father; but if his father were also a sage, he must first ransom his father and he ransoms his teacher afterward. (Talmud, Tractate Bava Metzia, 33a, Mishnah 11)

My point with these diverse examples is to suggest that the significance of the teacher-student relationship is universal, despite cultural differences in the form of education. Indeed, the form of education has been undergoing notable changes in Japan in recent years. Both the college and the primary school I cherish in my memory no longer exist, given the restructuralization of the educational system after World War II. Democratization of the authoritarian society was necessary, but it regrettably entailed a collapse of the "status" of the teacher vis-à-vis students. In addition, the transformation of the traditional extended family into a more nuclear family has probably had considerable impact on early education, especially when I think of the contribution my grandfather made to my growth. Yet, even with all these changes, I am inclined to feel that the significance of the teacher-student relationship is at least latently present in contemporary Japan.

My proposal is that the preconscious teacher transference should be considered as a possible part of the context for transference in any transcultural analysis, whatever the cultural interface. I am tempted to wonder about Freud's experience in regard to this preconscious teacher transference, since Freud experienced such strong relationships with his teachers, including Hammerschlag, Bretano, Brücke, Charcot, and Breuer (Jones, 1953). Of course, this question is misplaced, since Freud conducted his own analysis and did not have any analyst as his "teacher." But I have another, final question, which may not be displaced: Would Freud, with his rich experience of teacher-student relationships, have strictly advocated resolution of the teacher transference upon termination of a psychoanalysis?

NOTES

1. In gathering the information for this paper, I wish to acknowledge the kind help of Dr. Anna M. Antonowsky, Prof. Haruhiko Fujii, Prof. Yoshitaka Iriya, Prof. Takao Kashiwagi, Dr. J. Bradford Millet, Prof. Shoji Muramoto, Prof. Yasutaka Nagayama, Ms. Grace Nicotra, Prof. Sadao Okamoto, Ms. Yuko Okamoto, Mr. Micha Oppenheim, Mr. Tomiji Sukawa, Prof. Mikihachiro Tatara, and Prof. Shozen Yanagita. I also wish to thank Dr. Howard Davidman, Dr. Leah Davidson, Dr. Daniel M. A. Freeman, Dr. Mark Gehre, Dr. Raelene Gold, and Dr. John Speigel for their thoughtful critiques.

2. I am reminded here of Mikihachiro Tataro's (1980) doughnut theory, which can be graphically represented by three concentric circles enclosing each other.

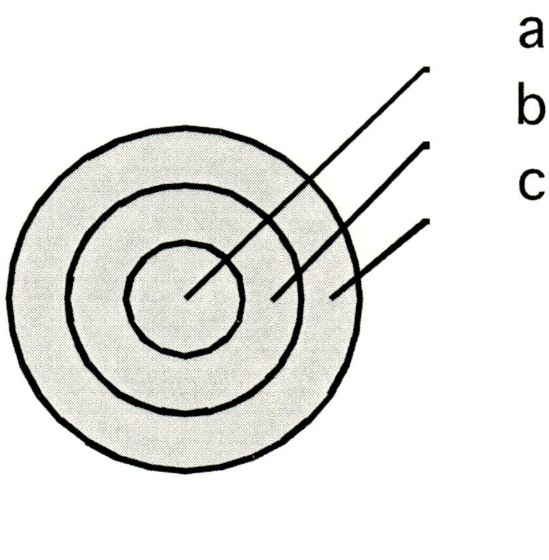

The center (a) represents the patient's primary territory, according to Tatara, consisting mainly of family members. He states that the anthropophobic patient "feels all right there, and there is no symptom formation." The next ring (b) is where the patient usually shows his symptoms and where he finds it most difficult to be. The area encompasses friends, acquaintances, and neighbors. Finally, in the outer ring (c)—the world of strangers—the patient can usually get along. Although he feels uneasy, this uneasiness is not evident.

3. The quotation, called *Dentaishi Hoshinsho*, was attributed to *Zenne-taisi* (497–569) and reflected Laotze's philosophy.

16

Naikan—A Buddhist Self-Reflective Approach: Psychoanalytic and Cultural Reflections

Adeline van Waning

Maple leaf
showing front
showing back
falling down

Ryokan (1857)

Psychoanalysis and Naikan—both are forms of self-reflection and introspection approaches. Psychoanalysis in this chapter is considered as more in the realm of shared exploration in a treatment (psychoanalysis, psychotherapy) context; Naikan can be seen, in addition to the therapeutic aspect, as a structured, clarifying meditation practice.

In this chapter I describe my experiences in the practice of Naikan, with some thoughts and associations connected with the process.[1] It is a description by a *gaijin* (foreigner), inevitably looking through culture-bound lenses, with the limitations and opportunities that this entails. The Naikan approach is compared, as far as possible, with psychoanalysis and forms of psychotherapy. Questions are posed about possible culture-bound aspects in the practice and the values that guide it, specifically in the field of ethics and infant psychology. Some core-Buddhist insights are presented, and Naikan as a spiritual path practice is explored. Six areas of difference in perspective that color the traditional psychoanalytic and psychotherapeutic worldviews, on the one hand, and the Naikan worldview, on the other, are then elaborated. Some conclusions then place Naikan in a larger context.

ON THE WAY OF NAIKAN SELF-REFLECTION

As a description will be given of some personal experiences in an intensive Naikan retreat at Nara Naikan Center, some information from this center is here provided. Nara Naikan Center, established in 1983, is led by Professor Yoshihiko and Mrs. Junko Miki, both clinical psychologists. Naikan is a structured way of self-reflection, introspection, self-discovery, and self-renewal, by way of examining our relationships with important people in our life—as the brochure says. It can help us to better see ourselves, our relationships, and the fundamental nature of human existence. Naikan (*nai* meaning "inside," *kan* meaning "observe"), as practiced in the present way, was developed and described by Ishin Yoshimoto in the 1940s. "From ancient times," Yoshimoto says, "many sages such as Buddha and Socrates have emphasized the importance of looking into oneself. I have just given shape to one particular method of introspection" (Miki, 1995, 1). Yoshimoto was a Buddhist in Jodo-shin, True Pure Land Buddhism, in Japan. He made an arduous training for the monks available to others in a way that more people could practice it and profit from it.[2]

An intensive Naikan retreat involves staying in a quiet place (usually for a week) and reflecting on one's life history from birth to the present time. Structure is provided by the facilitator, who guides one through—mostly—three-year periods of one's life at a time. One sits on a cushion in a comfortable position, surrounded by folding screens, one relaxes, and then thinks of oneself in relation to one's mother (or another person who nurtured one as a child) along the following questions: (a) What have I received from her? (b) What have I given to her? (c) What difficulties, troubles, burdens did I cause her? Later, one thinks of other persons—father, spouse, children, brothers or sisters, friends, and colleagues. Some deeper-going questions can be added afterward—for instance, about "lies and thefts."

One is asked to search for concrete examples illustrating each of these three aspects of the relationship. Usually, there is a three- to five-minute interview after every one or two hours of intensive Naikan. Watching television, listening to the radio, reading, and talking to others is not allowed during a Naikan intensive. Stimulation from the outside is kept to a minimum in order that one may wholly concentrate on the world of the mind. Going to the toilet and drinking water and tea is always possible.

SOME PERSONAL EXPERIENCES

Below, a more "embodied" idea of what Naikan entails is given, in presenting some parts of the report I wrote after the retreat in which I participated.

It is not my intention to burden the reader with personal biography; just a few ingredients are needed in order to be able to illustrate some of the Naikan process and the ambience.

It is a hot Sunday afternoon when I arrive at the large living house—Naikan Center in the quiet outskirts of Nara. I have had just one day to taste some of the atmosphere in the ambience that will hold me for a week: Nara, the first real capital of Japan in the eighth century that absorbed Buddhist influences from China, a process that laid the foundations for Japanese culture and civilization. In Nara, one cannot help but feel humble and impressed looking up into the serene face of the sixteen-meter huge bronze Daibutsu, the large Buddha statue in Todai-ji Temple. Daibutsu is surrounded, in the Nara-koen Park, with many other temples and about 1,200 deer that in old times were considered messengers of the gods. As I know that the coming week will offer me many, many hours of sitting and immobility, I love to roam around with the deer, before searching my way to the center.

Mrs. Miki shows me my room and I receive some instructions, with the help of an interpreter who will herself also take part in Naikan. The Japanese *naikansha*—Naikan participants—are introduced by way of a lecture. All of our sixteen participants have our own room. We turn out to be two thirds women, one third men; I'm the only non-Japanese. In the correspondence the Mikis and I had before, I've been told that I'll have a room of about eight *tatami* mats in size—at that moment intriguing information. I'm lucky—my comfortable tatami room has a balcony with a view on garden-greens, with sounds of cicadas. It contains a *byobu* (screen), a floor-chair, a low table, and a fan. Nothing more is needed. At night I spread a futon mattress with bedding on the spot where I sit at daytime, experiencing a twenty-four-hour around the clock Naikan flow.

We get a diary to hand in at the end, and taking notes is allowed. The first day we fill in a questionnaire about our purpose to do Naikan, with some specific questions about possible emotional, neurotic, physical problems; and a short sentence completion test with texts like: my mother . . . my father . . . my husband . . . from now on . . .

Mensetsu (interviews) are done by either Mr. or Mrs. Miki as the facilitator, the *shidosha*, the one who takes *mensetsu*. The ritual, eight times a day, makes for a vivid and dear memory now, afterward—the interpreter entering the room: "excuse me . . . (*sumimasen*)." We shift the *byobu* to the side, we organize the tape recorder and microphones, after which *shidosha*, interpreter, and I make a *gassho* (hand palms together) and deep bow (palms on the floor, forehead touching the floor). And then there's the question: "Tell me please, what relationship and years of your life did you examine during this period?" And my answer is, for instance: "I examined by relationship to my mother during my twelfth through fifteenth year, at high school. I received . . . from her, I gave her . . . and I caused her difficulty by . . ." The eight-times-a-day visits of the *shidosha* make up for forty-four times altogether in this one week.

Daily schedule is as follows: 6 a.m. we wake up with music, stimulating mixed old-new age sounds; 6:30, after a quick wash, and cleaning of the rooms, we start Naikan. We continue Naikan the whole day, formally up to 9 p.m., but also after that we are advised to keep going in the concentration flow. Some fifteen hours a day for more than six days makes for almost a hundred hours of focused meditation.

Meals are at 7:30, 12:00, and 6:00 p.m.: a few moments of some silent "external" contact with others when we collect our tray. The meals are nicely prepared, with varying dishes of delicious Japanese food. These are the moments of some culinary distraction, or better: vivid concentrated meditation for the senses. All rooms have a loudspeaker, and during the meals tapes are played with lectures, texts of radio programs, and personal accounts of former *naikansha* who tell their stories. At lunch on a tag on our tray a time is mentioned that each of us can shower in the afternoon during twenty minutes. Altogether, a sober, clear-cut program.

I'm told to examine my relationship with my mother, from ages 0–6, 6–9, 9–12, 12–15, 15–18, 18–22, 22–26, and 26–28; in this last year she died. At every *mensetsu* I name what I have discovered in relation to the three questions as mentioned. The *shidosha* listens carefully, and nods often as a sign of understanding. Most of the time there is nothing more to say, and I hear the next assignment. Sometimes a short clarification is requested. Most days the main feedback I receive is the respectful listening and nodding, bowing, and quitting again. Once I'm told that, also in relation to a deceased person, it is good to imagine what I might have wanted to give—the second question—also, if I regret not to have done that at the time.

More concrete memories turn up than I expected; in this it gets clear to me that I have many more memories of what my mother gave than what I gave to her. There has been much that I've taken for granted.

I make imaginary walks through our family's house, and see with children's eyes, at children's height, and remember many forms and materials, like the door handles, the feel of the textile on the chairs, the sound of the old refrigerator being closed.

On the second day I start also examining the relationship with my father. It feels very different to do Naikan with a person still alive or with one who died, where no direct contact can be made any more. Memories flow, organize themselves along the three questions, are told and received. After my father, talking about a former partner on the fourth day, many memories come up that I wasn't aware of. As before: some painful, some joyful, some highlights but also often about the "little things," no big deals.

When I'm told to start reexamination of the relationship with my mother at first a glimpse of disappointment comes up—"I wouldn't like a repetition"—but soon indeed I experience that I'm going much deeper, having new and more detailed memories, with more emotions, in a broader relational context.

If only these were the fruits of this week, then already I would experience it as very valuable. I feel some memories really come "from my belly," and from my body memory. "Going deeper" I feel, partly, as a sort of breathing process, of in and out, expansion and release, and certainly of letting come up and letting go, along the structure of the three questions; partly it can be actively done, partly it's just being receptive and open.

In the first days I've often named three examples of, for instance, what I received. Now I can only name one as it takes time to tell the context, with more color and feeling nuances. Also I see a shift away from stereotype to new and fresh, and from headlines to the details of daily life in those times. It is clear to me that there has been much day-to-day dedication, commitment, care, in the small things; I've many "just-so" and also happy memories "underneath" some big biographical facts. "Doing the best we could," by everyone in the family, I now experience as sort of natural perfection, "as it is" (which connects with the Japanese notion *arugamama*, as it is). I can now take each one's deeds just as they are without any conscious or unconscious bias or egocentric interpretation on my side. Being so involved with a number of people who were important in my life gives me a warm loving feeling toward my parents and siblings, with a deeply felt life. This gives a high degree of "intimacy": in this room only I can be seen now, but this room is inhabited with many of my inner representations of persons and dynamic relations, I'm "living" them right now . . . and in this way, I realize, sixteen silent rooms in this house are full of people, interactions, life!

It feels impressive to experience so many vivid, colorful memories of the different sense modalities: like the seeing of my mother's sewing box with which I played as a preschool child; the hearing of my father's early morning scrapings; the feeling of being lifted on my mother's right arm to put me on the backseat of the bicycle, as I was three; the taste of calcium tablets, of cod-liver oil, both so bitter, but so healthy for four-year-old children . . . the dark wet smell of the garage; the way I thought the world was turning as a six-year-old. . . .

On the fifth day I'm deeply into questions about death, very directly in relation to my mother, and also to others: they are experienced, now, as existential questions, in relation to impermanence; my meditation is about tolerating powerlessness, and gets a more positive touch, as well, as "celebrating uncertainty."

Feelings and memories present themselves to me now as a sort of a koan, a seemingly paradoxical question as used in Zen practice that can help to be able to transcend rational dualist thinking. How is it that death can feel so lively? I feel joyful, grateful with insights, also as if they have a sad taste. New memories, more refinement and differentiation, and more emotional context bring, as if naturally, more empathy and compassion, both in resting in my own—as well as stepping in the other person's shoes. . . .

"Lies and thefts" comes on the sixth day: I receive some explanation of what it means. They can be taken very literally, but also more metaphorically. As to lies, for instance: where did I cheat with others and myself (like saying I'm going to study, not doing it, and then finding a rationalization, and excuse)? As to thefts: theft can be the taking away of someone's pleasure in a joint activity, by being moody. We go along age lines; it is about taking responsibility, not about a specific relationship.

Finding examples of lies and thefts on one hand of course is frustrating for the self-image, on the other I experience a profound pleasure in the deepening of the process and the reassurance of "surviving" this, feeling regret about certain acts or indifferences while not losing compassion with myself within the context. And spontaneously sometimes ideas come up of ways of possible "reparation" of damage done, or at least of letting the person know that I regret something.

When there's four more *mensetsu* to go, we plan how to use them and how to come to a conclusion; in this I experience the Mikis' care and professional ability.

On the last, seventh day, to my surprise I can conclude that I've told some two hundred little "clinical vignettes" about myself (with forty-four times *mensetsu* and an average of four or five examples given). . . . For the *shidoshas* Mr. and Mrs. Miki this process must feel like playing simultaneous chess, playing with sixteen participants! With a different metaphor, they are the midwives who assist in the development of sixteen fresh life "narratives."

We are asked to fill out a questionnaire again; some examples of questions: "After Naikan, do you realize . . . that you have been self-centered, an irresponsible person, not considerate to others, that you have treated others badly. . . ."

I'm aware of a happy but also puzzling complementarity: my period of having been in psychoanalysis has taught me—to contrast, in a bit a crude way—about development, defense, and drama, Naikan showed me day-to-day dedication of others and habitual self-centeredness . . . and still, a feeling of calm at-homeness. Some days after, the feeling is that with Naikan, I feel more centered in *tanden* (the Japanese for a person's spiritual center, in the belly).

THE NAIKAN APPROACH: ABOUT SELF-CENTEREDNESS AND INTERDEPENDENCE

What has been described is the intensive Naikan retreat; other possibilities include daily Naikan (for instance, twenty minutes a day, writing down the answers to the three questions in connection with the day's events). One can do Naikan reflection on a specific person, or on a particularly difficult period in life—for instance, during an hour. Also jour-Naikan is done, with e-mail sending to the *shidosha*. In a less traditional way, one can also reflect on oneself in relation to, for instance, body parts (when being ill and healthy), pets, food, or even objects like a car and couch—in fact, our whole life-world.

In principle anyone can take part in Naikan, as Mr. and Mrs. Miki say. A person needs to have the motivation (and to participate in such a week requires some ego strength), but deeply depressive people, people who are suicidal or psychotic, are certainly advised not to do Naikan. The Mikis have an intake by telephone, and may advise a person to do counseling for some time before embarking on Naikan. The practice can also be combined with counseling.

Three stages are described in a Naikan week: the first, of aching legs, difficulty focusing, with uneasy feelings up to the tendency to quit. When one continues and gets used to the sitting position, gradually memories appear with greater clarity: unpleasant ones, which can be shocking and depressing, but also pleasurable discoveries. In the third phase, one can understand oneself much better; one may be able to discern a central problem in one's life, or specific patterns. The result is often that one experiences a sense of liberation, and a feeling of renewal.

The *mensetsu* interviews, it seems to me, have at least four functions: first, telling, in the ritual context, with receiving a new assignment, helps one to keep going; second, verbalization leads to appropriation ("I really did that") and taking responsibility, as well as—later—disidentification: things look more relative, not so heavy and "personal" anymore. Then, third, there is the function of realizing, sharing, and "surviving"; one gets no reproach, and is not excommunicated. Naikan in this way has aspects of the process of systematic desensitization, as applied in cognitive behavioral therapy: one does something, experienced as dangerous, and there is an antagonistic "relaxation" response that makes proceeding possible. And fourth, there is the witness-interviewer, who can effectively be revealed in a direct way by the *shidosha*; his or her questions support personal conscience.

One may wonder about this activity of conscience in *mensetsu*: in principle it is possible to "cheat"—not only to others, but certainly also to oneself—unconsciously. This touches a general question in psychology: how can we deal with our unconscious tendency for self-centeredness and embellishment, with which we make our memories and, namely, our role in them, just a bit nobler than it may have been in reality? Cognitive psychology has clearly shown how we subtly distort memories, give ourselves a more central role when things go well, and subtly hand over responsibility when things go less well.

How can one overcome one's unconscious defenses, I wonder; how can one draw oneself out of the mud, like Münchausen's Baron, pulling oneself up with one's own hands from one's own hair? Maybe we can say that the interweaving of different relations and perspectives, the multiple perspectives one develops during a Naikan week will help to develop a more truthful image than there might be when telling about one person; there is no escape from a more visible texture of patterns in relationships, no escape from the emerging picture of one's personally favored unconscious defense.

Nagayama (2000) sees the theme of "recollection of having given trouble to others" as closely related to psychological defense. In psychoanalysis the phenomenon of "transference" is used as the mirror for treatment, showing the patient's defenses and probing his or her unconscious inner discords. Naikan does much the same thing through the recollection of "having given trouble to others," says Nagayama. Also, it is his opinion that veteran Naikan interviewers find out whether the "trouble given to others," as presented, carries any unnecessary explanation, interpretation, or excuse. It seems Naikan can help a person to be able to let go of overdependent and defensive attitudes and take responsibility.

Nagayama (2000) names another link to psychoanalytic thinking: the realization that while one gave trouble in those early years, still one was accepted, helps to develop and support basic trust.

To examine, and reexamine relationships, to investigate lies and thefts, is a critical approach next to and including the third question about "which troubles I have caused others": it is like different threads weaving through each others, like the warp and the weft, creating a fuller and richer texture of a person's "life narrative."

In this, Naikan practice invites for a double awareness: to "content" of memories and to the working of the mind. The process of recovering concrete memories coincides with a deepening of insight in how we function in a psychological way, in processes like perception, attention, and selection, in emotion, identification, coping, and defense.

A core theme of experiential realization and clarification in Naikan is interdependence. Naikan addresses our personal life-history, and at the same times shows how much interconnected, interrelated, and dependent we've always been. This is done, as a start, with important people in our life. But, as was already mentioned, it can be expanded. We live under an illusion of independence. As Naikan clarifies in a very concrete way: our job description, our personalities, our titles, and our projects reinforce this illusion that we might be able to do our thing independent from others; in fact, in our life we can do nothing without being dependent on what others make and do.

As Unno (2006) vividly describes, "with intense self-reflection a meltdown occurs, while the circle of interaction with others is gradually widened" (162). As to the question "what have I given to . . ." we may notice that we are incapable of even an act of gratitude or compassion without concrete and consistent help from others. When giving an apple to a friend, it comes from an apple tree that has been raised in earth, with rain, sun, food, attention; a fruit vendor has taken care of it before we bought it with money we were given by others. We feed our dog with food prepared by others. We are part of the web of interconnectedness, with all the elements present to meet life's needs, at any moment.

In the words of Krech (2002): "Naikan broadens our view of reality. It's as if, standing on top of a mountain, we shift from a zoom lens to a wide-angle lens. Now we can appreciate the broader panorama; our former perspective is still included, but it is now accompanied by much that had been hidden. And what was hidden makes the view extraordinary" (26). He gives an example of interdependence in showing how, for instance, one can look at a book or article (in his case, a book on Naikan; in the present case a chapter). Krech (2002) states:

> I hope that my readers will take a moment to remember and thank all of the beings behind the scenes who made this article appear before them—the printer who runs the press that printed these pages, the truck driver who delivered this book to the store, the trees whose bodies were sacrificed to make these pages, the person who typeset the words, and the person who took time to edit the article so it could be read. And please remember the people who taught you to read. And perhaps those who manufactured your glasses or contact lenses as well. As we follow the complex web of connections between one heart and another, we may discover the true nature of this extraordinary universe and in doing so, we may come to rejoice in who we are and in the gift of life. (17)

NAIKAN, PSYCHOANALYSIS, AND PSYCHOTHERAPY

How does Naikan relate to psychoanalysis and some forms of psychotherapy? A differentiation may be made in the sense that Naikan can be cherished both as an ongoing (meditation) practice, and applied as a form of therapy. What follows is a more technical elucidation of the last aspect.

Psychoanalysis, with its setting, and Naikan, with its structure, can both be named self-exploration and introspection approaches. As different as they are, they both aim at a better understanding of our emotional life and problems that we experience, and, by understanding more of ourselves, to give room to our inner development and unfolding potential. In different ways both Naikan and psychoanalysis aim at better understanding of our early relationships with our parents, our caretakers. Psychoanalysis aims at (re)discovering and (re)constructing of these in interaction with a therapist who often will be a transference figure, who gets qualities ascribed that belonged to an important person earlier in our life; together the therapist and client seek to clarify, "interpret," and recognize patterns in how things have been. In Naikan it seems that important ingredients in the (re)discovering are memories becoming accessible with the help of an accepting facilitator-witness, and the trust that silence and serenity give room for the true self. Exploring relationships with important persons in the past means transforming our inner images and representations of our relationships with these persons now; it is healing in the present.

Different approaches in psychotherapy offer also some connections: earlier, in the context of Naikan, links with systematic desensitization and experiential avoidance have been named. It can be said that Naikan has aspects of a form of exposure therapy, as in cognitive-behavioral therapy: exposure to private events, including exposure to experiencing anxiety and guilt; to negative thoughts, feelings, and bodily sensations. With bringing up many autobiographical memories one creates a narrative-therapeutical context for one's life, which helps clarify implicit relation-representations as patterns.

Values as put forward in client-centered therapies are essential in Naikan—namely, respect and unconditional positive regard. And as the *naikansha* gets into deep meditation, perception is sharpened and refined, which enables the bodily senses to very subtle differentiations that, when made conscious, give valuable information; here's a link to body-oriented therapies.

The Naikan format with three questions offers a way of organizing information, like a "comb" they go through existing data. Included is the notion that we have been a burden to the other—this is often not much emphasized in conventional forms of psychotherapy. Included for being able to answer well is the necessity of stepping in the other's shoes, of developing empathy: doing Naikan means that one is doing empathy-practice.

About the structure of Naikan as a form of therapy, one may wonder why, next to the named three questions, there is no fourth included about burdens that others have caused us? It seems that our "inner software," our way of being "wired," our perceptional and attributional makeup automatically (and defensively) favors this last standpoint. In general we may say that this information about our feeling burdened is only too well-known to ourselves, and it will be getting through to the *shidosha* anyhow. Troubles caused to us are part of a balance, with the troubles caused by us on the other side. We mostly are only too well aware of troubles caused to us. As Reynolds (1991) clearly poses: "We are righting the misremembered balance by Naikan" (71).

Another aspect of this the question, having given troubles in one's early years, and still being cared for, is mirrored in a parallel way in the Naikan procedures themselves: one is telling about troubles that one gave, maybe telling about very self-centered behavior, and still the *shidosha* is respectfully bowing and serving food. This may help to suffer less of unconscious projected punitive self-criticism (Kris, 1990) in the sense that one thinks the other is criticizing oneself. It also helps one to integrate an attitude of compassion for oneself, which is anyhow necessary for being able to be with what is, not to have to flee for feelings of guilt or remorse, in experiential avoidance. So, next to empathy practice, Naikan provides a valuable compassion practice, for both oneself and the other.

Clarification in Naikan doesn't take place in a primarily verbal exchange. Nonverbal ingredients are important: the attitude and commitment of the guide shining through, the example of nonjudgmental awareness, the inner empathy and compassion practices, and the development of one's own inner witness. They can be seen as "tools for life," bringing more resilience and inner clarity.

The introspective-empathic attitude in witnessing has gotten more interest in psychoanalysis of late, one might say—namely, in the so-called two-person approach in psychoanalysis. In the more traditional one-person approach it was believed that the analyst could have privileged, more "objective" knowledge about the client. In the two-person approach the accent is more on the fact that in treatment two subjects with their complete beingness go in interaction and influence one another consciously and unconsciously, without privileged knowledge in the interpersonal field (McLaughlin, 1991; Renik, 1993). Witnessing is an important ingredient. It includes silent, active, nonintrusive involvement and listening to what cannot be verbalized (Felman and Laub, 1991). This witnessing is rooted in empathy and "holding" by a person, who can also let go. Self-definition and respect for the client are different, for both partners' aloneness, as well as awareness of the deep underlying connectedness of both subjects, can go together, so says Poland (2000). This way of witnessing can be recognized in Naikan in the guide as well as the participant, toward the participant's experiences.

The described form of attention has meditative qualities that for a long time have been recognized by analysts in the analytical process (Bion, 1970; Epstein, 1995; Coltart, 1996; Eigen, 1998; Van Waning, 2002, 2006). Indeed, in the words of Eigen, "there is a meditative dimension in psychoanalytic work" (11); this dimension can be found in the work of both therapist and patient.

HOW "CULTURE-BOUND" IS NAIKAN? ON BIAS, BURDEN, RESPONSIBILITY, AND GRATITUDE

Psychoanalysis is based in values like individualism, the value of reason, verbal communication, integration, personal responsibility, and making conscious what is unconscious (Cabaniss, Oquendo, and Singer, 1994). In many cultures other than "Western" (to use this generalization, for lack of a better denominator), also in Japan in part, different values flourish, with an important role, for instance, for the group, context, nonverbal communication, and acceptance of what is. Fujita (1986), in a somewhat polarizing way, states that in the West, human dignity is expressed in securing control over nature and environment, by human will and by expanding human activities; in the East one is more encouraged to tune in to nature, to adapt to the environment, and live in harmony with one's surroundings.

I felt touched hearing that Japanese *naikanshas* after a week retreat often say that they see themselves more as an individual with their own responsibilities, while Western participants describe a growth in empathy with others and greater sense of connectedness.

The field of intercultural ethics and morality that opens up as a result raises many interesting questions. For instance, how moralizing is Naikan? Naikan, with its Buddhist background, cherishes a positive view of mankind: one may have done a bad thing, but one can reconsider, make amends, change. As Wallace (2005) states:

> Buddhist psychology is primarily concerned with understanding mental states that by their very nature give rise to happiness, as well as those that result in misery and conflict. The former are said to be wholesome, and the latter are afflictive. This is a question of causality within the context of human experience, not morality imposed on humanity by an outside, moral authority. (141)

And Harvey (2000) adds that however much Buddhism may value genuine remorse, it does not encourage feelings of guilt, for such a heavy feeling, with its attendant anguish and self-dislike, is not seen as a good state of mind to develop, being unconducive to calm and clarity of mind. This, however, does not preclude that the questionnaire at the end of the one-week Naikan retreat, as described, carried a heavy moral tone: "After Naikan, do you realize . . . that you have been self-centered, an irresponsible person, not considerate to others, that you have treated others badly?" This is a way of speaking that Westerners are not very familiar with. What is the question's cultural baggage, how literally should it be taken, how far should it be seen as a positive admonition?

The measure in which confrontation with the truth of one's deeds, making a dedication for self-respect and honesty, or even self-reproach, can be experienced as either purifying and constructive, or inhibiting and undermining, will certainly differ by culture and by person. Also the evaluation of the meaningfulness to destroy the self-centered attitude will differ. As Miki states (1995), "one might tend to dismiss Naikan as simply Oriental or Confucian moralizing" (12), and some Westerners who are not amused may certainly do so, especially toward the third question. Some Westerners may find the whole approach too "soft" and superficial, when just looking (in a superficial way!) at gratitude, giving, and receiving, as in the first and second question. Also there may be a certain defensive cynicism: it may sound moralizing when having to acknowledge, when you have broken one leg, that you may be grateful that you still have another unbroken!

Anyhow, as for myself, getting more in tune with the three questions, with a wide-angle lens, has—paradoxically?—brought growing compassion for myself. In seeing things in context, I have not experienced them as closing off but as opening up to a wider scope.

I may at times have included a silent question like "What has been my way of coping with what I experienced as burdens in my life?" This is about compassionately exploring one's own responsibility anyhow, and would be suitable in the line of questions about lies and thefts. It does include the fact that as a young child, of course, we have been completely dependent, and may have been burdened. This brings us to another theme: early developmental psychology.

What Naikan does not emphasize is explicit attention for the earliest infant experiences before one's own conscious memory, attention, for instance, for real trauma caused by maltreatment or abuse by parents. This is in contrast to psychoanalysis, which, over the last few decades, has become greatly interested in infant development, early attachment styles, mentalization, and experiences in developmental phases earlier than those addressed in Naikan exploration. In most infant approaches, the (culture-bound) accent is less with empathy with others in one's young years, and more with empathy with oneself in the very early infant years. Well, some approaches serve better for some style of research or for some periods in life than with others, of course.

At the same time, in "the West" one can learn much of the Japanese psychoanalytical theory formation about *amae*, which can be seen as a specific dependency relationship, a form of dependency on the love of another, and a form of interaction—described as well for the infant-mother relationship as for two adults (Doi, 1973; Takemoto, 1986). Might there be some relationships, on the one hand, regarding the awareness of the all-over interconnectedness and dependencies in our life and, on the other, regarding the "holding" witnessing relationship—including the respect for the "aloneness" and "otherness"—of every Naikan participant?

As for morality and child development from a Western view, one may have a hard time with this emphasis on burden, responsibility, and gratitude, and the possible "moralizing" tone in the Japanese Naikan approach. Seen from a Japanese perspective there can be criticism of a (limiting) (over)individualizing in the West; maybe here as well, now on the Western side, a cultural blind spot and bias play a role.

In Western approaches separation and individuation are emphasized, and in a therapy context a focus many times may be on what parents have not been able to give, while we find in Naikan an emphasis on what they did give. Anyhow, on the "Western" end, a separation, if won by cultivation of anger and reproach, does not lead to real maturity and freedom. For real separation-individuation it is important that one can also empathize with one's parents as persons with positive and negative qualities, hope, anxiety, needs, and limitations, like everyone else.

Shidoshas who have worked internationally in guiding *naikanshas* state that all people universally basically share the same problems, in the origins and foundations of their lives, in relation with a mother and father and finding a relationship with them, with some cultural coloring in inner experience and outer presentation.

There are now more than forty Naikan centers in Japan and Naikan is used in mental health counseling, addiction treatment, rehabilitation of prisoners, coaching of adolescents, and in schools and business. There are centers also in the United States, and in Europe (in Austria and Germany).

NAIKAN: A TRANSCENDENT PATH?

Going with the natural refinement of memories, and the deepening of experiences and insights in doing a long Naikan retreat, has been an interesting, moving, and intriguing experience for me. Naikan can be viewed as a form of discursive meditation. The process-experience may by some be recognized as of a three-"level" format (of course, any model is a limited representation, just for temporary communication). "Level" is to be taken loosely—all levels interpenetrate, and are in flow.

The first "level" is about Naikan as a therapy in the conventional sense. Important aspects for the participant are the remembering and "appropriation" of dismissed aspects of self and the development of empathy and compassion for the other and oneself. The *shidosha* is the main witness, outside, while the witness inside the participant is mostly implicit.

Aspects of a second "level" start flourishing in the course of Naikan: this is where empathy and compassion deepen, and the realization of interdependence and gratitude becomes more profound. The field of nonjudgmental witnessing by the *shidosha* has invited the participant's inner witnessing to be more explicitly experienced. This leads to less robust identification, and more disidentification with one's biographical facts—meaning, of course, they are still there, but one is not only that—one is more a process of "transcending and including." At the same time there is more awareness of, and a shift in identification to, the spaces "in-between," as described, to the little, insignificant (do they exist?) day-to-day happenings in one's life that stand often for care and dedication.

The inner witness has always been there; in this process of waking up the Naikan witness, the ability to disidentify, to take a meta-position, is strengthened and liberated. Might one say that here the Naikan participant in some way can be said to become her or his own parent and therapist, and in this nonattached way—with a paradox—as yet contributes to her or his "secure attachment"?

A third "level" refers to the participant getting more experiences that don't have such a direct link with biographical facts; more existential themes present themselves. Identification fades and dissolves, one is now also a more "unselfconscious" witness that is part of a greater whole; the witnessing by the *shidosha* is also experienced in this way. This is a process of flow, of grace; one may experience being carried by manifestation, the cosmos, or the source, however one names it. Here interdependence may be experienced as a completeness, as truth, where feelings of pleasure or pain connected with one's biographical existence are transcended.

Again, this may be seen as "transcending and including"; still, one does what needs to be done: one washes the dishes, eats, one remembers one's biographical facts and the "in-between," but at these moments one is not identified with the conceptual loads that mostly burden the idea of who we are. We may speak here of a "non-self-centered subjectivity," characterized by clear, open presence, and attention to the other and oneself, with no defensive self-centered, self-attached agitation needed. Being aware that we are not separate beings but each have an impact on the entire web of relationships gives us a sense of responsibility that is both existential and civic in nature.

The suggestion is made here that Naikan, if practiced in a proper way with a good *shidosha*, has the potential to become a transcendent path. All three aspects/layers can be recognized, sometimes more thoroughly, sometimes fleetingly by moments. The first days take place in and revolve around the first level, with, for instance, the seeing of self-centeredness and self-criticism; a basic sense of autonomous, individual "sense of self" is kept intact. The need for this feels as an initial survival-reflex. An example of second-level experience is in the deeply felt interdependency-web with family members who all did "the best they could" in hard times, with so many day-to-day happenings of care; here is some shift to a broader identification, and disidentification. The third level is exemplified in the coming up of deeper existential questions in relation to impermanence, powerlessness, uncertainty, experienced as a truth, where no ego-reactivity reflex is needed.

A link may be suggested with psychoanalysis, in the sense that the first two layers may be recognized in psychoanalytical therapy-formation and canons. Engler (2003), writing about unselfconscious experience, hints in the same direction. He states that "there is no natural place for this mode of self-organization in the standard model of psychological functioning: It does not inform the core of psychoanalytic thinking about the person" (59).

As to the third existential "level," Naikan, based in Jodo-shin (True Pure Land) Buddhism, brings one more in contact with fundamental Buddhist insights.

First, interdependence is experienced in seeing a more complete picture, nourished by empathy. A more complete picture facilitates a mindful presence with what just is, without a need to judge, no comparison with any virtual, wished-for, or feared alternative.

With the flow of going a number of times through our life course, also the so-called three characteristics get to be lived experience. As to impermanence, the changing nature of life—all elements coming up, being, and vanishing—and the changing way of looking at it makes us see things more relatively. Kitayama (1998) elaborates how this truth of impermanence and transience is familiar in different Japanese contexts, and how it applies in the psychoanalytical field. He refers, for instance, to the Japanese word *mujo*, meaning "impermanence, transience, and mutability." It is originally a Buddhist term encompassing the doctrine that everything that is born must die and that nothing remains unchanged. Japanese have traditionally been keenly aware of the impermanence of things, and the sense of *mujo* has been a major theme in literature.[3]

Unease, suffering: any effort to seek the truth about our past must attempt to paint an accurate picture that includes everything, also the suffering, but not just the pain. The Naikan practice confronts one with one's illusions of deserving, being "entitled" to having no pain, no suffering!

Naikan also takes one somewhat away from a self-centred egocentric perspective, attached to the direct material world and image of oneself—while one becomes keenly aware, with doing Naikan, that there is not such a thing as a inherent separate self. I am not my (limited) self. In this context, Shore (1991) can be quoted: "Take a flower: where does it come from? Does it grow from out of itself? For the flower to be, it has to grow from a seed, from water and nutrients of the earth, from sunshine. A flower—just like everything—is not itself" (61). Interdependence of a flower-example seems easier for us to accept than the fact that also me, we, are not only a separate self, but that this self anyhow is co-constructed, influenced by so many conditions, in its temporary appearance.

Psychoanalysis, Naikan, and the spiritual path, in their different ways, share the commitment to experiential uncovery or recovery of truth. As Symington and Symington (1996) write, "the psychoanalyst Bion's attitude toward truth was the same as the one of the Buddha, who, at his dying, said that people should not just believe in his teachings, but have to explore and test these for themselves, with their own experiences" (178). Naikan, in my experience, has the potential of bridging the psychotherapeutic and the spiritual.

A SHIFT IN PERSPECTIVE

In comparing the conventional mental health approach with Naikan, Krech (2002) names six points of different emphasis (197–205). For clarity, the contrasts are emphasized; they are quoted, with some personal comments.

1. Conventional Approach—Focus on Feelings; Naikan—Focus on Facts

This doesn't mean that Naikan denies the value of feelings and emotions; they are important, but often we are so carried away with them that we fail to see the actual facts of a situation. With the first question, Naikan gives a clearer picture of the conduct of others toward us; with the second and third, of our conduct toward others. It's helpful to start with the facts.

2. Conventional Approach—Revisit How You've Been Hurt and Mistreated in the Past; Naikan—Revisit How You've Been Cared For and Supported in the Past

Again, there is no attempt to deny that we did experience pain, but rather we try to see this in the larger context, also including the love and care that others gave us. Naikan helps to get away from one-sided attention to a more complete picture. The care was just as real as the abuse; both need full attention.

3. Conventional Approach—The Therapist Validates the Client's Experience; Naikan—The Therapist Helps the Client Understand the Experience of Others

Naikan does this specifically with asking the third question: "What difficulties and troubles have I caused others?" To be able to answer the question, we must put ourselves in someone else's shoes.

4. Conventional Approach—Blame Others For Your Problems; Naikan—Take Responsibility for Our Own Conduct and the Problems You Cause Others

To really be able to open up for seeing which troubles we cause others and take responsibility, we do need first to have empathy and compassion for ourselves. This aspect cannot be overemphasized. The attitude of blaming others, attending to their limitations, wanting the other person to change: this is called *gaikan*, or "outside observation." As Krech elaborates about this "misdirection of attention," it doesn't lead very far, as we cannot control the actions of others, and the more we push, the more they resist. Also, even if we could change others, how could we know what is best for them? And certainly we distract ourselves from our own self-reflection and attention to what we are doing.

5. Conventional Approach—The Therapist Provides Analysis and Interpretation of the Client's experience; Naikan—The Therapist Provides a Structured Framework for the Client's Self-Reflection

The sober Naikan setting makes clear to the participant that he or she will not be "seduced" in the hope that the therapist "knows." This connects with what is called the "one-person" and "two-person" approach in psychoanalysis. Naikan can be seen as a "third way," the *shidosha* having an essential facilitating role in the process of the *naikansha*, whose inner witness is cultivated by inspiration of the outer witness.

6. Conventional Approach—Therapy Helps the Client Increase Self-Esteem; Naikan—Therapy Helps the Client Increase Appreciation for Life

Naikan, in fact, does not address the issue of self-esteem, at least not directly. Instead, it offers avenues for the realization of two issues, which are in fact more fundamental: having an accurate self-image, and the need to appreciate the world around us.

We can say that psychoanalysis, other than many other forms of therapy, also aims at truth about oneself, and can underscore what is written here about Naikan. One of the outcomes of Naikan self-reflection as well as psychoanalysis is that we come away with a more accurate self-image, and that we have less of a tendency to overestimate or underestimate ourselves. Still, interestingly, the manifestation of this will differ, as they depart from somewhat different values and views on the world and the position of the human in the world. In the relatively new movement of position psychology, gratitude and appreciation do receive a prominent place (Emmons and Shelton, 2002).

CONCLUDING REMARKS

Naikan is an open, accessible approach that offers itself for anyone, everyone, motivated to engage in self reflection and introspection. Naikan starts in a clear-cut way with the familiar facts of one's biography.

It is my experience that the seemingly and deceptively simple Naikan format harbors precious avenues for development and unfoldment.

Important aspects of the effectiveness of the Naikan therapy approach are, so it appears:

- In a structured way, the making explicit and the clarification of memories, which reveal implicit relation and interaction representations and patterns.
- The attitude of the respectful facilitator, who is a witness, who values effort and insight and doesn't judge.
- The internalizing of the facilitator-witness, which makes it easier to have empathy and compassion with oneself and others; in that way nourishing, strengthening, and liberating the—always present, but often obscured—inner witness.
- An integrated way of getting aware of "content" of memories and working of the mind.
- In the Naikan "laboratory" the development of, specifically, mindfulness, the capacity for witnessing, empathy, and compassion stand out. The deepening of the process over time helps in clearing defenses and obstructions; in that way it can be seen as a developmental path practice. Next to this there is the realization-unfoldment aspect revealing the always already present witness, with experiential existential insights.

Naikan supports a widening scope in awareness of interconnectedness, not only with people, but with all phenomena. The emancipatory movement from egocentric (me) to ethnocentric (us) may lead to a broader world-centric "all of us" as unfolding stages of consciousness (Wilber, 2006); it includes also an environmental, global life-world dimension. May Naikan contribute to this dearly needed movement.

NOTES

1. I would like to thank Gregg Krech and Ilse Bulhof for their valuable comments on an earlier version of this chapter.

2. More information on the Naikan approach can be found in Krech (2002), Murase (1993), Nagayama (2002), Reynolds (1980), Takemoto (1994), and Unno (2006).

3. The little poem that forms the epigraph of this chapter refers to coming, being, vanishing, and an attitude of nonattachment to this mutability. Showing both sides implies and emphasizes a sense of completeness to the process.

17

Psychoanalytic Therapy across Civilizations: Asians and Asian Americans

Alan Roland

> In order to understand who I was and who I would become, I would have to listen to voices . . . of my family, of Japan, of my own wayward and unassimilated past. In the word of the tradition, I was unimagined. I would have to imagine myself.
>
> David Mura (1991, 77)

In 1978, at the Conference of the International Psychoanalytic Association in New York City, I presented a paper, "The Familial Self, the Individualized Self, and the Spiritual Self: Psychoanalytic Reflections on India and America." The paper was written after eight months of clinical psychoanalytic research in India and well over twenty years of being a psychoanalyst in New York City. The chair of the panel was Dr. Nishizono (one of the disciples of Dr. Kosawa, the founder of psychoanalysis in Japan), the head of a major psychoanalytic group in Fukuoka, Japan. To my considerable surprise, Dr. Nishizono related that upon reading my paper he found that Indians and Japanese have a great deal in common. This seemed counterintuitive as at first glance they seem so different. The latter relationships are mainly rooted in Confucianism, the former in Hinduism. Our conversation fortified my resolve to conduct clinical psychoanalytic research in Japan, which I did during the summer of 1982. At that time, Dr. Mikihachiro Tatara (trained at the William Alanson White Institute and Austen Riggs) invited me to give seminars and supervise members of a group he ran of psychoanalytic therapists from Hiroshima and other Inland Sea cities. All of the psychoanalytic comparisons had been and still are between India and the West (Kakar, 1978), and Japan and the West (Doi, 1973, 1986) but never between Asian countries. By going to Japan, I could better assess the psychological commonalities and variations across Asian cultures for a comparative psychoanalysis.

Subsequent to my research work in India and Japan, I have worked in psychoanalytic therapy with a large number of Asians and Asian Americans—Indians and Japanese mostly but also Chinese, Koreans, and Vietnamese—some here temporarily in graduate school, most others as immigrants, some from third- or fourth-generation Japanese American families, some as 1.5s (those raised in early childhood in an Asian country but schooled in the United States when their parents immigrated), and some second-generation Asian Americans. Most have been seen in individual psychoanalytic therapy on a one-to-three-times-a-week basis, usually for prolonged periods of three or more years, occasionally in couples therapy where their partner is Euro-American.

CULTURAL SELF OF THE EURO-AMERICAN PSYCHOANALYTIC THERAPIST

It is not only the Asian immigrant or second generation in North America who is psychologically caught between civilizations, but also the Euro-American psychoanalytic therapist, once he or she begins to work with them. To understand someone from a radically different psychological universe, psychoanalytic therapists must begin to see themselves from a different perspective, to become aware of their own cultural selves as they differ from those of Asians. Otherwise, there is a strong tendency either to psychopathologize Asians or to see them as psychologically inferior, i.e., not being up to the psychoanalytic norms of development and functioning. Asian therapists trained in the West are not immune to this either as their training often pushes them to disown aspects of their indigenous self.[1]

It is difficult to be aware of the cultural and psychological baggage that we carry into the consulting room. Most of us are barely cognizant of just how deeply embedded sociocultural factors are in our psyche. And we rarely realize how profoundly Western cultural assumptions of individualism enter into the very nature of our psychoanalytic and psychological theorizing and norms, as well as therapy. A simple example is that of a Euro-American analyst considering it psychopathological for an Indian American man to have his parents arrange a marriage to a woman from India. He would be seen as surrendering his autonomy and having a problem with passivity (Cabaniss, Oquendo, and Singer, 1994). We are usually only aware of our cultural self through immigration or a sojourn in a radically different culture. Then one sees that a great deal taken for granted as being just the way things are universally is in fact only one particular way of life and being. This can well be a narcissistic wound to the Euro-American analyst.

I think this is the deepest level of why psychoanalytic therapists have usually only a limited interest in learning about those from other civilizations such as Asians.[2] It calls for self-examination different from the usual psychoanalytic one of delving into the unconscious. The cultural part of oneself is not repressed but rather can only be seen in perspective through comparative experiences. Our psychoanalytic emphasis, even in the relational schools and intersubjectivity, on autonomy of choices, self-direction, verbal communication, an I-self, a relatively constant identity that is self-created, and much more, are far more rooted in modern Western civilization and its culture of individualism than we realize. Psychoanalysts from Freud to a variety of current schools and theories have been engaged in a dialogue and dialectic with the modern Western culture of individualism: critiquing especially the concepts of the rational mind and the self-contained individual while at the same time unreflectingly carrying forth many of individualism's central values and ways of functioning (see Roland, 1996, 7–13, for a fuller discussion).

It is important to note that all of the major psychoanalytic writers who have delineated Asian psychological makeup have been involved in comparative experiences. Takeo Doi (1973, 1986) wrote seminal works on Japanese psychological makeup after he trained at the Menninger Foundation and the San Francisco Psychoanalytic Institute in the United States. Sudhir Kakar (1978, 1982, 1989, 1991) wrote extensively on the psychology of Indians after he worked under Erik Erikson at Harvard University and attended the Frankfurt Psychoanalytic Institute in Germany. This is not to mention a number of other Asian writers in the field of psychoanalytic therapy over the last few decades such as B. K. Ramanujam (1992), Taketomo (1989), Tang (1997), Tatara (1982), Tung (2000), Wong (2006), and Yi (1998), all of whom had training in the West.

Let me give an example of how an Indian encounter with American-style relationships can be easily misread by both patient and a Euro-American therapist.

Clinical Vignette: 1

Priya, an extremely bright and assertive Indian woman immigrant, was still very upset a year and a half later after a disastrous experience in a Yale M.B.A. course in which there was considerable interaction among the students, and between the students and a teaching assistant. Priya experienced the TA as constantly attacking her, and she found herself helpless to do anything about it. Finally, by the end of the course, she spoke to the instructor but by then it was too late. She felt embittered that the instructor had not come to her rescue earlier, since there is a strong expectation in Indian hierarchical relationships that the superior will take care of the subordinate.

Priya and her previous therapist had felt it was some kind of psychopathology that prevented her from defending herself and being more assertive with the teaching assistant since she was known to be highly assertive in voicing her ideas. I pointed out the key difference between asserting her ideas in a strong way and confronting a hierarchical superior, in this case, the teaching assistant. Confrontation with a superior is something that Indians learn from an early age never to do, but rather to be properly deferential. This made complete sense to her. She then mentioned that the instructor had to come to the class one day to ask the graduate students not to attack the teaching assistant so much. They were all fed up with her nasty treatment of them and so attacked her back. This was something that Priya from her Indian background could never think of doing.

This example raises an important issue: Is being open and empathic sufficient to work with someone from another civilization in psychoanalytic therapy, or does one have to consciously learn about the other? I doubt whether the usual, competent American psychoanalytic therapist would know the difference between asserting one's ideas and relating to a superior in an Indian manner. They might therefore come to some quite erroneous conclusion, including the possibility of some kind of psychopathology, rather than appreciating issues and problems of intercultural encounters. A deep-seated emotional problem might well be present in such encounters, but the intercultural issues must first be addressed. In fact, it is often only when the intercultural conflicts are empathized with and elaborated that deeper and more familial sources of emotional conflicts then become accessible (Roland, 1996, 85–86). An even more telling example was a minor incident with an Indian woman immigrant scientist.

Clinical Vignette: 2

Meena asked for directions to the subway from my office to go to a seminar at Columbia University. I told her it was very simple: just turn left when you leave the building, walk down West 9th Street to the end of the block at 6th Avenue, cross 6th Avenue and West 9th Street becomes Christopher Street, continue for two blocks to 7th Avenue, and the subway is on your left. She looked totally perplexed, obviously not understanding my directions. I reflected for a moment and then gave directions in an Indian manner: when you leave the building, go left to the end of the block where you see the small park on the right, continue going until you see another small park on your left, the subway is just beyond it. She smiled in a comprehending way. I had switched from giving directions in geometric space to giving one personalized landmark in relationship to another. I had earlier realized that all directions in India are given in the latter way, never in geometric space, signifying that the self is always experienced in a well-defined social matrix and not as an autonomous being in a relatively impersonal world. I strongly suspect that Euro-American psychoanalytic therapists of whichever persuasion would see her reaction to my initial directions as some kind of cognitive impairment or emotional problem.

NORMALITY-PSYCHOPATHOLOGY CONTINUUM

I would now like to proceed with the most difficult part of doing psychoanalytic therapy with someone from an Asian culture, especially if the psychoanalytic therapist is from a Euro-American background. When we work with patients in psychoanalytic therapy, we are always making implicit judgments as to what is normal in their relationships (including the one with the therapist) and work, and what may seem skewed or psychopathological. When these patients are from our own culture, we judge unreflectingly on implicit understandings of what goes or does not go in our culture, or what is generally considered normal or psychopathological. It is not that psychoanalytic therapy is a well-laid-out road map. It is indeed full of ambiguities and a great deal of uncertainty. However, in working with someone from a radically different culture, such as those from an Asian background, a Euro-American therapist may feel not only uncertain but at sea. This may be due to a different normality/psychopathology continuum from the one we are used to, and indeed from the norms of development, structuralization, and functioning that we have been taught in our psychoanalytic training. Plainly put, psychoanalytic norms of development and functioning are more Western-centric than most analysts realize regardless of their psychoanalytic orientation. This, I may add, is true in the general mental health field.

Clinical Vignette: 3

A simple example of this came from a colleague who was working with a second-generation Korean American psychologist in psychoanalytic therapy. Both she and her patient were keenly aware that there might be important cultural/psychological issues involved in her patient's emotional problems. However, neither of them could come up with anything. At the end of our conversation, she mentioned off-handedly that the one thing she really couldn't understand was her patient's emotional life. She had not realized that this was where the cultural/psychological factor was located.

As difficult as this other continuum may sometimes be to learn, even more difficult is to locate a patient's psychopathology on this different continuum.

And then there is the further issue of ascertaining the idiosyncratic, disturbed family relationships that have given rise to the patient's emotional problems. Understanding the unconscious factors is always a challenge in psychoanalytic therapy, but this is doubly difficult when working with someone from a radically different culture than oneself. I still struggle with this. I shall give another example.

Clinical Vignette: 4

Some years ago, I saw a Japanese man in psychoanalysis because of problems he was having in a doctoral counseling psychology program in New York City. His well-off family was subsidizing him in his graduate work, living expenses, and psychoanalysis. We agreed on a fee, my minimum fee at the time. Over a year later, he was granted a position by the university from which he earned a significant amount of money. As is customary after a year or two, especially when a patient's income increases, I ask for a small fee raise, usually $5 a session. He became indignant, telling me that he thought I knew about Japanese culture and the *amae* (dependency) relationship, that since he was dependent on me, I shouldn't raise the fee. This was even more important because his mother was not a nurturing person. Furthermore, that once a fee is set in Japan, it lasts a lifetime. However, should I insist on raising the fee, he would have to go along with it, as one must always obey what a superior wants. "It can't be helped."

Thus, he unreflectingly structured the therapy relationship as both a hierarchical intimacy relationship in which he is dependent and the therapist is nurturing, and a formal hierarchical relationship in which he as the subordinate has to obey the superior. This is totally consonant with Japanese hierarchical relationships. I found myself in the position of being highly uncertain whether the resistance to the fee raise was due to normal Japanese cultural expectations or to unconscious factors of which we were both unaware, or to a combination of the two. Furthermore, if I decided to raise the fee, he would have paid it, but would then have kept all feelings to himself in a very private self, also characteristic of Japanese.

I therefore decided not to raise the fee at the time but to keep a very close watch as to what money meant to him. It was only after well over a year later that it became apparent that money was a central dynamic in his family, especially with his mother, who bought off people right and left, including him. Instead of being emotionally nurturing, she would give him money to buy things. With this in mind, I told him that I thought it was very important that there be a fee raise, even if it was just 25 cents, for its symbolic meaning. It was a turning point in the therapy because the rage he had toward his mother began to be directed toward me in the transference. We could then analyze all kinds of defenses he had to contain his rage, including being very obsessive-compulsive. This resulted in significant change.

THE CLINICAL SITUATION

Relationship with the Therapist

I have found that one of the most crucial factors a Euro-American psychoanalytic therapist has to learn in working with Asians from any of their countries is the three psychosocial dimensions of their hierarchical relationships, especially the first two (see Roland [1988] for a much fuller description of Asian hierarchical relationships). These, of course, vary among the different South Asian and East Asian cultures but are in principle similar. How Asian patients relate hierarchically affects the psychoanalytic relationship to a considerable degree, as well as the transference, and is significantly different from how a Euro-American relates to the therapist. Already, in the case examples of Priya and Kondo cited above, hierarchical relationships played a major role in the therapy.

Euro-American psychoanalytic therapists are used to a relationship in which they consider both patient and analyst to be essentially equal although the latter is more knowledgeable psychologically. Furthermore, we assume a Western contractual relationship in which the patient pays a fee for our time, in which we are expected to be of help in their resolving their emotional conflicts, relationships, and self-feelings. In the current mode of psychoanalytic therapy, in contrast to the classical position, the analyst interacts much more with the patient but is still very much oriented toward the transference and in some schools equally to the transference/countertransference relationship.

By contrast, hierarchy in its different psychosocial dimensions structures the psychoanalytic relationship for Asians. In the formal psychosocial dimension of hierarchy, Asian patients observe the social etiquette of formal hierarchical expectations (related to age and gender) in which they are supposed to show deference, respect, and obedience to the superior, keeping disagreements and any negative feelings to themselves. I have never once in over thirty years of working with a few dozen Asian and Asian American patients been called by my first name. It is always "Dr. Roland," in contrast to most of my other American patients. What the Euro-American psychoanalytic therapist may not realize is that there is a deep-seated, culturally internalized reciprocity in the hierarchical relationship. For the subordinate, or patient, by displaying deference and respect, expects the superior, the psychoanalytic therapist, to be responsible and nurturing, and that each should maintain and enhance the esteem of the other. If any superior, including the psychoanalytic therapist, seriously lets the patient down, a great deal of anger can be generated. To understand the particular transference of an Asian patient, one must take into account how it is interacting with the hierarchical therapy relationship.

Thus, in the therapy relationship, Asian American patients will try to sense what the therapist expects of them while being polite and obedient. Indian immigrants, for instance, will often ask for a great deal of advice and guidance in handling their problems as they are used to this from family elders. I usually address this by telling them that I am sure that they have already gotten a great deal of advice from family elders and others but the problems still remain. They generally nod agreement to this. I then say that obviously there are deeper roots to their problems than they, others, or I am aware of. By working together and telling me whatever is on their mind, we can gradually learn what is causing their emotional problems.

The second psychosocial dimension is that of hierarchical intimacy relationships. Here, there is an expectation for caring, empathy, and closeness in insider relationships, particularly in the family, where outer ego boundaries are fluid, and much less in outsider relationships. In the therapy relationship, the timing of this varies considerably from South Asian to East Asian. With the former, if the patient senses you are concerned and empathic, and will keep their communications confidential, they may open up very quickly as they immediately establish a familial insider relationship, converting any significant outsider relationship into an insider one with the extended family. With Japanese patients, on the other hand, it often takes some time for the therapist to progress from an outsider relationship to an insider one. There is then an expectation for a close "we" relationship. For a Japanese man with a male therapist, once it becomes an insider relationship, the therapist is expected to become a mentor for life.

Congruent with both the dimensions of the formal hierarchy and hierarchical intimacy relationships, Asians and Asian American patients have a dual-self structure (Doi, 1986; Roland, 1988) that enters into psychoanalytic therapy in a major way. They all have a self that observes the social etiquette of formal hierarchical expectations, much more rigorously observed in Japan and Korea, less so in China, and even less in South Asian countries. All kinds of thoughts, feelings, and fantasies are kept in a private self and only revealed to those whom they sense are receptive to them. This private self also creates a personal space in the highly emotionally enmeshed hierarchical intimacy relationships in the family and group. In psychoanalytic therapy, the ability of Asian patients to keep thoughts and feelings secret goes far beyond what most Euro-American patients can do. One Indian woman patient, Shakuntala, saw a therapist in Bombay for one and a half years in twice-a-week psychoanalytic therapy, and, by report, kept her two most salient inner struggles secret because she sensed he wouldn't be receptive to them (Roland, 1988, 154–74).

The third psychosocial dimension is that of hierarchy by personal qualities. I have found persons from all different Asian backgrounds make quiet evaluations of the personal qualities of their superiors and others, reserving deeper respect and veneration for those with personal qualities they truly respect than simply for all superiors. Of course, the superior in the hierarchical relationship may indeed be a superior person but by no means always. Younger brothers, sisters, wives, and servants may all have superior qualities. Thus, the therapist will always be deferred to but not all will be really respected.

Anger

Anger in its various forms is highly important in psychoanalytic therapy, where gradually it is unconsciously displaced onto the psychoanalytic therapist in the transference from difficult past familial relationships. The case vignette above of Kondo illustrates this. Culture enters into the picture in a major way. My experience with most Euro-American patients is that they can openly express some disagreement, annoyance, or ambivalence toward me early on in the therapy process. Not so with my Asian and Asian American patients. They do express anger and even rage at another superior who has in some way mistreated or failed them, often from the beginning of treatment. However, there is no open expression of anger or ambivalence toward the therapist. Here, a Euro-American psychoanalytic therapist is at a disadvantage because someone from the patient's culture would more easily detect early disagreement or ambivalence, perhaps through a look or gesture or some subtle act of noncooperation.

In my experience with both an Indian and a Japanese man in New York City, it took approximately two years of intensive analytic work on a three-to-four-times-a-week basis for them to express even indirect criticism of me. This was followed by their coming in the following session in an anxiety state. I had to interpret that their anxiety was related to their criticism of me. This enabled them to be even more directly critical of me after a few more sessions, followed by another anxiety state, and then by interpretations connecting the two. Eventually, they became involved in an ongoing negative transference and transference neurosis (Roland, 1996). A Chinese American social scientist who had been in a long analysis reported the exact same experience to me. The difficulty Asian men have in expressing anger directly to a hierarchical superior is due not only to a very strict superego that inhibits any such direct expression but also to considerable anxiety that they will lose the nurturing relationship with the hierarchical superior. Asian women can also have a difficult time expressing anger or criticism directly to the therapist.

Clinical Vignette: 5

Kumiko, a highly successful third-generation Japanese American woman, had a tremendous angry outburst toward me in one session that became a turning point in the therapy. She had come to see me two years after her fiancé was killed in an auto accident and she was recovering from being highly distraught. She had become very involved with another man who in many ways was emotionally suitable for her but who was divorced with children and not making that much money. Her mother completely disapproved of the relationship because he wasn't Japanese American, was divorced with children, and didn't make a good living. Much of the therapy sessions were devoted to her conflicts over her mother's expectations and her own wishes for the relationship but with little resolution.

In one session, I asked her a question comparing her late fiancé with her current boyfriend. She flew into a rage over such an insensitive question, stormed out of the room, and declared she would never return. I felt a complete failure. But years of psychoanalytic work has taught me to pay close attention to my feelings as they usually reflect important issues going on in the transference. I gradually realized she had unconsciously induced in me her own self-feelings of failure that her mother conveyed to her on many occasions, including the current one of becoming involved with such an ostensibly unsuitable man. I phoned her and told her my thoughts. The interpretation was right on target. Her feelings of failure centered around many of her mother's expectations were worked through to a considerable extent and she was eventually able to marry this man.

Her way of expressing her anger and rage is another matter. It was characteristic of her that in all situations, including with her late fiancé, she could only express her anger by storming out of the relationship. For her, similar to the Asian male patients, anger was totally unacceptable in a hierarchical relationship. It was an uncontrollable outburst that catapulted her out of the relationship. We worked on her being able to express anger while still remaining with the person.

Communication

Nasir Ilahi[3] commented that the most difficult task for him when he first began seeing English and American patients in psychoanalytic therapy in London was realizing that all of the communications were verbal and that any nonverbal communication was usually unconsciously dissociated. He further elaborated that from his Pakistani background, he was accustomed to the conscious communication being more or less half verbal and half nonverbal, that one is always attuned to the conscious nonverbal communication (presentation to the Asian American Mental Health Professionals Discussion Group, 2002). This, of course, contrasts with the Euro-American psychoanalytic therapist, who is accustomed to the conscious communication in therapy sessions being verbal.

I have found, along with other Asian therapists, that one must be constantly attuned to the nonverbal in Asian patients but it is significantly different in Indians from Japanese. The former are far more verbally expressive than Japanese or Koreans, but the communication is multileveled in the sense that there are considerable facial and other gestures, moods, and actual behavior, all of which may or may not be congruent with the verbal. I have found that with most of my Japanese immigrant patients I must rely a great deal on a nonverbal empathic sensing, that when communicated verbally to the patient either evokes an elaboration of what I have said or a denial of its accuracy. There is a saying in Japanese that nothing important is ever to be communicated verbally.

In certain instances, particularly with East Asian patients, for the therapist to verbalize something when the patient is aware that the therapist knows this, is experienced by the patient to be insulting. May Ng, a Chinese American psychologist, related to me that she had just come from a session with a Chinese teenager at a clinic near Chinatown, New York City (personal communication). She gave him an interpretation and he responded with such anger that he threw a chair against the wall. She realized that he was not angry over the content of the interpretation but rather that he already knew that she knew this about him, and for her to verbalize it was highly insulting. I further found in commenting on a case in Japan with a woman from a traditional background, that not only was the psychoanalytic therapist aware of certain things months before the patient verbalized it, but the patient seemed also to be aware of what the therapist was thinking without her verbalizing it. Therapy had progressed well over a year and a half with a bare minimum of interpretations (Roland, 1988, 186–94).

THE BICULTURAL SELF

When we talk about psychoanalytic therapy with Asian Americans, we not only have to distinguish between persons coming from different East, West (e.g., Turkey), and South Asian cultures but also between the immigrant generation, 1.5s, and the second generation who are born here. All of them have a bicultural self, often with considerable turmoil, as the value systems and makeup of the self are significantly different from that of Euro-Americans. In fact, the 1.5 and second-generation Indians refer to themselves as ABCD, American-Born Confused Desi (Indian). In the immigrant generation, there is a need to combine a more individualized American self with their Asian familial self. In 1.5s and the second generation, although it can vary between them, they both have a strong internalized individualized self from American schooling and peer social life but also strong aspects of a familial self from their parents, which can also make for considerable conflict and confusion.

I have worked mainly with the Asian immigrant generation (those who have come after at least completing high school in their own country), but also with some 1.5s and occasionally with the second generation. What are some of the problems they encounter in their interface with American life? The vignette of Priya, an immigrant, illustrates how she was unable to cope in an American hierarchical relationship because of her Indian upbringing. In another case of a Japanese woman immigrant, Yoshiko, she was devastated by the occasional sharp criticism of her superior when she made one of her very few mistakes, in contrast to the other workers who made far more mistakes but let the criticism roll off them like water off a duck's back (Roland, 1996, 85–86). Unless the Euro-American psychoanalytic therapist is aware of the considerable differences in Asian and American hierarchical relationships and expectations, they might immediately seize on a psychopathological component rather than realizing that the clash of expectations and ways of relating has a strong existential component to it that must be dealt with in the therapy.

Central to Asians' reactions, no matter which country they are from, is the salient dimension of self-esteem or more accurately, we-self-esteem. They are not used to the direct criticism of American superiors nor what they often experience as an uncaring attitude, whether at work or in the university.

Clinical Vignette: 6

> One Indian woman, Veena, in a medical fellowship program after finishing her residency, had contracted to do an extra year at fewer hours because of having a toddler. The director of the program insisted she work the regular hours and had her repeat rotations she already had because he was short-handed. Both she and I were enraged. I felt it was a complete abrogation of the contractual relationship and that he was exploiting her. She, on the other hand, kept repeating "He doesn't respect me." The wound to her own esteem was enraging to her.

Still another problem of analysts not understanding Asian hierarchical relationships emerged years ago at the psychoanalytic institute of which I am a member, when one Indian woman was held up from becoming a member because all of the instructors' evaluations mentioned she rarely, if ever, spoke up in class. Her deferential attitude toward the instructors was completely misinterpreted as passivity, and it was judged that she needed more analysis. In reality, she was the administrator of a large clinic where she effectively dealt with a number of therapists.

On a more intrapsychic level, many Indian women are torn between relating in a modest, self-effacing manner and having to be highly assertive and verbally articulate in the workplace of American life. The internalized value systems and ways of relating from earlier life for immigrants and the later American ones that are also incorporated can result in considerable inner conflict and turmoil.

MAGIC-COSMIC AND THE SPIRITUAL SELF

The Asian self is both more horizontal and vertical than the typical Euro-American self. It is horizontal in terms of the self's enmeshment in the extended family, community, and group. It is vertical, especially in Indians, where there is an assumption of past and future lives, and a sense of personal destiny tied in to past lives and the effects of the planets, with the use of astrology, palmistry, psychics, and such to fathom one's destiny. Metonymic thinking where the transcendent and invisible world is also part of one's everyday experiences is integral to this way of thinking (Ramanujan, 1990). I have found with all of the Hindu Indian patients I have worked with, most with advanced degrees, that the assumption of personal destiny is very strong, and that astrology, psychics, palmistry, and such have often played a major influence in their life.

It is not only Euro-American psychoanalytic therapists who have difficulty in dealing with the assumptions of personal destiny, of the influences of planets and past lives, and of the use of astrology, palmistry, psychics, the spirit world, and such to ascertain one's destiny; it is also South Asian academic specialists. It is very difficult for the educated, more or less scientifically oriented Euro-American to entertain these notions given our Enlightenment heritage and the rational demystification of religion. Thus, the educated Westerner sees this as superstition, and it is mainly in the counterculture that astrology and such flourish.

I shall give a few brief examples out of many of how this magic-cosmic world has manifested in psychoanalytic therapy with Hindu patients.

Clinical Vignette: 7

> The very first Indian patient I saw, Ashis, came to psychoanalytic therapy for the first time in his life. He had intense identity conflicts but was in a highly optimistic mood, something rather unusual. His mood had resulted from his wife and mother going to the Brighu Temple in the Punjab with the exact minute of his birth. The temple priest then brought out a palm-leaf manuscript written three hundred years ago by a sage, Brighu. It not only told of Ashis's life up to then but also predicted that by the end of February (they had gone in December) his life would take a decided turn for the better. It was exactly the end of February when he began psychoanalytic therapy with me, and indeed from that time on, he moved on to a much better place. (Roland, 1988, 25–47)

The second example is of an Indian woman who was in therapy because of an overwhelmingly, verbally abusive husband.

Clinical Vignette: 8

Alka and I worked for a considerable period to help her recover from her battered emotional state and leave her husband. At one point, she gave her husband's and her own horoscope to a cousin in India, asking him to consult a good astrologer and find out what he thought about the marriage without telling him anything. The astrologer after looking at the horoscopes responded by saying in effect, "Who the hell arranged this marriage? It's a terrible one. The husband is very disturbed and she should leave him immediately. He has something growing behind his right eye, and if she stays longer, it will get worse and she'll find it harder to leave." It was already known that her husband had a brain tumor behind his right eye. The astrologer's report helped to confirm and fortify the patient's emerging desire to leave her husband, which she eventually did. Her marriage had been arranged by her father, who was indebted to the father of the man she married.

Clinical Vignette: 9

The third example involves an Indian man, Prakash, who regularly consulted psychics on his visits to India. They would give all kinds of directions and advice. I eventually noticed that he never followed any of it. The same pattern emerged in the psychoanalytic group he was in. He would importune the group members for advice on one matter or another but never follow it. Both were transference manifestations from his relationships with his seven older brothers and sisters, who would constantly advise, criticize, and direct him as a child. He would listen obediently but then never follow what they said.

For the Euro-American psychoanalytic therapist, it is first crucial to be open to any experience the patient has with the world of personal destiny, such as influences from the planets and/or past lives, and the predictions of astrology or palmistry. Otherwise, Indian patients will sense the therapist being unreceptive and simply keep this important realm out of the therapy. My own attitude is to put aside the issue of the validity or not of these notions but rather see how the patient responds to them and what effect it has on the patient. It is, after all, what we do in therapy with any experience.

Then there is a sense of a long spiritual evolution. Indians I have worked with all assume there is an inner spiritual reality but that it takes effort to realize it. Only a small number were actively involved in one discipline or another, some through their art, another through work and service, to realize this inner spiritual self. Not to recognize this other inner level of reality in therapy can be alienating to many Indian patients. In the last decade, many Euro-American psychoanalytic therapists have become much more open to the spiritual dimension, in good part due to the advent of Buddhism in the United States (Rubin, 1996).

TRAUMA AND IMMIGRATION

Another factor in working with Asian Americans that can be overlooked by the Euro-American psychoanalytic therapist is that of past trauma from their country of origin, or if they are Japanese North Americans from internment camps during World War II. Implicit in the working out of a bicultural self is the impact of immigration. Even when there are no financial problems, the inner emotional struggle and turmoil that living in a radically different culture entails can be considerable. The effects of immigration on therapy patients and their families enter into psychoanalytic therapy in a central way.

Clinical Vignette: 10

May, a Chinese immigrant woman who was married to an American man, was diagnosed by many therapists and psychiatrists as being borderline psychotic. She would fly into rages, seemingly on minor provocations, such as her neighbor honking her horn at 6:30 a.m. upon leaving their common driveway. As I worked with her, I asked about her childhood experiences in China. She told me that she was exposed to the Cultural Revolution from ages seven to seventeen. Across the street from her apartment building was a wealthy merchant's mansion. The Red Guard had killed him and then used the mansion to regularly torture people. Screams were heard day and night for ten years, severely traumatizing her. Thus, the neighbor honking at 6:30 a.m. awakening her from her sleep was experienced as the screams of people being tortured. She handled her extreme anxiety by flying into rages and attacking the other. Thus, this ongoing past trauma was misinterpreted by a few psychoanalytic therapists and psychiatrists because none had inquired into her prior experience before immigrating.

Clinical Vignette: 11

A Japanese Canadian woman, Sumiko, held a high executive position in a large American corporation. One of her major problems was compulsively working extremely long hours even when she could leave earlier. We had analyzed her incorporating her Japanese mother's typical attitudes of everything having to be done extremely well, but this had little effect on her compulsive work habits. It is only when we talked about her mother's experience of growing up during World War II in a Canadian internment camp where conditions were much more severe than in the United States, and where everything was confiscated from these families so they had nothing to return to when the war was

> over, that I understood more of the mother's nonnurturing nature. In effect, her mother had the usual high Japanese expectations but lacked the maternal nurturing qualities because of the childhood trauma she experienced in the internment camp and immediately afterward. As a result, Sumiko had to compulsively fulfill these high expectations because there was so little feeling of maternal warmth and love. Once this was understood, she was able to work fewer hours.

In two other cases of an Indian 1.5 and a second-generation woman, part of these women's problems with their mothers stemmed from the mother having a very difficult time with the immigration experience. In one case, the mother loved to manage the affairs of a large joint family in India, for which she was duly appreciated. Coming to the United States and living in a nuclear family with few other relationships and having to raise her children with little help, she felt very much put upon. This aggravated conflicts with her daughter. In the other case, the mother, upon immigration, had become depressed. This had an unconscious effect on her daughter of always having to take care of others with little thought for herself. In both cases, the Euro-American would have to pay considerable attention to the effects of immigration on the family as a whole, and then how it affected the patient.

CONCLUDING REMARKS

To conduct psychoanalytic therapy across civilizations, in this case Western psychoanalytic therapists with Asian patients, requires a twofold process. The first is to reexamine one's cultural self, and the developmental and other norms and assumptions of psychoanalytic theory and therapy as they are rooted in the modern Western culture of individualism. The second is to become acquainted with a different normality/psychopathology continuum than is common in the West, the three psychosocial dimensions of Asian hierarchical relationships as they affect the psychoanalytic relationship, the psychological importance of insider and outsider relationships, anger and its inhibitions and vicissitudes, and different modes of communication. Three other psychological dimensions of Asians are also discussed: the bicultural self of Asian Americans; the magic-cosmic, religion, and the spiritual self; and trauma and its effects from the indigenous country and from immigration.

NOTES

1. For approximately eleven years, Nasir Ilahi and I have run a monthly discussion group of Asian and Asian American Mental Health Professionals (social workers, psychologists, psychiatrists, and students in psychoanalytic training from East,

West, and South Asian countries) on "Cultural and Social Factors in Psychoanalytic Therapy." It clearly emerged that in none of their training programs was there any attempt to take into account Asian cultural/psychological factors. In fact, many had some kind of struggle not to pathologize or disavow aspects of their Asian self and upbringing.

2. A psychoanalytic theorist such as Philip Cushman (1995) has tried to take this into account through the concept of social constructivism.

3. While there has been a marked advance in the psychotherapy, counseling, and social work field in the last decade on cultural sensitivity and competence (Blustein and Noumair, 1996; Carter, 2005; Constantine, 2005; Laungani, 2004; D. W. Sue, 2003), it is still quite limited in psychoanalysis, regardless of the school or model. However, in the new New York State licensing law on psychoanalysis, psychoanalytic institutes will be required from 2007 onward to offer one course on social and cultural issues.

4. Mr. Ilahi is a Pakistani American psychoanalyst trained in the Independent School of the British Psychoanalytic Society.

References

Addis, S., and Hurst, G. C. (1983). *Samurai Painters*. New York: Kodansha International.

AFP (2008). China's suicide rate soaring [Electronic Version]. December 9. www.asiaone.com/News/Latest+News/Asia/Story/A1Story20081209-106506.html.

Akhtar, S. (1999a). *Immigration and Identity: Turmoil, Treatment, and Transformation*. Northvale, N.J.: Jason Aronson.

———. (1999b). The distinction between needs and wishes: implications for psychoanalytic theory and technique. *Journal of American Psychoanalytic Association* 47: 113–51.

Alexander, F. (1950). *Psychosomatic Medicine: Its Principles and Applications*. New York: W. W. Norton and Company .

Anderson, L. P. (1999). Parentification in the context of the African American family. In *Burdened Children: Theory, Research, and Treatment of Parentification*, ed. G. J. Jurkovic, 154–70. Thousand Oaks, Calif.: Sage.

Asahina, S. (1966). *Rinzairoku*, trans. Tokyo, Japan: Iwanami-Bunko.

Bahn, G. H. (2008). Holding environment. *Psychoanalysis* 19: 20–24.

Balint, M. (1959). *Thrills and Regressions*. London: The Hogarth Press.

Balmary, M. (1979). *L'homme Aux Statues*, trans. H. Iwasaki and T. Shobo. Paris: Grasset et Fasquelle, 1988.

Basho, M. (1991). *Narrow Road to the Interior*, trans. S. Hamill. Boston: Shambhala.

Bergman, A. (1997). Formal discussion of amae reconsidered. Presented at the American Psychoanalytic Association's Annual Meeting. May 1997.

Bion, W. (1962). *Learning from Experience*. London: Karnac Books.

———. (1970). *Attention and Interpretation*. London: Tavistock.

———. (1983). *Attention and Interpretation*. New York: Jason Aronson.

Blos, P. (1962). *On Adolescence: A Psychoanalytic Interpretation*. New York: The Free Press.

Blowers, G. (1993). Freud's China connection. *Journal of Multilingual and Multicultural Development* 14: 263–73.

——. (1994). Freud in China: The variable reception of psychoanalysis. In *Applying Psychology: Lessons from Asia-Oceania*, ed. G. Davidson, 35–49. Brisbane: Australian Academic Press.

——. (2004). Bingham Dai, Adolf Storfer, and the tentative beginnings of psychoanalytic culture in China: 1935–1941. *Psychoanalysis and History* 6: 93–105

Blowers, G., and Yuan, T. (2005). Psychoanalysis: China. In *International Dictionary of Psycho-analysis*. American Edition, ed. A. D. Mijolla, vol. 1, 285–87. Detroit: Macmillan Reference.

Blustein, D. L., and Noumair, D. A. (1996). Self and identity in career development: implications for theory and practice. *Journal of Counseling and Development* 74: 433–41.

Bowlby, J. (1958) The nature of the child's tie to his mother. *International Journal of Psychoanalysis* 39: 350–73.

——. (1963). Pathological mourning and childhood mourning. *Journal of the American Psychoanalytic Association* 11: 500–541.

Breuer, J., and Freud, S. (1893–1895). *Studien über Hysterie*. Frankfurt am Main: S. Fisher Verlag, 2007.

Cabaniss, D. L., Oquendo, M. A., and Singer, M. D. (1994). Values in transference and counter-transference: A study in transcultural psychotherapy. *Journal of the American Academy of Psychoanalysis* 22: 609–21.

Cao, X., and Gao, E. (1791). *The Story of the Stone*, vol. 1, trans. D. Hawks. Harmondsworth, UK: Penguin Books, 1973.

——. (1791). *The Story of the Stone*, vol. 5, trans. J. Minford. Harmondsworth, UK: Penguin Books, 1986.

Cao, Y. (1934). *Thunderstorm*. Peking: Chinese Literature Press, 1978.

Carter, R. T., ed. (2005). *Handbook of Racial-Cultural Psychology and Counseling: Theory and Research*. Hoboken, N.J.: John Wiley and Sons.

Caudill, W. (1972) Tiny dramas: vocal communication between mother and infant in Japanese and American families. In *Transcultural Research in Mental Health*, vol. II, ed. W. P. Lebra. Honolulu: University Press of Hawaii.

Center for Education Statistics. (2008). std.kedi.re.kr/index.jsp.

Chang, D. F., Tong, H., Shi, Q., and Zeng, Q. (2005). Letting a hundred flowers bloom: counseling and psychotherapy in the People's Republic of China. *Journal of Mental Health Counseling* 27: 104–16.

Chang, E. (1942). The golden cangue. In *Modern Chinese Stories and Novellas*, eds. J. S. M. Lau, C. T. Hsia, and L. Ou-Fan, 530–59. New York: Columbia University Press, 1981.

Chao, R. K. (1994). Beyond parental control and authoritarian parenting style: understanding Chinese American parenting through the cultural notion of training. *Child Development* 65: 1111–19.

Caho, R. K. (1995). Chinese American and European American cultural models of the self reflected in mothers' childrearing beliefs. *Ethos* 23: 328–54.

Chase, N. D. (1999). *Burdened Children: Theory, Research, and Treatment of Parentification*. Thousand Oaks, Calif.: Sage.

Chasseguet-Smirgel, J. (1984). *Creativity and Perversion*. New York: W. W. Norton.

Chen, N. (2003). Why psychiatry matters in China. *International Institute for Asian Studies* 30. iias.nl/index.php?q=newsletter-30.

Cho, D. Y. (1984). *More Than Numbers*. Waco, Tex.: Word Books.

——. (1995). Korea. In *Psychoanalysis International: A Guide to Psychoanalysis through-out the World*, vol. 2, ed. P. Kutter. Stuttgart–Bad Cannstatt: Frommann-Holzboog.

——. (2001). A psychoanalytic approach on Chang-Sup Sohn's three short stories. *Psychoanalysis* 12: 253–61.

Cho, H. (2002) Living with conflicting subjectivities: mother, motherly wife, and sexy woman in the transition from colonial-modern to postmodern Korea. In *Under Construction*, ed. L. Kendall. Honolulu: University of Hawaii Press.

Chodorow, N. (1978). *The Reproduction of Mothering*. Berkeley: University of California Press.

Chow, R. (1995). *Primitive Passions: Visuality, Sexuality, Ethnography, and Contemporary Chinese Cinema*. New York: Columbia University Press.

Chu, J. Y. (2004). *Filial Responsibilities in Chinese American Families: Definition, Affect, and Outcome.* Unpublished dissertation.

CIA World Factbook. (2008). www.cia.gov/library/publications/the-world-factbook/.

Claire, W. F. (1975). Report on a memorial service; a letter to Mark Van Doren. *Columbia Forum* (Winter 28).

Coltart, N. (1996). Buddhism and psychoanalysis revisited. In *The Baby and the Bathwater*, 125–39. London: Karnac Books.

Constantine, M. G., and Sue, D. W., eds. (2005). *Strategies for Building Multicultural Competence in Mental Health and Educational Settings*. Hoboken, N.J.: John Wiley and Sons.

Cooper, J. (1999). What is the right thing? A self-psychological discussion of Spike Lee's "Do the Right Thing." *Psychoanalytic Review* 86: 455–64.

Cox, H. (1995). *Fire from Heaven: The Rise of Pentecostal Spirituality and the Reshaping of Religion in the Twenty-First Century*. Cambridge, Mass.: Addision-Wesley Publishing.

Cushman, P. (1995). *Constructing the Self, Constructing America: A Cultural History of Psychotherapy*. New York: Addison-Wesley Publishing Co.

Dai, B. (1984). Psychoanalysis in China before the Revolution: A letter from Bingham Dai. *Transcultural Psychiatric Research* 21: 280–82.

Dalai Lama (1984). *Kindness, Clarity, and Insight*. New York: Snow Lion Publications.

Davies, R. J., and Ikeno, O. (2002). *The Japanese Mind: Understanding Contemporary Culture.* Boston: Tuttle Publishing.

Deleuze, G., and Quattari, F. (1977). *Anti-Oedipus: Capitalism and Schizophrenia*, trans. M. Seem and H. Lane. New York: Viking Press.

Deloria, E. C. (1988). *Waterlily*. Lincoln: University of Nebraska Press.

Deshimaru, T. (1982). *The Zen Way to the Martial Arts*. New York: E. P. Dutton.

——. (1983). *The Ring of the Way*. New York: E. P. Dutton.

——. (1985). *Questions to a Zen Master*. New York: E. P. Dutton.

Deuchler, M. (1977) The tradition: Women during the Yi Dynasty. In *Virtues in Conflict, Tradition and the Korean Woman Today*, ed. S. Mattielli. Seoul: Samhwa Publishing Company.

——. (1992) The pre-Confucian past: A reconstruction of Koryo society. In *The Confucian Transformation of Korea*. Cambridge, Mass.: Harvard University Press.

——. (1992). Neo-Confucianism: The ideological foundation of social legislation in early Choson. In *The Confucian Transformation of Korea.* Cambridge, Mass.: Harvard University Press.

——. (1992). Confucian legislation: The consequences for women. In *The Confucian Transformation of Korea.* Cambridge, Mass.: Harvard University Press.

Doi, T. (1956). Japanese language as an expression of Japanese psychology. *Western Speech* (Spring 1956).

——. (1962). Amae: A key concept for understanding Japanese personality structure. In *Japanese Culture: Its Development and Characteristics*, eds. R. J. Smith and R. K. Beardsley. Chicago: Aldine.

——. (1963). Some thoughts on helplessness and the desire to be loved. *Psychiatry: Journal for the Study of Interpersonal Processes* 26: 266–76.

——. (1964). Psychoanalytic therapy and Western man: a Japanese view. *International Journal of Social Psychiatry* 1: 13–18.

——. (1971). *The Anatomy of Dependence*, trans. J. Bester. Tokyo: Kodansha International, 1973.

——. (1973). Psychotherapy as "hide and seek." *Bulletin of the Menninger Clinic* 37.

——. (1973a). *The Anatomy of Dependence*. Tokyo: Kodansha.

——. (1973b). Omote and ura: Concepts derived from Japanese two-fold structure of consciousness. *Journal of Nervous and Mental Disease* 157: 258–61.

——. (1986). *The Anatomy of Self.* Tokyo: Kodansha.

——. (1989). The concept of amae and its psychoanalytic implications. *International Review Psycho-Analysis* 16: 349–54.

——. (1992). On the concept of amae. *Infant Mental Health Journal* 13: 7–11.

——. (1997). Some reflections on the concept of amae. Presented at the American Psychoanalytic Association Interdisciplinary Conference on Amae Reconsidered. May 1997.

Dornbusch, S. M., Ritter, P. L., Leiderman, P. H., Roberts, D. F., and Fraleigh, M. J. (1987). The relation of parenting style to adolescent school performance. *Child Development* 58: 1244–57.

Draeger, D. F., and Smith, R. W. (1980). *Comprehensive Asian Fighting Arts*. New York: Kodansha International.

e-Indices, Korean Government. (2008). www.index.go.kr/egams/default.jsp.

The Economist (United States). (2008). China healthcare: And now the 50-minute hour (electronic version). August 18. www.alacrastore.com/alacar/help/sample_eiuftxma_EN.pdf.

Editorial Committee of the Historical Sources of the Educational Institutions of Modern Japan, ed. (1956). *Historical Sources of Educational Institutions of Modern Japan*, vol. 6. Tokyo: Dainippon Yuben Kodansha Publishers.

Eigen, M. (1998). *The Psychoanalytic Mystic*. London: Free Associations.

Emmons, R. A., and Shelton, C. M. (2002). Gratitude and the science of positive psychology. In *Handbook of Positive Psychology*, eds. C. R. Snyder and S. J. Lopez, 459–71. Oxford: Oxford University Press.

Enchi, F. (1958). *Masks*, trans. J. W. Carpenter. New York: Vintage Press, 1983.

Engler, J. (1983). Vicissitudes of the self according to psychoanalysis and Buddhism: A development. *Psychoanalysis and Contemporary Thought* 6: 29–72.

——. (2003). Being somebody and being nobody: A re-examination of the understanding of self in psychoanalysis and Buddhism. In *Psychoanalysis and Buddhism—An Unfolding Dialogue*, ed. J. D. Safran, 35–79. Somerville, MA: Wisdom.

Epstein, M. (1995). Thoughts without a thinker—Buddhism and psychoanalysis. *Psychoanalytic Review* 92: 291–406.

Erikson, E. H. (1959). *Identity and the Life Cycle.* New York: International Universities Press.

Escoll, P. J. (1999). The "silent" parent and the unprotected, scapegoated child. In *At the Threshold of the Millennium*. vol. 2, eds. M. R. F. Brescia and M. Lemlij, 125–41. Lima: Sidea/Prom Peru.

Exploratory Committee to Korea. (2002). A summary of this committee's report to the Executive Council in July 2002. *International Psychoanalysis* 11: 42.

Faulkner, W. (1954). A rose for Emily. In *The Faulkner Reader*. New York: Random House.

Felman, S., and Laub, D. (1992). *Testimony: Crises of Witnessing in Literature, Psycho-Analysis, and History.* New York: Routledge.

Fenichel, O. (1931). Specific forms of the Oedipus complex. In *Collected Papers of Otto Fenichel First Series*, 204–20. New York: W. W. Norton, 1953.

Foucault, M. (1976). *The History of Sexuality: An Introduction*. New York: Vintage Books, 1980.

——. (1984). *The History of Sexuality: The Care of The Self.* New York: Vintage Books, 1988.

——. (1984). *The History of Sexuality: The Use of Pleasure*. New York: Vintage Books, 1990.

Freeman, D. M. A. (1993). Looking, precocious individuation and appeal behavior portrayed in Ukiyo-e Art of the 17th–19th centuries. Presented at the American Psychoanalytic Association Interdisciplinary Colloquium on Child Development and *Amae.* December 1993.

——. (1994). Early cognitive and visual individuation in Japanese child development. Presented at *Noguchi Kinen Kaikan*. August 1994.

——. (1997a). Emotional refueling in development, mythology, and cosmology: the Japanese separation-individuation experience. In *The Colors of Childhood*, eds. S. Akhtar and S. Kramer, 17–60. New York: Jason Aronson.

——. (1997b). Precocity, refueling and amae. Presented at the American Psychoanalytic Association Interdisciplinary Conference on Amae Reconsidered. May 17–18, 1997.

——. (1998). *Japanese Child-Rearing and Personality: Precocity, Individuation and Amae*. Tokyo: International House.

Freud, A. (1936). *The Ego and the Mechanisms of Defense*. New York: International Universities Press.

Freud, S. (1900). The interpretation of dreams. *Standard Edition*, 4 and 5. London: Hogarth Press.

——. (1905). Fragment of an analysis of a case of hysteria. *Standard Edition*, 7: 1–122. London: Hogarth Press.

——. (1908). Creative writers and daydreaming. *Standard Edition*, 9: 142–53. London: Hogarth Press.

——. (1912). Recommendations for physicians on the psycho-analytic method of treatment. *Standard Edition*, 2: 323–33. London: Hogarth Press.

——. (1913). Totem and taboo. *Standard Edition* 13. London: Hogarth Press.

——. (1914). On narcissism: an introduction. *Standard Edition*, 14. London: Hogarth Press.

——. (1935). Postscript (to an autobiographic study). *Standard Edition*, 20: 72. London: Hogarth Press.

Fromm, E., Suzuki, D. T., and DeMartino, R. (1960). *Zen Buddhism and Psychoanalysis*. New York: Harper and Row.

Fujita, C. (1986). *Morita Therapy—A Psychotherapeutic System for Neurosis*. Tokyo: Igaku-Shoin.

Fujiyama, N. (1997). The amae theory from the object-relational viewpoint. Presented at The American Psychoanalytic Association Interdisciplinary Conference on *Amae* Reconsidered. May 1997.

Fuligni, A. J., Tseng, V., and Lam, M. (1999). Attitudes toward family obligations among American Adolescents with Asian, Latin American, and European Backgrounds. *Child Development* 70: 1030–44.

Fuligni, A.J., Yip, T., and Tseng, V. (2002). The impact of family obligation on the daily activities and psychological well-being of Chinese American adolescents. *Child Development* 73: 302–14.

Gaddini, E. (1982). Early defensive fantasies and the psychoanalytic process. *International Journal of Psychoanalysis* 63: 379–88.

Gallimore, R., Goldenberg, C. N., and Weisner, T. S. (1993). The social construction and subjective reality of activity settings: implications for community psychology. *American Journal of Community Psychology* 21: 537–59.

Ganzarain, R. (1988). Various guilts within the Ajase complex, trans. K Okonogi. *Japanese Journal of Psychoanalysis* 32: 93–102.

Garrod A., and Kilkenny, R. (2007). *Balancing Two Worlds: Asian American College Students Tell Their Life Stories*. Ithaca, N.Y.: Cornell University Press.

Gay, P. (2006). *Freud: A Life for Our Time*. New York: W. W. Norton.

Gerlach, A. (1995). China. In *Psychoanalysis International: A Guide to Psychoanalysis throughout the World*, ed. P. Kutter, vol. 2, 94–101. Germany: Fromm-Holzoog.

——. (2006). Psychoanalysis training in China: Experiences of psychoanalytic therapy for the Chinese. Paper presented at the Congress Proceedings of First World Congress of Cultural Psychiatry, Beijing, China. Unpublished.

Goodhart, S. (1978). *Lhstas Efaske*: Oedipus and Laius' many murderers. *Diacritics* 8: 55–71.

Green, A. (1969). *The Tragic Effect: The Oedipus Complex in Tragedy*, trans. A. Sheridan. Cambridge: Cambridge University Press, 1979.

Greenberg, J. R., and Mitchell, S. A. (1983). *Object Relations in Psychoanalytic Theory*. Cambridge, Mass.: Harvard University Press.

Gu, M. D. (1993). A Chinese Oedipus in exile. *Literature and Psychology* 37: 1–25.

——. (2006). The filial piety complex: variations on the Oedipus theme in Chinese literature and culture. *Psychoanalytic Quarterly* 75:163–95.

Guntrip, H. (1961). *Personality Structure and Human Interaction*. New York: International Universities Press.

Ha, J. H. (2002). A psychoanalytic exploration of Korean folk tales. *Psychoanalysis* 13: 51–67.

Hahn, D. (1969). *Psychiatry*. Seoul: Ilchogak.

Han, S. H. (2005). Psychotherapy and medication. *Psychoanalysis* 16: 28–34.

Harvey, P. (2000). *An Introduction to Buddhist Ethics*. Cambridge: Cambridge University Press.

Hegel, G. (1807). *The Phenomenology of the Spirit*, trans. A. V. Miller. Oxford: Oxford University Press.

Hesse, H. (1915). Im Nebel, in *Die Gedichte von Hermann Hesse*, Fretz und Wasmuth Verlag, Zürich, 1942. See Das Lied des Lebens Die schönsten Gedichte von Hermann Hesse, und Vierre Auflage, Suhrkamp Verlag, Frankfurt am Main, 1987.

Hong, T. Y. (2007). Development of Freudian theory. *Psychoanalysis* 18: 28–32.

Hsia, C. T. (1961). *A History of Modern Chinese Fiction*. New Haven, Conn.: Yale University Press.

Hsu, F. L. K. (1981). *American and Chinese: Passage to Differences*, third ed. Honolulu: University of Hawaii Press.

Hume, D. (1787). *A Treatise of Human Nature*. Oxford: Oxford University Press, 1978.

Hurh, W. M. (1998). *The Korean Americans*. Westport, Conn.: Greenwood Publishing.

Hwang, I. K., and Yang, J. C. (2008). An essay on Freud's view of instincts and its interpretation through Yin-Yang Doctrine of Confucianism. *Psychoanalysis* 19: 46–53.

Illing, H. A. (1969). *Sigmund Freud: Briefe 1873–1939*. Frankfurt am Main: S. Fisher Verlag, 1980.

International Psychoanalytical Association. (2003). *Advisory Committee to Korea—Mandate*. January 2003.

Irigaray, L. (1974). *Speculum of the Other Woman*, trans. G. Gill. Ithaca, N.Y.: Cornell University Press, 1985.

Jameson, F. (1986). Third-world literature in the era of multinational capitalism. *Social Text* 15: 65–88.

Jeong, D. U. (2000). Psychoanalysis, Korea and Asia. *Psychoanalysis* 11: 167–68.

Jeung, R. (2005). *Faithful Generations: Race and New Asian American Churches*. New Brunswick, N.J.: Rutgers University Press.

Johnson, A., and Prince-Williams, D. (1996). eds. *Oedipus Ubiquitous: The Family Complex in World Folk Literature*. Stanford, Calif: Stanford University Press.

Johnson, F. A. (1993). *Dependency and Japanese Socialization*. New York: New York University Press.

Johnson, K., and Paulenich, C. (1991). *Beneath a Single Moon: Buddhism in Contemporary American Poetry*. Boston: Shambhala Publications.

Jones, E. (1953). *The Life and Work of Sigmund Freud*, vol. 1. New York: Basic Books.

Joseph, B. (1989). *Psychic Equilibrium and Psychic Change: Selected Papers of Betty Joseph*. London: Tavistock Books.

Juang, L. P., Lerner, J. V., McKinney, J. P., and von Eye, A. (1999). The goodness of fit in autonomy timetable expectations between Asian-American late adolescents and their parents. *International Journal of Behavior Development* 23: 1023–48.

Jurkovic, G. J., Thirkield, A., and Morrell, R. (2001). Parentification of adult children of divorce: A multidimensional analysis. *Journal of Youth and Adolescence* 30: 245–57.

Kakar, S. (1978). *The Inner World: A Psychoanalytic Study of Childhood and Society*. Delhi, India: Oxford University Press.

——. (1982). *Shamans, Mystics, and Doctors*. New York: Alfred A. Knopf.

——. (1989). *Intimate Relations: Exploring Indian Sexuality*. Chicago: University of Chicago Press.

——. (1991). *The Analyst and the Mystic*. Delhi, India: Viking by Penguin Books India.

Kaneko, T., ed. (1931). *Tanisho*. Tokyo: Iwanami-Bunko.

Kang, S. (2002). *Unveiling the Socioculturally Constructed Multivoiced Self: Themes of Self Construction and Self Integration in the Narratives of Second-Generation Korean American Young Adults*. Lanham, Md.: University Press of America.

Kapleau, P. (1965). *The Three Pillars of Zen: Teaching, Practice, Enlightenment*. Tokyo: Anchor Press/Doubleday.

Kawai, Y. (2005). Stereotyping Asian Americans: The dialectic of the model minority and the yellow peril. *Howard Journal of Communications* 16: 109–30.

Kaya, W. (1997). Amae in the life cycle: mourning and termination. Presented at the American Psychoanalytic Association's Interdisciplinary Conference on Amae Reconsidered. May 1997.

Kee, J. (1998). *(Re)sexualizing the Desexualized Asian Male in the Works of Ken Chu and Michael Joo*. Cambridge, Mass.: Harvard University Press.

Kernberg, O. F. (1980). *Internal World and External Reality*. New York: Jason Aronson.

——. (1991). Sadomasochism, sexual excitement, and perversion. *Journal of the American Psychoanalytic Association* 39: 333–62.

Kibria, N. (2002). *Becoming Asian American: Identities of Second Generation Chinese and Korean Americans*. Baltimore: Johns Hopkins University Press.

Kim, C. J. (1999). The racial triangulation of Asian Americans. *Politics & Society* 27: 105–38.

Kim, E. (1986). Asian Americans and Asian American Culture. In *Dictionary of Asian American History*, ed. H. C. Kim. New York: Greenwood Press.

Kim, H. N. (2001). Self-image of Tim Burton visualized in the movie *Scissorhands*. *Psychoanalysis* 12: 51–59.

Kim, I. J. (2004). *Korean Americans: Past, Present, and Future*. Elizabeth, N.J.: Hollym International.

Kim, I. J., Kim, L. I., and Kelly, J. G. (2006). Developing cultural competence in working with Korean immigrant families. *Journal Community Psychology* 34: 149–65.

Kim, J. Y., and Sung, K. (2000). Conjugal violence in Korean American families: A residue of the cultural tradition. *Journal of Family Violence* 15: 331–45.

Kim, M. K. (2005). Hidden resistance relating to the previous therapist. *Psychoanalysis* 16: 35–39.

Kim, R. Y. (2006). *God's New Whiz Kids?: Korean American Evangelicals on Campus*. New York: New York University Press.

Kirschner, S. R. (1990). The assenting ego: Anglo-American values in contemporary developmental psychoanalytic psychology. *Social Research* 57: 822–57.

Kirshner, L. A. (1991). The concept of the self in psychoanalytic theory and its philosophical foundation. *Journal of the American Psychoanalytic Association* 39: 157–82.

Kitano, H. H., and Daniel, R. (1995). *Asian Americans: Emerging Minorities, Second Edition*, 119. Englewood Cliffs, N.J.: Prentice Hall.

Kitano, H. H., Yeung, W. T., Chai, L., and Hatanaka, H. (1984). Asian-American interracial marriage. *Journal of Marriage and the Family* 46: 179–90.

Kitayama, O. (1985). Pre-oedipal "taboo" in Japanese folk tragedies. *International Review of Psycho-Analysis* 12: 173–86.

——. (1987) Metaphorization—making terms. *International Journal of Psycho-Analysis* 68: 499–509.

——. (1991). The wounded caretaker and guilt. *International Review of Psycho-Analysis* 18: 229–40.

——. (1993). On digesting ambiguous indebtedness. Presented at the 38th IPA Congress. Amsterdam, July 1993.

——. (1996). Prohibition and Transience. Presented at the 4th Delphi International Symposium.

——. (1997). Psychoanalysis in shame culture. *The Bulletin* 85: 47–50.

——. (1997). Amae and its hierarchy of love. Presented at the American Psychoanalytic Association Interdisciplinary Conference on Amae Reconsidered. May 1997.

——. (1998). Transience: its beauty and danger. *International Journal of Psycho-Analysis* 70: 937–53.

——. (2004). Cross-cultural varieties in experiencing affect. In *The Language of Emotions*, eds. S. Akhtar and H. Blum, 33–48. New York: Jason Aronson.

——. (2007). *Gekitekina Seishinbunseki-Nyuumon: A Dramatic Introduction to Psycho-Analysis*. Tokyo: Misuzu Shobo.

Klauber, J. (1968). The psychoanalyst as a person. In *Difficulties in the Analytic Encounter*, 123–39. New York: Jason Aronson.

Klein, M. (1935). A contribution to the psychogenesis of manic-depressive states. In *Love, Guilt, and Reparation and Other Works, 1921–1945*, 262–89. New York: Free Press, 1992.

——. (1946). Notes on some schizoid mechanisms. In *Envy and Gratitude and Other Works*. London: Virago Press, 1988.

——. (1946). The Oedipus complex in the light of early anxieties. In *Love, Guilt, and Reparation*, 370–419. New York: Dell.

——. (1948). On the theory of anxiety and guilt. In *Envy and Gratitude and Other Works*. London: Virago Press, 1988.

Kohut, H. (1971). *The Analysis of the Self*. New York: International Universities Press.

——. (1977). *The Restoration of the Self*. New York: International Universities Press.

Korea Tourism Organization. (2008). english.visitkorea.or.kr/enu/index.kto.

Korean Council of Deans of Medical College. (2008). www.meddean.or.kr/html/index.asp?

Korean Neuropsychiatric Association. (1958). Proceedings of symposium in commemoration of Sigmund Freud's one hundred and first birthday. *Psychoanalysis* 4:10–11.

Kosawa, H. (1932). Zaiakukannno nisyu (Two kinds of guilt conscience—Ajase complex). *The Japanese Journal of Psychoanalysis* 1: 5–9, 1954.

——. (1953). The Ajase story. In *Neue Folge der Verlesungen zur Einfuhrung in die Psychoanalyse*. S. Freud, 1932. Translator's afterword. Vienna: Internationaler Psychoanalyticher Verlag, 1933.

Krapf, E. E. (1955). The choice of language in polyglot psychoanalysis. *Psychoanalytic Quarterly* 24: 343–57.

Krech, G. (2002). *Naikan—Gratitude, Grace, and the Japanese Art of Self-Reflection.* Berkeley, Calif.: Stone Bridge Press.

Kris, A. O. (1990). Helping patients by analyzing selfcriticism. *Journal of the American Psychoanalytic Association* 38: 605–36.

Krühl, M. (1979). *Freund sein Vater*. Munden, Germany: C. H. Beck'esche Verlag.

Küng, H. (1970). *Freud and the Problem of God,* trans. E. Quinne. New Haven, Conn.: Yale University Press.

Kurtz. S.A. (1984). On silence. *Psychoanalytic Review* 71: 227–45.

Lacan, J. (1966). *Écrits: A Selection,* trans. A. Sheridan. New York: W. W. Norton, 1977.

———. (1973). *The Four Fundamental Concepts of Psycho-Analysis,* trans. A. Sheridan. Harmondsworth, UK: Penguin, 1977.

Larson, E. V., Levin, N. D., Baik, S., Savych, B. (2004). *Ambivalent Allies? A Study of South Korean Attitudes toward the U.S.* Santa Monica, Calif.: Rand.

Lau, J. S. M., Hsia, C. T., and Ou-fan, L., eds. (1981). *Modern Chinese Stories and Novellas*. New York: Columbia University Press.

Laungani, P. (2004). *Asian Perspectives in Counselling and Psychotherapy*. London: Brunner Routledge.

Lawrence, D. (2008). As stress grows, Chinese turn to Western psychotherapy. *International Herald Tribute: The Global Edition of the New York Times.* October 21. www.iht.com/articles/2008/10/21/asia/letter.php.

Lawrence, D. H. (1913). *Sons and Lovers,* eds. H. Baron and C. Baron. Cambridge: Cambridge University Press, 2002.

Lebovici, S. (1988). Fantasmatic interaction and intergenerational transmission. *Infant Mental Health Journal* 9.

Lee, B. W. (2008). A psychoanalytic comment on Woo Jang-Choon and the seedless watermelon. *Psychoanalysis* 19: 59–68.

Lee, M. S. (2007). Use of Countertransference. *Psychoanalysis* 18: 41–48.

Lee, S. J. (1996). *Unraveling the "Model Minority" Stereotype: Listening to Asian American Youth.* New York: Teachers College Press.

Lee, Y. S. (1930) Effects of psychotherapy on psychotic patients. *Byeol-Geon-Gon* 30: 55–61.

Lewis, C. S. (1960). *The Four Loves.* New York: Harcourt, Brace and Jovanovich.

Li, M., and Guan, L. (1987). Brief introduction of the Chinese Psychological Society. *International Journal of Psychology* 22: 478–82.

Liu, H. (1991). *The Obsessed,* trans. David Kuan. Beijing: Chinese Literature Press.

Liu, W., and Lo, I. Y., eds. (1975). *Sunflower Splendor: Three Thousand Years of Chinese Poetry*. Garden City, N.Y.: Anchor Press.

Lu, Xun. (1980). *Lu Xun lun wenxue yu yishu* [*Lu Hsun on Literature and Art*], eds. Z. Wu et al. Beijing: People's Literature Press.

McDougall, J. (1985). *Theaters of the Mind*. New York: Basic Books.

McGarvey, B. (2002). Korean Americans don't talk much about the gangsters in their midst. Philadelphiacitypaper.net.

McLaughlin, J. T. (1991). Clinical and theoretical aspects of enactment. *Journal of the American Psychoanalytic Association* 39: 595–614.

Maeda, S. (2003). Geironkaramita Shinri-mensetsu (Psychological Interview from *Artistic Point of View*). Tokyo: Seishin Shobo.

Mahler, M. S. (1961). On sadness and grief in infancy and childhood: Loss and restitution of the symbiotic love object. *Psychoanalytic Study of the Child* 16: 332–51.

Mahler, M. S., Pine, F., and Bergman, A. (1975). *The Psychological Birth of the Human Infant: Symbiosis and Individuation*. New York: Basic Books.

Mair, V., ed. (1994). *The Columbia Anthology of Traditional Chinese Literature*. New York: Columbia University Press.

Malinowski, B. (1929). *The Sexual Life of Savages*. London: Routledge.

Maruta, T. (1992). Does an American puppy amaeru? A comment on Dr. Doi's paper. *Infant Mental Health Journal* 13: 12–17.

Mason, R. H. P., and Caiger, J. G. (1997). *A History of Japan: Revised Edition*. Rutland, Vt.: Charles E. Tuttle Company.

Mathews, J. (2008). Asian American students and school stereotypes. Washingtonpost.com, January 8.

Meissner, W. W. (1984). *Psychoanalysis and Religious Experience*. New Haven, Conn.: Yale University Press.

Miki, Y. (1995). *Naikan Therapy, a Way of Self-Discovery and Self-Renewal*. Nara, Japan: Nara Training Center of Naikan Therapy.

Mitamura, T. (1963). *Kangan* (Eunuch). Tokyo: Chuko-shinsho.

Mizuta, I., Yokoi, K., and Inoue, Y. (1997). Some considerations on adaptive and maladaptive amae. Presented at the American Psychoanalytic Association Interdisciplinary Conference on Amae Reconsidered. May 1997.

Moser-Ha, H. (1999). The pre-oedipal father-son relationship in Korean myths and in the patient today. *International Journal of Psycho-Analysis* 80: 143–52

Mura, D. (1991). *Turning Japanese: Memoirs of a Sansei*. New York: The Atlantic Monthly Press.

Murase, T., ed. (1993). *Introduction to Naikan*. Tokyo: Seishinshobo.

Nagayama, K. (2000). *Naikan Therapy (Observing-Inside Therapy)*, summary lecture July 20, 2000, Tokyo.

Nakakuki, M. (1997). Amae and shibumi in healthy personality development of Japanese. Presented at The American Psychoanalytic Association Interdisciplinary Conference on *Amae* Reconsidered. May 1997.

National Institute of Korean History. (2008). Korean History Database. db.history.go.kr/.

Nishizono, M. (1998). Child rearing in Japan in transition. Presented at the American Psychoanalytic Association's Interdisciplinary Conference on Crosscultural Studies. May 1998.

Nordboe, D. J., Kantor, E. M., Barker, H., Ware, A., and Armistead, B. (2007). Immediate behavioral health response to Virginia Tech shootings. *Disaster Medicine and Public Health Preparedness* (Supplement 1): 31–32.

nytimes.com (1992). U.S. looks into Korean grocer's slaying of Black. *New York Times*, November 26, 1992.

Oe, K. (1964). *A Personal Matter*, trans. J. Nathan. New York: Grove Press.

O'Grady, M. (2008). The view from above. *Vogue*, April 2008.

Oh, S. H. (2000). The 34th Hamburg IPA congress in 1985. *Psychoanalysis* 11: 342–43.

Okano, K. (1997). Passivity in amae relationship and the fantasy of "genuine love." Presented at the American Psychoanalytic Association Interdisciplinary Conference on *Amae* Reconsidered. May 1997.

——. (1998). *Haji to Jikoai no Seishin-Bunseki (Psychoanalysis of Shame and Narcissism)*. Tokyo: Isawaki Gakujutsu Shuppansha.

Okimoto, J. T. (1997). A cultural comparison of the appeal cycle in American and Japanese dyads. Presented at The American Psychoanalytic Association, Interdisciplinary Conference on *Amae* Reconsidered. May 1997.

Okonogi, K. (1971). Dr. Heisaku Kosawa as a great pioneer of Japanese psychoanalysis. *Japanese Journal of Psychoanalysis* 15.

——. (1978). The Ajase complex of the Japanese (1): The depth psychology of the moratorium people. *Japan Echo* 5: 88–105.

——. (1978). The Ajase complex of the Japanese (2). *Japan Echo* 6: 104–18.

——. (1992). Amae as seen in diverse interpersonal interactions. *Infant Mental Health Journal* 13:18–25.

——. (1995). Japan. In *Psychoanalysis International: A Guide to Psychoanalysis throughout the World*, vol. 2, ed. P. Kutter. Stuttgart-Bad Cannstatt: Frommann-Holzboog.

Olinik, L. L. (1982). Meanings beyond words: psychoanalytic perceptions of silence and communication, happiness, sexual love and death. *International Review of Psycho-analysis* 9: 461–72.

Oliver, R. W. (1986). Transition and continuity in American-Korean relations in the postwar period. In *One Hundred Years of Korean-American Relations, 1882–1982*, eds. Y. B. Lee and W. Patterson. Tuscaloosa, Ala.: University of Alabama Press.

Park, Mia. (2001). *YELL-Oh Girls! Emerging Voices Explore Culture, Identity, and Growing Up Asian American*. New York: Harper Collins.

Parsons, M. (1992). The refinding of theory in clinical practice. *International Journal of Psychoanalysis* 73: 103–15.

Pashler, H. (1993). Doing two things at the same time. *American Scientist* 81: 48–55.

Pearson, V. (1991). The development of modern psychiatric services in China: 1891–1949. *History of Psychiatry* 2: 133–47.

Pfister, O. (1928). Die Illusion einer Zukunft. *Imago* 14: 100–141.

——. (1963). *Psychoanalysis and Faith: Letters of Sigmund Freud and Oskar Pfister*, ed. H. Meng and E. L. Freud. New York: Basic Books.

Pine, F. (1988). The four psychologies of psychoanalysis and their place in clinical work. *Journal of the American Psychoanalytic Association* 36: 671–96.

Plato. (1971). Phaedo. In *Plato 1*. trans. H. N. Fowler. Cambridge, Mass.: Harvard University Press.

Poland, W. (2000). The analyst's witnessing and otherness. *Journal of the American Psycho-analytic Association* 48: 16–35.

Pollock, G. H. (1988). Oedipus: The myth, the developmental stage, the universal theme, the conflict and complex. In *The Oedipus Papers*, eds. G. Pollock and J. Ross. New York: International Universities Press.

Pollock, G. H., and Ross, J. M. (1988). *The Oedipus Papers*. New York: International Universities Press.

Popp, C., and Taketomo, Y. (1993). The application of the core conflictual relationship theme method to Japanese psychoanalytic psychotherapy. *Journal of the American Academy of Psycho-analysis* 21: 229–52.

Qi, Z. (1985). *Lu You pingzhuan* [*A Critical Biography of Lu You*]. Hunan, China: Yuelu Shushe.

Rahula, W. (1959). *What the Buddha Taught*. New York: Grove Press.

Ramanujam, A. K. (1990). Is there an Indian way of thinking? An informal essay. In *India Through Hindu Categories*, ed. M. Marriott. London: Sage.

Ramanujam, B. K. (1992). Implications of some psychoanalytic concepts in an Indian context. In: *Psychoanalytic Anthropology after Freud*, ed. D. Spain, 121–35. New York: Psyche Press.

Ramzy, I. (1965). The place of values in psychoanalysis. *International Journal of Psychoanalysis* 46: 97–106.

Rank, O. (1912). *Das Inzest-Motiv in Dichtung und Sage: Grundzüge einer Psychologies des dichterischen Schafffens*. Leipzig: Franz Deuticke.

——. (1992). *The Incest Theme in Literature and Legend: Fundamentals of a Psychology of Literary Creation*, trans. Gregory G. Richter. Baltimore: Johns Hopkins University Press.

Raphael-Leff, J. (1989). Freud, Son of Jocasta. Presented to the International Conference on Prenatal and Perinatal Psychology. Amherst, Massachusetts. August 1989. Unpublished.

——. (1992). Mother of Ajase and Jocasta, 1991. Presented to The Tokyo Meeting of Infant Psychiatry. Tokyo, April 1992.

Ratcliff, C. (1982). *John Singer Sargent*. New York: Abbeville Press.

Reich, A. (1953) Narcissistic object choice in women. *Journal of the American Psychoanalytic Association* I: 22–44.

Renik, O. (1993). Analytic interaction: Conceptualizing technique in light of the analyst's irreducible subjectivity. *Psychoanalytic Quarterly* 62: 553–71.

——. (2006). *Practical Psychoanalysis for Therapists and Patients*. New York: Other Press.

Reynolds, D. (1980). *The Quiet Therapies*. Honolulu: The University Press of Hawaii.

——. (1991). *Thirsty, Swimming in the Lake—Essentials of Constructive Living*. New York: Quill.

Ricoeur, P. (1970). *Freud and Philosophy*, trans. D. Savage. New Haven, Conn.: Yale University Press.

Roland, A. (1988) *In Search of the Self in India and Japan*. Princeton, N.J.: Princeton University Press.

——. (1996). *Cultural Pluralism and Psychoanalysis: The Asian and North American Experience*. New York: Routledge.

——. (2003). Psychoanalysts and the spiritual quest: toward a new integration. In *Creative Dissent: Psychoanalysis in Evolution*, eds. A. Roland, B. Ulanov, and C. Barbre. New York: Praeger.

Ross, J. M. (1985). Oedipus revisited: Laius and the "Laius Complex." In *The Oedipus Papers*, eds. G. Pollock and J. Ross. New York: International Universities Press.

Rothenberg, A. (1976). Homospatial thinking in creativity. *Archives of General Psychiatry* 33: 17–26.

Rubin, J. (1996). *Psychotherapy and Buddhism: Toward an Integration*. New York: Plenum Press.

Rudnytsky, P. (1987). *Freud and Oedipus*. New York: Columbia University Press.

Rushdie, S. (1989). *The Satanic Verses*. New York: Viking.

Russell, S. R., Chu, J. Y., Crockett, L., and Lee, F. *Interdependent Independence: The Meanings of Autonomy among Chinese American and Filipino American Adolescents*. Under review.

Sandler. J. (1976). Countertransference and role-responsiveness. *International Review of Psycho-Analysis* 3: 43–47.

——. (1991). President's letter to Prof. Doo-Young Cho regarding a guest study group of the IPA, September 16, 1991. *International Review of Psycho-Analysis* 34: 11–14.

Saussy, H. (2008). Discussion: Psychoanalysis and China. Scientific session of the Association for Psychoanalytic Medicine, April 1, 2008. New York.

Schafer, R. (1983). *The Analytic Attitude*. New York: Basic Books.

Settlage, C. F. (2001). Defenses evoked by early childhood loss: Their impact on life-span development. In *Three Faces of Mourning: Melancholia, Manic Defense, and Moving on*, ed. S. Akhtar, 47–93. Northvale, N.J.: Jason Aronson.

Settlage, C. F., Bemesderfer, S., Rosenthal, J., Afterman, J., and Spielman, P. M. (1991). The appeal cycle in early mother-child interaction: Nature and implications of a finding from developmental research. *Journal of the American Psychoanalytic Association* 39: 987–1014.

Shairashi, H. (1997). Amae and sensitivity to others' feelings. Presented at the American Psychoanalytic Association's Interdisciplinary Conference on *Amae* Reconsidered. May 1997.

Shapiro, Y., and Gabbard, G. O. (1994). A reconsideration of altruism from an evolutionary and psychodynamic perspective. *Ethics and Behavior* 4: 23–42.

Sharpey-Schafer, J. (1984). *Soldier of Fortune: F. D. Millet, 1846–1912*. Utica. Privately printed.

Shimtuh, Korean American Domestic Violence Program. (2000). *Korean American Community of the Bay Area Domestic Violence Needs Assessment Report*. Oakland, Calif.: Author.

Shore, J. (1991). The source of Zen: who transmits what? *FAS Society Journal*. Kyoto, Japan, 1999, 55–69.

Siirala, M. (1969). *Medicine in Metamorphosis: Speech, Presence and Integration*. London: Tavistock Publications.

Sima, Qian. (1959). *Shiji* [*Records of the Grand Historian*]. Beijing: Zhonghua Shuju.

Siu, S. F. (1996). *Asian American Students at Risk: A Literature Review*. Baltimore: Johns Hopkins University Press.

Sluzki, C., and Veron, E. (1971). The double-bind as a universal pathogenic situation. *Family Press* 10: 397–410.

Smith, K. T. (1993). Epilogue: Korea today. In *Battle for Korea: A History of the Korean Conflict*, ed. R. J. Dvorchak. Conshohocken, Penn.: Combined Publishing.

So Chong-Ju, M. (1946). Beside a chrysanthemum. In *Midang So Chong-Ju: Early Lyrics 1941–1946*, trans. Bro. Anthony. Seoul: DapGae, 1993.

Sohn, J. W. (2005). Therapist-patient relationship in self psychology and intersubjectivity theory. *Psychoanalysis* 16: 13–27.

Sophocles. (1991). *Three Tragedies*, trans. David Grene (second ed.). Chicago: University of Chicago Press.

Spiegel, J. (1971). *Transactions: The Interplay between Individual, Family, and Society*, ed. J. Papajohn. New York: Science House.

Spitz, R. A. (1946). Anaclitic depression: an inquiry into the genesis of psychiatric conditions in early childhood. *Psychoanalytic Study of the Child* 2: 313–42.

Steinberg, L. (1996). Ethnicity and adolescent achievement. *American Educator*: 28–48.

Stern, D. N. (1985). *The Interpersonal World of the Infant*. New York: Basic Books.

Stern, D., Sander, L., Nahum, J., Harrison, A., Lyons-Ruth, K., Morgan, A., Bruschweler-Stern, N., and Tronick, E. (1998). Non-interpretative mechanisms in psychoanalytic therapy: The "something more" than interpretation. *International Journal of Psychoanalysis* 79: 903–22.

Stolorow, R. D., Brandchaft, B., and Atwood, G. E. (1987). *Psychoanalytic Treatment: An Intersubjective Approach*. Hillsdale, N.J.: Analytic Press.

Sue, D. W., and Sue, D. (2002). *Counseling the Culturally Diverse: Theory and Practice*. New York: Houghton Mifflin.

Sue, S. (1999). Science, ethnicity and bias: Where have we gone wrong? *American Psychologist* 54: 1070–77.

Sullivan, H. S. (1972). *Personal Psychopathology*. New York: W. W. Norton.

Suzuki, D. T. (1973). *Zen and Japanese Culture*. Princeton, N.J.: Princeton University Press.

Symington, J., and Symington, N. (1996). *The clinical thinking of Wilfred Bion*. London: Routledge.

Takemoto, T. (1994). Naikan and alcohol dependence: a case study. *Constructive Living Quarterly* 2 (1).

Taketomo, S. (1915). Banka (Requiem). In *Shishu* (Anthology). Tokyo: Shinchosha.

Taketomo, Y. (1986). Amae as metalanguage: A critique of Doi's theory of amae. *Journal of the American Academy of Psychoanalysis* 14: 525–44.

———. (1986a). Toward the Discovery of Self: A Transcultural Perspective. *Journal of the American Academy of Psychoanalysis* 14: 69–84.

———. (1986b). Amae as metalanguage: a critique of Doi's theory of amae. *Journal of the American Academy of Psychoanalysis* 14: 525–44.

———. (1989) An American-Japanese transcultural psychoanalysis and the issue of teacher transference. *Journal of the American Academy of Psychoanalysis* 17: 427–50.

———. (1990). Cultural adaptation of psychoanalysis in Japan, 1912–1952. *Social Research* 57: 951–91.

———. (1993). Amae interaction in childhood and through the life cycle. Presented at The American Psychoanalytic Association Interdisciplinary Colloquium. December 1993.

———. (1997). The suspension of formality in interpersonal relations: a review of interactional amae and intrapsychic amae. Presented at the American Psychoanalytic Association's Interdisciplinary Conference on *Amae* Reconsidered. May 1997.

———. (1999). "Interpersonal amae" and "intrapsychic amae"—the problem of the psychoanalytic concept of amae as an extension of ordinary language amae. In *Clinical Practice in the Japanese Language, Volume III: Amae*, ed. O. Kitayama, 61–62. Tokyo: Seiwa Shoten.

Tang, N. (1997). Psychoanalytic psychotherapy with Chinese Americans. In *Working with Asian Americans*, ed. E. Lee, 323–41. New York: The Guilford Press.

Tatara, M. (1980). Taijin-Kyofu-sho (Anthropophobia): A cross-cultural interpretation. Paper presented to the William Alanson White Institute.

Tezuka, C. (1997). An explication of the concept of amae with a particular emphasis on its interactional nature. Presented at the American Psychoanalytic Association Interdisciplinary Conference on *Amae* Reconsidered. May 1997.

Tillich, P. (1967). *Systemic Theology*. Chicago: University of Chicago Press.

Triandis, H. C. (1996). The psychological measurement of cultural syndromes. *American Psychologist* 51: 407–15.

Trulson, M. E. (1986). Martial arts training: a novel "cure" for juvenile delinquency. *Human Relations* 39: 1131–40.

Tung, M. (2000). *Chinese Americans and Their Immigrant Parents: Conflict, Identity, and Values*. Binghamton: Haworth Press.

Twemlow, S. W. (1994). Misidentified flying objects? An integrated psychodynamic perspective on near death experiences and UFO abductions. *Journal of Near Death Studies* 12: 203–84.

———. (1995). DSM IV from a cross cultural perspective. *Psychiatric Annals* 25: 46–52.

———. (2001). Training psychotherapists in the attributes of "mind" from Zen and psychoanalytic perspectives, part II: Attention, here and now, nonattachment, and compassion. *American Journal of Psychotherapy* 55: 22–39

Twemlow, S. W., and Sacco, F. C. (1996). Peacekeeping and peacemaking: The conceptual foundations of a plan to reduce violence and improve the quality of life in a midsized community in Jamaica. *Psychiatry* 59: 145–74.

Twemlow, S. W., Sacco, F., and Fonagy, P. (2008). Embodying the mind: Movement as a container for destructive aggression. *American Journal Psychotherapy* 62: 1–33.

Uba, L. (1994). *Asian Americans: Personality Patterns, Identity, and Mental Health*. New York: Guilford Press.

U.S. Census. (2000). www.census.gov.

U.S. State Department. (2006). travel.state.gov.

Unno, T. (2006). Naikan therapy and Shin Buddhism. In *Buddhism and Psychotherapy across Cultures—Essays on Theories and Practices*, ed. M. Unno, 159–68. Boston: Wisdom.

Ushijima, S. (1997). Amae, grandiose self, and preoedipal father. Presented at the American Psychoanalytic Association Interdisciplinary Conference on *Amae* Reconsidered. May 1997.

Van Waning, A. (2001). Naikan soul searching: Experiences, memories and musings by a Dutch psychotherapist and Zen practitioner, with a Japanese Buddhist introspection approach. *Journal of Contemporary Buddhism* (Winter/Spring 2001).

———. (2001). Psychoanalysis, peace and war: beyond heroism and tragedy. *Japanese Journal of Psychoanalysis* 45: 380–90.

———. (2002). A mindful self and beyond—sharing in the ongoing dialogue of Buddhism and psychoanalysis. In *Awakening and Insight: Buddhism and Psychotherapy East and West*, eds. P. Young-Eisendrath and S. Muramoto, 93–105. New York: Brunner-Routledge.

———. (2006). Buddhist psychology and defensive conditioning. In *Horizons in Buddhist Psychology: Practice, Research & Theory*, eds. M. G. T. Kwee, K. J. Gergen, and F. Koshikawa, 141–1953. Taos, N.M.: Taos Institute Publishing.

Waelder, R. (1936). The principle of multiple functions. *Psychoanalytic Quarterly* 5: 45–62.

Wallace, B. A. (2005). *Genuine Happiness—Meditation as the Path to Fulfillment.* Hoboken, N.J.: John Wiley.

Walsh, L. (1969). *Read Japanese Today.* Rutland, Vt.: Charles E. Tuttle Company.

Walsh, R. (1988). Two Asian psychologies and their implications for Western psychotherapists. *American Journal of Psychotherapy* 42: 543–60.

Walters, B. (2006). Movie review: *Dumplings. Time Out,* London: June 14–21, p. 12.

Wang, N. (1991). The reception of Freudianism in modern Chinese literature. *China Information* 5: 58–71, and 6: 46–54.

———. (1992). *Shenceng xinlixue yu wenxue piping [Depth Psychology and Literary Criticism].* Xi'an, China: Shanxi remin chubanshe.

WCP. (2008). Psychotherapy in China. www.wcp2008.org/inChina.htm.

Weber, M. (1958). *The Protestant Ethic and the Spirit of Capitalism.* New York: Scribners.

Weeks, G. G., and L'Abate, L. (1982). *Paradoxical Psychotherapy.* New York: Brunner/Mazel.

Wei-Ming, T. (1998). Confucius and Confucianism. In *Confucianism and the Family,* eds. W. H. Slote and G. A. DeVos. Albany: State University of New York Press

———. (1998). Probing the "three bonds" and "five relationships" in Confucian humanism. In *Confucianism and the Family,* eds. W. H. Slote and G. A. DeVos. Albany: State University of New York Press.

Wheelis, A. (1980). *The Scheme of Things.* New York: Harcourt Brace Jovanich.

Wilber, K. (1980). *The Atman Project.* Wheaton, IL: Quest.

———. (2006). *Integral Spirituality—A Startling New Role for Religion in the Modern and Postmodern World.* Boston: Integral—Shambhala.

Williams, G. (1997). No entry defences. *International Journal of Psychoanalysis* 3: 4.

Winnicott, D. W. (1935). The manic defense. In *Through Paediatrics to Psychoanalysis: Collected Papers,* 129–44. New York: Bruner/Mazel, 1992.

———. (1960). Ego distortion in terms of true and false self. In *The Maturational Process and the Facilitating Environment.* London: Hogarth Press, 1965.

———. (1963). Communicating and not communicating leading to a study of certain opposites. In *The Maturational Processes and the Facilitating Environment,* 166–70. New York: International Universities Press, 1965.

———. (1965). Ego distortion in terms of true and false self. In *The Maturational Processes and the Facilitating Environment.* New York: International Universities Press.

———. (1971). *Playing and Reality.* London: Tavistock.

———. (1977). *Piggle.* New York: International University Press.

Wittgenstein, L. (1956). *Remarks on the Foundation of Mathematics.* Oxford: Blackwell.

Wong, P. (2006). The Inscrutable Dr. Wu. In *Dialogues in Difference: Diversity Studies of the Therapeutic Relationship,* ed. C. Muran. Washington, D.C.: APA Books.

Wong, W. (1997). Covering the invisible "model minority." In *Facing Differences: Race, Gender, and Mass Media,* eds. S. Biagi and M. Kern-Foxworth. Thousand Oaks, Calif.: Pine Forge Press.

Wood, E. (1951). *Zen Dictionary.* Rutland, Vt.: Charles Tuttle Company.

Yamaguchi, S., Kim, U., et al. (1997). Use of the word "amae" in language and social interaction. Presented at the American Psychoanalytic Association Interdisciplinary Conference on *Amae* Reconsidered. May 1997.

Yamamura, M. (1975). Reviewing the 25 years of the Japan Psychological Association. *Japanese Journal of Psychoanalysis* 24: 215–19.

Yamazaki, M. (1971). *Gekitekina Nihonjin (The Dramatic Japanese People)*. Tokyo: Shinchosha

Ye, T. (1999). From the fifth generation to the sixth generation—an interview with Zhang Yimou. *Film Quarterly* 53: 2–13.

Yeh, S. (1932). Autumn. In *Modern Chinese Stories and Novellas*, eds. J. S. M. Lau, C. Hsia, L. Ou-fan Lee, et al., 117–22. New York: Columbia University Press, 1981.

Yi, K. (1998). Transference and race: An intersubjective conceptualization. *Psychoanalytic Psychology* 15: 225–38.

Ying, J. L., Chentsova-Dutton, Y., and Wong, Y. (2002). Why and how researchers should study ethnic identity, acculturation, and cultural orientation. In *Asian American Psychology: The Science of Lives in Context*, eds. G. C. N. Hall and S. Okazaki, 41–66. Washington, D.C.: American Psychological Association Press.

Yu, F. (1987). *Xinli fenxi yu Zhongguo xiandai xiaoshuo* [*Psychoanalysis and Modern Chinese Fiction*]. Beijing: Shehui kexue chubanshe.

Yu, J. (2002). Cultural differences in analytic practice: experience in interracial analysis. *Psychoanalysis* 13: 159–68.

Yu, T. (1921). Sinking. In *Modern Chinese Stories and Novellas*, eds. J. S. M. Lau, C. Hsia, L. Ou-fan Lee, et al., 125–41. New York: Columbia University Press, 1981.

Yuh, J. Y. (2004). *Beyond the Shadow of Camptown: Korean Military Brides in America*. New York: New York University Press.

Zane, N., Morton, T., Chu, J., and Lin, N. (2003). Counseling and psychotherapy with Asian Americans. In *Practicing Multiculturalism: Affirming Diversity in Counseling and Psychology*, ed. T. B. Smith. Boston: Allyn and Bacon.

Zeligs, M. Acting in. *The Journal of the American Psychoanalytic Association* 5: 685–706.

Zhang, J. (1992). *Psychoanalysis in China: Literary Transformations—1919–1949*. Ithaca, N.Y.: Cornell University Press.

Zhang, Y. (1990). Director. *Judou*. Sino-Japanese joint production. Xi'an Film Studio, China.

Zhou, M., and Gatewood, J. V. (2000). *Contemporary Asian America: A Multidisciplinary Reader*. New York: New York University Press.

Zilboorg, G. (1973). Masculine and feminine: Some biological and cultural aspects. In *Psycho-analysis and Women*, ed. J. B. Miller. New York: Penguin.

Index

About the Contributors

Salman Akhtar, M.D., professor of psychiatry, Jefferson Medical College; training and supervisor analyst, Psychoanalytic Center of Philadelphia, Philadelphia, Pennsylvania.

June Cai, M.D., fellow, American Psychoanalytic Association (2000–2001); senior medical reviewer, Food and Drug Administration, Silver Spring, Maryland.

Lois Choi-Kain, M.D., instructor of psychiatry, Harvard Medical School; medical and program director, the Gunderson Residence at McClean Hospital; candidate, Boston Psychoanalytic Society and Institute, Boston, Massachusetts.

June Y. Chu, Ph.D., director of Pan-Asian American Community House, adjunct faculty, Asian American studies, University of Pennsylvania, Philadelphia, Pennsylvania.

Daniel Freeman, M.D., faculty member, Psychoanalytic Center of Philadelphia; clinical associate professor of psychiatry, MCP-Hahnemann School of Medicine, Philadelphia, Pennsylvania.

Ming Dong Gu, Ph.D., associate professor of Chinese and comparative literature; director, Confucius Institute, University of Texas, Dallas, Texas.

Do-Un Jeong, M.D., member, Allied Centers Committee of the International Psychoanalytic Association; professor of psychiatry and behavioral science, Seoul National University College of Medicine, Seoul Republic of Korea.

Mikyum Kim, M.D., graduate, William Alanson White Institute; private practice of psychotherapy and psychoanalysis, New York.

Douglas Kirsner, Ph.D., professor of philosophy and psychoanalytic studies; program director, Psychoanalytic Studies School of International and Political Studies, Faculty of Arts and Education, Deakin University, Victoria, Australia.

Osamu Kitayama, M.D., supervising and training analyst, Japan Psychoanalytic Society; professor of psychoanalysis and chairman of the Department of Pyschology, Kyushu University, Fukuoka, Japan.

Heisaku Kosawa, M.D., deceased.

Mark Moore, Ph.D., director of psychological services, Joan Carnell Cancer Center, Pennsylvania Hospital, Philadelphia, Pennsylvania.

Monisha Nayar, Ph.D., faculty member, Psychoanalytic Center of Philadelphia; private practice of adult and child psychotherapy and psychoanalysis, Ardmore, Pennsylvania.

Keigo Okinogi, M.D., emeritus professor of psychiatry, Keio University, Japan; president, Kodera Foundation for Psychoanalytic Study; secretary, Japan Psychoanalytic Society, Japan.

Alan Roland, Ph.D., training analyst and faculty member, National Psychological Association of Psychoanalysis, New York.

David Sachs, M.D., chairman, Allied Centers Committee of the International Psychoanalytic Association; supervising and training analyst, Psychoanalytic Center of Philadelphia, Philadelphia, Pennsylvania.

Elise Snyder, M.D., president, China American Psychoanalytic Alliance; past president, American College of Psychoanalysts, New York.

Yasuhiko Taketomo, M.D., professor of psychiatry (emeritus), Albert Einstein College of Medicine, New York.

Stuart Twemlow, M.D., medical director of the Hope Program; director of the Peaceful Schools and Communities Project of the Child and Family Program, Menninger Clinic; professor of psychiatry of the Menninger Department of Psychiatry and Behavioral Sciences, Baylor College of Medicine; faculty member of the Houston-Galveston Psychoanalytic Institute.

Adeline van Waning, M.D., Ph.D., faculty member, Dutch Psychoanalytical Society, Amsterdam, Netherlands.